GORHAM AND COMPANY

MANUFACTURING SILVERSMITHS,

12 Steeple St.

PROVIDENCE, R.S.

TESTIMONIALS IN SILVER

EMBELLISHED with APPROPRIATE DESIGNS,

TO ORDER AT SHORT NOTICE

EVERY ARTICLE
GUARANTEED TO PROVE
AS REPRESENTED

THOMPSON & CROSBY
PROV R.I.

THE STOCK OF SILVER & SILVER-PLATED GOODS
AT THEIR WARE ROOM, COMPRISING NEARLY EVERY
ARTICLE DESIRED FOR ORNAMENT OR UTILITY,
CANNOT, FOR BEAUTY
OF DESIGN, QUALITY
AND
WORKMANSHIP,
BE SURPASSED BY ANY CITY

The above Cuts are only intended to represent a few
Establishment.
Dealers will find it convenient to be able to obtain at one place nearly every article in Silver, desired either
for ornament or utility. Prices low as work of equal merit can be obtained in the country.

Encyclopedia of
American Silver
Manufacturers

Encyclopedia of
American Silver
Manufacturers

Dorothy T. Rainwater

CROWN PUBLISHERS, INC., NEW YORK

Second Printing, May 1978

Encyclopedia of American Silver Manufacturers
Copyright © 1975 by
Dorothy T. Rainwater

Previous Edition Copyright © 1966 by
Dorothy T. Rainwater

Library of Congress Catalog Card Number: 75-18953
ISBN 0-517-521-458

Prepared and published by Everybodys Press, Inc.
Printed in the United States of America

This edition prepared for distribution by
CROWN PUBLISHERS, INC.

CONTENTS

Author's Preface

The identification and dating of American silver presents problems because, unlike England and a few other countries, no official stamps or date letters were used. Nor, was there ever established a guild hall for keeping records. Therefore, it is only through the identification of maker's marks and trademarks that the names of silversmiths and manufacturers can be traced.

The *manufacture* of silverware in the United States began about 1842. Prior to that time there were no real factories in this country. Almost all the silver was custom made with the buyer dealing directly with the silversmith. With the rise of manufactured goods, a new relationship of manufacturer-wholesaler-retailer-consumer developed. Many of these wholesalers and retailers had their own marks put on articles made for them or to be sold by them exclusively. In addition, there were some manufacturing companies who made nickel silver wares that were sold "in the metal" for plating by jobbing firms who then stamped them with their own or with retailers' marks. For the purpose of identification some of these trademarks are included. Many manufacturing jewelers also made various types of silver products. Some of the jewelry marks included in this book appear on silver articles and may, or may not, also be stamped "STERLING." The products of some foreign firms appear in such large quantities in this country that they have also been included. Most of them registered their trademarks in the United States Patent Office.

The first major effort to collect American silver manufacturers' trademarks was the publication in 1896, by the JEWELERS' CIRCULAR (now the JEWELERS' CIRCULAR-KEYSTONE) of *Trade-Marks of the Jewelry and Kindred Trades*. This was followed by editions in 1898, 1904, 1909, 1915, 1943, 1950, 1965, 1969, and 1973. Many of the trademarks illustrated here are from the 1896-1915 editions and are reproduced by the permission of the former Editor, Donald S. McNeil. Other trademarks were obtained from the United States Patent Office records, from silver and jewelry manufacturers, from old company catalogs, from actual pieces of silver and from photographs.

A number of trade journals and their related directories and indices are the principal source of trademarks and dates used in this book. The dates given are those of the various editions and are not to be construed as actual dates a particular company was in business unless specifically stated. To simplify the listings the following abbreviations are used:

AHR: American Horological Review
JBG: Jewelers' Buyers Guide

JC: Jewelers' Circular
JC&HR: Jewelers' Circular & Horological Review
JC-K: Jewelers' Circular-Keystone
JC-W: Jewelers' Circular-Weekly
JKD: National Jewelers' Trade and Trade-Mark Directory
JR: Jewelers' Review
JW: Jewelers' Weekly
KJI: Keystone Jewelers' Index
KS: The Keystone
NJSB: National Jewelers' Speed Book

This book could never have been written without the generous help of others. My deepest debt of gratitude is to Edmund P. Hogan of the International Silver Company who opened up the historical files to me and allowed me to draw freely from notes compiled by the late Wm. G. Snow. Mr. Hogan also has been unfailing in his encouragement and friendship.

A special note of thanks is due Kenneth K. Deibel, Dallas, Texas, for the loan of scarce and important research materials.

My sincere thanks go to Dr. Elliot A. P. Evans, Orinda, California, for notes about California silversmiths derived from his as yet unpublished material.

For biographical notes about some Boston silversmiths I am deeply indebted to J. Herbert Gebelein of that city.

The generosity of Charles A. McCarthy, Seattle, Washington, in supplying photographs from which I drew a number of the marks is exceeded only by his enthusiasm for the entire project. Both are much appreciated.

My warmest thanks and deepest appreciation go to the following librarians, representatives of silver manufacturers and collectors: A. Abrahamsen, John Arcate, James Avery, Swift C. Barnes, Fred M. Birch, John R. Blackinton, Patricia Blanchard, Mrs. H. Batterson Boger, RADM J. F. Bowling, USN, RET., Helen K. Butler, Louis Cantor, Nathalie Caron, Elizabeth T. Casey, Nancy F. Chudacoff, Bert Cohen, C. F. W. Coker, David M. Doskow, CMDR Frederick F. Duggan, Jr., Bernice Egbert, William Felker, George Fina, Michael C. Fina, Mrs. Olin M. Fisk, Mrs. Leonard I. Freedman, Paul A. Frey, George F. Gee, German Embassy, Herman W. Glendenning, Mrs. J. A. Greeley, Mrs. Mildred T. Guisti, Albert T. Gunner, Virginia Gunner, Margaret Smith Gunster, Robert Haftel, Nancy L. Harvey, Bruce A. Hauman, K. J. Herman, Beulah D. Hodgson, R. W. House, Rufus Jacoby, D. Wayne Johnson, K. Kovvalski, Charles Lamoureaux, Joan B. Lehner, Joseph McCullough, James D. McPherson, Helena Matlack, Mrs. William B. Mebane, Harold A. Milbrath, Dwane F. Miller, Mrs. Hester Miller, John G. Miller, Mrs. J. C. Mitchell, Dr. James Mitchell, B. J. Murphy, Dan Nagin, Helen Norris, Leonard E. Padgett, Don Parker, Enoch Pratt Free Library, Mrs. John H. Prest, Mrs. J. O. Randahl, Jr., Shirley Robertson, George S. Rogers, W. E. Rooks, Virginia Schmid, Stephen Schuldenfrei, Edwin Sellkregg, R. Champlin Sheridan, Jr., Jules Silverstein, Stanley S. Smith, Mrs. Clyde H. Smith, Charles C. Stieff II, Rodney G. Stieff, Peter J. Texier, Ernest T. Thompson, Jr., Le Roy Timmer, L. R. Titcomb, Albert S. Tufts, Ruth Van Meter, Mrs. Bert Welch, Rufus F. Wells, Elizabeth Willard, Harold Wolfson and Roland H. Wordwell.

Most of all, I am indebted to my husband, Ivan, who through the years has traveled thousands of miles with me, walked the halls of countless museums, tape recorded innumerable interviews and photographed thousands of silver articles and their marks to assist me, all with unfailing cheerfulness and good humor.

All photographs are by H Ivan Rainwater with the exception of the following—

Page 21: collection of Mr. and Mrs. A. Christian Revi; photos by Poist's Studios.

Page 39: photos by Lela Marshall Hine, Norfolk Museum of Arts and Sciences Norfolk, Virginia.

Page 78: photos by Richard Croteau Associates.

Page 79: collection of International Silver Company; photos by Richard Croteau Associates.

Page 105: collection of Mrs. James H. Sutherland; photos by Marshall Hunt.

Page 136: collection of Chatillon-DeMenil Mansion, St. Louis, Missouri.

Page 151: collection of and photos by Mr. and Mrs. Carl R. Almgren.

Pages 171 and 178: photos by Towle Silversmiths.

How to Use This Book

There are many tradenames used which do not include the name of the company concerned, these and brand names are grouped together in a separate section with the name of the company following. To locate the company that used the brand name DIAMOND EDGE, for instance, consult this alphabetical listing and find that it was used by the Shapleigh Hardware Company.

Most of the trademarks have letters or words giving at least a clue to the letter of the alphabet with which the company name begins; a few do not. These are grouped together in the back of the book with the company name and are also illustrated within the regular company listing.

Very few of the trademarks illustrated in this volume appear *exactly* as they do when actually stamped on a piece of silver. Allowance must be made for imperfect stamping, and very often, for simplification of the stamped mark. Many of the illustrations are from printed sources and show more detail than is possible when stamped on silver. Varying angles of light on a mark can cause it to have a different appearance also.

Lettering for some of the marks drawn from actual specimens was sometimes done by the author with Artype, Prestype or similar graphic art products.

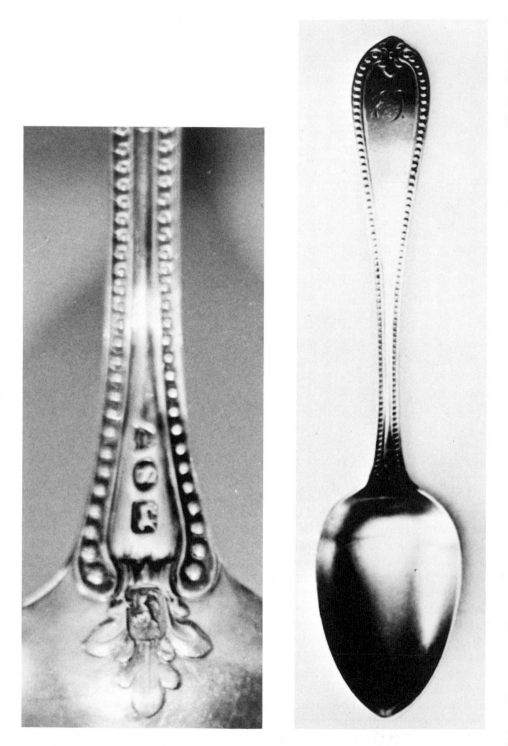

Maker's mark (George B. Sharp) and retailer (Bailey & Co.) both of Philadelphia, c. 1875.

A

ABBOTT SILVERSMITHS, INC.
New York, New York

Listed JBG 1957-61 as manufacturers of silverware.

ALBERT ABRECHT
Newark, New Jersey
also ABRECHT & COMPANY
also ABRECHT & SULSBERGER

Listed in the Jewelers' Weekly in 1896 as Abrecht & Sulsberger. Listed in JC as Abrecht & Co., 1896-1904; succeeded by Albert Abrecht before 1915. Manufacturers of sterling and plated silver, gold chains, pendants, scarf pins and brooches. Last listing found was 1936-37.

 A & S

ACADEMY SILVER CO. (Showroom)
New York, New York

Listed JBG 1957-61 as manufacturers of silverware.

ACME SILVER COMPANY
Toronto, Ontario, Canada

Manufacturers of silverplated wares c. 1885. Liquidated May 2, 1893. Sold to W. K. George and others who formed the Standard Silver Co., Toronto Ltd., later part of the International Silver Company of Canada Ltd.

ACME SILVER PLATE CO.
Boston, Massachusetts

Reported to have made plated silverware c. 1885. Not listed in U.S. Patent Office records.

C. C. ADAMS
Brooklyn, New York

"C. C. Adams, one of the largest and most prominent retail jewelers houses of Brooklyn, N. Y. have gone into the hands of a receiver. Stockholders are Sarah F. Adams, Cushing Adams, and Geo. S. Adams. The business was founded by the late Caleb Cushing Adams in 1887. He died Dec. 13, 1893, and since then the business has been in charge of his son, Cushing Adams." (JC 12-30-1896, p. 18)

The name is found impressed on flatware.

ADAMS, CHANDLER & CO.
Brooklyn, New York

Manufacturers of fine plated wares. They advertised in the *Watchmaker & Jeweler*, Nov. 1869, p. 43, a patent tilting ice water pitcher.

"John P. Adams [of Adams, Chandler & Co.], brother of Caleb Cushing Adams of Brooklyn, was recently deceased." (JCW, 2-7-1894, p. 6)

ADAMS & FARNSWORTH
Boston, Massachusetts

George Edward Adams and John C. Farnsworth were associated in the jewelry and silversmithing business from 1844 through 1848 (no directories available 1849-53), after which time Farnsworth was listed alone until 1857.

The firm began in 1839 under the name A. L. (Aaron L.) Dennison who was listed as an importer of watches. (It was Dennison who, in 1846, visited the Springfield Armory in Massachusetts and was impressed by the mass production or "interchangeable system" used there in the manufacture of weapons. Four years later he and others applied the same principles when they launched the American Horologe Co. in Roxbury, which eventually became the Waltham Watch Co.) By 1843 the firm had become A. L. Dennison, Adams & Co., jewelers, silversmiths and watchmakers. From 1846 to 1848 the firm name was Adams & Farnsworth.

| JOHN C. FARNSWORTH BOSTON |
| ADAMS & FARNSWORTH BOSTON |

GEORGE C. ADAMS
Baltimore Maryland

Listed in the 1864 Baltimore City Director as a silversmith.

ADAMS & SHAW
New York, New York
Newark, New Jersey

Caleb Cushing Adams president, was born in Newburyport, Massachusetts, March 25, 1833. He received his education at the famous colonial institution, Dummer Academy. While still a boy he started his business life in the employ of Joseph Moulton, an old jeweler in Newburyport. At the age of about 17 he went to New York City and became a salesman for Ball, Black & Co. where he remained about three years. His next post was Columbus, Georgia where he established a jewelry store. He sold his interest in a little more than a year and returned to New York in a position with Roberts & Bro. In 1858 he joined the Gorham Company as a traveler.

Thomas Shaw, head of the manufacturing, had learned electroplating at Elkington's of Birmingham, England, and came to America about 1860. He settled first in Providence, Rhode Island, where he worked for the Gorham Company, which was then trying to break into the trade in electroplate. In connection with Tiffany & Company Shaw formed the manufacturing company of Thomas Shaw & Company. By 1876 it was listed as Adams & Shaw. There was a notice (JC&HR, August 1876, p. 99) of the opening of the Adams & Shaw sample offices at No. 1 Bond St., New York City, for wholesale orders of sterling and electroplate. Following a fire in the Waltham Building, the factory moved to Newark, New Jersey and located at Park Street, corner of Mulberry, 1878-1895.

Both Adams and Shaw were skilled designers and both had worked for the Gorham Company. For 18 years Adams was the predecessor of Edward Holbrook as general manager there. Each had relatives associated in silversmithing. John P. Adams, brother of C. C. Adams, was owner of Adams, Chandler & Co., jewelers of New York City. Shaw had a son, Frank, also a fine designer, whose promising career was cut short.

In 1880 the Adams & Shaw Company was bought out by Dominick & Haff (Obit of Isaac Mills, JC&HR, 3-6-1895, p. 15). Their flatware patterns and dies were acquired from John R. Wendt & Co., New York, and eventually passed to Dominick & Haff. Following the closing of Adams & Shaw, Adams was connected with Leroy W. Fairchild & Co., and became buyer for N. Matson & Co., Chicago, Illinois. After about a year he became a partner in the Eugene Jaccard Jewelry Co., St. Louis, Missouri. In 1886 he again returned to New York City and formed the firm of C. C. Adams & Co., soon one of the leading jewelry firms there. He remained head of this firm until his death December 13, 1893.

WM. ADAMS
New York, New York

"William Adams, silversmith, New York City. Listed in directories there 1840-51. He was an Alderman (Ass't. 1840-42 and Alderman 1847-48). He learned the silversmith trade from Pierre Chicotree, Adams died about 1860." (JC&HR 8-5 1896)

In 1841 Adams reproduced the 46" mace of the House of Representatives, the original having been destroyed by fire when the British burned the Capitol in 1814.

WILLIAM ADAMS, INC.
New York, New York
Birmingham, England

Advertised that they are "Master craftsmen since 1854." (JC-K March 1966, p. 78) Importers of English Sheffield silverplate. Manufacturers of antique English silver and Sheffield plate.

In 1932 and 1950 registered a trademark in this country for which they claimed use since Dec. 1, 1899.

ADELPHI SILVER PLATE CO.
New York, New York

First record, 1890. Listed in the Jewelers' Weekly in 1896. Out of business between 1904-1915. John Schimpf & Sons, proprietors. They designed and made gold, sterling and plated silver holloware. Advertised "sterling silver mountings for cut glass a specialty."

(Quadruple Ware.)   STERLING ⁹⁹⁹⁄₁₀₀₀

(Quadruple Plate.)
(Holloware.)

(Special Goods in Holloware.)

ADIE BROTHERS, LTD.
Birmingham, England

Registered trademark in this country for flatware and holloware made of or plated with precious metal. Filed Sept. 1, 1948. Now part of British Silverware Ltd.

ALLAN ADLER, INC.
Los Angeles, California

Listed c. 1965-69 as manufacturer of sterling flatware, holloware and novelties.

ALLAN ADLER

AHRENDT & TAYLOR CO., INC.
Newark, New Jersey

First listed as Ahrendt & Kautzman; succeeded by Wm. G. Ahrendt and became Ahrendt & Taylor Co., Inc. between 1922-36. Not listed after 1943. Manufacturers and distributors of sterling silver novelties.

AKRON SILVER PLATE CO.
Akron, Ohio

"Akron Silver Plate Co., Akron, Ohio, in hands of receivers." (JC&HR 6-8-1898, p. 16)

ALBANY SILVER PLATE CO.
See Barbour Silver Co.
See International Silver Co.
See I. J. Steane Co.

ALBANY SILVER PLATE CO.
TRIPLE PLATE.

ALBERT BROS.
Cincinnati, Ohio

Wholesale jewelers who advertised that their silverplated holloware patterns were made especially for them. (JC&HR 11-6-1895, p. 35)

C. A. ALLEN
Chicago, Illinois

Specialized in plating pieces "in the metal" manufactured by others. Said to have been in the wholesale business from 1887 to c. 1900.

T. V. ALLEN CO.
Los Angeles, California

Listed as manufacturers of silver medals and trophies in 1931.

ALLSOPP-STELLER, INC.
Newark, New Jersey

The following company names were found:

Wordley, Allsopp & Bliss Co., Inc.	1915 JC
(Allsopp-Bliss Co. successors)	
Allsopp & Allsopp	1927 KJI
Allsopp-Bliss	1927 KJI
Allsopp Bros.	1927 KJI
Allsopp-Bliss Co.	1931 NJSB
Allsopp Bros.	1931 NJSB
Allsopp-Steller, Inc.	1943-1973 JC-K

Listed as manufacturers of sterling novelties. No answer to recent inquiries.

 (On sterling novelties)

ALVIN CORPORATION
Providence, Rhode Island
See Gorham Corporation

Organized as Alvin Mfg. Co., in Irvington, New Jersey by Wm. H. Jamouneau in 1886. Jamouneau was president until his retirement in 1898. A note in JC&HR (4-19-1893, p. 44) states that "The Alvin Mfg. Co., has been changed to the Alvin-Beiderhase Co.," Wm. H. Jamouneau, Henry L. Leibe and George B. Beiderhase, all of Newark, incorporated to manufacture metal, plated and other goods and novelties." In 1895 the Alvin factory was moved from Irvington, New Jersey to Sag Harbor, Long Island. It was purchased by Joseph Fahys & Co., watch-case manufacturer in 1897 and operated as a branch of that firm c. 1898-1910. The name of the company was changed to the Alvin Silver Co. in 1919. They were makers of sterling silver flatware, holloware, dresserware, silver deposit ware and plated silver flatware. Certain assets, dies and patterns were purchased by the Gorham company in 1928 and the name changed to the Alvin Corporation. It still functions as a division of the Gorham company.

In addition to the manufacture of electro-plated wares by the old methods, the Alvin company patented (January 5, 1886) a new process for depositing pure silver on both metallic and non-metallic surfaces. The first articles produced in this country by the process were cane and umbrella handles. In this process, the article was first coated with silver and afterwards a part of the coating was cut away, thus exposing the base, as in pierced work.

CHRONOLOGY

Alvin Mfg. Co.	1886-1893
Alvin-Beiderhase Co.	1893-1919
Alvin Silver Co.	1919-1928
Alvin Corporation	1928-present

ALVIN
long life Plate
ALVIN PATENT
ALVIN STERLING

SHERWOOD SILVERPLATE
STEGOR SILVERPLATE

SILVERPLATE

ALVIN-BEIDERHASE CO.
New York, New York
See Alvin Corp.

Made Official World's Fair souvenir spoons for the Columbian Exposition held in Chicago 1893-94.

AMERICAN RING CO.
Waterbury, Connecticut

Manufacturers of plated silverware c. 1920.

AMERICAN SILVER CO.
Bristol, Connecticut
See Bristol Brass & Clock Co.
See Holmes & Tuttle Mfg. Co.
See International Silver Co.

Established in 1901 as successor to Holmes & Tuttle Mfg. Co. and Bristol Brass & Clock Company. Bought by International Silver Co. in 1935.

(Reg. May 6, 1930)

"WORLD BRAND"

INDEPENDENCE BRAND

ASC (Stamped on Nickel Silver Wares.)

AMERICAN SILVER CO.
12 DWT.
A. S. CO.
BRISTOL CUTLERY CO.
NEW ENGLAND CUTLERY CO.
OLD ENGLISH BRAND, B.
BEACON SILVER CO.
CROWN SILVER CO.
1857 WELCH-ATKINS
EASTERN SILVER CO.
H. & T. MFG. CO.
NEW ENGLAND SILVER PLATE CO.
PEQUABUCK MFG. CO.
ROYAL PLATE CO.
WELCH SILVER
CROWN SILVER PLATE CO.
STERLING PLATE ◁ B ▷
(Flatware.)

AMERICAN SILVER PLATE CO.
See Simpson, Hall, Miller & Co. .)

AMERICAN STERLING CO.
Naubuc, Connecticut
See F. Curtis & Co.
See Thomas J. Vail
See Williams Bros. Mfg. Co.)

Successors to the Curtisville Mfg. Co. in 1871 when they took over the property of Thomas J. Vail, manufacturer of German silver and plated ware. In business till 1880 when it was bought by James B. and William Williams and the name changed to Williams Bros. Mfg. Co.

AMES MFG. COMPANY
Chicopee, Massachusetts

Nathan Peabody Ames and James Tyler Ames, founders of the Ames Mfg. Co., in 1829, began with the production of swords and sabers, many of which were presentation pieces for such eminent figures as Ulysses S. Grant and Zachary Taylor.

It was at the Ames company that the process of electroplating was introduced into the United States, according to Chicopee historian, Ted M. Szetela. His account says that Charles R. Woodworth, an artist employed by Ames, was the pioneer plater of the country. They made silver services for the leading hotels of the country. Among the elaborate plated silverware they exhibited at the New York World's Fair, 1853-54, were a wine cooler, a sword and standing salt cellar.

James T. Ames became head of the company after the death of his elder brother in 1847.

In 1853, the company added the manufacture of bronze statuary becoming the first company in the United States to cast bronze statues. The bronze doors of the United States Capitol in Washington, D.C., were cast at Ames from designs by Thomas Crawford, American sculptor. These were commissioned in 1853. The East doors were installed in 1868 and the West doors in 1905. Both doors are made up of panels which depict scenes of important events in American history.

During the Civil War, Ames became the largest producers of light artillery and third largest supplier of heavy ordnance.

James T. Ames retired in 1874 and was succeeded by his son-in-law, Albert C. Woodworth. The company was later owned by Emerson Gaylord and James C. Buckley and went out of business in 1920. It is thought that they discontinued the manufacture of silverplated wares about 1872. The silverplate aspect of the business is believed to have been transferred to the Meriden Britannia Company while the sterling and bronze departments were transferred to Providence where the Gorham Company developed them in later years. No records in the Meriden Britannia Company offices substantiate this.

AMITY SILVER INC.,
Brooklyn, New York

Manufacturers of sterling silver c. 1950.

AMSTON SILVER CO., INC.,
Meriden, Connecticut

Manufactuers of sterling and plated wares. Listed 1965 JC-K as a division of Ellmore Silver Co. Out of business c. 1960. Flatware dies purchased by Crown Silver Co., Inc.

STERLING   FINE SILVER PLATE

ANCHOR SILVER PLATE CO.
Muncie, Indiana and St. Paul, Minnesota

Listed in 1898 and 1904 JC. Listed in 1909 JC as out of business.

ANCHOR SILVER PLATE CO.
(On Quadruple Plate.)

INDIANA BRAND   **ANCHOR BRAND**
(On Triple Plate.)   *(On High Grade Novelties.)*

ANCHOR SILVERWARE CO.
Oswego, New York

"The company formerly known as the Seliger-Toothill Novelty Company will hereafter be known as the Anchor Silverware Co. The former were a stock company incorporated in New Jersey with head offices in Newark and factory in Oswego, N. Y." (JC&HR 11-11-1896, p. 6)

ANCO SILVER CO.
New York, New York

Manufacturers of sterling silverware c. 1920-1927.

DAVID ANDERSEN
Oslo, Norway

Established in 1876 as retail and manufacturing firm by David Andersen. Especially noted for filigree work and enamel. Firm presently directed by sons, grandson and great grandson. Distributed in the U.S. by the Norwegian Silver Corporation.

L. D. ANDERSON JLY. CO.
Reading, Pennsylvania

In business c. 1910. Louis D. Anderson was listed in the Reading City Directories from 1914-1939 as a manufacturer of jewelry and souvenir spoons. Listed again 1941-44. No further listing and no record of store.

L. D. A.

ANDOVER SILVER COMPANY
Andover, Massachusetts

Manufacturers of silverplate c. 1950.

ANDOVER SILVER PLATE CO.
See R. Wallace & Sons Mfg. Co.

APOLLO SILVER CO.
New York, New York
See Bernard Rice's Sons

Succeeded by Bernard Rice's Sons before 1899. Sterling dies now owned by Garden Silver Co.

ARCHIBALD-KLEMENT CO., INC.
Newark, New Jersey

Successor to C. F. Kees & Co. c. 1909. No record after 1922. Trademark used on sterling and gold lorgnettes.

ARGENTUM SILVER COMPANY
New York, New York

Listed 1958 JBG and 1965-73 JC-K. Recent inquiry returned by post office as undeliverable.

DEKRA

ARISTON SILVERSMITH CORP.
New York, New York

Listed 1931 NJSB as manufacturers of sterling silver holloware.

〉ARISTON〉

JAMES R. ARMIGER
Baltimore, Maryland

Successors to Justis & Armiger in 1892. Armiger was born in Baltimore in 1835. He received his training as a watchmaker from his foster father, John F. Plummer, jeweler. Was later employed by Canfield Bros. & Co., Baltimore. During the early part of the Civil War he moved to Magnolia, Harford County, Maryland, remaining there only a year. He returned to Baltimore and once again entered the employ of

Canfield, where he remained until May 1, 1878 when he went into partnership with John C. Justis, the firm succeeding Justis & Co. This partnership continued for 14 years when Justis retired and Armiger conducted the business until his death February 23, 1896 in a fire that destroyed his home.

According to an article in the JCW (2-5-1919) the Armiger company was a direct descendant of the B. Larmour & Co., in business in Baltimore at least as early as 1869. This article states that in 1874 the Larmour firm was succeeded by W. M. Justis and was styled Justis & Co. A few years later James R. Armiger became associated with the business and it was then known as Justis & Armiger. This was succeeded by James R. Armiger in 1892 and was incorporated as the James R. Armiger Co. in 1896. It continued to be listed in Baltimore City Directories to 1936.

ARROWSMITH SILVER CORP.
Brooklyn, New York

Listed as manufacturers of sterling silver c. 1960-66. Succeeded by Garden Silversmiths Ltd.

ART CRAFT PRODUCTS CO.
Sycamore, Illinois

Listed 1927 KJI as manufacturers of art metal novelties; silver deposit ware and silverplated holloware.

ART MFG. CO.
Meriden, Connecticut
See International Silver Co.

Name used on sterling silver match boxes.

ART MFG. CO.

(Match Boxes.)

THE ART SILVER SHOP
Chicago, Illinois

Listed in 1922 JC as The Art Silver Shop. Makers of handwrought sterling silverware, bar pins, ring and novelties. Still in business as Art Metal Studios. No address in 1974.

ART STAMPING & MFG. CO.
Philadelphia, Pennsylvania

Listed in 1909 JC as manufacturers of sterling and plated silverware. No record after 1915.

A. S. & M. CO.

ART STERLING SILVER CO., INC.
New York, New York

Their 1968 catalog says "Manufacturing & Importers of Fine Sterling Silver." About half the catalog is devoted to Judaica. Some other articles made by Weidlich Sterling Company. No reply to recent inquiry.

ARTCRAFT SILVERSMITH CO., INC.
New York, New York

Listed with manufacturers of sterling holloware 1927 KJI and 1931 NJSB.

ASSOCIATED SILVER CO.
Chicago, Illinois

Listed 1915 and 1922 JC, 1922, 1931 KJI as manufacturers of plated silver flatware.

SILVERSEAL

YOUREX

H. F. ATKINSON & CO.
Baltimore, Maryland

Listed in Baltimore City Directories 1887-1889 under plated silverware.

ATTLEBORO CHAIN CO.
Attleboro, Massachusetts

Listed in JC 1909-1915. Trademark used on sterling dresserwares.

ATTLEBORO MFG. CO.
Attleboro, Massachusetts

Listed in JC 1898-1915, as manufacturers of sterling silver novelties. Out of business before 1922.

(Novelties.)

AULD CRAFTERS, INC.
Columbus, Ohio

Manufacturers of pewterware. No reply to recent inquiry.

AURORA SILVER PLATE CO.
Aurora, Illinois
See Mulholland Bros., Inc.

Organized under charter from Illinois Legislature in 1869 when the city's industries were few in number and the population of the city was only 10,000. It employed 65 people at the start. The company was an important factor in the development of the city. Its rolling mill was "the only one west of Cincinnati" at that time. They made plated silver flatware and holloware. Succeeded by Mulholland Bros., Inc. between 1915-1922.

Built on Stolph's Island, the business was founded by J. G. Stolph (president for several years), Charles L. Burphee, Daniel Volintine, George W. Quereau, A. N. Shedd, D. W. Young, Charles

Wheaton, Samuel McCarty, M. L. Baxter, William Lawrence, William J. Strong and James G. Barr.

(*On Best Grade.*)   (*Holloware.*)

1869
AURORA SILVER PLATE M'F'G. CO.
12 Dwt.
(*Flatware.*)

AVERBECK & AVERBECK
New York, New York

"Manufacturers of Easter spoons, book marks, paper cutters, etc." (Adv. JCW 3-30-1898, p. 14)

JAMES AVERY, CRAFTSMAN, INC.
Kerrville, Texas

James Avery taught design at the Universities of Iowa, Colorado and Minnesota from 1946-54. He first set up shop with a small investment and built a workbench and a few hand tools, and "with a few scraps of silver and copper set up shop in a garage near Kerrville, Texas." For three years he worked alone and in 1957 hired his first employee. Today there are more than 125 designers, craftsmen, management and support personnel. Their work is primarily jewelry of gold and sterling silver, much of it handcrafted and with a sculptural look. Their outstanding line is their Christian jewelry, all of it symbolic and inspirational.

J. A. BABCOCK & CO.
New York, New York

"J. A. Babcock & Co., manufacturers of silver plated ware, have dissolved. The business is continued by Wm. Tuscano under the style of the Knickerbocker Mfg. Co." (JC&HR 2-7-1894, p. 94)

BACHRACH & FREEDMAN
New York, New York

Listed in 1896 JC under sterling silver. Succeeded by E. & J. Bass in 1900.

BAILEY, BANKS & BIDDLE CO.
Philadelphia, Pennsylvania

CHRONOLOGY

Bailey & Kitchen	1832-46
Bailey & Company	1846-78
Bailey, Banks & Biddle	1878-94
Bailey, Banks & Biddle Co.	1894-present

On September 20, 1832 Joseph Trowbridge Bailey and Andrew B. Kitchen formed a partnership under the firm name of Bailey & Kitchen for the manufacture and sale of silverware, jewelry and kindred articles and began business at 136 Chestnut Street, Philadelphia.

Mr. Kitchen died in 1840 but the business was continued under the same name until 1846, when E. W. Bailey, formerly of Maiden Lane, New York, the brother of J. T. Bailey, and Jeremiah Robbins and James Gallagher formed a new partnership under the name of Bailey & Company and continued business at the same location until 1859 when they constructed a new building at 819 Chestnut St.

Joseph Trowbridge Bailey, II entered the business in 1851 and was admitted into partnership at the age of twenty-one in 1856. His father died March 15, 1854.

In 1878 Joseph T. Bailey, II, George Banks of J. E. Caldwell & Co. and Samuel Biddle of Robbins, Clark & Biddle, formed a partnership under the name of Bailey, Banks and Biddle. Mr. Biddle retired in 1893 and on March 2, 1894 the business was incorporated with J. T. Bailey, II as president, Charles W. Bailey as vice-president and treasurer and Clement Weaver as secretary.

In 1903 and 1904 a new modern 10-story building was erected at 1218-20-22 Chestnut Street with a floor space of 76 x 230 feet and an eight-story factory.

In old City Directories the firm was listed primarily as jewelers but from 1839 through 1846 they were listed as jewelers and silversmiths. Brief mentions in old trade journals tell about the factory buildings (1868) and new buildings (1903-04) but they neglected to say whether these factories were for the manufacture of jewelry or silverware. George Sharp is known to have made silver for them and much of it is found bearing his personal stamps as well as "Bailey & Co."

In 1871 Bailey & Company published their *History of Silver, Ancient and Modern*. This is a 54-page booklet measuring about four by six inches. There is only one illustration of a Bailey & Company article but on p. 21 there is the statement, "The Advent of Messrs. Bailey & Company, in the year 1832, with new and improved machinery, created quite a revolution in the art of manufacturing silverware. They immediately took the lead in this department of industry which they have steadily maintained.

"They claim the distinction, and without cavil, of having first introduced silver of the full British standard of 925-1000 the American standard being but 900. The advantages of raising the standard are that it prevents the importation from abroad, and especially from British workshops, for purchasers are assured by a guarantee of receiving silver, pure as that stamped by the English government. Besides, the quality of the silver renders the article more brilliant, whiter, and more susceptible of a higher finish, and obviates discoloration from exposure."

And on a later page, "Messers Bailey and Company, formerly Bailey & Kitchen, as old and reliable manufacturers of Silverware for the past *forty years*, desire, in connection with the foregoing interesting sketch, to direct especial attention to the following list of articles with prices appended." Eighteen pages of price lists follow.

Silverplated ware received attention also for toward the back of the brochure we find, "PLATED WARE—Of our own manufacture, of every style, constantly in store and warranted equal to any sold in this country. Guaranteed in every particular. Information sent upon inquiry."

ROSWELL & B. M. BAILEY
Woodstock, Ludlow & Rutland, Vermont

In 1837-72 with partners, Parmenter & Parker, made silverware. The Baileys' apprentices made doll-size spoons as evidence of their craftsmanship and were allowed to sell them for their own profit for 25¢ each.

Roswell Bailey established his own large shop in 1839 and kept a dozen journeymen and apprentices busy. He was in business until 1875.

BRADBURY M. BAILEY
Ludlow and Woodstock, Vermont

A brother-in-law of Roswell Bailey of Woodstock, he worked as a silversmith in Ludlow before moving to Rutland in 1852. Closed his business in 1885. Born 1824-died 1913.

BAIRD-NORTH CO.
Providence, Rhode Island

Advertised that they manufactured and sold direct to the user. Advertised 200 page free catalog in 1912. Basically they were distributors.

BAKER-MANCHESTER MFG. CO.
Providence, Rhode Island
See Manchester Silver Co.

A short-lived concern in operation from c. 1914-1915 to the early 1930s. Manufacturers of sterling silver fancy flatware, souvenir spoons, holloware and novelties.

BALDWIN & CO.
Newark, New Jersey

CHRONOLOGY
Taylor, Baldwin & Co.	c. 1825-41
Baldwin & Co.	c. 1841-69

Manufacturing jewelers around 1840-69. Established by Isaac Baldwin, formerly with Taylor, Baldwin & Co. c. 1825-41. (He had also been a partner with James M. Durand in Baldwin & Durand c. 1845-50.) After the death of Isaac Baldwin, the business was continued by his son, Wickliffe. Sold to Thomas G. Brown in 1869.

BALDWIN & CO.

BALDWIN, FORD & CO.
New York, New York
See Cohen & Rosenberger
See Ford & Carpenter

Listed in the 1896 JC as Baldwin, Ford and Co. Succeeded by Ford & Carpenter before 1904. They, in turn, were succeeded by Cohen & Rosenberger before 1915. Baldwin, Ford & Co., whose factory was in Providence, Rhode Island, advertised that they made "the only one piece stud in the market," patented May 6, 1884.

BALDWIN & JONES
See Shreve, Crump & Low Co., Inc.

BALDWIN & JONES

BALDWIN, MILLER CO., INC.
Indianapolis, Indiana

First established in 1883. Manufacturers, wholesalers and jobbers of silverware, jewelry, clocks, and appliances. Their early trademarks have been found on souvenir spoons. Still in business.

B. M. CO.
Not used after 1915

B. & M.
Present trademark

BALDWIN & MILLER INC.
Newark, New Jersey

Manufacturing silversmiths. They manufacture sterling and pewter holloware, novelties and special trophy items—cups, trays, etc., to order.

The company was founded by Fred W. Miller, Sr. and Milton Baldwin. It began as a partnership in 1920 supplying retail stores with special order sterling silver holloware and stock items. Following Mr. Baldwin's death in 1939 the Miller family purchased all stock in the business. The firm is now in the third generation and is still in the hands of the Miller family.

Not related to Baldwin, Miller Co., Indianapolis, nor to Baldwin & Co., Newark.

B & M
(On sterling and on pewter)

BALDWIN SILVER CORP.
New York, New York

Listed JBG 1957-61 as manufacturers.

BALL, BLACK & COMPANY
New York, New York
See Black, Starr & Frost, Ltd.

Successors to Ball, Tompkins & Black in 1851. Partners were Henry Ball and William Black. In the 1860s they bought Reed & Barton wares "in the metal" and operated their own plating establishment. Succeeded by Black, Starr & Frost in 1876.

EDWARD BALL CO.
New York, New York

Manufacturers of sterling silverware. Listed JKD 1918-19 as silversmiths.

BALL, TOMPKINS & BLACK
New York, New York
See Black, Starr & Frost, Ltd.

Successors to Marquand & Co. in 1839. Partners

were Henry Ball, Erastus O. Tompkins and William Black. Succeeded by Ball, Black & Co. in 1851.

THE BALLOU MFG. CO.
Attleboro, Massachusetts

Manufacturers of gold, gold-filled and sterling silver jewelry, materials and findings. Listed in JC 1915 and 1922; JKI 1927.

BALTES-CHANCE CO., INC.
Irvington, New Jersey

Manufacturers of sterling silver novelties. First record found in early 1920s. Succeeded by Baltes Mfg. Co. before 1927.

BALTIMORE NICKEL PLATING WORKS
Baltimore, Maryland

Listed in Baltimore City Directories 1874-1886 as silverplaters.

BALTIMORE SILVER CO.
Baltimore, Maryland

Listed in Baltimore City Directories 1906-1908 as silverplaters. Successors to Baltimore Silver Plating Co.

BALTIMORE SILVER PLATE CO.
Baltimore, Maryland
See Balt. Silver Plating Co.

Listed in Baltimore City Directories as silverplaters 1894-1907. Succeeded by Baltimore Silver Plating Company.

BALTIMORE SILVER PLATING CO.
Baltimore, Maryland

In business from 1905-1907 as successors to the Baltimore Silver Plate Company which was first listed in 1894. Succeeded by the Baltimore Silver Co.

BALTIMORE SILVERSMITHS MFG. CO.
Baltimore, Maryland
See Heer-Schofield Co.
See Schofield Co., Inc.

BALTIMORE STERLING SILVER BUCKLE CO.
Baltimore, Maryland

Listed c. 1900-1904 at the same address as the Baltimore Sterling Silver Co.

BALTIMORE STERLING SILVER CO.
Baltimore, Maryland
See Stieff Co.

C. A. BAMEN
Boston, Massachusetts

Listed as specialist in plating c. 1860.

BANCROFT, REDFIELD & RICE
New York, New York
See Bernard Rice's Sons

In the 1860s they purchased Reed & Barton wares "in the metal" and operated their own plating establishment. Predecessors of Redfield & Rice, Shepard & Rice and Bernard Rice's Sons.

BARBOUR BROS. CO.
Hartford, Connecticut
See Barbour Silver Co.
See I. J. Steane & Co.

Samuel L. Barbour, of Chicago, moved to New Haven, Conn. about 1881-82, to join his brother Charles who was in business there. They marketed the plated silverware produced by I. J. Steane & Co. Succeeded by Barbour Silver Co. in 1892.

BARBOUR HOBSON CO.
Hartford, Connecticut
See Barbour Silver Co.

The Barbour Hobson Company was organized in 1890 for manufacturing sterling silver. The interests of I. J. Steane, the Barbour Bros. Co. and the Barbour Hobson Co. were so nearly identical that it was thought best to unite them and the Barbour Silver Co. was the result.

BARBOUR SILVER CO.
Hartford, Connecticut
See International Silver Co.

When the Barbour Silver Co. was organized in 1892 by Samuel L. Barbour, Isaac J. Steane and J. L. Dalgleish, they succeeded I. J. Steane & Co., Barbour Hobson Co. and Barbour Bros. Co. In August of 1893, they took over at least some of the machinery and stock of the Hartford Silver Plate Co., organized in 1882 and believed to have been carried on for a short time under the name of Hartford Silver Co.

When the International Silver Co. was formed in 1898, Samuel L. Barbour, who had been active head of the Barbour Silver Co. for several years, continued as manager of that branch (known as Factory "A") and was made a director of the new company and remained in that capacity for several years after the plant was moved to Meriden to the buildings formerly occupied by the Meriden Silver Plate Co.

BARBOUR SILVER Co.
QUADRUPLE PLATE

B. S. C.

Samuel L. Barbour was born in Norwalk, Conn., about 1865 and died in San Francisco, Nov. 11, 1925. He was identified with A. I. Hall & Son.

One of the original companies to become part of the International Silver Co. in 1898.

BARDEN, BLAKE & CO.
Plainville, Massachusetts
See Chapman & Barden

B. B. & CO.
STERLING.

BARKER BROS. SILVER CO., INC.
New York, New York
See Ellis-Barker Silver Co.

Sterling and plated silver wares; wholesaler and importer. Registered trademark Feb. 10, 1935 for silverplated holloware and flatware for table, toilet, or ornamental use. Claims use since Oct. 1, 1934.

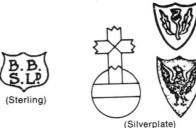

(Sterling)

(Silverplate)

C. E. BARKER MFG. CO.
New York, New York
(Quadruple Plate)

Manufacturers of sterling (?) and plated silverware. First listed in JC in 1896. Out of business before 1915.

GEORGE BARRETT
Baltimore, Maryland

Listed in the Baltimore City Directories 1873-1898 as silverplaters (electroplate) Successors to Barrett & Rosendorn who were first listed in 1871 as silversmiths.

BARRETT & ROSENDORN
Baltimore, Maryland

Listed 1871-1872 as silversmiths and silverplaters (electroplaters). Succeeded by George Barrett in 1873.

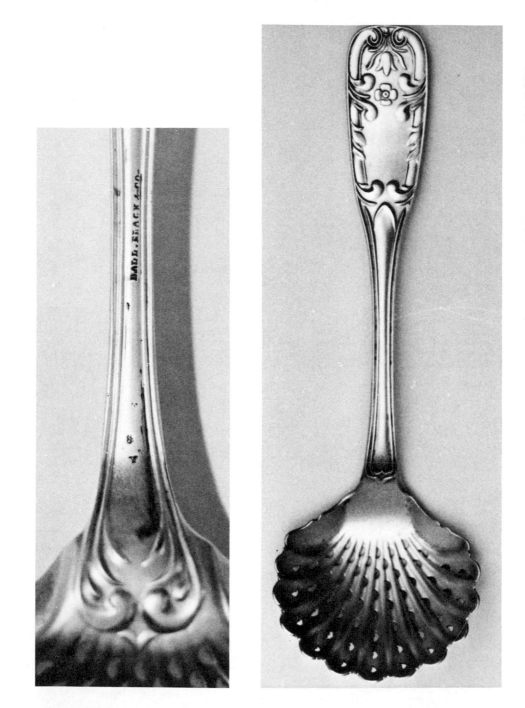

Pierced ladle marked with the retailer's stamp "Ball, Black & Co." The pattern was designed and patented by Michael Gibney, New York, December 4, 1844, Patent Design No. 26 — the first patented flatware design in this country. Some other pieces in this pattern also bear the mark of the letter "Y" and a cryptic little symbol which may be an ampersand.

L'art nouveau candlestick made by the Barbour Silver Plate Company c. 1900-1905.

H. F. BARROWS & CO.
North Attleboro, Massachusetts

In business since 1851. Listed in 1896 JC under sterling silver and under jewelry in all subsequent listings. Still in business as manufacturers of jewelry in sterling silver and gold filled, 10k and 14k gold. A new line of religious medals and symbols was added c. 1965.

 Sterling.

N. BARSTOW
Providence, Rhode Island

Successors c. 1904 to Barstow & Williams.

BARSTOW & WILLIAMS
Providence, Rhode Island
See N. Barstow Co.

About 1880 Nathaniel Barstow began the manufacture of jewelry and in 1888 Walter S. Williams joined him to create the firm of Barstow & Williams. They added the manufacture of silver novelties to their line which then formed a complete line of jewelry and silver ornaments. Apparently Williams dropped out because by 1904 the firm name was once again N. Barstow & Co.

E. BARTON & COMPANY
New York, New York
See Black, Starr & Frost, Ltd.

In business 1815-1823. Partners were Erastus Barton and Isaac Marquand.

BASCH BROS. & CO.
New York, ew York

Listed in 1904 JC under sterling silverware. Out of business before 1915.

E. & J. BASS
New York, New York

Manufacturers of sterling silver wares, sterling silver deposit wares and plated silver and jewelry. In business from 1890-c. 1930.

"E. & J. Bass, New York manufacturers of silver novelties, announce they have purchased from Reeves & Browne, Newark, N.J., the entire outfit of tools and dies used in the manufacture of silver novelties and have purchased the dies, tools, trademarks, etc., of Bachrach & Freedman." (JC-W 5-9-1900, p. 33)

THE BASSETT JEWELRY CO.
Newark, New Jersey

Manufacturers of sterling silver and gold jewelry. Listed in JC 1896-1943.

They took over the plant and stock of Kent & Stanley in 1894.

J. C. BATES
Northfield, Vermont

Advertised in 1859 and 1860 that he sold watches, jewelry, silver, clocks, toys and fancy goods.

BATES & KLINKE, INC.
Attleboro, Massachusetts

Established in 1919 as a die cutting and jobbing firm by Harold Bates and Oscar F. Klinke. Both are accomplished die cutters who served their apprenticeship before World War I. After serving in the army, they started business in November, 1919. The company was incorporated in 1929. The company gradually moved into the jewelry business. They now manufacture convention and special jewelry and souvenir spoons, mostly of sterling silver.

BATTIN & CO.
Newark, New Jersey

Listed in JC 1896-1922. Manufacturers of 14k and sterling silver match boxes, cigarette cases, eyeglass cases, belt buckles and pocket knives. KJI 1927.

BAY STATE JEWELRY & SILVERSMITHS CO.
Attleboro, Massachusetts

Patent No. 104,012. Registered April 27, 1915. Application filed October 20, 1914. Serial No. 82,010. Trademark used continuously since August 1, 1914. For jewelry and precious metal ware; silver novelties, match boxes, purses, dresserware, cigarette cases, vanity cases and coin holders. Filed by Carrie L. Saart, Treasurer.

BAY STATE SILVER CO.
North Attleboro, Massachusetts

In business 1890-93. Made bracelets and novelties. (JC-W 4-13-1898, p. 28)

BEAUCRAFT INC.
Providence, Rhode Island

Listed 1950-65 as manufacturers of sterling novelties. ⓣ

Registered trademark, below 1948 for costume jewelry. Claims use since Aug. 5, 1947.

BECHARD MFG. CO.
Chicago, Illinois

PORTSMOUTH

Manufacturers of plated wares c. 1940-45.

BECHT & HARTL, INC.
Newark, New Jersey

Manufacturers of sterling silver c. 1935-50.

ERNST GIDEON BEK, INC.
Pforzheim, Germany
See Binder Bros., Inc.

Manufacturers of sterling silver, gold and platinum mesh bags. Prior to World War I, Bek's was represented in the United States by Binder Bros., Inc. Following the war, Binders purchased the Bek stock from the alien custodian. The Germany company is thought to be still in operation. Pforzheim is the center of the German silver industry.

BELKNAP HARDWARE & MFG. CO.
Louisville, Kentucky

1840 W. B. Belknap Co.

Silverplated flatware with their imprint was sold. Identical patterns bore the imprint of the Rockford Silver Co. and were probably made by the Williams Bros. Co. The Belknap Co. is still in business.

BELL BROS.
Ogdenburg, New York

"Bell Bros. silver ware factory, Ogdensburg, N.Y. has been sold. Purchasers are Messrs. Tucker & Parkhurst, Concord, N.H." (JC-W 3-3-1898, p. 17)

GEORGE BELL CO.
Denver, Colorado

Retail jewelry company. Listed in JC 1904-1922. Their trademark was found on souvenir spoons.

O. E. BELL COMPANY
Cincinnati, Ohio
See Cincinnati Silver Co.

Founded in 1892 as the Cincinnati Silver Company. O. E. Bell was general manager in 1898 and took over the company in 1899. They were manufacturers of plated silver holloware and novelties. Out of business c. 1900.

BELL TRADING POST
Albuquerque, New Mexico

A division of Sunbell Corporation. In business since 1932. Manufacturers of sterling silver, turquoise, copper and nickel silver jewelry and souvenir spoons.

W. BELL & COMPANY
Rockville, Maryland

Founded in 1950 by Walter Bell. For several years operated as a catalog source for high-quality, high-value gift items and premiums. Sales efforts formerly directed primarily toward businesses and organizations. In 1971 their marketing activities were expanded and services extended. Nine showrooms are scattered throughout the country.

Besides sterling, silverplate and pewter is made by several outstanding firms under their own names and trademarks, they also market WARWICK sterling silver and SOMERSET silverplated holloware in exclusive designs made for them by various manufacturers.

Warwick (Sterling Silver)

Somerset (Silver Plated Holloware)

BENEDICT MFG. CO.
East Syracuse, New York

Organized in 1894 with M. Stewart Benedict as president. Incorporated in 1902 and reorganized in 1906 as T. N. Benedict Mfg. Co. Their principal business at the start was silverplated holloware and they continued this line of goods which was adapted to household purposes and gradually included a line of holloware for hotel and restaurant use. Later they added a line of holloware plated on a nickel silver base, and a variety of equipment for soda fountains, including flatware. In 1910 they established a branch factory in Canada. They continued to produce lines mentioned above until 1942 when much of their plant facilities was converted to war work. Out of business in 1953.

In the consolidation of January 1912, they absorbed the Hamilton Silver Mfg. Co. of New York, the Benedict Dunn Co., Bridgeport, Connecticut, and the Benjamin Clark Silver Co., Ottawa, Illinois (founded 1890). Most of these factories were moved and merged with the East Syracuse plant.

BENEDICT PERIOD PLATE
GEORGIAN
CHIPPENDALE
BERKELEY
INDESTRUCTO
M. S. BENEDICT QUADRUPLE PLATE
(Above on silverplated holloware)

REVERE
STANDISH
(Above on pewter)

BENEDICT & MCFARLANE CO.
Bridgeport, Connecticut

"The Benedict & McFarlane Co. has been organized to manufacture silverplated flatware. The company gets its name from M. S. Benedict of the M. S. Benedict Mfg. Co., Syracuse; and F. H. McFarlane, treasurer and manager of the Bridgeport Silver Plate Co. of Norfolk, Virginia. The Benedict Mfg. Co. will purchase the entire outfit of the new company." (JW 10-4-1899, p. 9)

BENEDICT-PROCTOR MFG. CO.
Trenton, Ontario, Canada

Listed 1920 to present as manufacturers of plated silverware.

T. N. BENEDICT
East Syracuse, New York
See Benedict Mfg. Co.

BENNETT-MERWIN SILVER CO.
New Milford, Connecticut
See Merwin-Wilson Co., Inc.

U. S. Patent No. 91,548, May 13, 1913, registered for use on plated silver flat, hollow and tableware.

WM. BENS CO., INC.
Providence, Rhode Island

Listed 1915-c. 1920 as manufacturers of sterling silver dresser-ware.

FREDERICK BERENBROICK
Weehawken, New Jersey

Established c. 1840 at 15 John Street (New York?) by Frederick Berenbroick, the pioneer maker of filigree in the United States. In 1858 the business was taken over by his nephew, Gottlieb Berenbroick, who made filigree and silver jewelry and novelties at 78 Duane St. in 1889, at death of Gottlieb, the business was taken over by Berenbroick & Martin, Frederick Berenbroick and Max Martin. Max Martin retired in 1919 and Frederick Berenbroick continued. The last listing found was 1935. He manufactured reproductions of old Dutch, English and French silverware.

ODO BERGMANN
Baltimore, Maryland

Listed in Baltimore City Directories 1897-1900 under silverware, solid and plated.

BERNDORF METAL WORKS
Berndorf, Austria
(Arthur Krupp)

Manufacturers of plated silverware c. 1910. No record after 1915.

SAMUEL E. BERNSTEIN
New York, New York
See National Silver Co.

Founded in 1890 and succeeded by the National Silver Company in 1904.

BEVAN & CO.
Baltimore, Maryland

Listed in 1872 Baltimore City Directory as silverplaters.

BIGELOW, KENNARD CO., INC.
Boston, Massachusetts

CHRONOLOGY

John Bigelow	1830
Bigelow & Bros.	c. 1840-50
Bigelow Bros. & Kennard	c. 1845
Bigelow, Kennard & Co.	c. 1863
Bigelow, Kennard & Co., Inc.	c. 1912
Bigelow Kennard Co., Inc.	1937

"Wm. H. Kennard, b. Portsmouth, N.H. Oct. 14, 1842, d. July 1891. In 1840 went with Low, Ball & Co., predecessors of Shreve, Crump & Son [Sic!]. In

1847, with his brother, M. P. Kennard, became member of Bigelow Bros. & Kennard, later changed to Bigelow, Kennard & Co." (JW 7-15-1891)

I. BIGGERS SILVER CO.
Taunton, Massachusetts

Manufacturers of silverplated novelties c. 1895.

I. BIGGERS SILVER CO. TAUNTON

BIGGINS-RODGERS CO.
Wallingford, Connecticut

Founded May 18, 1894 to manufacture sterling, silverplated and metal goods. Founders were Henry E. Biggins, president, former superintendent of Hartford Silver Plate Co., Frank L. Rodgers, treasurer, descendant of Joseph Rodgers, of Joseph Rodgers & Sons, well-known English firm and Henry B. Hall, secretary, formerly with R. Wallace & Sons. They purchased the machinery of the Hartford Silver Plate Co. and installed it in their new factory building. Succeeded by Dowd-Rodgers Co., c. 1915-20.

D

BINDER BROS. INC.
New York, New York

Prior to 1919, Binder Brothers Incorporated were the exclusive American agents for Ernst Gideon Bek, Inc., Pforzheim, Germany. To their knowledge the Bek Company is still doing busines in Germany today.

Since 1919, when Binder Brothers Incorporated purchased the Ernst Gideon Bek stock from the alien custodians who had taken it over during World War I, Binder has manufactured, imported and had made up exclusively under its own trademark, jewelry, watchbands, sterling novelties, etc.

JAMES BINGHAM
Philadelphia, Pennsylvania

Listed from 1896 to c. 1910 as manufacturer of sterling silverware and jewelry.

FRED M. BIRCH CO., INC.
Providence, Rhode Island

Manufacturer of gold filled and mens' sterling jewelry only from 1959 to 1971. Have since diversified and are now making ladies' gold filled and sterling lockets, crosses, pins, etc.; also brass items.

BIRMINGHAM SILVER CO., INC.
Yalesville. Connecticut

Successors to Goldfeder Silverware Co. Manufacturers of sterling silver and silverplate.

"... Sol Goldfeder — newly married and with $150 in his pocket — launched a small silver hol-

lowware company anyway. He still recalls his first order. 'It was $30, may be $31. We sold it to M. A. Cohen & Sons.' The sale was a good omen. Soon Goldfeder owned a prospering factory in Brooklyn. In 1957, after 25 years there, his firm, now named Birmingham Silver Co., shifted operations to Yalesville, CT. Now the firm has added a New York address." (JC-K July 1974, p. 223)

(Sterling & silverplate)

(Silverplate)

BIXBY SILVER CO.
Providence, Rhode Island

Listed in JC as manufacturers of sterling silverware 1896-c. 1909.

B. S. C.

SPE ET LABORE

BLACK, STARR & FROST, LTD.
New York, New York

CHRONOLOGY

Marquand & Co.	1810
Ball, Tompkins & Black	1839
Ball, Black & Co.	1851
Black, Starr & Frost	1876
Black, Starr, Frost-Gorham Inc.	1929
Black, Starr & Gorham, Inc.	1940
Black, Starr & Frost, Ltd.	1962

Black, Starr & Frost traces its history to Marquand & Paulding who began their partnership in Savannah, Georgia in 1801. Several related firms were established in Savannah, New Orleans and New York. For a complete account see *The Silversmiths of Georgia*, by George Barton Cutten.

The present firm does not manufacture items but uses the trademarks shown.

B S & F

Black Starr

Black, Starr & Frost Ltd

R. BLACKINTON & CO.
North Attleboro, Massachusetts

Founded in 1862 by Walter Ballou and Roswell Blackinton in North Attleboro, Massachusetts and has been owned and operated by members of the same two families to the present day. The original trademark ⟶B⟵ was used till c. 1900. Their products have consisted mostly of sterling silver and 14 karat gold novelties, flatware, holloware and dresserware, with a small amount of costume jewelry.

Bought by Wells, Inc. Attleboro, Mass. June 1967.

About 1965-66 their *Marie Louise* flatware pattern was sold to the U. S. State Department for use in all United States embassies throughout the world.

PONTIFEX
(On dresserware)

MARIE LOUISE
(On dresserware)

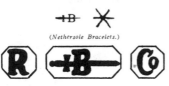

(Nethersole Bracelets.)

W. & S. BLACKINTON CO.
Meriden, Connecticut

Founded in 1865 by the Blackinton brothers who specialized in gold jewelry. Acquired by the Ellmore Silver Co. in 1938. While owned by Ellmore, operations expanded to include plated silver holloware. Production was curtailed during World War II and resumed with new lines in 1945. Independently owned since 1961. Incorporated between 1961-65. Purchased by Raimond Silver Mfg. Co., Meriden, Connecticut in 1966 and moved to Chelsea, Massachusetts.

W. & S. BLACKINTON

BLACKSTONE SILVER CO.
Bridgeport (Stratford), Connecticut

Started by E. H. H. Smith, formerly of Meriden, Connecticut, when he did business alone or under the name E. H. H. Smith Silver Co. The firm went into receivership April 12, 1914 and was reorganized as Blackstone Silver Co. It was backed to some extent by Albert Pick & Co., Chicago, for whom it had been making hotel ware. The Blackstone Silver Co. was sold in 1943 to Bernstein (of National Silver Co.?)

CHARLES BLAKE
Baltimore, Maryland

Silverplaters listed in Baltimore City Directories as Charles Blake 1868-1876, and as Charles W. Blake 1877-1886.

JAMES E. BLAKE CO.
Attleboro, Massachusetts

The Manufacturing Jeweler (10-25-1894) called James E. Blake one of the "pioneer silversmiths of Attleboro." It commented on the increased use of silver for useful and ornamental purposes and credited the firm of Blake & Claflin as being one of the most successful in its efforts in that direction. James E. Blake, senior partner, was born in Chicopee Falls, Massachusetts in 1851. In 1879 he was married to a daughter of C. H. Sturdy, a member of the old firm of Sturdy & Bros. & Co., manufacturing jewelers, established in Attleboro in 1859. In 1880 he joined the Sturdy firm and the following year entered into partnership with Edward P. Claflin, the foreman of the old firm, and Albert W. Sturdy, one of the Sturdy brothers under the firm name of Blake & Claflin. Blake & Claflin thus succeeded to the business of Sturdy Bros. & Co. About 1889 the firm began the manufacture of articles in silver, match boxes being among their first products. Various other novelties

were added from time to time. In 1898 James E. Blake, William H. Blake and Lefferts S. Hoffman filed papers of incorporation under the name James E. Blake Co. The firm name continued to be listed until 1936.

On January 31, 1905 they were granted a patent (No. 44,102) for the manufacture of sterling silver and silver inlaid with 14k gold cigarette and vanity cases, match boxes, men's belt buckles and pocket knives.

Their factory building is now occupied by Bates & Klinke.

PORTER BLANCHARD
Pacioma, California

Silversmith and pewterer.

E. A. BLISS CO.
Meriden, Conecticut
See Napier Company

Used on World's Fair souvenirs, Chicago, 1893 (U. S. Patent 18,479, September 30, 1890.)

Founded in 1875 by E. A. Bliss and J. E. Carpenter in North Attleboro, Massachusetts when they took over the Whitney & Rice Co. where Bliss had been a traveling salesman: succeeded by E. A. Bliss in 1883. Moved to Meriden, Connecticut in 1890. Began the manufacture of sterling silver in 1893. Succeeded by Napier-Bliss Co., c. 1915.

(Stamped on
Nickel Silver Wares.)

Used on World's Fair souvenirs,
Chicago, 1893 (U. S. Patent
18,479, September 30, 1890.)

L. D. BLOCH & CO.
New York, New York

Manufactured plated silver novelties c. 1920.

BONTON
B
SILVERPLATE

BLUE RIBBON SILVER MANUFACTURERS, INC.
New York, New York

Max Sherman, Brooklyn, New York received Design Patent No. 59,036, Assignor Blue Ribbon Mfgrs. Sept. 13, 1921. He also received Design Pat No. 62,036, March 6, 1923, for fruit basket, pierced design; not assigned.

J. C. BOARDMAN & CO.
S. Wallingford, Connecticut

The company was founded in 1950 by Joseph C. Boardman. Originally located in New Haven, Connecticut and moved to Wallingford, Connecticut in 1962. They originally manufactured silverplated novelties and unweighted (no artificial weight such as pitch or plaster of Paris) sterling holloware. Boardman was one of the first American manufacturers to recognize the revival of pewter in 1956 and today manufactures America's most complete pewter line — more than 300 items. Today they also continue to make the finest quality sterling holloware. With the increased price of silver, the temptation to weight the product is something to which all but a few in the industry have succumbed. Although the name is the same, they are not direct descendants of the Thomas and Sherman Boardman line.

LUTHER BOARDMAN & SON
East Haddam, Connecticut

The company was founded by Luther Boardman in the 1820s; became L. Boardman & Son between 1840-44 and went out of business about 1905.

Luther Boardman was born at Rocky Hill, Connecticut, December 26, 1812. He was apprenticed to Ashbil Griswold at Meriden, Connecticut, where he learned the britannia trade. In 1833 he worked for Burrage Yale at South Reading, Massachusetts and became owner of the shop in 1836. In 1837 he returned to Meriden and married Lydia Ann Frary. In 1838 he worked for Russell & Beach at Chester, Connecticut and later made britannia spoons in his own shop there. In 1842 he moved to East Haddam, Connecticut. Most of his work after this time was silverplated britannia.

In 1864 his son was made a partner and the name of the firm changed to L. Boardman & Son which was continued for some time after his death in 1887. In 1866 a new plant was built for making nickel silver, silverplated spoons. The business was discontinued shortly before the death of Norman S. Boardman in 1905.

L. BOARDMAN & SON

Z. BOSTWICK
new York, New York

Zalmon Bostwick advertised in *The New York Mercantile Register* 1848-49 as "successor to Thompson," and that he "Would inform the public generally that he has made extensive preparation for the manufacture of SILVER WARE, in all its branches . . ." Listed in New York City Directories 1851-52.

F. L. BOSWORTH CO.
Minneapolis, Minnesota

Founded 1900. Jobbers and wholesale jewelers. They bought wares "in the metal" from manufacturers and plated them in their own shop. Succeeded by P. M. Vermaas c. 1915. Vermaas was president when Bosworth died in 1914.

BOTT SILVERSMITHS, INC.
New York, New York

Listed 1961 JBG as manufacturers of silver wares.

D. C. BOURQUIN
Port Richmond, N.Y.

Founding date not known. Listed in JC 1904, under sterling and jewelry. Out of business before 1909. Trademark identical to Wortz & Voorhis.

BOWLER & BURDICK CO.
Cleveland, Ohio

Listed in JC 1904-1922. Wholesaler whose trademark was found on souvenir spoons. In business before 1890.

JACK BOWLING
Philadelphia, Pennsylvania

Silversmith, designer and lecturer on silver and silver work. His own works are included in the permanent collections of the Honolulu Academy of Arts and the Library of Congress. He has won numerous awards for excellence and is noted especially for his handwrought ecclesiastic silver.

Admiral Bowling, while still a lieutenant, gained an international reputation as an engraver and print maker but found rough seas unsuitable for the pursuit of these skills. He turned then to metal work and started with the handiest material — tin cans, and soon graduated to gold and silver. He made a silver ladle while at sea on an anti-submarine patrol in 1943 and was impressed with the time and patience required. It was then that he selected his "turtle" maker's mark, chosen because of its significance that "slow and steady does it." — a most appropriate symbol on handwrought silver. The two stars were added on his promotion to Rear Admiral and retirement from the Navy in 1947. In addition, he engraves "jack bowling — philadelphia" and the date of completion on finished articles when suitable. This is not a stamp but an actual signature.

The turtle mark used with 14K, 10K on gold; with STERLING on silver.

WM. N. BOYNTON
Manchester, Iowa

Registered trademark June 27, 1882 for manufacture of gold, silver and plated ware. This is essentially the same trademark used by the United States Jewelers' Guild until c. 1904. This latter mark was also used by J. H. Purdy & Co., wholesale and retail jeweler in Chicago, listed c. 1896-1924. It was also used by others who belonged to the Guild.

BRAINARD & WILSON
Danbury, Connecticut

Listed 1909-1922 in JC under plated silver art wares.

B. & W.

(On Silver Plated Art Ware.)

W. J. BRAITSCH & CO.
Providence, Rhode Island

Silversmiths before 1895. They were manufacturers of sterling dresserware. In 1898 they introduced a new type of dresserware of 14k gold plate which they guaranteed to wear ten years. An ingot of gold was welded to an ingot of gun metal, both were then rolled into sheets of the desired thickness and then made into backs for brushes, mirrors, trophies, etc. They were hand chased and either a gold or gold plated shield was inserted. The process was somewhat related to the "Old Sheffield Plate" process. Out of business before 1922.

TRADE MARK
STERLING

E. P. BRAY & DAUCHY
New York, New York

Advertised in *Harper's Weekly* (12-4-1858) as "Agts., Manufacturers . . . We *Manufacture* and *Plate* our own Ware, and are thus enabled to offer. . . . Coffee, Tea, and Hot Water Urns. . . . Liquor, or Cordial Stands; Magic perfumery and Cigar Stands with Thermometer attached; Magic Castors and Egg Stands combined; complete with Cups and Spoons; Fillagree [sic!] Card and Sugar Baskets; Wine Syphons; Champagne and Hock Bottle Holders; New Style French 3 and 4 Ring Breakfast Castors, & c, &c."

RAYMOND BRENNER, INC.
Youngstown, Ohio

Registered trademark for sterling silverware, silver-plated holloware, flatware and table cutlery. Claims use since August 29, 1949.

CHAS. C. BRIDDELL, INC.
Crisfield, Maryland
See Towle Silversmiths

Started in business c. 1900 and originally made oyster knives and other seafood tools and implements for the watermen who worked the lower Chesapeake Bay area. In 1905 the firm registered the trademark "Carvel Hall" to be used on cutlery, machinery and tools. The name, Carvel Hall, was

DIVISION OF TOWLE SILVERSMITHS

chosen many years ago by a designer for the company who was visiting Annapolis. While there, he noticed the elegant designs on the massive doors of the Carvel Hall Hotel and returned to Crisfield with the suggestion that the name be used on the line of knives being made by the firm. They now make a dozen lines of dinner knives and carving knives. Carvel Hall is now a Division of Towle Silversmiths.

BRIDE & TINCKLER
New York, New York

Wholesalers of sterling silverware and jewelry. Listed JC 1896-1922.

BRIDGEPORT SILVER CO.
Bridgeport, Connecticut

In business in 1880. President, James Staples; sec-treas., superintendent, Samuel Larkin. About 1882 there was a report that they were to merge with the F. B. Rogers Silver Co. Business continued until 1884 or longer.

BRIDGEPORT SILVER PLATE CO.
Bridgeport, Connecticut
Lambert's Point, near Norfolk,
West Virginia

Incorporated January 15, 1891 with George A. Leonard of Boston as president; treasurer, F. H. MacFarlane; sec., Thomas F. MacFarlane. Moved to Lambert s Point, near Norfolk, West Virginia in 1898 although in 1910 there was a MacFarlane Mfg. Co. listed in the Bridgeport Directory. In 1894 there was a Bridgeport Silver Plate Co., probably controlled by MacFarlane. In 1913 there was a firm, MacFarlane, Brothers Mfg. Co. In August 1913 the deeds, tools, etc., were given to the Newfield Silver Co.

BRINSMAID
Burlington, Vermont

CHRONOLOGY

Pangborn & Brinsmaid	1833-43
J. E. Brinsmaid & Brothers	1843
Brinsmaid & Bros.	1843-1850
Brinsmaid, Brother & Co.	1850-1854
James E. Brinsmaid	1854-1884
Brinsmaid & Hildreth	1854-1902

The Brinsmaid name has been connected with silversmithing in Burlington since c. 1795 when Abram Brinsmaid, from Great Barrington, Massachusetts, settled there. His three sons, James Edgar, Sedgwick Swift and William Bliss, set up in business in 1843 at the old stand of Pangborn & Brinsmaid under the name J. E. Brinsmaid & Brothers, a name soon shortened to Brinsmaid & Bros. Sedgwick left the partnership in 1850 and the two remaining brothers took into partnership Chester Hildreth under the new firm name of Brinsmaid, Brother & Co. In 1854 James Edgar announced that he was opening his own business as successor to Brinsmaid, Brother & Co. William Brinsmaid and Chester Hildreth went into business together under the name of Brinsmaid & Hildreth. Both new firms claimed to be successors to Pangborn & Brinsmaid, Brinsmaid & Bros. and Brinsmaid, Bros. & Co. James

E. Brinsmaid retired in 1884. Brinsmaid & Hildreth business continued until 1902 when it was sold to Nelson A. Bero.

A. Brindsmaid B & H

Brinsmaid's, B⊖D Brinsmaid

Brinsmaid & Hildreth

BRISTOL BRASS & CLOCK CO.
Bristol, Connecticut
See American Silver Co.
See International Silver Co.

1857 WELCH-ATKINS
NEW ENGLAND SILVER PLATE CO.
H. & T. MFG. CO.
WELCH SILVER
ROYAL PLATE CO.

Organized in 1856. They furnished Holmes & Tuttle with their metal. Successor to Holmes & Tuttle Mfg. Co. in 1857. In 1901 became The American Silver Co. which was bought by International Silver Co. in 1935. Bristol Brass & Clock Co. owned the entire stock of American Silver Co. until 1913 when a distribution of stock was made.

Makers of silver tableware, solid and plated.
Patent 26,297, March 26, 1895.

1857 WELCH-ATKINS
NEW ENGLAND SILVER PLATE CO.
H. & T. MFG. CO.
WELCH SILVER.
ROYAL PLATE CO.

Trade Mark. 1850 BRISTOL. 1857 Diamond Brand.

Windsor Table Patterns.

BRISTOL MFG. CO.
Attleboro, Massachusetts

Founding date not known. They were manufacturers of plated silverware, cut and plain glass. Succeeded by Bristol Silver Co. c. 1895.

SILVEROIN
Novelties

GERMAN SILVER
(On Mesh Bags.)

BRISTOL SILVER COMPANY
Attleboro, Massachusetts

Successors to Bristol Mfg. Co. Out of business before 1915.

(Sterling Finish.)

BRISTOL SILVER CORP.
Taunton, Massachusetts
See Poole Silver Company, Inc.

BRITANNIA ARTISTIC SILVER
See M. T. Goldsmith

BRITANNIA ARTISTIC SILVER

BRITANNIA METAL CO.
See Van Bergh Silver Plate Co.

BRODGERS SILVER CO.
Taunton, Massachusetts

The trademark shown here has previously been attributed to a "Brodgers" Silver Company. It is actually the trademark of F. B. Rogers Silver Company of Taunton, Massachusetts, successor to the West Silver Company.

THOMAS F. BROGAN
New York, New York

Listed JC 1896-1930 under sterling silverware and jewelry.

D. L. BROMWELL, INC.
Washington, D.C.

Founded in 1873 by James Bromwell as a small silver and nickel-plating plant. Wet cells were used for the electroplating process, but the buffing wheels that were used to develop the gleaming finish employed a huge mastiff dog, named Cleo, as the motive power. So well did Cleo love the work that it was a problem getting the dog out of the wheel when his efforts were no longer needed. An old-style gas engine was installed later to replace Cleo's power potential, but it broke down periodically and Cleo was allowed to return to the beloved wheel.

James Bromwell's shop, which was capable of making or repairing almost anything, soon became the popular refuge of inventors, who would bring their problems there to be solved. One inventor was trying to develop a gramophone at about the time Edison was perfecting his. While working with the inventor on the basis of a coated cylinder to retain the sound impressions, James discovered how to plate babyshoes with precious metals, a branch of the business which is still active.

Requests for repair and replacement of antique door knockers, fireplace andirons, fenders and fire tools led to new fields and the development of a bewildering array of metal products spread the fame of the establishment all over the country.

In 1907 James Bromwell died, and his son, Dwight, took over the business. His own son, Berton also began to learn the business, but his interests were in its administration. In 1924 the firm was incorporated under its present name. It is presently operated by the fourth generation of Bromwells. They no longer do their own plating and now specialize in fireplace fixtures.

J. T. BROMWELL
Baltimore, Maryland

Listed in the Baltimore City Directories 1881-1888 under the name T. T. Bromwell, silver plater; listed 1889 as Bromwell Plating Works; 1898-1901 as John T. Bromwell and 1902-04 as Bromwell Plating Works.

BRONZART METALS CO.
New York New York

Listed among manufacturers of silver c. 1940.

BRONZART

BROOKLYN SILVER CO.
See Schade & Co.

"Satin finish" on plated silver patented in 1870 by James H. Reilly.

BROOKLYN SILVER PLATE CO.
Brooklyn, New York

In business c. 1890. "Brooklyn S.P. Co. Quadruple Plate" mark used on napkin rings made by E. G. Webster & Son c. 1895-1900.

BROWER & RUSHER
New York, New York
See Walter S. Brower

Listed in New York City Directories 1837-1842 as retailers for S. D. Brower; Hall, Hewson & Co.; Hall, Hewson & Brower.

WALTER S. BROWER
Albany, New York

CHRONOLOGY	
Carson & Hall	1810-1818
Hall & Hewson	1818-1829
	1842-1847
Hall, Hewson & Co.	1839-1842
	1847-1850
Hall, Hewson & Merrifield	1845
Hall, Hewson & Brower	1849-1850
Hall & Brower	1852-1854
Hall, Brower & Co.	1854
S. D. Brower & Son	1850
Walter S. Brower	1850

The history of the Walter S. Brower company of Albany, New York can be traced to Carson & Hall (Thomas Carson & Green Hall, 1810-1818); Hall & Hewson (Green Hall & John D. Hewson, listed in City Directories 1818-1829; 1842-1847); Hall, Hewson & Co. (Green Hall, John D. Hewson and S. Douglas Brower, listed in the City Directories 1839-1842; 1847-1850); Hall, Hewson & Merrifield (Green Hall, John D. Hewson & Thomas V. Z. Merrifield, in business c. 1845); Hall, Hewson & Brower (Green Hall, John D. Hewson & S. D. Brower listed in the City Directory 1849-1850); Hall & Brower (Green Hall & S. Douglas Brower, listed in the City Directories 1852-1854); Hall, Brower & Co. (Green Hall and S. D. Brower, listed in City Directories after 1854); S. D. Brower & Son (S. D. Brower & Walter S. Brower, in

business around 1850) and finally Walter S. Brower, who began around 1850 in Albany. Walter S. Brower was the son of S. Douglas Brower, who had been apprenticed to Hall & Hewson before setting up his own shop in Troy, New York in 1834. S. Douglas retired to a farm temporarily and then returned to silversmithing with the firm of Hall, Hewson & Brower c. 1849-50. Father and son were in business together soon afterwards. Walter S. Brower retired in 1898.

BROWN & BROS.
Waterbury, Connecticut

Established in 1851. They originally produced brass and German silver. September 21, 1875 they registered a patent for brass, German silver and plated silver goods. In 1874 they engaged LeRoy S. White, who had been with Rogers & Brother for 17 years and earlier with Hartford Mfg. Co., to start making silverplated flatware. The business continued for about ten years but was not too successful and the entire business discontinued in 1884 or 1885. No successor of their silverplated line was recorded. In 1886 Randolph and Cough took over the plant but evidently did not continue making silverplated flatware.

THOMAS G. BROWN & SONS
New York, New York

(Goods made for Gorham Mfg. Co.)

CHRONOLOGY	
Hinsdale & Taylor	1807-1817
Taylor, Baldwin & Co.	1817-1841
Baldwin & Co.	c. 1840-1869
Thomas G. Brown	1869-1881
Thomas G. Brown & Sons	1881-c. 1915

Manufacturers of some sterling goods for Gorham Mfg. Co., which were so marked.

"Justus Verschuur, for several years connected with the Alvin Mfg. Co., is now connected with Thomas G. Brown & Sons." (JC&HR 3-18-1896, p. 24)

"William A. Brown, New York, formerly of Thomas G. Brown & Sons, and Frederick, T. Ward, formerly of Cox, Cooper, Ward & Young, have formed a partnership and started in business to manufacture high class novelties in sterling silver." (JC&HR 3-25-1896, p. 24)

"This concern started in Newark c. 1801-02 and has been in existence for 98 or 99 years, thus outdating all others." (Letter from T. G. Brown & Sons, JC-W 5-16-1900, p. 52)

The sons were Thomas B. and William A. Brown.

(Goods made for Gorham Mfg. Co.)

THOMAS J. BROWN
Baltimore, Maryland

Listed in Baltimore City Directories 1867-1874 as a goldsmith and silversmith. The company name was changed to Thomas J. Brown & Son in 1875 and continued under this listing through 1883.

BROWN & SHARP
Warren, Rhode Island
Pawtucket, Rhode Island
Providence, Rhode Island

"Brown & Sharp, established in 1804 by David Brown, jeweler and silverware, in Warren, Rhode Island. When business failed he traveled through the valley of the Connecticut and ground razors and fine cutlery. He also carried with him silverware of his own manufacture. He followed this itinerant occupation for 3 years. In 1828, he moved from Warren, Rhode Island to Pawtucket, R.I. and five years later, in 1833, formed a co-partnership with his son Joseph P. Brown and not long afterwards founded in Providence the establishment which became incorporated in 1868 as Brown & Sharpe Mfg. Co. still in business in 1919." (JC-W 2-5-1919)

BROWN & WARD
New York, New York
See Thomas G. Brown & Sons

Listed JC 1896 under sterling silver. Out of business before 1904.

BROWNE, JENNINGS & LAUTER
New York, New York
See Jennings & Lauter

BRUN-MILL CO.
Pittsfield, Illinois

Manufacturers of plated silverware c. 1920.

FRED BUCHER
Baltimore, Maryland

Listed in Baltimore City Directories 1877-79 as a goldsmith and silversmith.

BUCK SILVER COMPANY
Salamanca, New York

Listed as Buck Silver Company c. 1900-1914 when it became Buck Plating Co. Out of business before 1922. According to an unidentified newspaper clipping dated 1908, they made an extensive line of plated holloware.

BUCKER & ROHLEDER
Baltimore, Maryland

Listed in Baltimore City Directories 1901-04 as silverplaters.

SILAS E. BUCKER
Baltimore, Maryland

Listed in Baltimore City Directories 1907-13 as a silverplater.

CALEB H. BURGESS
Baltimore, Maryland

Listed in 1864 Baltimore City Directory as a silverplater. Listed as Caleb H. & John Burgess 1865-1883 — Caleb H. Burgess 1884-89.

JOHN BURGESS
Baltimore, Maryland

Listed in 1864 Baltimore City Directory as a silverplater.

OWEN D. BURGESS
Baltimore, Maryland

Listed in Baltimore City Directories 1894-1899 as a silverplater.

CHAS. B. BYRON CO.
New York, New York

Successors to Bryon & Vail Co. before 1909.

BYRON & VAIL CO.
New York, New York
See Chas. B. Byron Co.

Succeeded by Chas. B. Byron Co. Founding date not known. Manufacturers of sterling silverware, gold and platinum cigarette and vanity cases, match boxes and powder boxes.

J. E. CALDWELL & CO.
Philadelphia, Pennsylvania

"Caldwell & Bennett predecessors of J. E. Caldwell." (JC&HR 8-28-1895, p. 15) Jewelers, silversmiths and antiquarians since 1839.

J. E. C. & CO.

CAMDEN HALL INC.
New York, New York

Importers. Listed JC-K 1964 in New York; no further listing.

J. D. CAMIRAND & CO.
Montreal, Canada

Manufacturers of plated silver c. 1920.

A. CAMPBELL
Chicago, Illinois

Listed in Chicago City Directories 1853-1855 as a silverplater.

ARCHIBOLD CAMPBELL
Baltimore, Maryland

Listed in 1864 Baltimore City Directory as a silverplater.

JAMES J. CAMPBELL
Baltimore, Maryland

Listed in Baltimore City Directories 1874-1877 as silverplaters.

SAMUEL K. CAMPBELL
Baltimore, Maryland

Listed in 1864 Baltimore City Directory as a silverplater.

CAMPBELL-METCALF SILVER CO.
Providence, Rhode Island

Founded by Ernest W. Campbell and Joseph M. Metcalf. Campbell was born in Providence, Rhode Island April 11, 1860. Studied art at Brown University. Started in silver manufacturing business as a designer and superintendent at "one of the prominent Providence silver manufactories" [probably Gorham]. Metcalf was born in Brooklyn, Connecticut in 1861 and received his education in Providence. His first business experience was as a salesman for a drug firm. Campbell and Metcalf joined together under the name Campbell-Metcalf Silver Company in 1892 to manufacture sterling silver goods.

"The Campbell-Metcalf Silver Co. was adjudged insolvent." JC&HR 6-8-1898, p. 17) In 1900 Campbell designed silverware for W. H. Manchester Co.

CANADIAN JEWELERS, LTD.
Montreal, Quebec

Manufacturers of silver deposit ware c. 1915-1920.

DEPOS-ART

CANADIAN WM. A. ROGERS CO., LTD.
Toronto, Canada
See Oneida Silversmiths
See Wm. A. Rogers Co.

"HEIRLOOM" "WM. A. ROGERS" (R) Wm. A. Rogers

W. R. ☼   1881 (R) ROGERS (R) A1

CANFIELD & BROTHER
Baltimore, Maryland

Ira B. Canfield and William B. Canfield, silversmiths in Baltimore c. 1830.

CANFIELD BRO. & CO.
Baltimore, Maryland

Ira B. Canfield, Wm. B. Canfield and J. H. Meredith. Importers and manufacturers of watches, jewelry and silverware, "Albata & Plated ware." Listed in Baltimore City Directories 1850-81. Succeeded by Welsh & Bro.

OSCAR CAPLAN & SONS
Baltimore, Maryland

Silversmiths, established 1905.

CALBERT MFG. CO.
New York, New York

Listed JC 1915 as manufacturers of plated silver. Out of business before 1922.

GONDOLA SILVER

DAVID CARLSON
Gardner, Massachusetts

Listed KJI 1927 as manufacturer of handwrought sterling silverware.

CARON BROS.
Montreal, Canada

Listed in JC as manufacturers of metal products and jewelry. Their trademark has been found on souvenir spoons.

Their catalog of 1878 features sterling silver, electroplate, ormolu, etc., "of British manufacture."

CARPENTER & BLISS
North Attleboro, Massachusetts
See Napier Company

Began business as Carpenter & Bliss in 1875 in North Attleboro, Massachusetts. Succeeded by E. A. Bliss Co. in 1883.

M. W. CARR & CO., INC.
West Somerville, Massachusetts

Listed from c. 1920 to the present as manufacturers of bag frames, dorine boxes, vanity cases, match boxes, jewel boxes, Dutch reproductions, pewterware, photo frames and other novelties. No response to inquiries.

CARR CRAFT

SANDERS W. CARR
Baltimore, Maryland

Listed in 1876 Baltimore City Directory as a silverplater. Succeeded by W. S. Carr & Co. in 1877.

W. S. CARR & CO.
Baltimore, Maryland

Successors to Sanders W. Carr, silverplater, first listed in 1876 Baltimore City Directory. In business through 1886.

JOHN CARROW
Philadelphia, Pennsylvania

In business about 1884.

JOHN CARROW. PHILA. QUAD. H.W.M.

CARTER-CRUME CO.
Niagara Falls, New York

Listed in the Niagara Falls City Directory as the earliest manufacturers of salesbooks in this country.

Succeeded by American Salesbook Co., now Moore Business Forms, Inc.

They were also listed in the 1898 JC as manufacturers of plated flatware.

These two trademarks were registered at the U. S. Patent Office for use on plated flatware.

The Niagara Silver Co. (Wm. A. Jameson, manager) was a branch of Carter-Crume.

EXTRA {COIN SILVER N2.12} PLATE

U. S. Patent 30,185, June 15, 1897 to be used on spoons, forks, knives and plated flatware.

RSMC

U. S. Patent 30,962, December 14, 1897, to be used on blades of knives, shanks of spoons and forks.

H. A. CARY CO.

"H. A. Cary formerly of Phelps & Cary Co. has gone into business for himself. Incorporated at Albany [New York] Friday. They will engage in the business of silversmithing." (JC-W 6-6-1900, p. 34)

LEWIS CARY
Boston, Massachusetts

Silversmith c. 1820. One of his apprentices was Newell Harding.

CASTLE SILVER CORP.
New York, New York

Manufacturers of silverplated wares c. 1950.

CATTARAUGUS CUTLERY CO.
Little Valley, New York

In 1904 advertised "Manufacturers of fine cutlery since 1876." No record after 1910.

YUKON SILVER
98-100 FINE.

CELLINI CRAFT, LTD.
Evanston, Illinois
See The Randahl Shop

Manufacturers of sterling and silverplated holloware c. 1940-50.

CENTRAL STERLING CO.
Brooklyn, New York
See J. Wagner & Son, Inc.

Discontinued between 1909-14

CENTURY SILVER MFG. CO.
New York, New York

Listed 1927 and 1931 KJI as manufacturers of silverplated wares.

CHAPIN & HOLLISTER CO.
Providence, Rhode Island

Listed in JC 1915-22. Manufacturers of gold, silver and gold-filled knives and jewelry.

C. &. H. Co.

CHAPMAN & BARDEN
Attleboro, Massachusetts
See Barden, Blake & Co.

C. & B.

CHARTER COMPANY
See International Silver Company

Trademarks used on sterling reproductions of early Colonial silver. Made in the Barbour Silver Co. plant c. 1930-33. When that division was closed, the Charter line was moved to the sterling division in Wallingford. Discontinued about 1942.

BENJAMIN K. CHASE
Rutland, Vermont

Went into business in 1869 as a silversmith and jeweler after serving as a captain in the Union Forces in the Civil War. Advertised gold and silver goods and watches.

JOHN CHATTELLIER
Newark, New Jersey

Manufacturer of sterling cigar, cigarette and clock cases, razor sets, jewel, match and cigarette boxes, picture frames and watch cases.

CHELTENHAM & CO., LTD.
Sheffield, England
See National Silver Co.

CHICAGO MONOGRAM STUDIOS
Chicago, Illinois

Listed 1922 JC as manufacturers of sterling, 10, 12 and 14k gold buckles, belt and trouser chains. Successors to Chicago Monogram Jewelry Works. William Nicholls registered their Silvergrams

Silvergrams

trademark in 1948 and claimed that it had been in use since Oct. 23, 1947. It was for monograms in the form of initials made of, or plated with precious metal, to be attached to automobiles.

CHICAGO SILVER CO.
Chicago, Illinois

Listed in business c. 1925-1950 as manufacturers of sterling silverware.

SAMUEL CHILD & CO.
Baltimore, Maryland

Listed in Baltimore City Directories 1868-1886 as silverplaters.

CHRISTOFLE
Paris, France

Founded in 1839 by Charles Christofle. He was the founder of the plated and gilded silverware industry of France. He bought up all the French electroplate patents then extant and started his own silver and gold plating industry. Later he branched out into sterling and gold wares. Workmanship of the Christofle firm has always been outstanding. The firm is still considered one of the leaders in world silver design. They are represented in the U. S. by Christofle at Baccarat, New York.

July 9, 1949 Christofle filed application for a trademark in the U. S. to be used on gold and sterling silver flatware and holloware.

CHURCH & ROGERS
See Rogers Brothers

LOREY CHURCHILL
Baltimore, Maryland

Listed in Baltimore City Directories 1864-1868 as a silverplater.

CINCINNATI SILVER CO.
Cincinnati, Ohio
See O. E. Bell Co.

FREDERICK H. CLARK
Newark, New Jersey

Listed in JC 1915 as manufacturer of sterling silverware. Out of business before 1922.

GABRIEL D. CLARK
Baltimore, Maryland

Silversmith in Baltimore 1830-1896, associated with James A. Foxcroft 1831-1839 in the firm of Foxcroft & Clark. Born 1813 — died 1896.

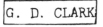

CLARK & NOON
Newark, New Jersey

First listed in JC as W. F. Cory & Bros., Newark, N.J. in 1896. Clark & Noon are listed as successors in 1915 and not listed after 1922. Makers of sterling silverware and 14 and 18k gold jewelry.

BENJAMIN CLARK SILVER CO.
Ottawa, Illinois
See Benedict Mfg. Co.

CLIFF SILVER CO.
New York, ew York

They advertised (Antiques, Nov. 1929, p. 407) that they specialized in "Reproducing by hand sterling or Sheffield Plate." The ad says "Established 1905."

CLIMAX MESH BAG CO.
Newark, New jersey

Listed in JC in 1915. Out of business before 1922.

COBB, GOULD & CO.
Attleboro, Massachusetts
See Wallace Silversmiths
See Watson Co.

Founded in 1874 in Attleboro, Massachusetts. Succeeded by Watson & Newell in 1894; the Watson Company in 1919 and Wallace Silversmiths in 1955.

HERBERT COCKSHAW, JR.
New York, New York

Listed in 1904 as Howard & Cockshaw; Herbert Cockshaw successor in 1915 and Herbert Cockshaw, Jr. in 1936-37 in the Jobbers' Handbook.

CODDING BROS. & HEILBORN
North Attleboro, Massachusetts

Codding Bros. & Heilborn were manufacturers of silver novelties, founded in 1879 in North Attleboro, Massachusetts. In 1882 their business was burned out and they erected a new factory that same year. Leo A. Heilborn was admitted to the firm in 1891. In 1895 the members of the firm were Arthur E. Codding, James A. Codding, Edwin A. Codding and Leo A. Heilborn. C. A. Vanderbilt (q. v.) was in charge of the domestic trade office from 1893. "Codding Bros. & Heilborn, Providence, incorporated for the manufacture and selling of jewelry and silverware and novelties." (JC 4-28-1897, p. 28) The firm went out of business in May 1918.

C. B. & H.
STERLINC.

D. D. CODDING
North Attleboro, Massachusetts

Listed in JC in 1896 as manufacturers of sterling silverware. Out of business before 1904.

STE*RLING
D. D. C.

COHANNET SILVER CO.
Taunton, Massachusetts

Catalog published 1896. Illustrated candlesticks, fern dishes, shaving mugs, tea sets, pickle casters with glass inserts, etc.

A. COHEN & SONS CORP.
New York, New York

Founded in 1911 by Hyman J. Cohen, Samuel Cohen, Harry Cohen and Abraham Cohen. They are the largest wholesale jewelry distributors in the world catering to the retail jewelers. A division of Cohen-Hatfield Industries, Inc. Wholesalers of sterling and silverplated holloware and flatware which is produced under contract for them.

CROSBY   KRANSHIRE

L. H. COHEN
New York, New York

Listed in the Jeweler's Weekly 1896 as manufacturers of sterling silverware. Listed in JC 1904. Succeeded by L. H. Cohen Co., Inc. between 1909-1915. Last listing was in 1922.

COHEN & ROSENBERGER
New York, New York

Listed in JC as Baldwin, Ford & Co. 1896; Ford & Carpenter in 1904 and Baldwin, Ford & Co. 1915-1943. Advertised imitation pearls, novelty jewelry and beads. Listed in sterling silver section until 1943.

S. COHEN & SON
Boston, Massachusetts

A jobbing concern that specialized primarily in plating about 1856.

J. J. COHN
New York, New York

Listed in Jewelers' Weekly, 1896 in sterling section. Also listed in JC 1896, leather goods.

L. COHN
Baltimore, Maryland

Listed in 1868–69 Baltimore City Directory as a silverplater.

WILLIAM H. COLE & SONS
Baltimore, Maryland

Listed in 1895 Baltimore City Directory. Advertised plated silverware.

ALBERT COLES & CO.
New York, New York

New York silversmiths. Listed in city directories from 1836 to 1880 The factory was at 6 Liberty Place. This was a large factory and the silver was sold to numerous retailers who, in turn, stamped their own names on pieces that Coles had actually manufactured. Coles was succeeded in business by Morgan Morgans who, in turn, sold out to Geo. W. Shiebler in 1876. Coles' spoon designs were continued by the Shiebler company for many years, some of them being quite popular as late as 1895. From 1880 until his death November 27, 1886, Coles was listed only at his residence, 225 West 39th St.

COLONIAL SILVER COMPANY, INC.
Portland, Maine

Successor to the Stevens Silver Co. in 1899. They were manufacturers of plated silverware and pewter. Gold and silver and nickel plating done to order. In business until 1943.

COLONIAL SILVER CO.

(Nickel Silver Hollowware)

(Plated holloware)

(On white metal)

COLONIAL SILVER CO.
(White Metal Hollowware)

COLUMBIA MFG. CO.
Gowanda, New York

"The Columbia Mfg. Co. of Gowanda, N.Y., has been incorporated with a capital stock of $15,000 for the purpose of manufacturing plated ware. The company will at once begin constructing a factory." (JW 6-1-1892)

COLUMBIA SILVER CO.
Brooklyn, New York

Listed 1957-61 JBG as manufacturers of silver.

COLUMBIA SILVERSMITHS
New York, New York

Listed 1957-61 as manufacturers of silver.

COMMONWEALTH SILVER CO.
Los Angeles, California

Manufacturers of sterling silverware 1905-c. 1920.

CONCORD SILVERSMITHS, LTD.
See Ellmore Silver Co., Inc.

Began as Concord Silver Co., in 1925 using the old Durgin factory. In 1939 a new concern was organized under the name of Concord Silversmiths, Ltd., and bought the plant, machinery, tools of the Concord Silver Co., then in bankruptcy. They were to manufacture heavy sterling flatware only. In September of 1942 they discontinued the manufacture of sterling for the duration of the war. Ellmore Silver Co. took over the business and produced their patterns. Dies purchased by Crown Silver Co.

CONTINENTAL MFG. CO.
New York, New York

Listed 1927 KJI as manufacturers of silverplated flatware and holloware.

CONTINENTAL SHEFFIELD SILVER CO.
Brooklyn, New York
See Continental Silver Co.

CONTINENTAL SILVER CO.
New York, New York

The Continental Silver Co. of New York and the Continental Sheffield Silver Co. are related. the former being the sales office of the latter. Listed as manufacturers of plated silver holloware on nickel silver base c. 1920 to 1950.

JOHN COOK
New York, New York
See Theo. Evans & Co.

John Cook, foreman for Wm. Gale & Son, 1855, patented a design for "Table-Set for Silver and Plated Ware," Design Patent No. 3384, February 23, 1869. Partner with Theo. Evans in Theo. Evans & Co.

P. A. COON SILVER MFG. CO.
Syracuse, New York

Manufacturers of plated silverware. Successor to

Albert G. Finn Silver Co. between 1904 and 1909. Out of business before 1915.

CORONET SILVER CO., INC.
Brooklyn, New York

Manufacturer of silverplated wares c. 1950.

CORONET

CORTLAN & CO.
Baltimore, Maryland

Listed in Baltimore City Directories 1868-1870 as silverplaters.

W. F. CORY & BRO.
Newark, New Jersey
See Clark & Noon

 STERLING.

Not used after 1904

COSMOPOLITAN SILVER CO.
New York, New York

Adv. in 1922 KS says "Newest Designs in Sheffield Hollow Ware plated on copper." Possibly jobbers or importers. Listing in 1924 KS says they were manufacturers of plated silver holloware.

S. COTTLE CO.
New York, New York
See Howard Sterling Co.

Established 1865. I. N. Levinson, President. H. S. Morris, Sec'y-Treas. Makers of 14k gold and sterling silver novelties. Not listed after 1920.

S. Cottle invented the machine for making a collar button which became the specialty of Howard & Son about 1880.

"S. Cottle, manufacturer of paper knives, pen trays, penwiper stands, letter files, candlesticks, mounted inkstands in sterling silver, etc. Shubael Cottle retired in 1878 and the firm continued as Hale & Mulford. Six years later L. J. Mulford retired and Seth W. Hale & Co. succeeded. This firm continued two years, at which time Mr. Hale assumed the management of *The [Jewelers] Circular.*" (JC&HR 2-4-1894, p. 4) [This account does not agree wth the listings which continue as S. Cottle Co. until c. 1915.]

M. A. COURTRODE
New York, New York

Listed JKD 1918 as silversmiths.

COWLES MFG. CO.
Granby, Connecticut
See International Silver Co.
See Rogers Brothers

Rev. Whitfield Cowles began silverplating in 1843. After he died his son, William B. Cowles, continued the experiments. In 1845 the Cowles Mfg. Co. was organized with Asa Rogers, James H. Isaacson and John D. Johnson. They used German silver as the base for their silverplated wares. In business only a few years.

The Cowles' business led to the first real development in commercial silverplating in this country.

W. I. COWLISHAW
Boston, Massachusetts

Cowlishaw was in business at least as early as 1898 and was known especially for his pewter reproductions of early pieces which were made by the traditional methods of casting and spinning.

He was succeeded by Morton Wheelock c. 1930. Wheelock continued to use the Cowlishaw name but changed the mark to a shield with the name enclosed. He made newer forms rather than reproductions and continued the business until the 1940s. Pieces marked with small circular mark with initials "W.I.C." and an eagle. (Used c. 1898-1930)

(Used c. 1930-c. 1940-45)

COYWELL SPECIALTY CO.
New York, New York

Listed in 1915 JC as manufacturers of sterling silverware. Out of business before 1922.

COYWELL
PLATNOID

CRAIG SILVER CO.
Bridgeport, Connecticut

"A concern operating under the name of Craig Silver Co. has been in existence [in Bridgeport] for some time." (JW 6-6-1894)

CRAIGHEAD SILVER PLATE CO.
Bridgeport Connecticut

"The report of the receiver is that employees of the defunct concern received only 7 percent of the money they earned." (JC&HR 12-4-1895, p. 17)

CRESCENT SILVERWARE MFG. CO., INC.
Port Jervis, New York

Founded in 1922 in New York City. Moved to Port Jervis, New York in 1939. Manufacturers of silverplated holloware and during their early years also made pewter and chrome-plated items. For the past forty years have made only silverplated holloware. At the present time they manufacture about 450 different items. They took over the Knickerbocker Silver Co.

CRESCENT

CROMWELL PLATE CO.
Cromwell, Connecticut
See Barbour Silver Co.
See I. J. Steane & Co.

Organized in 1881 to manufacture a variety of silverplated wares. Sold to I. J. Steane & Co. before 1885.

CROWN MFG. CO.
North Attleboro, Massachusetts

Listed in 1915 JC as manufacturers of plated silverware. Out of business before 1922.

C. M. C.

CROWN SILVER CO., INC.
Brookline, Massachusetts

Listed 1936-37 Jobber's Handbook and 1950 JC-K as manufacturers of plated wares.

CROWN SILVER INC.
New York, New York

The Hasselbring Silver Company, founded in Brooklyn about 1890 by John Hasselbring; the Revere Silver Company, successor to Revere Silversmiths Inc., founded in Brooklyn about 1914 and the Wolfenden Silver Company, successor to J. W. Wolfenden Corporation became divisions of the Crown Silver Inc. in 1955. Manufacturers of sterling silver wares. They own the dies of Amston Co. and bought the F. M. Whiting Co. dies for sterling flatware when the Ellmore Silver Co. went out of business in 1960.

CROWN SILVER PLATE CO.
Bristol, Connecticut
See American Silver Co.

CROWN SILVER PLATE CO.
New York, New York
See J. W. Johnson

"There is no longer any Crown Silver Plate Co. but J. S. Johnson stamps this name on plated silver ware." (JC&HR 4-17-1898, p. 23)

CROWN SILVER PLATE CO.
Toronto, Ontario

Listed in JC 1909-15. Out of business before 1922.

H. C. CULMAN
Honolulu, Hawaii

Listed JC 1909. Out of business c. 1917. Manufacturing jewelers. Trademark found on Hawaiian souvenir spoons.

H. C.

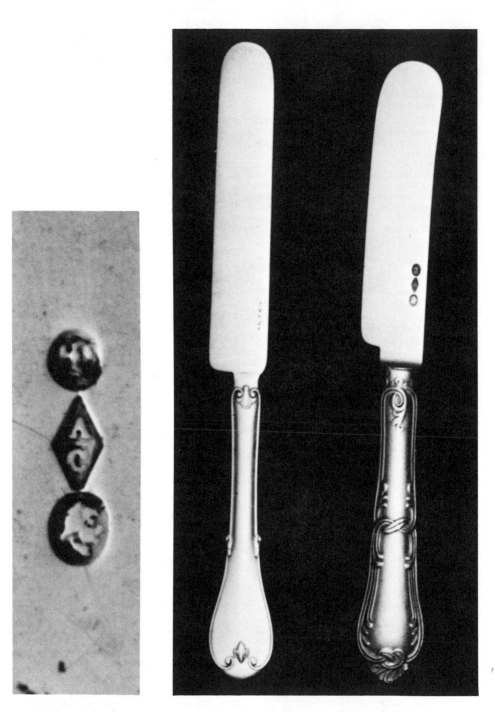

The trademark of Albert Coles, New York silversmith 1860-1880, consisted of an eagle, Coles' initials and a rather strange looking head. These "pseudo hallmarks" were quite common among New York silversmiths c. 1825-1860.

Sugar sifter in *Prince Albert* design by Henry Hubbard, New York City silversmith c. 1855. The form is based on *Fiddle Tipt* pattern while the design elements are derived from the *Kings* and *Queens*. The same design is found in English silver under the name *Albert*, made by C. J. Vander, Ltd. makers of hand forged silver. It was also shown in an Elkington & Mason Co. catalog of 1851 and described as one of "the current styles in silver-plated wares. The "pseudo hallmarks" accompanying the stamp of Rudd & Scudder are typical of those used in New York and elsewhere around the middle of the nineteenth century.

J. F. CURRAN & CO.
New York, New York

Silverplaters c. 1860-1900.

CURRIER & ROBY
New York, New York
See Elgin Silversmith Co., Inc.

Manufacturers of sterling silver holloware. Listed JC and JC-K 1904-1950. Currier was Ernest M. Currier, silversmith and author of *Marks of Early American Silversmiths.* Currier & Roby succeeded the George A. Henckel & Co., in 1940. Now a division of Elgin Silversmiths Co.

Numerous Currier & Roby products made since the late 1920s bear also a Gebelein (q.v.) stamp as retailer.

CURTIN & CLAKE HARDWARE CO.
St. Joseph, Missouri

Listed in JC 1909-22 as silverplaters.

CURTIS & DUNNING
Burlington, Vermont

Lemuel Curtis and Joseph N. Dunning advertised that their "silver spoons are made from crowns, without the least alloy." In partnership 1822-32.

F. CURTIS & CO.
Connecticut
See American Sterling Co.
See Williams Bros. Mfg. Co.

Frederick and Joseph S. Curtis, brothers who manufactured German silverware, spoons and spectacles in Hartford, moved to Glastonbury. The first notice of the partnership appeared January 24, 1848. Company offices remained at Hartford while manufacturing operations were begun at Curtisville — that section of Glastonbury which today comprises a part of Naubuc. The company name was changed to Curtisville Mfg. Co. "The Memorial History of Hartford County" states that at Curtisville was manufactured the first German Silver in America. The silver-white metal, an alloy of copper, zinc and nickel, was hauled by wagon to Waterbury and there rolled to the desired thickness. *(Retrospect,* A publication of the Historical Society of Glastonbury, No. 10, Feb. 1948.)

H. H. CURTIS & CO.
North Attleboro, Mass.

The earliest record found was a Patent Office registration of the trademark in the name of Curtis and Wilkinson, November 3, 1891, to be used on jewelry, table and flatware. The company was sold at auction in May 1915.

Note that the trademark is similar to those of the W. H. Glenny & Company and the Waldo Foundry.

H. H. C. CO.
(German Silver Bags.)

JAMES CURTIS
Chicago, Illinois

Listed in 1854-1855 Chicago Directory as a silverplater.

CURTISVILLE MFG. CO.
Connecticut
See American Sterling Co.
See F. Curtis & Co.
See Williams Bros. Mfg. Co.
See Thomas S. Vail

Successor to F. Curtis & Co. of Hartford and Glastonbury. F. Curtis & Co. was reorganized on September 18, 1854 under the name Curtisville Mfg. Co. with Charles Benedict as President and R. F. Fowler, Sec. and Treas. By 1857 the locale was called Curtisville and had its own postmaster. In 1859, Thomas J. Vail assumed the Presidency and the Curtis family no longer appeared in the Hartford listings.

D

DAMAKS REFINING CO.
New York, New York

Manufacturers of sterling holloware c. 1950.

THE DANFORTH COMPANY
See Merwin-Wilson Co., Inc.

DANIEL AND ARTER GLOBE NEVADA SILVER WORKS
Birmingham, England

The Daniel and Arter Globe Nevada Silver Works produced great quantities of flatware bearing their trademarks and various tradenames which included the word "silver." These terms refer to alloys, none of which contain any silver, though some were plated with it.

ALUMINUM SILVER
ARGENLINE
BURMAROID
INDIAN SILVER
JAPANESE SILVER
LAXEY SILVER
NEVADA SILVER

DART CRAFTSMAN CORP.
New York, New York

Manufacturers of silverplated novelties c. 1950.

A. DAVIS CO.
Chicago, Illinois

Successors to M. C. Eppenstein & Co. before 1904. Out of business shortly afterwards.

R. COIN   R. SPECIAL

DAVIS & GALT
Philadelphia, Pennsylvania

Registered U. S. Patent No. 22,275, January 3, 1893 for manufacture of sterling silverware. Patent Office records show this trademark in use since July 21, 1888. Listed in JC 1896-1915. Out of business between 1915-22.

Junius H. Davis and Charles E. Galt first listed in 1889 as Davis & Galt in the Philadelphia City Directory. In 1887 and 1888 the Directories list Junius H. Davis as a silversmith with no associate. The 1880 Directory lists Hamilton & Davis (Matthew F. Hamilton and Junius H. Davis) as silversmiths.

"Davis & Galt have dissolved partnership." (JC&HR 5-30-1894, p. 30)

"Wm. Linker of Davis & Galt, has returned from a successful business trip." (JC&HR 3-4-1896, p. 25) Apparently, the company itself continued for some time after the partnership was dissolved. Charles E. Galt was related to the Galt family (See Galt & Bro.) in Washington, D.C. He was mentioned in a Dec. 19, 1902 newspaper item about the Washington Galts as being deceased. Junius H. Davis was associated with M. F. Hamilton in the firm of Hamilton & Diesinger.

DAWSON COMPANY MANUFACTURERS
Cleveland, Ohio

DAWCO

Organized in the middle 1920s by Irwin H. Dawson to make fraternity, school, fraternal and other special pattern jewelry and allied products. These include plaques, pins, emblems, medals, trophies and some other items of sterling silver, gold plate and other metals. Sterling silver plaques with crests and trademarks thereon are one of their specialties.

JAMES J. DAWSON CO.
New York, New York

Listed in JC 1904 in plated silverware section. Out of business before 1915.

NORTH AMERICA

DAY, CLARK & CO.
Newark, New Jersey
New York, New York

Manufacturers and distributors of sterling and jewelry. The trademark was first used in 1895. Last record found was 1935.

E. L. DEACON JEWELRY CO.
Denver, Colorado

Listed in JC 1909; Eugene L. Deacon, successor before 1915 with address given as Los Angeles, California.

E. L. D.
(Souvenir Spoons.)

I. N. DEITSCH
New York, New York

Listed in JC 1904-15 as manufacturers of sterling silverware. No records after c. 1920.

DEITSCH BROS.
New York, New York

Patent Office records show they were manufacturers of leather articles with sterling silver mountings, September 8, 1896. Listed in JC 1896-1922.

DELAWARE SILVER CO.

Found on grape design sterling and plated flatware of c. 1895-1900.

DELAWARE SILVER CO.

DELLI SILVERPLATE
San Francisco, California

Succeeded by Leonard Silver Mfg. Co. 1974.

DEPASSE MFG. CO.
New York, New York

Manufacturers of sterling silver deposit and gold encrusted glassware. Listed in JC 1909-15. Succeeded by Depasse, Pearsall Silver Co. before 1922.

DEPASSE, PEARSALL SILVER CO.
New York, New York

Successors to Depasse Mfg. Co. between 1915-1922. Last record was 1935.

DERBY SILVER CO.
Derby (Originally called Birmingham),
Connecticut
See International Silver Co.

Founded in 1873 by Edwin N. Shelton, Watson J. Miller and Thomas H. Newcomb, silverplaters of holloware. They made decorative wares of sterling silver.

U. S. Patent No. 15,642, June 26, 1888, registered by Watson J. Miller and Henry Berry for M & B sterling trademark to be used on forks, spoons, tea sets, brushes, mirrors and pitchers.

One of the original companies which formed the International Silver Co. in 1898.

Sterling mark not used after about 1895. Another Derby Silver Co. mark c. 1900-1904 had the anchor & crown with Derby Silver Co., Derby, Conn. around the edge.

Their first few years were largely devoted to the production of flatware as they had purchased from the bankrupt Redfield & Rice concern their tools and material. They gradually dropped flatware and started silverplated holloware which continued under the direction of Colonel Watson J. Miller who came from New York in 1879. They put out a large line of plated dresserware. The factory continued to operate in Birmingham (Derby) until July 1933 when it was consolidated with other plants in Meriden.

(Pewter Holloware)

ALDEN
(Pewterware)

ADAM DEUPERT
Baltimore, Maryland

Listed in Baltimore City Directories 1875-1882 as a gold and silversmith (gold leaf).

DIAMOND SILVER CO.
Lambertville, New Jersey

In business in the 1930s. Clipping from the *Lambertville Beacon*, New Jersey (1-4-1949) says that the Diamond Silver Co. is now part of Ecko Products Co., Chicago, Illinois. (Nickel silver and silverplated flatware)

MISS SARAH B. DICKINSON
Niagara Falls, New York
See Mrs. Sarah B. Dickinson Wood
See Thomas V. Dickinson

THOMAS V. DICKINSON
Buffalo, New York
See Mrs. Sarah B. Dickinson Wood

U. S. Patent No. 19,905, registered July 21, 1891 for silver, flat and tableware. The mark is the same as that used by Mrs. Sarah B. Dickinson Wood.

RICHARD DIMES COMPANY
South Boston, Massachusetts

Founded in 1908, according to one account and in 1923 by another. Sold to the King Silver Company in October 1955, which was acquired by Rogers, Lunt & Bowlen (Lunt Silversmiths) soon afterwards. They made sterling silver holloware and flatware and the ℞D trademark is registered with the U. S. Patent Office, No. 755,049, by Rogers, Lunt & Bowlen for use on sterling holloware and novelty items.

Manchester Silver Company in 1955 or 1956 acquired the tools, dies and rights to the flatware patterns formerly produced by Richard Dimes. Richard Dimes in 1890 started the holloware room of the Towle Mfg. Co. He later went to Frank W. Smith Co. and finally started his own business.

AUGUST DINGELDEN & SON
New York, New York

Listed in 1931 as manufacturers of sterling silverware.

ERIK MAGNUSSEN

DIRIGO DISTRIBUTING CO.
New York, New York
See Dirilyte Co. of America
DIRIGOLD

DIRILYTE COMPANY OF AMERICA, INC.
Kokomo, Indiana

Began in 1926 under the tradename DIRIGOLD. Their wares are of gold color, not plated, but solid metal developed in Sweden. Objection to the name was raised by the U. S. Patent Office as it implied that gold was included in its composition when there was none. In 1937 the name was changed to DIRILYTE. Both flatware and holloware are still being made. Since 1961 a process called Bonded Protection has been used to protect the finish which is tarnish free but loses its luster in the dishwasher. Dirilyte made prior to 1961 may have this finish applied at the factory.

DIRKSEN SILVER FILIGREE CO.
Freeport, Illinois

Founded by Gerritt Dirksen, born Emden, Germany 1818. Though a silversmith by trade when he and his wife came to this country c. 1844 they settled on a farm in Ridott Township, Illinois. Several years later they moved to Freeport where he established a grocery business and was first listed in the city directories in 1872. In the back of the store Dirksen set up a small silversmith shop where he created many pieces of filigree ware. By 1890 the silverware business had prospered so that the grocery line was terminated and the entire two-story frame building converted into a silver filigree factory. This business was given a tremendous boost by the World's Columbian Exposition held in Chicago 1893-94. Gerritt and his two sons designed, made and exhibited some very elaborate pieces in a booth at the Fair. The elder son, John, a jewelry salesman, sold the Dirksen line with his other merchandise and Richard D., the younger son, assisted his father and eventually managed the shop. The elder Dirksen's work was more delicate than that of his son or the other employees. The 1900-01 city directory lists the firm as Dirksen Silver Co. (G. and R. D. Dirksen). The following year R. D. Dirksen is listed as proprietor. The elder Dirksen died in 1903. Demand for the delicate filigree work lessened and in 1905 the company closed. Dirksen filigree silver is plentiful in the Freeport, Illinois area and pieces are included in the collections of the Stephenson County Museum.

D. S. F. CO.

J. DIXON & SONS
Sheffield, England

Established in 1806 by James Dixon as silversmiths and were among the first in Britain to manufacture "Old Sheffield Plate" and britannia wares. They were the leading makers of the britannia and silverplated wares imported into this country in the period from the 1830s to the 1860s. At least one large American firm frankly copied Dixon designs as fast as they reached this country. Registered U. S. Patent No. 14,806 for the manufacture of silver, nickel-silver, britannia and plated goods, Oct. 11, 1887. In 1930 the Dixon firm took over the goodwill of William Hutton & Sons. Dixon's is now run by fifth generation descendants of the founder.

PLATED SILVER   STERLING SILVER

JAMES M. DIXON
Chicago, Illinois

Listed in 1854-55 Chicago Directory as a silverplater.

DODGE, INC.
Los Angeles, California

Listed in city directories 1940s to present in Chicago, Dallas, Los Angeles, Miami and Newark, as manufacturer to wholesaler. Sterling and silverplate.

(Sterling)

(Silverplate)

DOMINICK & HAFF
Newark and New York
See Reed and Barton

CHRONOLOGY

Wm. Gale & Son	1821
Gale & North	1860
Gale, North & Dominick	1868
Gale, Dominick & Haff	1870
Dominick & Haff	1872
Dominick & Haff, Inc.	1889

The firm of Dominick & Haff was established by H. Blanchard Dominick, descendant of George Dominick, French Huguenot, who came to this country in 1740 and Leroy B. Haff who first entered the silversmithing business in the retail department of William Gale in 1867. In their early days they devoted themselves to the manufacture of small silverwares and became especially noted for their vinaigrettes, chatelaines and other fancy articles. Following a disastrous fire in 1877, they moved to a new factory and began to manufacture all kinds of articles in silver. Other moves were necessitated by the growing firm which eventually manufactured a general line of silverware.

The complicated inter-relationships of silversmiths and silver manufacturing is amply demonstrated by the history of Dominick & Haff whose beginnings can be traced back to William Gale & Son, silversmiths in New York in 1821. The succession of firm names was Gale & North; Gale, North & Dominick; Gale, Dominick & Haff; and in 1872 Dominick & Haff. William Gale had been an apprentice of Peter & John Targee, silversmiths in New York (John Targee, w. 1797-1841; Peter Targee, w. 1809-11; together, 1809-16), who had succeeded to the business of John Vernon, New York silversmith (w. 1787-1816). In 1879 Dominick & Haff bought out the business of Adams & Shaw (which had been founded about 1873 by Caleb Cushing Adams, for 18 years the general manager of the Gorham Company, and Thomas Shaw, an Englishman employed by the Gorham Company, until in connection with Tiffany & Company, he formed the manufacturing firm of Thomas Shaw & Company) the tools, fixtures, and patterns that related to the manufacture of silverware (the rest went to the Whiting Mfg. Co.), and which Adams & Shaw had previously purchased from John R. Wendt & Company, of New York. Dominick & Haff, was in turn, sold to Reed & Barton in 1928 and consolidated with that firm. There were also connections with the McChesney Company, formed in 1921 by Samuel D. McChesney whose brother was Wm. F. McChesney, treasurer and later president of Dominick & Haff. At the death of Samuel D. McChesney, his business was taken over by Dominick & Haff. What was left of that business was acquired by Reed & Barton in 1928.

D. & H.

DORLING COMPANY OF AMERICA, INC.
Jenkintown, Pennsylvania

Registered trademark for use on flatware. Claims use since August 24, 1949.

DORST CO.
Cincinnati, Ohio

Successors (?) to Jonas, Dorst & Co. in business 1896. Manufacturers and retailers of sterling and plated silverware, and jewelry. Succeeded c. 1940 by Dorst Jewelry Co. which is still in business.

STERLING SILVER

LENORE DOSKOW, INC.
Montrose, New York

Founded in 1934 by Lenore and David Doskow. All pieces are designed by Leonore Doskow and made under her supervision. The company moved from New York City in 1942 and occupied its own building in Montrose, N.Y. They manufacture sterling and gold jewelry and novelty items. The line today comprises two thousand sterling silver pieces ranging from boxes to yoyos. Concentration is on the unusual—sets of measuring spoons, cookie cutters, melon scoops, collar stays, toothpicks, sport jewelry, desk accessories, etc.

LEONORE DOSKOW
HANDMADE STERLING

DOWD-RODGERS CO.
Wallingford, Connecticut

Listed in the City Directory 1915/16-1937. Not listed in 1939. Directories published every two years. Jobbers of plated silverware. Listed as manufacturers of silverplated wares 1922 KS.

TRADE **D** MARK

DROBENARE BROS. INC.
New York, New York

Listed directories 1960s through 1973 as manufacturers of sterling silver. Inquiry returned by post office as undeliverable.

THE DUHME COMPANY
Cincinnati, Ohio

Herman Duhme (b. Germany 1819) started his business career in 1839 when he opened the Duhme & Co. in Cincinnati, Ohio. It became the Duhme Jewelry Co. c. 1887-1890 and was incorporated Jan. 22, 1898 for the manufacture of gold and silver arti-

cles. A notice in the *Jewelers Circular* (1-26-1898) states that "The Duhme Company have purchased the mfg. concern of Neuhaus, Lakin & Co. and will remove the plant to their building and begin the mfg. of sterling silver." Four months later there was a note that "The Kecks are in full possession of Duhme firm. Duhmes to open again under the name Duhme Bros." About 1893 the title of the firm was again changed to The Duhme Company and this listing continued in the city directories until 1907.

RUFUS DUNHAM
See Stevens and Smart
See New England Silver Co.

Made britannia and plated ware 1863-1875. In 1877 the company became Rufus Dunham & Sons and continued this same name until 1883 with sons Joseph S., Charles A. and John associated with the firm. In 1894 Joseph S. formed the New England Silver Company.

DUNKIRK SILVERSMITHS, INC.
Meriden, Connecticut

Successors c. 1945-50 to Gold Recovery & Refining Corp.

BENEDICT DUNN
See Benedict Mfg. Co.

L. F. DUNN
Niagara Falls, New York

Registered U. S. Patent No. 10,65 for the manufacture of knives, forks and spoons, Dec. 4, 1883. Not listed in City Directory (1886 Directory is the earliest available).

DURAND & COMPANY
Newark, New Jersey

CHRONOLOGY	
James M. Durand	1838
Durand & Annin	1852
Durand, Carter & Co.	1859
Durand & Co.	1864
Durand & Co., Inc.	1892-1919

The firm of Durand & Co., manufacturing jewelers and silversmiths 1838-1919, was a culmination of seven successive generations of manufacturing jewelers. The Durand name is a very old one, dating back to 1100 A.D. in France and Italy; Durante being the Italian spelling of the name of which "Dante" is a corruption.

For many generations the Durands were identified with the artistic side of the jewelry trade as watchmakers, engravers, jewelers and silversmiths, sometimes one man being proficient in all these. Dr. Jean Durand, the Huguenot progenitor of the Durand family in America, was born in France in 1667 and came to this country in 1685. He died in Derby, Connecticut in 1727. His son, Samuel, born in Derby in 1713, was the first of the Durands in America to engage in jewelry manufacturing. He left Derby in 1740 for New York where he stayed for ten years as a farmer, watchmaker and jeweler. In 1750 he moved to Newark and then to South Orange where he died in 1787. John Durand, son of Samuel, was a jeweler and watchmaker. During the Revolutionary War he was highly praised by George Washington for his skill in repairing field glasses. John Durand's son, Henry, was a manufacturer of jewelry, silverware and crystals for watches. James Madison Durand, son of Henry Durand, founded the firm of Durand & Co. in 1843. He learned his trade with Taylor & Baldwin of Newark. From 1820 to 1840 he was engaged as an engraver, engine turner, watchcase maker and jeweler. His son, Wickliffe Baldwin Durand, became head of the partnership in 1880. Harry Durand entered the partnership in 1882 as purchaser and became secretary and treasurer. Harry Durand, Jr., was interested in the selling end of the business. Wallace Durand was associated with his father and brothers in the firm and became its president in 1892. Perhaps the best known of the Durand family was Asher Brown Durand (1796-1886) who was first an engraver. He later took up the engraving of plates from which pictures were printed. Many of these are in the National Portrait Gallery, the most famous one being Trumbull's "The Signing of the Declaration of Independence." From 1835 he devoted his time to painting, mainly landscapes, and with Thomas Cole is credited with founding the Hudson River school of painting.

Among the many items made by the Durand company were scarfpins, silver links, studs, collar buttons, brooches, pendants, necklaces, lorgnettes, vanity cases, purses, mouchoir bags, rings, vest chains, cigarette cases and other novelties.

DURGIN & BURTT
St. Louis, Missouri
See F. A. Durgin

Listed in St. Louis City Directory 1859-60 as manufacturers of silver and plated silverware.

F. A. DURGIN
St. Louis, Missouri

Founded by Freeman A. Durgin in St. Louis in 1858. The 1859-1860 St. Louis Directory lists him as a member of the firm, Durgin & Burtt. From 1863-1888 he was in business for himself. From 1888-1911 he was a salesman for the Jaccard jewelry firm. It has not been definitely established that he was actually a manufacturer of silver and plated silverware as he advertised, or whether he was a wholesaler or retailer for others. Much silver, especially flatware, is found with his name.

F. A. DURGIN
ST. LOUIS

WM. B. DURGIN CO.
Concord, New Hampshire
Providence, Rhode Island
See Gorham Corporation

Founded in 1853 by William B. Durgin in Concord, New Hampshire. Durgin had been born in Compton

Village, New Hampshire in 1833 and left his mountain home at the age of 16 to seek his fortune in Boston. He apprenticed himself to Newell Harding. On completion of his apprenticeship he set himself up in business in Concord. He soon purchased the tools of two jeweler-spoonmakers of that town. Not long afterwards he also bought the tools of a retail jeweler in Claremont, New Hampshire. His initial order was given by Carter Bros., then in business in Concord and later in Portland, Maine. This order was for six sets of teaspoons. During his early days as a spoon maker, Durgin would make up a lot of spoons and pack them in a handsatchel or small trunk and start out with a horse and wagon to sell them, sometimes taking old silver in barter. Durgin was noted for the fine quality of his silver spoons and was soon able to set up a shop which grew rapidly into a factory which made sterling flatware, gold, silver and plated tableware, jewelry and similar articles. The Durgins, father and son, continued in the business until their deaths, both in 1905, in which year the ownership passed out of the family. It was purchased by the Gorham Company but continued to operate in Concord until 1931 when it was moved to Providence, Rhode Island.

DISCOVERY
(Discontinued.)
CROMWELL
WATTEAU

DURHAM SILVER CO.
New York, New York

Listed in directories in the 1950s and 60s as manufacturers.

JOSEPH DYAR
Middlebury, Vermont

Advertised from 1822 through 1845 that his table and tea spoons, cream and salt spoons, sugar tongs, thimbles and gold beads were of first quality and workmanship. He was born in 1804 and died in 1851.

EAGLE SILVER CO.
Providence, Rhode Island

Listed in Providence City Directories 1922-1953 as manufacturers of silver novelties. Owners— Memelaus Sava and Ignatius H. Findan. Manufactured sterling silver cigarette cases, vanity cases, whiskey flasks, match safes, 14k gold inlaid and onyx inlaid wares.

E.S.C.O.

EAGLE SPOON COMPANY
Bridgeport, Connecticut

"Articles of association of the Eagle Spoon Company were filed in Bridgeport last week. The purpose of the association is to manufacture and sell all kinds of personal property, including spoons and forks and other flatware. Stockholders are William H. Waterman, Hartford; George C. Edwards and C. A. Hamilton, Bridgeport; and James G. Ludlum and Thomas B. Lashar." (JC-W 5-30-1900, p. 47) Succeeded by Housatonic Mfg. Co.

EAGLE STERLING CO.
Glastonbury, Connecticut

Successors to W. L. & H. E. Pitkin July 1, 1894. Organized in 1894 by William H. Watrous and others to manufacture silverware. Listed in 1896 JC in plated silver section. Out of business before 1904.

GEORGE EAKINS
Philadelphia, Pennsylvania

Advertised in *Jewellers, Silversmiths & Watchmakers*, December 1877 as "Mfg. of silver plated ware and dealer in cut glass bottles."

EARLY AMERICAN PEWTER CO.
Boston, Massachusetts

Advertised in the 1940s.

EASTERLING COMPANY
See Westerling Company

(Used since December 1944)
(Sterling silver flatware
and holloware)

EASTERN CAROLINA SILVER CO.
Hyattsville, South Carolina

EASTERN CAROLINA SIL. CO.

Made silverplated holloware c. 1900.

EASTWOOD-PARK COMPANY
Newark, New Jersey

Manufacturers of exclusive designs in sterling silverware, dresserware, novelties, mesh bags and jewelry for the wholesale trade.
Listed JC 1909-1915. Out of business before 1922.

ECCLESIASTIC SILVERSMITHS
Wallingford, Connecticut

"International Silver Company sold its Ecclesiastic division to Ecclesiastic Silversmiths, a new company in Wallingford, Connecticut. The new com-

pany will be a division of Lamson-Goodnow Mfg. Co., which is affiliated with Voos Industries, Inc. (JC-K April 1969, p. 144)

ECKFELDT & ACKLEY
Newark, New Jersey

Listed in 1896 Jewelers' Weekly in sterling silverware section. Listed 1898-1915 JC as jewelers. Last record found c. 1935.

EDSON MFG. CO.
New York, New York
Newark, New Jersey

"The Edson Mfg. Co., New York, was incorporated Feb. 16, 1893 for the manufacture of silver novelties with a factory in Newark. Franklin Edson, Sr., president; Albert E. Coon, sec. & treas., and Henry T. Edson, Manager." (JC&HR 3-1-1893, p. 28)

EDWARDS, HORTON & EDWARDS
Chicago, Illinois

Silversmiths c. 1850.

EISENBERG-LOZANO, INC.
New York, New York
See Samuel Kirk & Son
See Kirk International

Founded by Arthur Eisenberg and Neal Lozano in 1953. Purchased by The Kirk Corporation in 1970 after the deaths of the founders.

WM. J. EISENHARDT
Baltimore, Maryland

Listed in Baltimore City Directories 1887-1888 as a silverplater.

M. EISENSTADT JEWELRY CO.
St. Louis, Missouri

M. Eisenstadt Company (Wholesale distributors of silverware and jewelry). Founded in 1853 by Michael Gabriel Eisenstadt. First appeared in St. Louis directory in 1866. From 1904 is listed as M. Eisenstadt Manufacturing Co., and from 1908 on they are listed as manufacturers of jewelry, jobbers of watches and importers of diamonds in the 1920s, 1930s and 1940s they are listed as M. Eisenstadt Mfg. Co. and they are still in business as M. Eisenstadt, wholesale jewelry.

(Used since 1892)   (Plated silver holloware)

ELDRIDGE & CO.
Taunton, Massachusetts

Listd in Taunton City Directories from 1800-1884 as silver manufacturers "at Britanniaville, near R. R. crossing Reed & Barton."

ELECTROLYTIC ART METAL CO.
Trenton, New Jersey

Listed in JC 1915 with manufacturers of sterling silverware. No record after 1920.

ELEDER-HICKOK CO.
Newark, New Jersey
See Hickok-Matthews Co. Silversmiths

Originally Lebkuecher & Co.; the name was changed by law to F. A. Lester after 1915 and was taken over by the Eleder Co. in 1918. By 1922 it had become the Eleder-Hickok Co. It merged with the Matthews Company after 1931 to form the Hickok-Matthews Company, manufacturers of sterling silver novelties.

WM. R. ELFERS CO., INC.
New York, New York

Listed in 1931 NJSB and KS as manufacturers of sterling silver holloware, candlesticks, vases, salt and pepper shakers, sherbet compotes, centerpieces, etc.

ELGIN-AMERICAN MANUFACTURING COMPANY
Elgin, Illinois

Began business in 1887. An undated Elgin-American catalog in the writer's possession (with illustrations of souvenirs engraved "Remember the Maine" and desk calendars dated January 1898) includes flatware of plated silver, smoking sets, jewel cases, bracelets, dresser sets, match safes and novelties.

Registered U. S. Patent No. 103,053, March 16, 1915 for manufacture of silverware.

Became a division of Illinois Watch Case Company before 1950. Observed its 65th anniversary in 1952. This is the last record found.

On plated silver knives about 1898

ELGIN SILVERSMITH CO., INC.
New York, New York
See Redlich & Co.

Founded by two partners, Ludwig & Redlich, and operated under that name until 1892 when Mr. Ludwhen he sold his interest to three of his old employees and it became Redlich & Co., Inc. It was taken over by Elgin Silversmith Co., Inc. in 1946. Products are sterling flatware, holloware and 14k goldwares. The Redlich trademark has not been are sterling silverware, holloware and 14k goldwares. The Redlich trademark has not been changed and is stil used by the firm to the present day. Currier & Roby is now a Division of Elgin Silversmiths.

(Sterling)

ELKINGTON & CO., LTD.
Birmingham, England

George Richards Elkington was apprenticed at 14 to his two uncles, Josiah and George Richards to learn silverplating. This was in 1815 and the silver-plating process he learned was "close plating"—hammering thin layers of silver over base metal, with adhesion being by soldering. His cousin, Henry Elkington, joined him about 1829-30 in the making of small articles. They were constantly doing research towards better methods of gilding base metals. Between 1836 and 1839 the firm of G R & H Elkington took out various patents, including one for "electro-gilding." Therefore, they are usually credited with the invention of electroplating. John Wright discovered the need for cyanide of potassium in the plating solution and submitted his process to the Elkington company who embodied it in their patent of 1840. This process was available to other manufacturers on a royalty basis. A third partner, Josiah Mason was admitted in 1842 and the firm became Elkington, Mason & Company. Beginning then, their electroplate was marked with "E & Co" in a shield, and "E M & Co" in three separate shields, together with their company date letters. Mason left the firm about 1859 but his initial was not dropped from the marks until 1864. The Crown, long used as part of many silverplaters' marks, was dropped from Elkington's "E & Co" mark in 1896.

In 1963 Elkington and Mappin & Webb merged to form British Silverware Ltd. Soon afterwards they acquired Walker & Hall, Adie Bros., and Gladwyn Ltd. Products of all four firms are now sold under the Elkington name.

Through changes in Elkington's trademarks it is possible to date their products with reasonable accuracy. They first used "E & Co., crowned" within a shield and ELEC TRO PLATE. In 1842 a series of numbers was added to the trademark. The numbers ran from 1 to 8 with the number 6 being reversed. In 1849 letters of the alphabet were substituted for the numbers, beginning with the letter K. A new series of letters began in 1865 with a change in the trademark. Letters B, C, and J were omitted. The letter Q was not used by the sheet department and used on only part of the cast articles. The letter Q as well as R was used from 1900 onwards. Both numbers and letters are enclosed within shapes that aid in their dating.

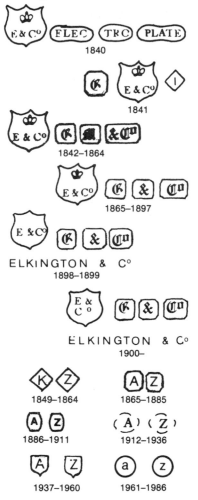

1840

1841

1842–1864

1865–1897

ELKINGTON & C°
1898–1899

ELKINGTON & C°
1900–

1849–1864

1865–1885

1886–1911

1912–1936

1937–1960

1961–1986

ELLIS SILVER COMPANY, INC.
New York, New York
See Ellis-Barker

Established in New York c. 1900 as a branch of Ellis & Co., Birmingham, England.

ELLIS-BARKER SILVER COMPANIES
Birmingham, England
New York, New York

The Ellis-Barker Company can trace its history to a partnership c. 1820 by partners Barker and Creed. It became Barker Bros. (William and Matthias Barker) c. 1860. Encouraged by their success in England,

they opened an American branch in 1897 (Samuel Buckley & Co., New York) where a full line was introduced. Among the pieces offered were trays, candelabra, candlesticks, plates, urns and bottlestands. These articles were copper, heavily electroplated with silver and mounted with handles, borders and edges of sterling silver. In 1921 Barker Bros. was joined by Levi & Salamon, specialists in dresserware and by Potosi Silver Co., spoon and fork makers. In 1931 they purchased the Ellis Silver Co. (Ellis & Co., Birmingham, being the parent) and the firm has been known since then as Ellis-Barker. They are noted especially for their beautiful reproductions of antique silver.

FOR SILVER AND ELECTROPLATED TRAYS, WAITERS, CANDLESTICKS, CANDELABRA, DINNER SETS, FLOWER-STANDS, COFFEE AND TEA SERVICES, VASES, WINE-COOLERS, TEA-URNS, INK-STANDS, DECANTER-STANDS, DINNER-PLATES, MEAT-DISHES, ENTRÉE DISHES, BOTTLE-STANDS, CAKE-BASKETS, SIPHON-HOLDERS, BOWLS, JUGS, TEA-CADDIES, BOXES, FRUIT-STANDS, AND FRUIT-BASKETS.
Claims use since October 1906.

FOR TRAYS, WAITERS, CANDLESTICKS, CANDELA-BRA, DINNER SETS, FLOWER-STANDS, DINNER-PLATES, BOTTLE-STANDS, VASES, TEA AND COFFEE SERVICES, WINE-COOLERS, TEA-URNS, INK-STANDS, DECANTER-STANDS, MEAT-DISHES, CAKE-STANDS, SIPHON-HOLDERS, FRUIT STANDS AND BASKETS, BOWLS, JUGS, TEA CADDIES, BOXES, AND ENTRÉE-DISHES, ALL MADE OF PRECIOUS METALS OR PLATED WITH PRECIOUS METALS.
Claims use since August 1912.

FOR CAKE-BASKETS, CRUETS, CUPS, DISH-COVERS, MEAT-DISHES, ENTRÉE-DISHES, EGG-FRAMES, TEA AND COFFEE SERVICES, WINE-COOLERS, INKSTANDS, LIQUOR-FRAMES, MUSTARD-POTS, MUFFINEERS, SALT-CELLARS, SAUCE-BOATS, SOUP-TUREENS, SIPHON-STANDS, SWEET-DISHES, TEA-URNS, TOAST-RACKS, TEA-CADDIES, TRAYS, VASES AND WAITERS, ALL MADE OF SILVER OR PLATED WITH SILVER.
Claims use since November 1912.

FOR SILVER-PLATED HOLLOWARE.
Claims use since 1912.

FOR SILVER PLATED HOLLOWARE AND FLATWARE.
Claims use since Mar. 2, 1932.

J. E. ELLIS & CO.
Toronto, Canada

James E. Ellis moved from Liverpool, England, to Canada in 1848 and was associated with Rossin Bros. until 1852. He bought into that business that year. Ellis' son joined him in 1862. The firm name became J. E. Ellis & Co. in 1877 when M. T. Cain became a partner. It continued until 1901 when it was sold at auction.

P. W. ELLIS
Toronto, Canada

In business c. 1876 as a partnership of Philip W. Ellis and Matthew C. Ellis (nephews) of Toronto silversmith James E. Ellis). The company was incorporated in 1901; liquidated in 1928 and taken over by Birks.

They were importers and wholesalers of watches, clocks, sterling and plated silverware, china and cut glass, artware, jewelry, diamonds, tools, materials and supplies.

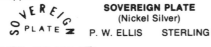

SOVEREIGN PLATE
(Nickel Silver)

P. W. ELLIS   STERLING

ELLMORE SILVER CO., INC.
Meriden, Connecticut
See Concord Silver Co.
See G. H. French & Co.
See Frank M. Whiting Co.

Founded c. 1935 by I. A. Lipman who rented space in the old C. F. Monroe factory and took over F. M. Whiting Co. of N. Attleboro, G. H. French & Co., New York and Concord Silversmiths, Ltd., Concord, New Hampshire about 1939. Whiting had been making sterling flatware and some holloware. French made novelties and dresserware. With these lines added, the Ellmore company increased production and established branch offices in New York, Los Angeles and Chicago. The W. S. Blackinton Co. became a division of the Ellmore co. in the 1940s. The Ellmore Co. went out of business in 1960. The Blackinton Co. was purchased by Raimond Silver Mfg. Co., Meriden, Connecticut, in 1966 and moved to Chelsea, Massachusetts. The sterling flatware dies of the Whiting Company were bought by the Crown Silver Co., New York. It is believed that they are no longer being used.

SILVER HARVEST
HARVEST
(Used since 1950)

ARNOLD ELTONHEAD
Baltimore, Maryland

Listed as a silversmith in the 1850 census. Born Pennsylvania.

EMPIRE ART METAL WORKS
New York, New York

Listed 1909 JC in plated silver section.

EMPIRE CRAFTS CORP.
Newark, New Jersey

Manufacturers of silverplated flatware 1930s to 1950s. Later controlled by Oneida Silversmiths.

NOBILITY PLATE

(Silverplate)

(Sterling)

EMPIRE SILVER PLATE CO.
Brooklyn, New York

Advertised in 1896 JW and JC&HR as manufacturers and importers of silverplated hollowares. Last record found 1931.

ENGLISH SILVER MFG. CORP.
Brooklyn, New York
See Leonard Silver Mfg. Co.

Manufacturers and importers of silverplated wares from c. 1950. Still in directories. No answer to recent inquiry.

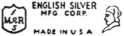

ENTERPRISE PLATING WORKS
Baltimore, Maryland

Listed in Baltimore City Directories 1894-1916 as silverplaters.

M. C. EPPENSTEIN & CO.
Chicago, Illinois
See A. Davis & Co.

Earliest record found was Patent Office Registration No. 24,525, April 17, 1894 for use on plated silver tableware. Succeeded by A. Davis & Co. c. 1904.

R. COIN.

GEORGE C. ERICKSON
Gardner, Massachusetts

George Erickson was born in Sweden and came to this country when six months old. He served his apprenticeship under Arthur J. Stone where he developed into a master craftsman in the production of sterling silver flatware. In 1932 Erickson bought from the heirs of the late David Carlson, the shop which Carlson had run for several years and even during Depression days was able to build a successful business. His first trademark "G. C. E." used in 1932, was soon changed to "Erickson Sterling" which is still used today. Erickson's work has graced the table of a United States President, Governors and Senators and other notables.

G. C. E. (Used 1932)

Erickson Sterling (now used)

ETON SILVER INC.
Glendale, New York

Listed directories from the 1960s to the present as manufacturers and importers. No reply to recent inquiry.

EUREKA MFG. CO.
Taunton, Masschusetts

Listed directories from the 1950s through the 1960s as manufacturers of silverware.

EVANS & ANDERSON
Newark, New Jersey

Horace B. Anderson and Theodore Evans, silversmiths, worked 1864-c. 1866. Listed Newark City Directory as "Evans and Anderson, Successors to Henry Evans. Dealers in Clocks, Watches, Jewelry, etc., and manufacturers of Sterling silver ware." Succeeded by Horace B. Anderson and operated under his name.

EVANS & ANDERSON

EVANS CASE CO.
North Attleboro, Massachusetts

Listed in the 1920s as D. Evans Case Co. Still in business as a division of the Hilsingor Corp., Plainville, Massachusetts.

THEO. EVANS & CO.
New York, New York

"Theodore Evans was the son of Henry Evans. He succeeded his father as Evans & Anderson (1864-66), in New York City. Theo Evans & Co. (Theo. Evans and John Cook) since 1855." (JC&HR 6-30-1897, p. 33)

"An old-time silversmithing house was that of Theodore Evans & Co. who started business in 1855 at 6 Liberty Place, New York. The firm was composed of Theodore Evans and John Cook. Mr. Evans was a salesman for Wm. Gale & Son from 1850 to 1855, while Mr. Cook was foreman for the same firm, but in '55 they joined forces and started for themselves, soon doing a large southern business in flat

and hollow wares. They manufactured many of the old patterns: Plain, Tipped, French Thread, Plain Thread, Oval Thread, Mayflower, Shell, Grape, as well as a patented one named Ribbon. . . . Many of their goods are still extant in the south.

"In 1865 the firm name was changed to Evans & Cook, Jas. E. Johnson having been admitted as a special partner. In 1869 Mr. Evans retired and John Cook continued for several years. In their prosperous days everything in their line, from a thirty inch tray to a salt spoon, could be found in their safes, and in no instance was a piece issued which was not up to the standard at that time—that of New York coins. They lost heavily through the war, as most of the silverware houses did, the south before the war being fond of luxuries." (JC&HR 6-30-1897, pp. 33-34)

T. EVANS & CO.

OTTO G. FABER
Baltimore, Maryland

Listed in Baltimore City Directories 1895-1910 as a silversmith, goldsmith and jeweler. Some of his pieces bear a marked similarity to designs made by Samuel Kirk & Son.

WILLIAM FABER & SONS
Philadelphia, Pennsylvania

Silversmiths and Silverplaters 1828-1887.

FAHYS WATCH-CASE CO.
New York, New York

Listed in 1896 as Jos. Fahys & Co.; 1922 as Jos. Fahys & Co., Inc. Design patents Nos. 32,914, July 10, 1900 and 38,583, May 28, 1907 for spoons, forks or similar articles were taken out by Fred Habensack, Sag Harbor, New York and assigned to the Fahys Watch-Case Co.

FAIRCHILD & CO.
New York, New York

CHRONOLOGY	
Randall & Fairchild	1837
LeRoy W. Fairchild	1843
LeRoy W. Fairchild & Co.	1867
L. W. Fairchild	1873
L. W. Fairchild & Sons	1886
LeRoy Fairchild & Co.	1889
Fairchild & Johnson	1898
Fairchild & Company	1919

Founded in 1837 as Randall & Fairchild in 1843, known as Randall & Fairchild. In 1843, known as LeRoy W. Fairchild; 1867-1873 as LeRoy W. Fairchild & Co.; 1873-1886 as L. W. Fairchild; 1886, L. W. Fairchild & Sons; 1889 it was incorporated as LeRoy Fairchild & Co.; in 1896 Harry P. Fairchild bought out the business and in 1898 he formed the corporation of Fairchild & Johnson. In 1919 it was known as

Fairchild & Co., and went out of business c. 1922. Makers of sterling silverware.

F

L. W. FAIRCHILD & CO.

FAIRCHILD & JOHNSON CO.

LEROY C. FAIRCHILD CO.
New York, New York

"Leroy C. Fairchild Co., manufacturers of gold pens and novelties recently incorporated. Directors are Julia L. M. Fairchild, W. Clifford Moore and Leonard S. Wheeler. They purchased the machinery, tools, etc. used by the defunct Leroy W. Fairchild & Co. Leroy C. Fairchild, prsident of the old company, is now in charge of the new corporation's selling and manufacturing departments. (JC&HR 6-9-1897, p. 23)

FARBER BROS.
New York, New York

Manufacturers and jobbers of plated silver holloware c. 1920-1950. Now a division of LCA Corp.

Silvercraft

(On silverplated holloware)

FARRINGTON & HUNNEWELL
Boston, Massachusetts

Silversmiths 1838-85. Great quantities of flatware turn up with their (Star) F & H (Star) trademark, often accompanied by the mark of another as retailer.

FEDERAL SILVER COMPANY
New York, New York

Listed from c. 1920 to 1961 as manufacturers of sterling and plated wares.
The trademark at right appears under the name Jones & Woodland, Newark, New Jersey in 1896-1915 JC and 1950 JC-K.

FEDERAL SILVER CO. E.P.C.

(On silverplate)

(On sterling)

W. J. FEELEY CO.
Providence, Rhode Island

One account says that the company was founded in 1875 by Michael Feeley. Another says it was established by W. J. Feeley in 1875 and incorporated in 1892. Acording to this account, W. J. Feeley was born in Providence January 19, 1855 and learned the trade of silversmithing from Knowles & Webster; worked several years as a journeyman before beginning business on his own account.

They were manufacturers of gold and silver ecclesiastical goods. City Directories list the company from 1875 to 1920 as manufacturing jewelers and silversmiths. Listed in 1936-1937 Jobbers' Handbook.

ALBERT FELDENHEIMER
Portland, Oregon

U. S. Patents registered April 28, 1891 and January 1892 for sterling souvenir flatware and jewelry. Became A. & C. Feldenheimer between 1896-1904. Last record c. 1904.

FRANCES FELTEN
Winstead, Connecticut

Pewterer, currently in business.

FENNIMAN CO.
New York, New York

Listed JC 1915 in sterling silver section. Out of business before 1922.

PETER FERRARI
Baltimore, Maryland

Listed in Baltimore City Directories 1887-89 as a silverplater.

FESSENDEN & COMPANY
Providence, Rhode Island

CHRONOLOGY
Whiting, Fessenden & Cowan	1858
Wm. P. Fessenden & Co.	1860
Fessenden & Company	1860

In April 1858 William B. Fessenden who had at one time been a member of the firm of Whiting, Fessenden & Cowan, moved to Providence and established a silverware factory there. He took into partnership his son, Thomas F. and started as Wm. P. Fessenden & Co., in the manufacture of fancy flat and staple hollowares. In 1860 the father sold out his interest to his son and retired. Soon afterwards, Thomas took Giles Manchester as partner, who remained in charge of the manufacturing department until his death in 1886. In 1876, Silas H. Manchester, a brother of Giles, joined the firm and later became a

925 STERLING 1000

partner and assumed management. Silas Manchester became sold owner about 1895. On his death in 1905 the company was incorporated. It continued to be listed in business until 1922.

MARSHALL FIELD & CO.
Chicago, Illinois

Began business in 1864 as Farwell, Field & Company. In 1865 the company became Field, Palmer & Leiter; Potter Palmer sold out his interests in 1866 and the firm name became Field, Leiter & Company. Marshall Field became sole owner in 1881 and gave the firm its present name.

Marshall Field's was one of the first large department stores to have many articles stamped with trademarks registered for its own use. U. S. Patent No. 146,536, September 6, 1921, was registered for their use on silverware, both sterling and plated.

An advertisement in a 1966 Chicago(?) paper read as follows: "Silver is a glittering thread interwoven with the history of Britain. The ancient craft of the English silversmith has been regulated by Royal Ordinances and Acts of Parliament since the late 12th century. Since 1935, the Marshall Field & Company hallmark has been registered at the Worshipful Company of Goldsmiths in London. In all the world, we are one of the few non-British companies privileged to have our own shield put on silver made for us in England. This mark of quality distinguishes a pattern of silver flatware made expressly for Field's in England."

(Used since June 1935)
(On sterling silver table articles)

FIFTH AVENUE SILVER CO., INC.
Taunton, Massachusetts

The company was founded September 1948 by Manuel J. Andrade of Taunton, a spinner by trade. It was first named the Pilgram Silver Company, that name being soon changed because of a conflict with a tradename already in use. The name was changed to Prospect Silver Company in the early 1950s but was again changed to Fifth Avenue Silver Company. In 1960 the company changed ownership and was incorporated. The new owners are Leon J. and Mildred A. Bunk and Frank and Joanna Todorsky. Mr. Bunk is general manager and president. From the beginning the company has been manufacturers and wholesale distributors of silverplate and pewter hollowares.

5 TH AVE	5 TH AVE
SILVER CO.	SILVER CO.
SILVER PLATED	SILVER ON COPPER

LEXINGTON
PEWTER
(On pewter)

HARVEY FILLEY & SONS
Philadelphia, Pennsylvania

Silver platers c. 1859-c. 1900.

FILLEY & MEAD
Philadelphia, Pennsylvania
See John O. Mead

FILLEY, MEAD & CALDWELL
Philadelphia, Pennsylvania
See John O. Mead

FILLKWIK CO.
Attleboro, Massachusetts
See Shields Inc.

MICHAEL C. FINA CO., INC.
New York, New York

Founded December 1935 by Rose Fina and Michael C. Fina. Manufacturers and wholesalers of sterling and silverplate holloware.

WILLIAM C. FINCK CO.
Elizabeth, New Jersey

Listed in JC 1896-1904. Out of business before 1915. Manufacturers of sterling silverware. Among their products were sterling souvenir spoons.

FINE ARTS STERLING SILVER COMPANY
Morgantown, Pennsylvania

Founded in Philadelphia in 1944 by Jerry N. Ashway. They are sole distributors of six sterling flatware patterns manufactured by the International Silver Company and distributed through direct sales.

The company was moved from Philadelphia to Morgantown, Pennsylvania in 1972.

The founder and board chairman, aged 66, died November 1973 at his home in Glenside, Pennsylvania

(Used since January 24, 1949
on children's tableware)

ALBERT G. FINN SILVER CO.
Syracuse, New York
See P. A. Coon Silver Mfg. Co.

Manufacturers of plated silverware. Founding date not known. Listed JC 1904. Succeeded by P. A. Coon Silver Mfg. Co. between 1904-1909.

ALBERT G. FINN SILVER CO.
CRESCENT SILVER CO.

FISHEL, NESSLER & CO.
NEW York, New York
See Majestic Mfg. Co.

Manufacturers of sterling silver and rhinestone-set jewelry, platenoid rhinestone-set jewelry, plated jewelry and card jewelry. Registered U. S. Patent No. 23,016 for use on jewelry, May 16, 1893. Last listing found was 1936-1937.

"Established over 45 years." (Adv. KJ 1931)

FISHEL NESSLER CO.,
184 Fifth Ave.,
NEW YORK.

(This trademark also found with "J. O. - N. Y." on the center strip.)

FISHER SILVERSMITHS, INC.
Jersey City, New Jersey
New York, New York

Successors to M. Fred Hirsch Co. Manufacturers of sterling and silver plated flatware and holloware since 1936 or earlier. Still in business.

(On sterling)

FISHER, COLTON & KINSON
Montpelier, Vermont

"Fisher, Colton & Kinson, silverplaters, Montpelier, Vermont, have sold out to Fisher & Colton." (Jeweller, Silversmith & Watchmaker, Nov. 1877)

FLAGG & HOMAN
Cincinnati, Ohio
See Homan Mfg. Co.

(Pewter)

W. L. FLETCHER
South Chatham, Massachusetts

Pewterer, currently in business.

FLORENCE SILVER PLATE CO.
Baltimore, Maryland

Listed in Baltimore City Directories 1894-1942 as silverplaters. No City Directories available 1942-1955.

FOOT & COLSON
Chicago, Illinois

Listed in 1854-1855 Chicago Directory as silverplaters. In 1856 Foot was listed as working alone.

E. B. FLOYD
Burlington, Vermont

Worked as late as 1868 in coin silver.

FORBES SILVER CO.
Meriden, Connecticut
See International Silver Co.

Organized in 1894 as a department of Meriden Britannia Co. for holloware silverplating. One of the original companies which formed the International Silver Co.

(This mark sometimes used with the words SHEF-FIELD REPRODUCTION.)

FORD & CARPENTER
New York, New York
See Cohen & Rosenberger

Succeeded Baldwin, Ford & Co. between 1896 and 1904 and were succeeded by Cohen & Rosenberger before 1915.

BEN FORMAN & SONS, INC.
New York, New York

In directories 1950s and 1960s as manufacturers of silverwares.

FOSTER & BAILEY
Providence, Rhode Island
See Theodore W. Foster & Bro. Co.

Theodore W. Foster and Samuel H. Bailey. Succeeded by Theodore W. Foster & Bro. Co.

THEODORE W. FOSTER & BRO. CO.
Providence, Rhode Island

Established January 1, 1873 under the name White & Foster. Walter E. White had been listed previously as a jeweler from 1869-1872. The name was later changed to White, Foster & Co. and in 1878 when White withdrew, the name became Foster & Bailey. (S. H. Bailey) In May 1898 the company was incorporated under the name Theodore Foster & Bros., Co. They were among the largest manufacturers of jewelry and sterling silver goods in Providence. Among the goods were gold filled, electroplated and sterling silver vanity cases, cigarette cases, clock cases, ecclesiastical goods, cigar and cigarette holders, knives, medals, pens and pencils, photo frames, dresserware and candlesticks for which U. S. Patent 28,069, April 17, 1896 was registered. This last listing continued until 1951.

F. & B.

J. F. FRADLEY & CO.
New York, New York

In 1867 or 1868, J. F. Fradley who had completed his apprenticeship as a chaser in the silverware factory of Wood & Hughes, opened a small workshop and began doing chasing for the trade. He soon had a staff of 25-30 chasers in his employ.

In 1870 he opened a small factory for the production of gold-beaded canes. This venture was so successful that in 1873 he moved to larger quarters and added all kinds of silver novelties to his productions. The business was incorporated in 1890. Fradley retired in 1902 but the firm continued under the same name with Geo. F. Fradley, a son of the founder. The last record found was 1936. Among the articles made were 14k gold and sterling silver cane and umbrella handles; 14k dresserwares and novelties; sterling photo frames, vases, desk accessories and other novelties.

TRADE MARK

AUG. C. FRANK CO., INC.
Philadelphia, Pennsylvania

Founded in 1894 by a German-born engraver, August Conrad Frank. As his two sons, Herman and Edwin, grew up he taught them engraving and brought them into the company. In 1942 the business was made a partnership with the father and two sons under the Aug. C. Frank name. Today, Edwin Frank is the only survivor. The senior Frank died Oct. 31, 1946 at the age of 83, and the eldest son, Herman, died May 24, 1966 at the age of 68. The present firm was incorporated May 1, 1971.

The Frank company had a fine tradition of excellent medallic work in the Philadelphia area. Custom medals, sports awards, badges, advertising coins and plaques were produced.

On September 15, 1972 the Frank company medal division was purchased by Medallic Art Company of Danbury, Connecticut. The dies, medal presses and other equipment were immediately moved to their Danbury, Connecticut factory. The purchase did not include the non-medallic business of the Aug. C. Frank firm, which will continue in other areas in which it engages, including plastic thermomolding, light metal stamping and their tool and die business.

(Trademark shows the motif of a hand-operated medal screw press.)

THE FRANKLIN MINT
Franklin Center, Pennsylvania

The Franklin Mint was founded in 1963 by Joseph M. Segel and has become the world's largest and foremost private mint. It is the principal operating division of the Franklin Mint Corporation and the only non-government mint in the United States that produces legal tender for foreign countries. It is best known for its many series of commemorative and art medals, which are usually struck in sterling silver and issued in limited editions.

The Franklin Mint specializes in *proof-quality* coins and medals. *Proofs* bear the "FM" mark and are characterized by flawlessly minted detail on a brilliant, mirror-like background and are highly prized by collectors everywhere.

The Franklin Mint is the official minter for many important series of commemorative medals such as those for the Bicentennial Council of the Thirteen Original States, the White House Historical Association, Postmasters of America, the National Governors' Conference, the National Audubon Society and the United Nations.

In 1973 they entered the field of signed art prints with the formation of the Franklin Mint Gallery of American Art. Early in 1974 they began the publication of luxury editions of books of proven literary importance and the creation of limited edition sculptures of fine pewter. On July 10, 1973 they dedicated the Franklin Mint Museum of Medallic Art which houses a most complete collection of Franklin Mint issues.

Their extensive sculpturing and engraving staff is augmented by more than 100 distinguished sculptors working in their own studios, thus making the Mint an important patron of the arts and largely responsible for the modern renaissance in medallic art.

FRANKLIN SILVER PLATE COMPANY
Greenfield, Massachusetts
See Lunt Silversmiths

Incorporated in Greenfield, Massachusetts in 1912. Ceased operations between 1920-22. They were manufacturers of plated silver holloware. The trademark was taken over by Rogers, Lunt & Bowlen (Lunt Silversmiths) c. 1922, but with minor exceptions has not been used.

TRADE MARK

FRARY & CLARK & SMITH
Meriden, Connecticut

In business c. 1850-65. Merged with Landers & Smith in 1865 to form Landers, Frary & Clark.

FRENCH & FRANKLIN
North Attleboro, Massachusetts

Listed in Jewelers' Weekly, 1896 as manufacturers of sterling silverware.

G. H. FRENCH & CO.
North Attleboro, Massachusetts
See Ellmore Silver Co., Inc.

Earliest record found c. 1920. Manufacturers of sterling silver novelties, cigarette and vanity cases, cups and tableware. Succeeded by Ellmore Silver Company, Inc., between 1935-43.

FRIED, MILLS & CO. INC.
Irvington, New Jersey

Listed in JC 1915 in sterling silver section. Last record found c. 1935.

FRIEDMAN SILVER CO., INC.
Brooklyn, New York
See Gorham Corporation

Creators of fine holloware since 1908. Bought by the Gorham Corporation in 1960.

BENJAMIN FROBISHER
Boston, Massachusetts

Benjamin Frobisher was a silversmith and jeweler. Though britannia wares are generally thought not to have been made in this country until 1835 or afterwards, according to the late Carl Dreppard, Frobisher advertised them as early as 1829.

FERD. FUCHS & BROS.
New York, New York

Ferdinand Fuchs and his brothers came to this country from Germany about 1835. They were in business first in Boston and later moved to New York. The firm was composed of Ferdinand and Rudolph Fuchs and was established in 1884 for the manufacture of sterling silverware. Richard Fuchs was sales representative in Baltimore, Philadelphia and the West. Piérre Joseph Chéron designed some of their wares. They were out of business before 1922.

FUCHS & BEIDERHASE
New York, New York

Founded by Rudolph Fuchs and George B. Beiderhase in 1891. Makers of sterling holloware, cups, napkin rings, dresserware, library articles and novelties. Succeeded by Alvin Mfg. Co. before 1896.

"Rudolph Fuchs, president of Fuchs & Beiderhase, silversmiths, died Thursday morning. Only 34 years old he had been connected with the silverware business for 18 years. He served his apprenticeship with B. D. Beiderhase & Co., New York and was afterwards connected with Adams & Shore [Shaw?], Dominick & Haff and J. F. Fradley & Co. When he left the latter firm in 1884 he went into partnership with his brother under the firm name of Ferdinand Fuchs & Bro. The partnership was dissolved in 1891, and Mr. Fuchs and Mr. Beiderhase formed the firm of Fuchs & Biederhase, incorporated last April. Mr. Fuchs was president." (JC&HR 1-18-1893, p. 5)

G

JOHN GAILLISSAIRE
Baltimore, Maryland

Listed in Baltimore City Directory as silverplater in 1864.

GALE & HAYDEN
New York, New York

Gale & Hayden are mentioned (JC-W 7-20-1904) as "a firm of the first half of the last century in New York." Possibly retailers as some flatware sold by them bears marks of Gale & Hughes. Gale & Hayden obtained Design Patents #149 and #150, September 11, 1847 for flatware.

WM. GALE
New York, New York
See Gorham Corporation
See Graff, Washbourne & Dunn

CHRONOLOGY

William Gale NYC Directory	1824-1850
Gale & Stickler (Wm. Gale & John Stickler)	1822-1823
Gale & Moseley (Wm. Gale & Joseph Moseley)	1828-33
Gale, Wood & Hughes (Wm. Gale, Jacob Wood, Jasper W. Hughes)	1836-45
Gale & Hayden ("first half of last century") (Patent Office records Sept. 11, 1847)	
Gale & Willis (NYC Directory 1840)	
Gale & Hughes (Wm. Gale & Jasper W. Hughes)	1845-50
William Gale & Son (Wm. Gale & Wm. Gale, Jr.)	1850-60
William Gale, Son & Co.	1860
Gale & North	1860
Gale, North & Dominick	1868
Gale & Corning (W. Gale, Jr. & Edward Corning)	1868-69
Gale, Dominick & Haff (Wm. Gale., Jr., H. Blanchard Dominick & Leroy B. Haff)	1870-71
Dominick & Haff	1871-1899
Purchased by Reed & Barton	1928
Wood & Hughes (Jasper W. Hughes, Chas. Wood & S. T. Fraprie)	1850
Wood & Hughes (Chas. Wood S. T. Fraprie, J. W. Hughes & Chas. W. Hughes)	1856
Wood & Hughes (Chas. Wood, S. T. Fraprie, Henry Wood & D. E. Hughes)	1871-99

Succeeded by Graff, Washbourne & Dunn 1899-1961
(Chas. Graff, W. L. Washbourne &
Clarence or Cleveland(?) A. Dunn)
Purchased by the Gorham Corporation in 1961
William Gale invented and patented a process for making spoons with ornamental patterns. This entailed cutting the ornament on rollers, both the upper and lower rollers being cut with the pattern. This made the production of pattern spoons much less expensive than the former method of hand hammering patterns by the use of dies. During the fourteen years Gale controlled this patent he became the largest manufacturer of spoons in the country. The process was superseded by the mechanical perfection of the drop hammer, spoons then being made from flat dies, the upper and lower dies containing the ornament. Shaped dies were a still later development.

GALT & BRO., INC.
Washington, D.C.

CHRONOLOGY

James Galt	1802-47
M. W. Galt & Bro.	1847-79
M. W. Galt, Bro. & Co.	1879-92
Galt & Bro.	1892-34
Galt & Bro. Inc.	1934-present

James Galt moved from Georgetown to Alexandria in 1802 and established his business which included the making of watches, and later fine silver pieces.

In 1847 James Galt died and ownership of the business passed into the hands of M. W. Galt and William Galt, his sons. Among their patrons were Abraham Lincoln and Jefferson Davis. In 1879 William Galt withdrew from the firm. The following year M. W. Galt retired and turned over to Norman Galt, grandson of the founder, the responsibility for maintaining the prestige and respect which the House of Galt had earned. He was assisted by Henry C. Bergheimer.

About 1900, Galt and Brother was chosen to execute a bowl which was presented to Postmaster Charles Emory Smith for his efforts in establishing a rural mail system. This piece of work brought a special congratulatory note from President Roosevelt in 1902, the one hundredth anniversary of Galt and Brother.

In 1908 Norman Galt died and Henry C. Bergheimer became the first to manage the business without bearing the founder's name. That year they began automobile delivery service. In 1923, Henry C. Bergheimer died and the management was carried on under William H. Wright. In 1934 Galt & Brother was incorporated when Norman Galt's widow, Edith Bolling Galt Wilson (Mrs. Woodrow Wilson), turned the firm over to the employees.

U. S. Patent No. 19,421, May 5, 1891. Portrait of Christopher Columbus, a copy of M. Maelia's engraved picture of Columbus published by Joseph Delaplaine, Philadelphia and later given to the U. S. Navy Department.

U. S. Patent No. 20,448, December 8, 1891. Landing of Columbus. Facsimile of the famous painting later placed in the U. S. Capitol.

Both trademarks were used in gold, silver and plated silver articles, presumably of the souvenir type.

The George and Martha Washington medallions were registered trademarks for use on souvenir spoons conceived by M. W. Galt. The first of these was a ladle that was an exact facsimile of the Washington ladle preserved in the National Museum, with the addition of the Washington medallion stamped in the bowl.

GALT & BRO.

ALBERT J. GANNON
Philadelphia, Pennsylvania

The Philadelphia City Directory lists Albert J. Gannon as a salesman in 1905; as a silversmith between 1906-1910 and lists Albert J. Gannon Company, silversmiths from 1911-1914. This is the last listing.

GARDEN SILVERSMITHS
New York, New York

Listed in directories 1960s and in 1973 JC-K. Successors to Arrowsmith Silver Corp. They own the dies for sterling silver wares formerly made by Apollo and Bernard Rice's Sons.

GARRETT & SONS
Philadelphia, Pennsylvania

In the 1860s they purchased Reed & Barton wares "in the metal" and operated their own plating establishment.

GEBELEIN SILVERSMITHS
Boston, Massachusetts

Gebelein Silversmiths was founded by George C. Gebelein who was born near Bayreuth, Bavaria, in 1878 and was brought to this country when a year old so his training was entirely American. he was apprenticed at the age of 14 to Goodnow & Jenks (q.v.). He concluded his apprenticeship in November 1897 and went to work for Tiffany & Company in their new (1895) factory at Forest Hills, New Jersey. He returned to New England to work for William B. Durgin (q.v.) in 1900 before starting out for himself as a member of The Handicraft Shop of Boston at the end of the year 1903, then setting up the shop of his own at the foot of Beacon Hill in 1909 where it remained until forced to move in 1968.

Besides making fine reproductions and adaptations, Gebelein was a collector and dealer in old American and European silver, becoming a recognized authority on silver. He was one of the early recipients of the medal for excellence presented by the Society of Arts and Crafts of Boston. The Williamsburg Communion set is one of his best-known productions.

His son, J. Herbert Gebelein, followed him in the silversmithing craft and is usually noted for the excellence of his work. After the father's death in 1945, the company was incorporated under family directorship as Gebelein Silversmiths Inc.

The customary marking on sterling silver from 1908-09 has been:

    1. Incised surname without outline;
    1.Incised name in cut-cornered rectangle;
    3. Small surname (raised capitals in rectangle) STERLING (and usually) Boston.

In some instances, in emulation of the Colonial practice, this last mark was struck without STERLING unless the customer preferred it. More cases of the omission of the STERLING mark occurred since the addition of another stamp (about 1929) enclosing the name GEBELEIN in oval cartouche. Used mostly in its largest of three sizes, this mark was intended in general to go on entirely hand-fashioned pieces.

Other marks:

1904-08 G or GG (incised) with H anvil S (raised in outline) Year STERLING or COIN.

In 1908 G or GEBELEIN H anvil S.

From 1908 GEBELEIN (in cut-cornered rectangle, incised) (2 sizes; continued in use).

From 1909 GEBELEIN (incised, no outline) STERLING Boston (incised) (medium and small continued in use).

Another old stamp GEBELEIN (raised letters in rectangle).

A small G (for marking small areas) (incised in Old English—Gothic text capitals).

The mark above includes a G, the outline beaded at top, bottom and sides. Not used on solid silver as a rule but on work in metals other than gold and silver such as the specialty of Gebelein, hand-hammered silver-lined copper bowls, or some few silver-plated or pewter specialties.

(On hand-forged special order flatware, forks and spoons)

GELSTON & GOULD
See Gould & Ward

GEM SILVER CO.
See International Silver Co.

Trademark of Wilcox Silver Plate Co. for dresserware and several flatware patterns.

GEM SILVER CO.

GENOVA SILVER CO., INC.
New York, New York

Manufacturers of sterling silver c. 1950.

ARTHUR R. GEOFFROY
New York, New York

Listed in JC 1896 as manufacturer of sterling silverware. Out of business before 1904. Advertised as maker of wares in sterling silver for the trade only.

GERITY PRODUCTS, INC.
Toledo, Ohio

Their advertising reads, "Custom platers since 1898." No answer to recent inquiries.

GERMAN SILVER
See Holmes & Edwards

GEORGE E. GERMER
Boston, Massachusetts

George E. Germer was the son of a Berlin jeweler and was born in 1868. Even before his apprenticeship, he showed a love of silver. Otto Gericke of Berlin, was his teacher and from him he learned chasing and modeling. He came to the United States in 1893 and for nearly 20 years worked in New York, Providence and Boston. After 1912 he worked independently, producing mostly ecclesiastical silver. During his latter years, he moved his shop to Mason, New Hampshire and produced more silver for churches, some of which is now in museums.

MICHAEL GIBNEY
New York, New York

Michael Gibney was listed in the New York City Directories 1836-45 and 1849-51. He was issued the first Design Patent for a flatware design in this country (Design Patent No. 26, Dec. 4, 1844). Pieces in this pattern are marked "Ball, Black & Co.," "Ball, Thompkins & Black," with a "Y" or completely unmarked. Gibney was also issued other Design Patents. One, *Tuscan* (Design Patent No. 59, July 10,

1846) was designed at the request of E. K. Collins, noted shipbuilder, who wished to equip a new vessel with a silver service with "a pattern different from the old ones then prevailing." The order was placed through Marquand & Co. It was later marketed by them and eventually became one of the first standard patterns issued by the Whiting Mfg. Co.

Gibney was a designer for the trade as well.

F. S. GILBERT
North Attleboro, Massachusetts

Listed JC 1904 as manufacturer of sterling silverware. Out of business before 1915.

STERLING **G**

GILBERTSON & SON
Chicago, Illinois

In business in the 1920s as silversmiths, platers and finishers, mesh bag repairers and electroplaters.

GINNELL MFG. CO.
Brooklyn, New York

Listed in JC 1915-22 as a manufacturer of sterling silverware and jewelry.

G. MFG. CO.

GLASTONBURY SILVER CO.
Chicago, Illinois

Listed in JC 1922-1950 as manufcturers of plated silver flatware and holloware. Between 1931-1950 the company name became Glastonbury, Inc.

ARROW PLATE
(On plated flatware)

GEE-ESCO

R. GLEASON & SONS
Dorchester, Massachusetts

Began with Roswell Gleason who was a tin worker in 1822. He was first listed as a pewterer about 1830. he was noted for the extremely fine quality of his work. This quality was carried over into britannia work later when the business became one of the largest and most important in Dorchester. After 1850 their products were mostly silverplated. the business closed in 1871.

Used on plated silver. Attributed to Manhattan Silver Plate Co. in 1904 JC.

HERMAN W. GLENDENNING
Gardner, Massachusetts

Herman W. Glendenning is a silversmith. As a young boy he lived across the street from Arthur J. Stone

(q.v.) whose shop he entered in 1920 to learn silversmithing. He was first instructed in making flatware, forging with a three or four pound hammer. He then progressed to holloware which he still prefers as there is more variety in its design and execution. When he was judged proficient, he was permitted to put his "G" under the Stone trademark and eventually attained his goal of "Master Craftsman."

After Stone's retirement, Mr. Glendenning became the designer and producer of holloware at the Erickson Shop (q.v.) where he worked for about thirty-five years. In 1971 he retired from the Erickson Shop but is currently teaching a young man silversmithing with the view to having him take over the business, including tools and patterns.

Glendenning Sterling Handwrought

(Used since 1955)

W. H. GLENNY & CO.
Rochester, New York

Wholesale and retail silverware and jewelry. Note similarity of trademark to that of The Waldo Foundry, Bridgeport, Connecticut, and H. H. Curtis & Co., North Attleboro, Massachusetts

ESTABLISHED 1876

W. H. GLENNY, SONS & CO.
Buffalo, Nw York

"W. H. Glenny Sons & Co., was established in 1840 in Buffalo, New York, as a crockery and glassware business. Branch stores were opened in St. Paul, Elmira and Rochester. St. Paul and Elmira stores closed several years ago but the Buffalo and Rochester stores continued until 1898 and were operated by the sons. At the time of closing of the entire business it was operated by William H. Glenny, Bryant B. Glenny, W. Henry Glenny and Francis Almy and William Keagey." (JC&HR 2-2-1898, p. 23)

They were wholesalers of silverware, including souvenir spoons stamped with their trademark.

GLOBE ART MFG. CO.
Newark, New Jersey

Listed in JC 1915-1922 as manufacturers of sterling silver and plated silverware.

GLOBE SILVER CO.
New York, New York

Listed in directories 1957-61 as manufacturers.

JACOB GMINDER
Baltimore, Maryland

Listd as a silverplater 1867-1901 in Baltimore City Directories.

ALEXANDER GOLDMAN
Ne York, New York

Listed directories 1920s and 1930s as manufacturer of sterling holloware, sterling religious articles.

GOLD RECOVERY & REFINING CORP.
New York, New York

Manufacturer (?) of sterling and silverplate c. 1940-45. Succeeded by Dunkirk Silversmiths, Meriden, Conn.

GOLDFEDER SILVERWARE COMPANY, INC.
Yalesville, Connecticut

Established in 1932. Manufacturers of silverplated hollowares, namely candelabra, trays, water pitchers, champagne buckets, vegetable platters, combination platters, lazy susans, punch bowls and cups, tea sets, sugar and creamers, tea kettles and gravy bowls.

Trademark issued to Sol Goldfeder, New York. Succeeded by Birmingham Silver Co. No answer to recent inquiries.

(Used since Jan. 1, 1947)

GOLDMAN SILVERSMITHS CO.
New York, New York

Manufacturers (?) of sterling silver articles c. 1940-45.

M. T. GOLDSMITH
Brooklyn, New York

Established in 1864 by Marcus Goldsmith as Goldsmith Brothers Smelting & Refining Company, Lexington, Kentucky. In 1882, his sons, Moses and Simon, succeeded to the business and in 1884 moved to Chicago. In 1909, the New York branch was opened by Simon. They were known as leaders in smelting and refining gold, silver and platinum. Listed by JC as out of business in 1909.

BRITANNIA ARTISTIC SILVER

GOLDSMITH'S COMPANY OF CANADA, LTD.
Toronto, Canada

Listed in JC 1915-1922 in the plated silver section.

NICKELITE SILVER
SHEFFIELD CUTLERY

GOLDSTEIN & SWANK CO.
Worcester, Massachusetts

Listed in JC 1915-1922 as makers of plated ware, jewelers and special order work.

Became Goldstein, Swank & Gordon before 1936. This is the last record found.

GOODBY MFG. CO.
San Francisco, California

Listed in the 1931 JKI as special order work in silver holloware and gold ware; gold and silver plating, repairing and refinishing.

A. E. GOODHUE
Quincy, Massachusetts

In 1950 JC-K and 1957 JBG under sterling and silverplate.

GOODNOW & JENKS
Boston, Massachusetts

Successors to Kennard & Jenks. They were established in 1893 to manufacture and sell sterling silverware. Walter R. Goodnow, formerly of Bigelow, Kennard & Co., was a financial partner only. Barton Pickering Jenks, son of the gifted designer Lewis E. Jenks of Kennard & Jenks, received his degree in architecture from M.I.T. about 1890 after beginning his college career for a year at Harvard.

Goodnow & Jenks were the principal silverware manufacturers of their time in Boston, concerned mainly with holloware. In 1904 or 1905 Jenks resigned and went to work for Wm. B. Durgin Co.

One of the senior silversmiths at Goodnow & Jenks was George F. Hamilton, Irish-born 1831, who arrived in Boston as a boy where he served his apprenticeship with Charles West (also possibly with Newell Harding whose Court Avenue address was nearby). Hamilton had been with Haddock & Andrews (Henry Haddock, 1811-92, apprenticed to Moses Morse, Boston; Henry Andrews, 1809-93) and with Haddock, Lincoln & Foss, before going with Goodnow & Jenks. When Goodnow & Jenks closed, Hamilton went with the Tuttle Silver Co.

Another silversmith at Goodnow & Jenks was Adolph Krass, born in Westphalia, Germany, in 1833. He came to this country at the age of about twenty and was first employed by Ferdinand Fuchs & Bros. (q.v.). It was Krass from whom George C. Gebelein (q.v.) obtained special attention during his apprenticeship at Goodnow & Jenks August 1893 to November 1897.

GOODWILL MFG. CO.
Providence, Rhode Island

Listed 1927 KJI as manufacturers of flatware, dresserware and holloware.

FREDERICK GORDON
Baltimore, Maryland

CHRONOLOGY

George B. Gordon	1864-79
Gordon & Company	1880-94

| F. S. Gordon | 1894-97 |
| Frederick Gordon | 1898-99 |

Silverplaters.

GORHAM CORPORATION
Providence, Rhode Island
(Division of Textron)

CHRONOLOGY

Gorham & Webster	1831-1837
Gorham, Webster & Price	1837-1841
J. Gorham & Son	1841-1850
Gorham & Thurber	1850-1852
Gorham & Company	1852-1865
Gorham Mfg. Company*	1865-1961
Gorham Corp.	1961-present

* Or Lion and Anchor

Jabez Gorham, founder of the Gorham Corporation, was born in Providence, Rhode Island in 1792 and at 14 began his seven year apprenticeship to Nehemiah Dodge. After serving his apprenticeship, he formed a partnership with Christopher Burr, William Hadwen, George C. Clark and Harvey G. Mumford about 1815-1818 at which time he purchased his own shop to manufacture small items and became known for his '"Gorham chain," unequaled at the time.

With Stanton Beebe he made jewelry until 1831 with Henry L. Webster, formerly with Lewis Cary in Boston, joined the firm to make silver spoons. The firm name was changed to Gorham & Webster. In 1837, the firm was called Gorham, Webster & Price. When Gorham's son, John joined the firm in 1841, the name was changed to Jabez Gorham & Son. John Gorham quickly recognized the advantages of machinery and as a result the Gorham Company was among the first to introduce factory methods to augment hand craftsmanship in production of silverware. He designed and made much of the machinery himself if none was available to suit his purposes.

In 1850, three years after Jabez Gorham retired, the company name was Gorham & Thurber. By 1852, it was Gorham & Company. The firm was chartered by the Rhode Island Legislature as the Gorham Manufacturing Company in 1863 and organized as a corporation in 1865. In 1868, they abandoned the coin silver standard (900/1000) and adopted the sterling standard of 925/1000 fine silver. At the same time, the familiar trademark—a lion, an anchor and a capital G—was adopted for use on all sterling articles. Ecclesiastical wares of gold, bronze, stone, wood and sterling were added in 1885. *L'art nouveau* designs of the talented English artist, William Christmas Codman, were added under the name "Martelé" in the late 19th century.

By 1863 the company decided to use its facilities for making electroplated silverwares using nickel silver as the base. Made entirely of nickel silver, these wares were processed by the same general methods used in making sterling silverware, even to the use of silver solder in assembling the component parts. The tooling and die work occupied about two years so that it was not until 1865 that the first of their silverplated line was marketed. They ceased production of their silverplated flatware May 1, 1962 but their silverplated holloware continues to be an important part of their output.

Holding companies were chartered in New York during 1906 and 1907 for the purpose of acquiring the Whiting, Durgin and Kerr companies. These corporations in the order of their formation were known as the Silversmiths Stocks Company and The Silversmiths Company. In the reorganization of the Company in 1924, the Silversmiths Company was purchased, its assets taken over and the company dissolved. The Gorham Company then operated as subsidiary divisions, the Whiting Mfg. Co. (moved to Providence in 1925); William B. Kerr Company, (moved to Providence in 1927); and William B. Durgin Company, (moved to Providence in 1931).

About 1913 the Gorham interests expanded to include the Mt. Vernon Company Silversmiths, Inc., which had resulted from the merging of the Roger Williams Silver Company of Providence, Rhode Island, the Mauser Manufacturing Company of Mt. Vernon, New York and Hayes & McFarland of New York City.

The Alvin Silver Company was acquired in 1928 and its title changed to The Alvin Corporation. Its products are made at the Providence plant though it functions as an organization separate from The Gorham Company.

The Gorham retail store at 5th Avenue and 47th Street in New York merged with Black Starr and Frost in 1929 under the new firm name of Black, Starr and Frost-Gorham Inc. In 1962 The Gorham Company sold its interests and the name became Black, Starr & Frost, Ltd.

In 1931 the McChesney Company of Newark, New Jersey was purchased and its tools and dies moved to Providence.

The Quaker Silver Company of North Attleboro, Massachusetts was purchased in 1959, the Friedman Company of Brooklyn, New York in 1960 and Graff, Washbourne & Dunn of New York in 1961. The Gorham Company was sold to Textron, Inc. in 1967.

At all periods the Gorham Company has been noted for the fine quality of its die work as well as superior design and fine finishing of all products.

Gorham's familiar trademark was registered (#33.902) Dec. 19, 1899 at which time it was stated that it had been in use since January 1, 1853. The Gorham Company now states that this trademark was used as early as 1848 and that from 1848 to 1865 the lion faced left rather than right.

TRADE MARK

STERLING

TRADE-MARK.

STERLING

GORHAM MFG CO

GORHAM (Gold)

Martelé

• GORHAM (art bronzes) (Bronze)

950-1000 FINE

(Plated silver)

GORHAM
(Pewter)

GORHAM ELMWOOD PLATE

NEWPORT STERLING
TWINKLE STERLING
VOGUE

BANQUET PLATE
ELMWOOD PLATE

SUFFOLK SILVERPLATE (Tradename used with Gorham's silverplate mark and METROPOLITAN MUSEUM REPRODUCTION)

Athenic

STERLING
(Sterling silver)

The Athenic trademark was used on articles that are Art Nouveau in feeling but Greek in inspiration. Sterling silver is combined with other materials.

A.	1868		1885		1902		1918
B.	1869		1886		1903		1919
C.	1870		1887		1903		
D.	1871		1888		1904		1920
E.	1872		1889		1905		1921
F.	1873		1890		1906		1922
G.	1874		1891		1907		
H.	1875		1892		1908		1923
			1893		1909		1924
I.	1876		1894		1910		
J.	1877		1895		1911		1925
K.	1878		1896		1912		1926
L.	1879		1897		1913		1927
M.	1880		1898		1914		
N.	1881		1898		1915		1928
O.	1882		1899		1916		1929
P.	1883		1900				1930
Q.	1884		1901		1917		1931

Holloware year markings have been used since 1868. Letters of the alphabet A through Q were used from 1868 through 1884 at which time symbols were adopted for each year until 1933 at which time they were discontinued. In January 1941, year markings were resumed on sterling holloware except lower priced items.

During 1933 year marks were discontinued.

1932   1933

January 1941 year marking was resumed on Sterling Holloware except lower priced items.

1941

The square frame indicates the decade of the 40s. The numeral indicates the year of the decade.

The pentagon indicates the decade of the 50s. The numeral indicates the year of the decade.

1950
1951

The hexagon indicates the decade of the 60s. The numeral indicates the year of the decade.

O   1960   1961

The heptagon indicates the decade of the 70s. The numeral indicates the year of the decade.

O   1970   1971

This marking will be used only on heavy sterling items such as tea sets and on specially made sterling items for individual consumers. The Christmas items such as the Snowflake will be back stamped with a four digit numeral to indicate the year of production.

At one time flatware was made in as many as five different weights for the same pattern. The letters below are those used to indicate these weights:
T   for Trade
M   for Medium
H   for Heavy
EH   for Extra Heavy
Regular weight had no marking.

JOHN T. GOSWELL
Baltimore, Maryland

Listed in Baltimore City Directories 1864-1868 as silverplaters.

GOTHAM SILVER CO., INC.
New York, New York

Manufacturers of plated silver holloware c. 1920. Last record found was 1950.

WEAR-WELL

GOULD, STOWELL & WARD
Baltimore, Maryland

James Gould A. Stowell, Jr., William H. Ward, silversmiths and dealers in jewelry. Advertised silverware made to order. Listed in Baltimore City Directory 1855-1856.

GOULD & WARD
Baltimore, Maryland

James Gould and William H. Ward were successors to Gelston & Gould, silversmiths, c. 1810-1820. Became Gould, Stowell & Ward, c. 1855.

GRAF & NEIMANN
Pittsburgh, Pennsylvania

Manufacturers of silverware c. 1900.

GRAFF, WASHBOURNE & DUNN
New York, New York
See Gorham Corporation

The predecessors of Graff, Washbourne & Dunn may be traced back to William Gale who was active in silversmithing in New York in 1833. He was followed by the firm of Wm. Gale & Son, then Gale, Wood & Hughes, and Wood & Hughes. In 1899, Wood & Hughes sold their factory to Graff, Washbourne & Dunn who at once incorporated. Charles Graff was president, designer and factory manager. Clarence A. Dunn was vice-president and treasurer, also manager of the business and general executive. William L. Washbourne was secretary and in charge of sales. Graff died in 1931 and Washbourne in 1941. Dunn acquired the stock of both and in 1942 became

— 61 —

Salt dishes, probably c. 1865. Made by the Gorham Company. Note that the trademark of the "Lion, anchor & G" is not enclosed in cut-corner squares and shield as are most later ones.

Tea and coffee service, probably late 19th century. The Gorham Company trademark on the tea and coffee pots include the capacity of each.

sole owner and then sold his entire holdings, including the corporate name to Harrison W. Conrad, who became president and Eugene Rossi, who became treasurer. The company was purchased by the Gorham Corp. in 1961. Graff, Washbourne & Dunn were makers of sterling silver holloware and novelties.

GRANAT BROS., INC.
San Francisco, California

Registered trademark for use on silver flatware, silver services, jewelry and novelties made wholly or partly of precious metal. Published Dec. 6, 1949.

(Used since Aug. 1, 1929)

GREATREX LTD.
New York, New York

Trademark registered May 29, 1951 for use on sterling silver, silverplated and silver mounted flatware and holloware.

(Used since 1947)

GREEN-SMITH CO.
Denver, Colorado
See Frederick L. Smith

GREGG SILVER CO., INC.
Taunton, Massachusetts

Manufacturers of silverplated holloware c. 1950.

F. L. GREGORY
Niagara Falls, New York

Listed in the 1886 Niagara Falls City Directory as makers of silver and plated silverware.

CHARLES W. GRESHOFF
Baltimore, Maryland

Gold and silversmith. Listed in Baltimore City Directories 1888-1898.

FRANCIS A. GRESHOFF
Baltimore, Maryland

Gold and silversmith. Listed in Baltimore City Directories 1864-1885. Succeeded by Francis A. Greshoff & Son in 1887. This listing continued through 1894.

GRIFFON CUTLERY WORKS
New York, New York

Began business before 1904 as Silberstein, Hecht & Company, soon succeeded by A. L. Silberstein and has been Griffon Cutlery Works since 1915.

GRIFFIN SILVER PLATE CO.
Elgin, Illinois

"The Griffin Silver Plate Co.'s factory, Elgin, Illinois, has started up with a small force of hands." (JC&HR 2-1-1893, p. 17)

ED. GRONEBERG
Baltimore, Maryland

Listed in 1855-1856 Baltimore City Directory as a manufacturer and dealer in fine gold jewelry and silverware.

GROSJEAN & WOODWARD
New York, New York

Their partnership was listed in Boston in 1840. Charles Grosjean and Eli Woodward were silversmiths in New York from 1852 to 1862. Charles Grosjean was a silversmith in Würtemberg, Germany. He came to New York in 1836 and died on January 30, 1865. Their "G & W" mark is to be found on many silver articles sold through Tiffany & Co., around 1852-53.

Charles Grosjean (son?) designed and patented the Tiffany Indian Dance spoons February 10 and 17, 1885 as well as several full line flatware patterns of theirs.

G & W

LEWIS GUIENOT
Baltimore, Maryland

Listed in Baltimore City Directories 1870-1877 as a gold and silverplater.

A. T. GUNNER MFG. CO.
Attleboro, Massachusetts

Albert T. Gunner was born January 23, 1897, in Wallingford, Connecticut, second son of Charles R. and Etta (Simmons) Gunner.

He attended public school in Providence, Rhode Island and Attleboro, Massachusetts, and, in 1919, took night courses in Accounting in New York City.

On July 5, 1912, he went to work to learn a trade as a spinner at the Watson Company in Attleboro, Massachusetts. Later he worked for F. W. Whiting Company in North Attleboro as foreman of the Spinning Department.

In 1918 he enlisted in the Army and was stationed in New York City with the Chemical Warfare Service. He was a Sergeant at the end of the war.

He then went to work as a metal spinner for the Gorham Company in New York City. Upon leaving that company, he was employed by Graff, Washbourne & Dunn as a spinner.

In 1920 he returned to Attleboro and started his own business for the manufacture of sterling silver holloware. It has been in operation ever since.

In 1921 Mr. Gunner married Grace Elizabeth Mahler of New York City.

An ancestor by the name of Gunner, who was in the agricultural business was given an order by the King of England in 1660 to supply cannon for the army. In recognition for this, he received the coat of arms which has been passed down in the family. The Latin inscription on it says, "We are known by our deeds." In Birmingham, England, there is a Gunner's Lane named after this ancestor.

H

J. H. FERD. HAHN
Baltimore, Maryland

Listed 1899-1911 Baltimore City Directory as a silverplater and metal worker.

HALL BROS. & CO.
Pittsburgh, Pennsylvania

H. B. & Co.

Wholesale and retail outlet in business c. 1910-1915.

HALL, BOARDMAN CO.
New York, New York
Philadelphia, Pennsylvania

Hall, Boardman & Company and its successor, Hall and Boardman, are listed in the Philadelphia and New York City Directories from 1845 through 1856 as makers of britannia wares. The New York firm apparently was solely a retail outlet.

HALL, ELTON & CO.
Wallingford, Connecticut
See International Silver Co.
See Maltby, Stevens & Curtiss
See Watrous Mfg. Co.

In 1837 Deacon Almer Hall, William Elton and other formed the firm of Hall, Elton & Co. for the manufacture of German silver flatware and britannia ware. In 1890 the company was purchased by Maltby, Stevens & Curtiss which was in turn purchased by Watrous Mfg. Co. In 1898 they were one of the original companies to become part of the International Silver Co.

Registered U. S. Patent, January 20, 1873 for use on flatware.

They made britannia spoons at least until 1875.

(German Silver Flatware.)

WILBUR B. HALL
Meriden, Connecticut

Specialist in silverplated peppers and salts, napkin rings, cups and other small articles. He was the son of Lewis Hall, superintendent of Wilcox Silver Plate Co. The business started in 1886 and continued for about 50 years. (*Meriden Journal,* Anniversary Issue, April 17, 1936)

HALLMARK SILVERSMITHS, INC.
New York, New York

An advertisement by Hallmark appeared in the *Saturday Evening Post* in 1917. The Hunt Silver Co., Inc. and Hallmark Silversmiths, Inc., merged in 1954 to form Hunt-Hallmark Co. Officials, Carl K. Klein, Joseph C. Hirsch and Irving L. Hirsch.

HALLMARK

CHARLES W. HAMILL & CO.
Baltimore, Maryland

Charles W. Hamill, manufacturer of silverplated wares was born in Baltimore, Maryland, March 2, 1845. After eleven years working for someone else he entered business for himself in 1876 with ten employees. His business increased rapidly so that by 1878 he had 40 employees. The company was listed in Baltimore City Directories from 1877 to 1884 inclusive.

C. A. HAMILTON
Waterbury, Connecticut
See Rogers & Hamilton

U. S. Patent No. 13,289, May 11, 1886 was registered by Charles Alfred Hamilton, president of Rogers & Hamilton, president of Rogers & Hamilton, for the manufacture of spoons, knives, forks, ladles, cheese-scoops, tea sets, casters, pitchers. waiters and napkin rings.

HAMILTON & DIESINGER
Philadelphia, Pennsylvania
See M. F. Hamilton & Son

Hamilton & Diesinger were successors c. 1895 to Hamilton & Davis (Matthew F. Hamilton and Junius H. Davis) listed in Philadelphia City Directories in 1880. Davis was associated briefly with Charles E. Galt in the firm of Davis & Galt (q.v.). Hamilton & Diesinger were manufacturers and retailers of both sterling and silverplated wares. The partnership was dissolved in 1899 when Hamilton's interest were bought out by Diesinger. Hamilton and his son then opened their own business under the name M. F.

Hamilton & Son (q.v.). In 1900 Diesinger sold what remained of the Hamilton & Diesinger business to Gimbel Bros.

HAMILTON & HAMILTON, JR.
Providence, Rhode Island

Registered U. S. Patent Office, No. 49,473, February 6, 1906.

This manufacturing jewelry business was established January 1, 1871 by R. S. Hamilton, R. S. Hamilton, Jr., and George C. Hunt. They began the manufacture of ladies' jewelry sets, lace pins and gentlemen's chains — all of solid gold. Six months later they began the manufacture of rolled plate chains. They advertised that they were the first makers of gold filled chains. April 27, 1886 they registered a patent for jewelry, chains, trimmings, cuff buttons, bracelets, lockets, cigarette holders and cases, knives and novelties. Listed from 1921-1935 as Hamilton & Hamilton Jr., Inc. Ralph S. Hamilton is still listed as a manufacturing jeweler not associated with a particular firm. "Hamilton & Hamilton began in 1870 as Hamilton & Hunt. The firm became Hamilton & Hamilton in 1883." (JW 3-30-1892)

"Ralph Spence Hamilton, senior member of Hamilton & Hamilton, Jr., died at the residence of his son, Ralph H. Jr., early Tuesday. He was born in St. Louis, Missouri, June 14, 1829. When quite young his parents moved to New Orleans. At age nine he accompanied his parents to Jamaica, where his father became interested in the cultivation of sugar and owned extensive plantations. Here he remained until about 16 years of age, when he started out for himself. He went to New York and apprenticed himself to learn the jewlery business. He adopted his pursuit from the interest which had been manifested in watching the native Indians of Jamaica fashion ear-rings and other trinkets out of metal by the crude mthod of hammering. Having concluded his apprenticeship, he went to Attleboro in the early 60's where he engaged in business for himself. In 1870 he removed to this city [Providence] and with J. Hunt formed the well known concern of that period, Hamilton & Hunt, which began the manufacturing business on a small scale on Potter Street. The business grew rapidly and new and larger quarters had to be obtained, and the firm removed to 226 Eddy St. where it remained for more than a decade.

"The firm of Hamilton & Hunt was dissolved by mutual consent early in 1883, and on July 10 of that year the firm of Hamilton & Hamilton, Jr. was organized, Mr. Hamilton taking his eldest son, Ralph S. Hamilton, Jr. into partnership with him. The business increased steadily so that when the Enterprise Building was erected in the Spring of 1888 the factory was removed to the new building." (JC&HR 2-8-1893, p. 14)

★H&H

★H&H

HAMILTON MINT
Arlington Heights, Illinois

The Hamilton Mint was organized in 1972 by a group of men with experience in art and minting who chose to found a new private mint specializing in medallions, ingots, plates and art forms honoring man's most noteworthy accomplishments in graphic arts and sculpture.

Their first major offering was announced August 1972 and was a series of three plates adapted from Picasso paintings in the National Gallery of Art, Washington, D.C.

M. F. HAMILTON & SON
Philadelphia, Pennsylvania

Successors to Hamilton & Diesinger before 1904 and out of business before 1909.

HAMILTON MFG. CO.
Chicago, Illinois

"The Hamilton Mfg. Co., Chicago, incorporated Wednesday to manufacture silverware with C. Van Allen Smith, Arthur R. Wells and Frederick H. Gade." (JC&HR 5-1-1895)

HAMILTON MFG. CO.

HAMILTON SILVER MFG. CO.
New York, New York

Absorbed by T. N. Benedict Mfg. Co., in 1912 and moved to East Syracuse, N.Y.

HAMILTON SILVER MFG. CO.
New York

JAMES B. HAMLIN
North Bridgton, Maine

Pewterer. Currently in business.

HAMMERSMITH & FIELD
San Francisco, California

John A. Hammersmith and Hampton S. Field were listed in city directories from at least 1899 to 1908 but had terminated before 1915. Attributed to their shop are trophies for the K. T. Conclave and some souvenir spoons with the seal of the State of California on the handle.

HAMPSHIRE SILVER CO.
New York, New York

In directories c. 1950s through 1960s as manufacturers.

HAMPTON ROADS CUTLERY CO.
Norfolk, Virginia

Listed in JC 1915 and JKI 1918-19 as Hampton Roads Silver Company, manufacturers of silverplated ware and table cutlery.

A. L. HANLE, INC.
New York, New York

Currently listed as pewterers. Hanle & Debler, Inc. listed as same address.

HANLE & DEBLER, INC.
New York, New York
See Samuel Kirk & Son

Listed 1950-73 JC-K as manufacturers of sterling. Succeeded by Kirk Pewter.

NEWELL HARDING & COMPANY
Haverhill & Boston, Massachusetts

Newell Harding (b. 10-20-1796, Haverhill, Mass.) was a silversmith. He was apprenticed to his brother-in-law, Hazen Morse. He went into business for himself in 1822. Under his own name and later as Newell Harding & Co, he made plain spoons in a factory in Court Street, Boston. The firm had a high reputation and did considerable business. Harding sold his business to Ward & Rich in 1832. Ward retired in 1835 and Obadiah Rich continued it until 1849 when he also retired.

Ensko *(American Silversmiths & Their Marks III)* credits Harding with introducing power to the rolling of silver.

Gibb *(The Whitesmiths of Taunton)* identifies the Harding company as one of those who operated its own silverplating establishments and purchased goods "in the metal."

HARPER & McINTIRE CO.
Ottumwa, Iowa

Silverplaters c. 1920.

HAR-MAC

HARRINGTON & MILLS
Baltimore, Maryland

Listed in Baltimore City Directories 1868-1874 as silverplaters.

R. HARRIS & CO.
Washington, D. C.

Established in 1874-1876. Manufacturing jewelers and silversmiths according to their catalog E, published c. 1898. No trademark but the company name. Still in business.

HARRIS & SCHAFER
Washington, D. C.

Listed in the Washington, D.C. Directories 1880-1938 as Harris & Schafer, Jewelers.

Edwin Harris was born in Charles County, Maryland in 1831. Educational facilities were limited at that time, so at a very early age he went to work in the store of Galt Bros. of Washington. He was taken into partnership in 1870 and remained there in that capacity for nine years. He then sold his interest and started a store of his own.

Charles A. Schafer, the junior partner, was born at Boonsboro in Washington County, Maryland. He moved to Washington, D.C. when ten years of age. He attended both Gonzaga College and Georgetown University. He entered the employ of Galt Bros. in 1849 and remained with that firm for

thirty years, mastering the jewelry making and watchmaking business. When Harris opened his own store, Schafer chose to join him as a partner.

Trademarks were registered at the U. S. Patent Office in 1891 and 1892 for gold, sterling silver and plated silver flat and tableware. These trademarks were used on souvenir silver. It is doubtful if Harris & Schafer did any manufacturing themselves. They were noted, however, for the fine quality of silver, jewelry, watches, diamonds, artwares and crystal and glassware they sold. Much of it was imported from the finest houses in Eruope.

HARRISON & GROESCHEL
New York, New York

Listed in JC 1896 in sterling silver section. Out of business before 1904.

LUCIUS HART MFG. CO.
New York, New York

Lucius Hart is listed in New York City Directories 1828-1850. The earlier listings are in connection with Timothy Boardman, pewterer, under the name Boardman & Hart. By 1850 the Boardman name was dropped and the listing was Lucius Hart, Britannia Ware Manufacturer. After 1863 the listing was Lucius Hart & Company. During the 1860s Hart bought many of Reed & Barton's wares "in the metal" and operated his own plating establishment in New York.

R. H. & A. W. HART
Brooklyn, New York

Silverplaters c. 1860.

HARTFORD HOLLOWARE CO.
Hartford, Connecticut

Reportedly, as off-shoot by some workmen previously in business with other Hartford silverware companies. In operation c. 1888-1901.

HARTFORD MANUFACTURING CO.
Hartford, Connecticut
See Bernard Rice's Sons

Organized September 23, 1854 by E. W. Sperry. Listed in city directories 1854-62 inclusive. The 1863

Hartford directory does not contain the Hartford Mfg. Co. but on March 23, 1863 the Hartford Plate Co. was organized to make German silver goods with Sperry listed as a member of the firm. The Hartford Plate Co. was organized by Redfield & Rice of New York.

HARTFORD SILVER PLATE CO.
Hartford, Connecticut
See Barbour Silver Co.
See International Silver Co.
See I. J. Steane Co.

Listed in Hartford City Directories from 1882 through 1894. Each listing accompanied by a half or full page advertisement.

The 1882 listing says they were manufacturers of fine electroplated holloware. Incorporaters: James G. Batterson, E. N. Welch, Henry C. Robinson, W. H. Post, Jonathan Goodwin, James L. Howard and Rush P. Chapman.

They advertised "Everything in silver plate." Absorbed by Barbour Silver Co. in 1893 which became part of the International Silver Co. in 1898.

"The Hartford Silver Plate Co. are engaged in refinishing and replating the beautiful candelabra of the White House, Washington, D.C." (JC&HR) 9-21-1892, p. 30)

HARTFORD STERLING COMPANY
Philadelphia, Pennsylvania
See I. J. Steane Co.
See Tennant Company
See Phelps & Cary Co.

Successors(?) to the Tennant Co., New York, 1900.

The Philadelphia City Directories list the Hartford Sterling Company from 1901-1924. In 1901 and 1902 the listing refers to foreign plated ware. Subsequent listings are for plated ware. The 1907-1912 Directory lists Isaac J. Steane (probably Isaac J. Steane, Jr.), president, Arthur B. Wells, secretary and Jacob S. Hecker, treasurer.

"The Hartford Sterling Co. has purchased the plant and business of Phelps & Cary Co. of New York and also Jacob S. Hecker & Co.. mfgrs. of silver plated holloware. H. A. Cary went into business for himself." (JC-W 7-4-1900, p. 23)

The upper trademark is identical to those of The Tennant Co. and Phelps & Cary Co., with the exception of the initials in the shield.

HARVEY & OTIS
Providence, Rhode Island

Manufacturing jeweler and silversmith. Listed JC 1896 to present.

H-O

HASKELL, BEECHER & CO.
Baltimore, Maryland

Listed in Baltimore City Directories 1885-1886 as silverplaters.

HENRY C. HASKELL
New York, New York

Listed in JC in sterling silver and jewelry sections 1896-1904. Out of business before 1915.

JOHN HASSELBRING
Brooklyn, New York
See Crown Silver Inc.

Founded about 1890 by John Hasselbring. Purchased by Crown Silver Inc. about 1954-1955 and is now a division of that company in New York. Their products are silver peppermills, bar accessories, silver trimmed salad bowls and silver trimmed cutlery.

Another trademark, containing a deer head, has been reported but not found.

HATTERSLEY & DICKINSON
Newark, New Jersey

William Hattersley is listed as a silversmith 1854-61 and as "Britannia metal works" 1852-53, as a partner in Hattersley & Dickinson 1854-56 and with Hattersley & Son J., britannia metal workers 1856-61. Charles Dickinson is listed under britannia metal 1850-57. The Patent Office records show that they were granted a patent (Design Patent No. 657, July 4, 1854) for the ornamental design for a tea or coffee pot, the type of metal not specified. This tea and coffee service is illustrated in the E. Jaccard catalog of 1856 under Solid Silver Tea Ware.

HAVONE CORPORATION
New York, New York

Listed JC 1915 in sterling silver section. Patents and trademarks taken over by Elgin-American Mfg. Co., Elgin, Illinois.

Elgin-American manufactures match boxes, vanity, poto and cigarette cases, belt buckles, cuff links, traveling clocks, photo lockets and knives.

HAWTHORNE MFG. CO.
New York New York

Manufacturer of sterling silverware. Listed in JC 1904 as out of business.

HAYDEN MFG. CO.
Newark, New Jersey
See G. W. Parks Co., Inc.

Gold and silversmiths c. 1893. Manufacturers of sterling silverware and jewelry. Succeeded by G. W. Parks Co., Inc. between 1904 and 1909.

WILLIAM W. HAYDEN CO.
Newark, New Jersey
See G. W. Parks Co., Inc.

Listed in JC 1904 in sterling silver section. Out of business before 1909.

HAYES & MCFARLAND
Mount Vernon, New York
See Gorham Corporation
See Mt. Vernon Silversmiths, Inc.

In 1903 merged with the Mauser Manufacturing Company of New York and the Roger Williams Silver Company of Providence, Rhode Island to form the Mt. Vernon Silversmiths Company which was purchased by the Gorham Corporation in 1913.

J. R. HAYNES
Cincinnati, Ohio

Listed in Cincinnati City Directories 1850-1859 as a silversmith who operated a silverware factory.

HAYNES & LAWTON
San Francisco, California

Silverplaters, not manufacturers. In 1864-65 listed in San Francisco city directory as dealers; in 1869 as agents for electrotyping work; 1870 Benjamin Haynes & Orlando Lawton; 1871 as prop. of Pacific Plate Works; 1874 no longer listed.

"Silverplating under the older methods has been practiced in San Francisco for a number of years, the articles being made of equal quality to the same work imported. During the past year, however, a new branch of the business, viz. electrotyping has been introduced in San Francisco by the Pacific Plate Works, Haynes & Lawton being the agents. By this process excellent work is done, the designs being elegant and the standard coating of metal of a purity and thickness not to be excelled." (Henry Langley, *The Pacific Coast Almanac for 1869*, S. F. 1869, p. 69)

C. E. HAYWARD COMPANY
Attleboro, Massachusetts
See Walter E. Hayward Co., Inc.

HAYWARD & SWEET
Attleboro, Massachusetts
See Walter E. Hayward Co., Inc.

WALTER E. HAYWARD CO., INC.
Attleboro, Massachusetts

Established in 1851 as Thompson, Hayward & Co., in Mechanicsville. Charles E. Hayward and Johnathan Briggs became partners in 1855. Charles E. Hayward was one of seven children of Abraham Hayward, captain of a privateer during the War of 1812. When Charles was 17 he was apprenticed to Tifft & Whiting to learn jewelry making.

The Hayward and Briggs partnership was dissolved in 1855 and Walter E. Hayward became associated with his father under the name of C. E. Hayward Co.

In 1887 the younger Hayward accepted George Sweet as a partner and the firm became Hayward & Sweet Company. The firm name became Walter E. Hayward Co. before 1904. Frank J. Ryder and Charles C. Wilmarth, both already associated with the firm, purchased the company in 1908.

Ryder bought out Wilmarth's interest in 1917 and remained sole owner until incorporation in 1921. Frank J. Ryder, Sr. died in 1943 and three years

Hayward

HAYWARD

later his son, Frank, Jr., became president and part owner; acquiring full ownership in 1949. They are still in business manufacturing religious items of sterling silver and gold and gold-filled jewelry.

HENRY HEBBARD
New York, New York
See Geo. W. Shiebler & Co.

Silversmith, listed New York City directories 1847-51 as Henry Hebbard & Co. Records in the U. S. Patent Office indicate that he was associated with John Polhemus (q.v.) in 1855 when the two obtained design patents for flatware later made by Geo. W. Shiebler & Co. Some later flatware design patents obtained in Hebbard's name from c. 1853 through 1869 were made by the Whiting Mfg. Co.

JACOB S. HECKER & CO.
Philadelphia, Pennsylvania

Manufacturers of silverplated holloware. Purchased by Hartford Sterling Co. in 1900.

HEER BROS. CO., INC.
Baltimore, Maryland

Listed in the Baltimore City Directories 1927-1928 as manufacturers of silverware.

HEEREN BROS & CO.
Pittsburgh, Pennsylvania

Mentioned as makers of a silver trophy cup. (JC-W 5-9-1900, p. 7)
Adv. (JR 1887) says they are manufacturers of "silver and plated ware."

HEER-SCHOFIELD CO.
Baltimore, Maryland
See Schofield Co., Inc.

HEINTZ ART METAL SHOP
Buffalo, New York

Listed in JC 1915-1922 in the plated silver section. Became Heintz Bros. Mfg. before 1935. This is the last listing found. Manufacturers of art metal goods and novelty jewelry.

HEIRLOOM
See Oneida Silversmiths

Heirloom is a trademark acquired by Oneida Silversmiths in 1929 through the acquisition of Wm. A. Rogers, Ltd.

HEIRLOOM

HEMILL SILVERWARE INC.
New York, New York

Manufacturers (?) or silverplaters c. 1920-1930.

SHEFFIELD H. S. Co.

SUSSEX

THE HEMMING MFG. CO.
Montreal, Canada

Listed in JC as manufacturers of sterling silverware and jewelry c. 1909. Out of business before 1915.

GEORGE A. HENCKEL & CO.
New York, New York
See Currier & Roby, Inc.

Manufacturers of small articles in sterling silver for the trade only. Listed in JC 1909-1922. Succeeded by Currier & Roby, Inc. before 1943.

HENNEGAN, BATES & COMPANY
Baltimore, Maryland

Established as jewelers and silversmiths in Wheeling, West Virginia, by James T. Scott in 1857. In 1859 William H. Hennegan, a native of Rochester, New York, went to Wheeling from St. Louis and became associated with Scott. The firm's name was changed to James T. Scott & Co. In 1864 they opened a wholesale house in Pittsburgh with Hennegan in charge; Scott remained at the Wheeling store. The Pittsburgh house was known as Scott & Hennegan. This partnership was dissolved in 1869 and Hennegan took over the Wheeling business. In 1866 James O. Bates was admitted to partnership and in 1869 John D. Reynolds joined the firm as jeweler. In 1874 Hennegan and Reynolds moved to Baltimore and opened a jobbing firm; Bates remained in charge of the Wheeling store until it was sold in 1874 to Jacob W. Grubb. Bates then moved to Baltimore where the business was for some time both wholesale and retail. The wholesale business was dropped and only the retail remained. The last listing found in Baltimore City Directories was for c. 1930.

HENNEGAN, BATES & CO.

HERBST & WASSALL
Newark, New Jersey

Listed JC 1904-1922 as manufacturers of sterling

silver goods, 14k gold ware and novelties. Last record found was 1931.

F. A. HERMANN CO.
Melrose Highlands, Massachusetts

Founded 1908 by F. A. Hermann. Manufacturers of sterling barrettes, brooches, bar pins, baby pins, bracelets, pendants and bookmarks, mostly enameled and handpainted.

GEORGE E. HERRING
Chicago, Illinois

Registered U. S. Patent No. 59,353 January 8, 1907 for use on imitation silverware. Out of business before 1915.

YOUREX

HIBBARD, SPENCER, BARTLETT & CO.
Chicago, Illinois

Trademark registered May 15, 1906 (No. 52,721) to be used on plated silver holloware, flatware and tableware. Used continuously since April 1, 1905. Application filed by A. M. Graves, secretary.

Trademark registered on August 7, 1906 (No. 55,072) to be used on jewelry, solid and plated, precious metalware—silver and plated silver holloware. Used continuously since May 1884. Application filed by A. C. Bartlett, president.

This hardware firm took the entire first production of steel traps made by the Oneida Community — the success of this enterprise eventually led to Oneida's silversmithing business.

GEORGE W. HICKOK & CO.
Santa Fe, New Mexico

"Manufacturers of filigree spoons and everything in the filigree line." Century Magazine, April 1892. Montezuma spoon marked "Copyrighted".

HICKOK MATTHEWS COMPANY
Newark, New Jersey
See Eleder-Hickok Co.
See Lebkueker & Co.

Formed by the merger, between 1931-1943 of the Eleder-Hickok Company, manufacturers of sterling silver novelties and the Matthews Company (incorporated in 1901). They are manufacturers of sterling holloware and presentation pieces.

Purchased in 1965 by Wolfgang K. Schroth from David M. Warren, Jr., president and owner.

Mr. Schroth was born in Frankfort, Germany and received his training under August Bock and Emil Woerner. He formed his own silver company there, but came to this country in 1955 and joined Tiffany and Company as their silversmith. In 1961 he joined Hickok-Matthews as manager and silversmith. One of the country's foremost silversmiths, Mr. Schroth lectures extensively on that subject.

(On novelties)   (On holloware)

HIGGINS, MARCHAND & CO.
Philadelphia, Pennsylvania

Charles E. Marchand, Delaware City, Delaware, was granted a spoon Design Patent, No. 2,788, August 27, 1867, which was assigned to Higgins, Marchand & Co.

HI-GRADE SILVER CO., INC.
New York, New York

Listed in 1927 KJI as manufacturers of sterling silver holloware.

H. M. HILL & CO.
Lynn, Massachusetts

Registered U.S. Patent No. 19,221, March 24, 1891 for manufacture of sterling souvenir flatware.

Herbert H. Hill, native of Barnstead, New Hampshire, moved to Lynn, Massachusetts c. 1889. There, he learned the jewelry and watchmaking business from John M. Humphrey with whom he was in business for about three years. Hill bought the business when Humphrey sold out and continued to operate it until 1914 when he moved to Centre Barnstead.

MAX HIRSCH
Philadelphia, Pennsylvania

Listed as manufacturer of silverplated articles c. 1920. The trademark indicates fittings for leather goods.

M. FRED HIRSCH CO., INC.
Jersey City, New Jersey

In business c. 1920-1945 as manufacturers and jobbers of sterling silverware.

Succeeded by Fisher Silver Co.

ST. JAMES   M. F. H. Co.
VIOLET

HIRSCH & OPPENHEIMER
Chicago, Illinois

Manufacturing jeweler and special order work. Listed JC 1904-22 and KJI 1927.

HIPP & COBURN
Chicago, Illinois

STERLING HIPP & COBURN   CHICAGO

(Cameo marks on commemorative spoon)

CHARLES E. HOCHHAUS
Baltimore, Maryland

Listed in Baltimore City Directories 1870-1871 as a silverplater.

F. B. HOFFMAN & CO.
Baltimore, Maryland

Listed in Baltimore City Directories 1870-1871 as silverplaters.

FREDERICK S. HOFFMAN
Brooklyn, New York
See Clarence B. Sebster

Listed in JC 1896 in sterling silver section. Other sources indicate that these trademarks were used also on 14 and 18k gold and silver novelties and on silver mountings for leather goods. Succeeded by Clarence B. Webster beofre 1904.

HOFFMAN MANUFACTURING CO.
Newark, New Jersey

Listed 1927 KJI as manufacturers of sterling silver dresserware, vanity and cigarette cases, tableware and novelties.

MAX HOFFMAN
Newark, New Jersey

Jeweler and silversmith c. 1848-51. Advertised as manufacturer of jewelry, silverware, and metal gilding.

HOLBROOK, WHITING & ALBEE
North Attleboro, Massachusetts
See Frank M. Whiting Co.

HOLBROOK MFG. CO.
Attleboro, Massachusetts

Founded by Harry R. and Charles L. Holbrook. Listed in Attleboro City Directories from 1905-1916 as manufacturers of special machines and novelties.

HOLBROOK & SIMMONS
See Thornton & Company

H. & S.

Successors to Holbrook, Dagg & Co. "Holbrook & Simmons, manufacturing silversmiths, 427 E. 144th Street, New York, have dissolved by mutual consent, Henry B. Simmons retiring. The remaining partners, Eugene C. Holbrook and William H. Thornton, will continue the business as before under the firm name of Holbrook & Thornton [later Thornton & Co.]. (JC&HR 5-2-1896, p.20)

WILLIAM HOLBROOKE
Baltimore, Maryland

Listed 1850 census as a silversmith. Born Maryland.

JOHN HOLIDAY
Baltimore, Maryland

Listed in Baltimore City Directory in 1872 as a silverplater.

HOLMES, BOOTH & HAYDENS
Waterbury, Connecticut

Organized by Israel Holmes in 1853 to roll brass. They made plated silver copper sheets for photography which produced a better and less expensive photograph than copper plate.

During the Civil War they made brass buttons for both military and civil uniforms, brass fittings and kerosene lamps. After the war they went into the nickel-silver business and turned out huge quantities of knives, forks and spoons for silverplating.

Brought by Rogers and Hamilton c. 1886, which later became part of International Silver Company.

H. B. & H. A. 1.
SHEFFIELD PLATED CO.
STERLING SILVER PLATE CO.
UNION SILVER PLATE CO.

WM. HOLMES
ROBERT HOLMES
Baltimore, Maryland

William Holmes, founder of the silver manufacturing business of that name in Baltimore, was born in Sheffield, England July 27, 1816 and died in Baltimore April 7, 1883. Holmes' family had been in the silver manufacturing business in Sheffield and it was there that he learned the trade he established in Baltimore. There is a listing in Baltimore City Directories 1847-1848 as "Wm. Holmes, brass founder, patent, windlass maker, composition and iron caster," which the family feels is a different William Holmes as their records show the silver manufacturer arriving in Baltimore in 1852.

William Holmes and his wife, Ann, had at least six children, four of whom were boys. All four sons learned some branch of the silver manufacturing and plating trade. Samuel specialized in chasing, William, Jr., in buffing and polishing, Robert specialized in spinning, molding and other manufacturing processes and John was listed in City Directories as a gilder.

The manufacturing business established by William Holmes was financially successful for a number of years but failed about 1855 on account of a dishonest bookkeeper. For some years the Holmes' business was dormant until Robert decided to establish a repair, replating and limited manufacturing business. (Ledlie I. Laughlin in his *Pewter in America*, Vol. II, says that Robert Holmes & Sons were makers of britannia ware in 1853 and 1854.) This new business was started in his home but as the business grew activities were transferred to more suitable locations.

William Holmes was listed in Baltimore Directories from 1865-76 at "over 12 Bank Lane" and at 46 N. Holliday, the latter apparently a factory or business location as the residence was 820 W. Baltimore. Samuel Holmes and George Holmes were listed as electroplater and britannia worker at the N. Holliday address. Other locations and company names listed were Holmes Bros. & Co., 1877-90; Holmes Nickel Plate Co., 1886; Robert Holmes, 1894; Holmes Plating Works., successor to Robert Holmes, 1895-96 and Holmes & Son, 1896-1940.

Robert Holmes had six children, three boys and three girls. All three boys entered the repair establishment with their father. They were Robert Frederick, W. Grover and Morris. Robert Frederick became the plater. Grover inherited the business after the deaths of his father, Robert Frederick and Morris, the youngest. This was carried on principally as a general repair business until Grover retired on account of age in 1960. The business was then placed in the hands of W. Stanley Rauh who had been with the firm for almost forty years. Following Mr. Rauh's death about 1967 the tools and dies were purchased by the Stieff Company of Baltimore.

WM. HOLMES

HOLMES & EDWARDS SILVER CO.
Bridgeport, Connecticut
See International Silver Co.

The Holmes & Edwards Silver Co. was started in Bridgeport, Connecticut in 1882, having taken over a business run under the name of Rogers & Brittin,

XIV

ROLLED PLATE, HOLMES & EDWARDS
ORIENTAL
MEXICAN CRAIG
EDWARDS
B. S. CO.
XIV. HOLMES & EDWARDS

INLAID

HESCO

HE

VIANDE

STRATFORD SILVER PLATE CO.

STRATFORD SILVER CO.

STRATFORD PLATE

Ⓔ STERLING INLAID

Ⓔ HOLMES & EDWARDS HE
SILVER – INLAID

STRATFORD SILVER CO AXI

STRATFORD SILVERPLATE

WALDO HE

HOLMES & EDWARDS
INLAID

which had been in existence about two years. At first, their business was largely the making of moderate priced flatware, sometimes producing the blanks, oftentimes buying the blanks from other makers, plating and marketing them. Edwards saw a notice in a newspaper of a new patented idea of inserting a piece of sterling silver in the backs of spoons and forks prior to their being plated. This was patented by William A. Warner of Syracuse. Edwards immediately secured rights to the patent from Warner and put out a line of Holmes & Edwards sterling inlaid flatware in which the idea was utilized. The Holmes & Edwards plant was taken over by the International Silver Company in 1898 though it continued to operated in Bridgeport until moved to Meriden in 1931.

HOLMES & TUTTLE MFG. CO.
Bristol, Connecticut
See American Silver Co.
See Bristol Brass & Clock Co.
See International Silver Co.

Organized by Israel Holmes in 1851. Made plated silver knives, forks and spoons. Taken over by Bristol Brass & Clock Co., in 1857 and operated as their silverware department until 1901 when it became the American Silver Company which was bought by International Silver Co. in 1935.

HOLMES & TUTTLE

H. & T. MFG. CO.

HOMAN MANUFACTURING COMPANY
Cincinnati, Ohio

Established in 1847 by Henry Homan and Asa F. Flagg.

The Cincinnati City Directories of 1842-1843 and 1846 list Asa F. Flagg as a britannia manufacturer. An English potter, he went to Cincinnati to form a partnership with Homan for the manufacture of pewter. Flagg was so devoted to his work that he was known locally as "Pewter" Flagg.

Under the firm name Homan & Co. (pieces are also found marked Flagg & Homan), they made britannia ware until Flagg's retirement in 1854.

M. Miller joined the firm and remained a co-partner until the death of Henry Homan in 1865.

Homan's widow, Margaret, with their sons, Frank (who died in 1880), Louis and Joseph T., managed the firm until her retirement in 1887.

About 1864 the company gradually changed from the manufacture of pewter, britannia and German silver to electroplated silverware. They also advertised that they did gold plating.

Their regular products were ecclesiastical wares, registered U. S. Patent 27,974, March 17, 1896, (chalices, patens, beakers, tankards, baptismal bowls, alms dishes and candlesticks); Ohio-Mississippi river boat equipment (bowls, pewter plates, beakers, trenchers, chargers, tea sets and swivel lamps); bar equipment and articles for domestic use (tea and coffee sets, cups, ewers and basins, warming pans, pitchers, jugs, sugar sifters, pewter combs, spectacle frames, clockweights and buttons).

Around 1896 the name of the firm was the Homan Silver Plate Company which was succeeded by

Homan Manufacturing Company between 1904 and 1915. Out of business in 1941.

HOMAN & COMPANY CINCINNATI

(Nickel Silver.)

(Popular Price Goods.)

HOMAN & COMPANY CINCINNATI

OUTFIT.

(Church Goods.)

MADE IN USA

HOME DECORATORS, INC.
Newark, New Jersey

Registered trademarks for use on silverplated flat and hollow tableware.

State House ⚓ Sterling

PRESTIGE ★ ★ ★ ★ *PLATE*

(Used since Feb. 4, 1944)

DISTINCTION

(Used since March 20, 1950)

GEO. E. HOMER
Boston, Massachusetts

George E. Homer established a jewelry business with his brother, Joseph J., in 1875. The business grew rapidly and additional stores were opened in Providence, R. I., Portland, Me., and Lowell, Taunton, and Ayer, Mass. These were discontinued after Joseph's death, before 1922. The same year George completed a new building for his store at 45 Winter Street, Boston. The firm is still in business. Many souvenir spoons bear the Homer trademark.

(Souvenir Spoons.)

HOPEWELL SILVER COMPANY
See Reed & Barton

HOPEWELL SILVER CO.

HOPKINS & BRIELE
Baltimore, Maryland

Listed in Baltimore City Directories 1879-1886 as gold and silversmiths.

J. SETH HOPKINS & CO.
Baltimore, Maryland

Listed in Baltimore City Directories 1887-1888 under plated silverware.

HORTON & ANGELL
Attleboro, Massachusetts

Manufacturers of gold and silver goods. Listed J C-K 1896. Founded 1870. Now called Horton Angell.

HOTCHKISS & SCHREUDER
Syracuse, New York

David Hotchkiss and Andrew B Schreuder, silversmiths c. 1850.

E. V. HOUGHWOUT & COMAPNY
New York, New York

In the 1860s they purchased Reed & Barton wares "in the metal" and operated their own plating establishment.

HOUSATONIC MFG. CO.
New Haven, Connecticut

Registered trademark No. 40,725 on July 7, 1903 for use on tableware, spoons, knives, forks, table tongs of plated ware. Used continuously in their business since April 1, 1902. Edgar A. Russell, Treasurer.

"Articles of association [were drawn for] the Housatonic Mfg. Co., Wallingford, Conn., for the making of 'German silver, brass and other metals, silverware and other goods made in whole or in part of metal, glass, china, queensware, wooden or any other kind of goods to use in combination with above.' by C. A. Hamilton, N. Y., F. W. Carnell and E. A. Russell, Waterbury; Waterbury Brass Co.; Birmingham Brass Co. and C. E. Minor, New Haven." (JC&HR 9-30-1896, p. 13)

HOWARD & CO.
New York, New York

Established as silversmiths c. 1866. Last listing 1922.

HOWARD & CO.
1903. STERLING
NEW YORK.

HOWARD & CO.

HOWARD & COCKSHAW CO.
New York, New York
See Herbert Cockshaw, Jr.

HOWARD CUTLERY CO.
New York, New York

Manufacturers of plated silver knives and holloware. Successor to E. Magnus before 1896. Out of business before 1909.

(*Knives.*)   (*Hollowware.*)

HOWARD & SCHERRIEBLE
Providence, Rhode Island
See Howard Sterling Co.
See Roger Williams Silver Co.

HOWARD & SON
Providence, Rhode Island
See Howard Sterling Co.
See Parks Bros. & Rogers

The trademark is similar to that used by Parks Bros. & Rogers — a four-leaf clover partially encircled by the word "sterling" in a horseshoe arrangement.
Registered U. S. Patent No. 15,614, June 19, 1888 for useful or ornamental articles made of solid silver.

HOWARD STERLING CO.
Providence, Rhode Island
See S. Cottle

CHRONOLOGY

H. Howard & Co.	1878-79
Howard & Scherrieble	1879-84
Howard & Son	1884-89
The Sterling Co.	1886-91
Howard Sterling Co.	1891-1901

Established January 1, 1878 as H. Howard & Co., with Hiram Howard, A. J. Scherrieble and Arnold Nicoud, to manufacture plated jewelry. January 1, 1879 Arnold Nicoud withdrew and a limited partnership was formed with Sterns Hutchins. The firm name was Howard & Scherrieble until the expiration of the limited partnership on January 1, 1884, when Hutchins retired and Stephen C. Howard, son of the senior member of the firm was admitted as a partner. On February 5, 1884, Scherrieble withdrew and the firm name was changed to Howard & Son. In July 1886 a department was established for the manufacture of sterling silverware and was conducted under the title of The Sterling Company. During the Fall of 1888 the firm discovered that their combined industries had outgrown their limited accommodations, and on January 1, 1889 they moved to a new factory. In January 1891 the concern was incorporated as Howard & Son and continued under that name until December 1891 when they disposed of the electro-

plated goods branch of the business to Parks Bros. & Rogers, and at the same time the name of the corporation was altered to that of Howard Sterling Co. The company went into receivership about 1901-02. Some of the patterns and dies were sold to the Roger Williams Silver Company and others.

Lever cuff and collar buttons were specialties of this company. One, in particular, the "Sensational" collar button, was constructed of rolled gold plate, the shoe and post were drawn from a single piece of stock, while the top or head was made from another piece and firmly secured without the use of solder — all the work being done by a machine invented for the purpose by S. Cottle (q.v). They also made great quantities of silverware, both table and ornamental.

 (used since 1894)

TRADE MARK

1776

H. G. HUDSON
Amesbury, Massachusetts

Trademarks in 1896-1904 editions of J C-K were parts of the designs used on the souvenir spoons sold by H. G. Hudson honoring John Greenleaf Whittier, "the Quaker Poet," who moved to Amesbury in 1836 after serving in the Massachusetts legislature. U. S. Patent Office also registered No. 19,959, August 4, 1891, for the manufacture of flatware, spoons, knives, forks and ladles. It is doubtful that Hudson did the manufacturing himself as numerous examples of these spoons bear the mark of the Durgin Company, now a Division of The Gorham Company.

J. B. HUDSON
Minneapolis, Minnesota

Founded in 1886 by Josiah Bell Hudson, retail jeweler. Owned by Dayton Co. since 1929. Now a divison of Dayton Hudson Jewelers, a part of Dayton Hudson Corporation. Retailers of sterling, silverplate and pewter holloware flatware, novelties and importers of their own exclusive line.

J.B.Hudson

JBH

WALTER HUNOLD
Providence, Rhode Island

First listed in Providence City Directory in 1903 as Walter Hunold. About 1920 listed as Nussbaum & Hunold (B. Nussbaum, W. Hunold, J. Nussbaum), manufacturing jewelers. From 1921-1925 the listing was Walter Hunold. This is the last listing.

GEORGE J. HUNT
Boston, Massachusetts

George J. Hunt was born in Liverpool, England in 1865, serving the usual seven years' apprenticeship in one of the leading silversmith concerns of that city. In 1885 he came to the United States and worked in several silver factories. In 1905 he opened his own ship in Boston. His real love was teaching others the craft of silversmithing and this became his major interest. He was also a jeweler.

WM. E. HUNT CO.
Providence, Rhode Island

Listed 1927 KJI as manufacturers of sterling silver and white metal novelties.

HURLY SILVER CO.
Scriba, New York
See Benedict Mfg. Co.

Established in 1890 as John Hurly Silver Co. Purchased by Benedict Silver Co. in 1894.

J. H. HUTCHINSON & CO.
Portsmouth, New Hampshire

Registered U.S. Patent No. 19,770, June 30, 1891, for use on spoons, forks, bells, plates and holloware of sterling silver and plated silver. This drawing of "Old Constitution" is the trademark registered. It is doubtful if Hutchinson company actually manufactured any of the silverware. Souvenir spoons sold by him bear the Durgin Company mark. Out of business before 1915.

"John H. Hutchinson, B. Nelson, New Hampshire, June 6, 1838. Graduated from Dartmouth College. Took up residence in St. Johnsbury, Vermont where he began the merchant tailoring business and married Mary E. Graham a week before he was commissioned a lieutenant of Co. G, Third Vermont Volunteers and left for the front. Soon after reaching Washington he was commissioned a captain in the signal corps, was later aide-de-camp on the staff of General McClellan.

"After he was mustered out of the service he returned to St. Johnsbury and on May 18, 1868 moved to Portsmouth, New Hampshire and started in the jewlery business under the firm name of Rowell & Hutchinson. Later he purchased the interest of the senior partner and became associated with James R. Connell and so continued for about ten years. Fifteen years ago last January this firm dissolved and each continued in the business, Mr. Hutchinson retaining the old stand and continuing there until two years aga Last November he removed to the present location. Meanwhile he had associated his daughter and son-in-law with him in the firm. He also established a large florist business. He was active in various civic and charitable organizations. He died Monday morning [June 9] at his summer home." (JC&HR 7-16-1897, p.6)

OLD CONSTITUTION

WM. HUTTON & SONS, LTD.
Sheffield, England

Silversmiths, cutlers and electroplaters established in 1800. Limited since 1893 in which year they absorbed Fanell, Elliott & Co. Made sterling silverware, nickel spoons and forks and steel cutlery. Last listing in 1922.

Registered U. S. Patent 40,657, June 23, 1903 for silver and plated silver tableware.

Family disagreements in the 1920s caused the firm's demise; its goodwill was transferred in 1930 to James Dixon.

HYDE & GOODRICH
New Orleans, Louisiana

Hyde & Goodrich were in business at least as early as 1816. The earliest New Orleans City Directory available is for 1822 which lists James N. Hyde & C. W. Goodrich, at "15 Chartres Street; jewelry, military and fancy hardware." The firm name Hyde & Goodrich first appears in the 1838 Directory. Their advertisement in the *New Orleans Merchants' Diary and Guide*, 1857-58, says, "The largest importers of jewelry, watches, plated-ware, guns and pistols and the only manufacturers of gold and silverware in the South-West," with the added claim "established forty years in New Orleans." They went out of business in 1866

IDEAL SILVER COMPANY
Portland, Connecticut

A short-lived company, manufacturers of silverware about 1905-06.

IKORA
New York, New York
See Württembergische Metallwarenfabrik

Distributors for Württembergische Metallwarenfabrik (WMF).

IMC Mint Corp.
Salt Lake City, Utah

No response to inquiries.

J. T. INMAN & CO.
Attleboro, Massachusetts

They were listed in JC 1896-1922 as manufacturers of sterling silver and plated silver cigarette cases, link buttons, buckles, vanity cases, dorines (powder boxes), bar pins, cuff and collar pins and souvenir goods.

Listed in the Attleboro City Directories 1892-1944 as manufacturing jewelers with James McNerney as owner. Listed from 1944-1963 with Roy W. Inman.

When the Watson Company went out of business about 1955, the Inman Company bought some of the souvenir spoon dies (The Wallace Company took over the old Watson business). These dies were used by the Inman Company until 1964 when Whiting & Davis Co. purchased the company and integrated the complete manufacturing facilities into its own plant.

GOLDEYE

STERLING.

INMAN STERLING

INTERNATIONAL SHEFFIELD WORKS, INC.
New York, New York

Listed in 1927 and 1931 KJI as manufacturers or plated silver holloware, pewterware and pewter lamps.

INTERNATIONAL SILVER CO.
Meriden, Connecticut

The International Silver Company was incorporated in 1898 by a number of independent New England silversmiths whose family backgrounds began with the earliest American settlers. International Silver has become not only world renowned for the quality of its fine silver, it has also become the world's largest manufacturer of silverware.

The history of International Silver Company and its predecessors is a history of America's silversmithing. Early records of this industry started with Ashbil Griswold who in 1808 set up his pewter shop in Meriden, Connecticut, soon expanding his business to include britannia ware. Meriden became the center of pewter, britannia ware and silver manufacturing through the efforts of Griswold and other independent makers who joined together to finance the Yankee peddlers responsible for selling and bartering these wares.

About the same time, the growing demand for coin silver led the three Rogers brothers, Asa, Simeon and William, to open their workshop in Hartford, Connecticut. The high cost of coin silver, as well as its impractical nature for constant use, led to experimentation in the new process of electroplating spoons and forks with pure silver.

In 1847 they perfected this process and marketed their first silverware under the firm name of Rogers Bros. Their fine workmanship and high quality material soon established the name of the Rogers Bros. line throughout the country. This reputation is maintained today.

Britannia, more brilliant, harder and more resistant to wear than pewter, was replacing pewter in many American homes. Several small factories in Meriden turned to the production of this new ware, most of which was marketed by Horace C. and Dennis C. Wilcox under the name of H. C. Wilcox & Co. The Meriden Britannia Company which followed in 1852, offered German silver holloware and flatware for silverplating by 1855.

In 1862, the Rogers brothers, who had been making and selling plated silver ware in Hartford, were moved to Meriden and added to the Meriden Britannia Company. Their 1847 Rogers Bros. trademark was an important addition.

Other silversmiths, who had set up small shops in Connecticut, soon realized they could all work more efficiently and supply the demands of the public

better by combining into one organization. The scope of the Meriden Britannia Co. had become international with the establishment of London and Canadian branches and sales offices in New York, Chicago and San Francisco. The Meriden Britannia Co. was the leading spirit in the formation of The International Silver Company in November 1898.

Among the many independent companies which then or later became part of The International Silver Company, either directly or indirectly through Meriden Britannia Co., were the American Silver Co., Bristol, Conn. established in 1901; Barbour Silver Co., Hartford, 1892; Derby Silver Co., Birmingham, 1873; Forbes Silver Co., Meriden, 1894; Hall & Elton Co., Wallingford, 1837; Holmes & Edwards Silver Co., Bridgeport, 1882; Holmes & Tuttle, Bristol, 1851; International Silver Co. of Canada, Ltd., Inc., 1922; La Pierre Mfg. Co., Newark, 1895; Maltby, Stevens & Curtiss, Shelton, 1879; Manhattan Silver Plate Co., Brooklyn, 1877; Meriden Britannia Co., Meriden, 1852; Meriden Britannia Co., Ltd., Hamilton, Ont., 1879; Meriden Silver Plate Co., Meriden, 1869; Middletown Plate Co., Middletown, 1864; Norwich Cutlery Co., Norwich, 1890; Parker & Casper, Meriden, 1867; C. Rogers & Bros., Meriden 1866; Rogers Cutlery Co., Hartford, 1871, W. Rogers Mfg. Co., Ltd., Niagara Falls, 1911; Rogers Bros., Hartford, 1847; Rogers & Bro., Waterbury, 1858; Rogers & Hamilton Co., Waterbury, 1886; Rogers, Smith & Co., Wallingford, 1856; Simpson Nickel Silver Co., Wallingford, 1871; Standard Silver Co. of Toronto, Co., Ltd., 1895; Watrous Mfg. Co., Wallingford, 1896; E. G. Webster & Son, Brooklyn 1886; E. G. Webster & Bro., Brooklyn, 1863; Webster Mfg. Co., Brooklyn, 1859; Wilcox Britannia Co., Meriden, 1865; Wilcox Silver Plate Co., Meriden, 1867; Wilcox & Evertsen, New York, 1892 and William Rogers Mfg. Co., Hartford, 1865.

By 1900, the Meriden-Wallingford area of Connecticut had became a center for silver craftsmanship. Almost the peak of production was reached shortly before World War II.

Today the International Silver Co. is not only the world's largest manufacturer of fine tableware, it makes a broader variety of products than any other silverware manufacturer.

The Ecclesiastic division was sold to Ecclesiastic Silversmiths.

The Hotel Divison specializes in flatware and holloware designed for use by hotels, restaurants, airlines, railways, steamships and institutions.

It is one of the few silver manufacturing companies to maintain an historical library which houses a large collection of Victorian silverplate made by International Silver Co. predecessors.

They continued marks of predecessors after 1898. The International Silver Co. mark was not used until after 1928 on flatware.

In 1925 the International Silver Company introduced a sterling pattern with an imprint of a pine tree on the back of the handle. The pine tree was similar to that on the pine tree shilling made famous through the tradition that the Mint Master, John Hull, gave his daughter her weight in shillings as a dowry upon her marriage to Samuel Sewall. When the silver pattern was introduced, the International Silver Company secured permission from the United States Treasury to reproduce in silver, the original pine tree shilling which was first made by John Hull in 1663. The reproductions were distributed for advertising.

Lord Robert pattern tea pot, one of the International Silver Company's current sterling productions. Note the 20th century use of the pattern name stamped on the bottom of the pot.

Silverplated, swirled and fluted design coffee pot made by Meriden Britannia Company c. 1896.

International Silver Company weight markings on sterling flatware

The use of letters to indicate the various weights in sterling patterns cannot be answered in a general way as there are some exceptions. Variations occur, depending upon the pattern. For both Wilcox & Evertsen and Simpson, Hall, Miller & Company, in 1899 none of their price lists show what symbols or letters were used. The different weights are listed but not the symbols used.

In 1904 Simpson, Hall, Miller & Company pattern teaspoons were listed as light, medium, heavy, extra heavy and massive. In 1906 there were listed medium, heavy, extra heavy, massive and extra massive (in some patterns). In 1906 the weights were listed as trade, medium, heavy and extra heavy and in 1910 the listing was the same with the addition of massive.

In Wilcox & Evertsen patterns, in 1899 were listed regular, medium, heavy and extra heavy with a footnote to the effect that the regular weight was "small size." (Probably the five o'clock teaspoon size.) In 1901 there were listed medium, heavy, extra heavy and massive and in 1906, regular, medium, heavy and extra heavy.

Not until 1920 did the old price lists show the letters and these were basically for standard patterns. The following seem to be the most commonly used:

Teaspoon (five o'clock)	A
Trade	B
Regular	C
Heavy	D
Massive	E

In some patterns B was sometimes called medium, C was sometimes heavy and A was called regular.

For example:

Deerfield (1913) teaspoons were made in A, B, C and D weights; the only other pieces made in different weights were the dessert and tablespoons and the dessert and dinner forks, all made only in A and B weights.
Pantheon (1920) teaspoons were made in B, C, D and E weights; the other four items listed above were made only in B and C.
By 1941 only teaspoons were made in more than one weight with no consistency in the system of marking. The letters R and H were used for Regular and Heavy and also E for Extra Heavy. *Prelude* (1939) and *Gadroon* (1933) teaspoons were made in R and H. *Richelieu* (1935) and *Colonial Shell* (1941) were made just in H and E; *Continental* (1934) was made in R, H and E.
Empress (1932) and *Fontaine* (1924) had teaspoons made in Regular, Heavy and Extra Heavy but these weights were represented by the letters C, D and E. After 1945 extra weight teaspoons were discontinued but some patterns are heavier than others. Patterns are separated into Groups I through IV, all teaspoons within a group being the same weight.

GRADE MARKINGS FOR 1847 ROGERS BROS. SILVERPLATED FLATWARE

The base metal used for these goods is 18% nickel silver — practically indestructible . . . . The plating on a spoon or fork is .999 pure silver.

There are three grades of plate with marks as follows:

XS
1847 ROGERS BROS. TRIPLE

This is the grade ordinarily sold and more than sufficient for any except especially hard wear. Teaspoons are plated not less than six ounces and Table Spoons not less than twelve ounces to the gross (other staple pieces in proportion).

XS
1847 ROGERS BROS. XII TRIPLE

The Tea spoon are plated not less than six ounces and Table Spoon not less than twelve ounces to the gross, and in addition the parts most exposed to wear bear an additional double plating.

xs
1847 ROGERS BROS. Quintuple

This is the heaviest grade of silver plate made and is required only by those who desire something extraordinarily heavy. It is used for the most part by hotels, railroads, etc., where the silver is subjected to constant and hard use. Teaspoons are plated not less than ten ounces and Table Spoons not less than twenty ounces to the gross (other staple pieces in proportion).

The above from an early 1900 pamphlet issued by the International Silver Company.

INTERNATIONAL STERLING

INTERNATIONAL SILVER COMPANY

INTERNATIONAL STERLING

INTERNATIONAL STERLING

IS

INTERNATIONAL STERLING

Wilcox IS

INTERNATIONAL SILVER COMPANY

I.S.CO.   INTERNATIONAL SILVER CO.

INTERNATIONAL S. CO.   INTERNATIONAL

L STERLING   I.S. CO.

INSICO

L ROGERS *L* STERLING   R. & B.

INTERNATIONAL SILVER COMPANY

LA PIERRE

WILCOX & EVERTSEN

INTERNATIONAL BC STERLING

1847 STERLING

1847 ROGERS BROS. STERLING

BREWSTER
(Pewter holloware)

TRADEMARKS ON SILVERPLATE

ALBANY SILVER PLATE
AMERICAN SILVER CO.
AMSILCO
ATLAS SILVER PLATE
AVON SILVER PLATE
BS CO.
CAMELIA SILVERPLATE
CARV-EZE
COURT SILVER PLATE
CROWN SILVER CO.
DEEP SILVER
DEERFIELD SILVER PLATE
EASTERN SILVER CO.
1847 ROGERS BROS.
1865 WM. ROGERS MFG. CO.
EMBASSY SILVER PLATE
GEM SILVER CO.
HOLD-EDGE
HOLMES & EDWARDS
HOLMES & TUTTLE
H. & T. MFG. CO.
INDEPENDENCE TRIPLE
INLAID
INSICO
INTERNATIONAL
INTERNATIONAL SILVER CO.
I.S.CO.
I.S. CO.
KENSICO
KENSINGTON SILVER PLATE
MANOR PLATE
MELODY SILVER PLATE
N.E.S.P. CO.
NEW ENGLAND SILVER PLATE

NO-TARN
OLD COMPANY PLATE
PALLADIANT
R. & B.
R. C. CO.
REVELATION SILVER PLATE
ROGERS CUTLERY CO.
ROGERS & HAMILTON
ROYAL PLATE CO.
SILVER WELD (knives)
SOUTHINGTON COMPANY
STRAND
STRATFORD PLATE
STRATFORD SILVER PLATE CO.
SUPER-PLATE
SUPERIOR
SUPREME SILVER PLATE
VIANDE
VICTOR S. CO.
WILCOX SILVER PLATE CO.
WM. ROGERS MFG. CO.
WM. ROGERS & SON
WORLD
X S TRIPLE

INTERNATIONAL SILVER COMPANY OF CANADA, LTD.
Hamilton, Ontario
See International Silver Co.

Began with the establishment of the Meriden Britannia Co. Ltd. at Hamilton, Ontario in 1879. Organized to take care of the Canadian business of the International Silver Co. Was incorporated in 1925.

INTERNATIONAL-COMMONWEALTH SILVER CO.
New York, New York

Listed in JC 1915-1922 as successor to International Silver Deposit Works, founding date unknown.

POPPY
(Deposit Ware.)

J

D. C. JACCARD & CO.
See Mermod, Jaccard & King

A. JACOBI
Baltimore, Maryland
See Jenkins & Jenkins

Founded in 1879 as manufacturing silversmiths. Company name changed to Jacobi & Co. in 1890.

JACOBI & COMPANY
Baltimore, Maryland
See Jenkins & Jenkins

Successors to A. Jacobi in 1890; reorganized as Jacobi & Jenkins in 1894.

JACOBI & JENKINS
Baltimore, Maryland
See Jenkins & Jenkins

Successors to Jacobi & Co. in 1894; succeeded by Jenkins & Jenkins in 1908.

Members of the firm were A. Jacobi, W. Armour Jenkins and W. F. Jacobi. In 1895 they advertised that they were "the only silversmiths in Maryland making and retailing their own work exclusively — all articles of sterling silver."

RUFUS JACOBY
Silver Spring, Maryland

Silversmith, specializing in handwrought liturgical articles. Many of his chalices are a combination of silver and Macassar ebony. Though he fashions all his silver entirely by hand, his work is the essence of modern simplicity and functional design.

JACOBY HANDMADE STERLING

GUY S. JENKINS
New York, New York

Listed JKD 1918-19 as manufacturer of silverplated holloware.

JENKINS & JENKINS
Baltimore, Maryland

CHRONOLOGY

A. Jacobi	1879-90
Jacobi & Co.	1890-94
Jacobi & Jenkins	1894-1908
Jenkins & Jenkins	1908-c. 1915

Originally founded as A. Jacobi in 1879, manufacturing silversmiths; changed to Jacobi & Co., 1890; reorganized as Jacobi & Jenkins in 1895; succeeded by Jenkins & Jenkins in 1908. The tools and dies were purchased c. 1915 by the Schofield Company, Inc. of Baltimore manufacturers of silverware and jewelry. The Schofield Co. was bought by Oscar Caplan & Sons in 1965 and in 1967 sold the Stieff Co., all of Baltimore.

LEWIS E. JENKS
Boston, Massachusetts

Listed in Boston City Directory 1875 to 1885 at same address as Farrington & Hunnewell. He was also a member of the partnership of Kennard & Jenks which was bought by the Gorham Company c. 1879-80.

JENNINGS & LAUTER
New York, New York

Listed in JC 1896 as Reeves & Sillcocks; succeeded by Reeves & Browne before 1904; by Browne, Jennings & Lauter before 1915 and by Jennings & Lauter before 1922. Listed in sterling silver section.

JENNINGS BROS. MFG. CO.
Bridgeport, Connecticut

Manufacturers of silverplated toilet ware, shaving stands, shaving sets, casseroles, table holloware, clocks, lamps, Sheffield reproductions.

1890 JENNINGS BROS. A1

JENNINGS SILVER CO.
Irvington, New Jersey

Manufacturers and jobbers of sterling and plated silver holloware. Listed JC 1915-1943.

J.S.C.

JENNINGS
(On sterling)

JESCO
(On silverplate)

GEORG JENSEN, INC.
Copenhagen, Denmark

Founded by Georg Jensen (b. 8-31-1866; d. 1935) who opened his first tiny shop at 36 Bregade, Copenhagen, in 1904. Twenty-five years later he had a staff of 250. There are now branches all over the world. Among the world's leaders in production of modern silver, they turned to stainless steel during World War II when silver was not available. Georg Jensen was on of the most influential designers of modern silver.

GEORG JENSEN Inc.
(On base metals)

(On articles made of or plated with precious metals)

Claims use on goods made of bronze since December 1932; on goods made of aluminum since April 1936; on goods made of pewter since October 1936; and on goods made of stainless steel since November 1940.

The above trademarks all registered in the U.S.

THE JEWELERS' CROWN GUILD
Rockford, Illinois

The Jewelers' Crown Guild appears to have been successor December 21, 1892 to the Watchmaker's and Jewelers' Guild of the United States which had been formed in 1879. The object of this organization was to combat the "catalogue nuisance," or underselling by firms who sold through catalogs and did not have the expense of maintaining retail outlets — a problem that jewelers still face today. The goods were to be distributed through certain jobbing houses who were bound by Guild restrictions to sell only to Guild members and were required to mark all goods passing through their hands as Guild goods, with certain private marks. The Guild adopted distinctive marks which were to be stamped on all Guild goods. Thus all goods were stamped by both manufacturer and with quality marks, and their course would be easily traced through the various channels of trade in order to fix responsibility. The idea never won complete acceptance and seems to have been of short duration as no record of it has been found after 1904. The old Guild mark was composed of lines, and it was discovered that it broke the plating on certain goods, consequently the Guild adopted as its mark the device used by J. H. Purdy when he was chief distributor for the Guild. The device was adopted by Purdy when two doves flew down and lit on his outstretched hand when he stood in front of a store in Manchester, Iowa, where he had just completed a successful business arrangement for the Guild. Perhaps Mr. Purdy had been recently hearing Lohengrin; at any rate, the incident so impressed him that he accepted it as an omen, and immediately adopted it as his private device until it was later adopted by the Guild.

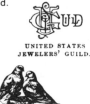

UNITED STATES
JEWELERS' GUILD.

UNITED JEWELERS' GUILD.

C. C. JOHNSON
Chicago, Illinois

Listed in 1854-1855 Chicago Directory as a silverplater.

E. S. JOHNSON & CO.
New York, New York

Listed in 1896-1922 JC in sterling silver and jewelry sections.

JOHNSON & GODLEY
Albany, New York

Samuel Johnson and Richard Godley listed in Albany City Directories 1843-1850 as producing factory-made silver. Their marks consisted of the two surnames in addition to "pseudo hallmarks."

JOHNSON, HAYWARD & PIPER CO.
New York, New York

Listed in JC 1904-1915 in plated silver and jewelry sections. Were probably distributors.

DUTCH SILVER NOVELTIES

J. W. JOHNSON
New York, New York

Founded in 1869 by J. W. Johnson who had as a boy worked for J. A. Babcock & Co. in the plating shop. Johnson was an agent for the Middletown Plate Company after working for Babcock.

By 1919, the J. W. Johnson company was operated by the founder's son, Harry F. Johnson, still under the same name.

They were jobbers who specialized in plating and were also wholesalers of plated silverware. Last listed in 1950.

"There is no longer any Crown Silver Plate Co. but J. W. Johnson stamps this name on plated silver ware." (JC&HR 4-17-1898, p. 23)

CONNECTICUT PLATE CO.
(Hollowware.)

CROWN SILVER PLATE CO.
(Flatware.)

ROYAL PLATE CO.
(Flatware.)

J. H. JOHNSTON & CO.
New York, New York

Established in 1844 according to their advertisement in *Harpers Weekly* 1898.

"J. H. Johnston & Co. insolvent. J. H. Johnston, president of the company started in business about 1860, succeeding Many & Lewis. About 1888 he opened the present store at 15th St. and Union Square which he conducted while Albert E. Johnston conducted the Bowery store. The latter store was given up about 1882, and the same year the business was incorporated as J. H. Johnston & Co., with J. H. Johnston becoming president and A. E. Johnston, treasurer." (JC&HR 1-13-1897, p. 17)

"A new corporation, J. H. Johnston Co. formed of creditors of the old company." (JC&HR 3-17-1897, p. 9)

Out of business between 1904 and 1915.

C. B. M. C.
C. P. F.
DUPICATE WEDDING PRESENTS

A. H. JONES CO. INC.
Meriden, Connecticut

Listed as manufacturers of plated silver shakeless cellars and novelties 1918-31.

JONES, BALL & POOR
JOHN B. JONES CO.
JONES, LOW & BALL
JONES, SHREVE, BROWN & CO.
JONES & WARD
See *Shreve, Crump & Low Co., Inc.*

JONES & WOODLAND
Newark, New Jersey
See Federal Silver Co.

A. R. JUSTICE CO.
Philadelphia, Pennsylvania

The Philadelphia City Directories list the A. R. Justice Company from 1881 (hardware) through 1935-1936. The 1882 listing is in the name of Alfred R. Justice, cutlery. In 1885, the names of F. Millwood & Herbert M. Justice are added. In 1886 is the first reference to plated ware. The 1892 listing is A. R. Justice & Company (with C. Arthur Roberts added to those mentioned), silverware and cutlery. By 1895 there is reference only to silverware and plated ware and in 1899 the reference is to silversmiths. In 1910-1911 silverware and cut glass are mentioned. Further listings mention only silverware.

(The name is often spelled Justus.)

(Pearl Handled Knives.)

HICKS SILVER CO.
(Hollowware.)

MEDFORD CUTLERY CO.
(Pearl Handled Knives.)

RIVERTON SILVER CO.
(Hollow and Flatware.)

JUSTIS & ARMIGER
Baltimore, Maryland
See James R. Armiger

First listed in the Baltimore City Directory in 1891 as manufacturers of silverware, solid and plated. Succeeded by James R. Armiger in 1893.

JUSTIS & ARMIGER
TRIPLE PLATE
BALTIMORE

K

THE KALO SHOP
Chicago, Illinois

Listed JKD 1918-19 as manufacturers of sterling and plated wares.

KANN BROS. SILVER CO.
Baltimore, Maryland

CHRONOLOGY

Kann & Sons	1870–1885
Kann & Sons Mfg. Co.	1885–1896
Kann Bros. Silver Co.	1899–1913

Originally founded as Kann & Sons. Listed in Baltimore City Directories from 1877 but advertisements say "Established 1870." Succeeded by Kann & Sons Mfg. Co., 1885 and by Kann Bros. Silver Co. 1899.

The firm continued to be listed as silverplaters through 1913.

E. M. KARMEL & CO.
Brooklyn, New York

Listed JC 1915-1922 in sterling silver section.

J. KATZ & CO.
Batlimore, Maryland

Listed in Baltimore City Directories 1901-1904 as silversmiths.

ERNEST KAUFMANN
Philadelphia, Pennsylvania

Listed Philadelphia City Directory only 1855 "brit. — tin." Advertised in *The Watchmaker & Jeweler* June 1870. Adv has illustration of "Kaufman's [sic!] Patent Butter Dish." Also says "Manufacturers of superior silver plated & Britannia Ware. Established in 1857." Several patents in his name.

C. F. KEES & CO.
Newark, New Jersey

Successor, before 1904, to Henry I. Leibe Mfg. Co. and were succeeded by Archibald, Klement Co. c. 1909. They were manufacturers of sterling silver and gold lorgnettes and related items.

KELLEY & MCBEAN
New York, New York

Listed in the 1900 Niagara Falls City Directory as makers of silver and plated silverware.

"Henry Kelley, senior member of Kelley & McBean, manufacturers of silver plated goods, and inventor of considerable prominence, died a few days ago. He was born in Toulon, Illinois. Fifteen years ago he moved to Niagara Falls where he continued to live. For many years he was superintendent of the Oneida Community mill. In 1892 he launched out with F. Woolworth under the name Kelley & Woolworth in the designing and manufacture of [silver and silverplated] novelties. The firm was changed about a year ago by the retirement of Mr. Woolworth and the succession of H. W. McBean." JC&HR 3-2-1895, p. 5)

JACK KELLMER CO.
Philadelphia, Pennsylvania

Wholesale and retail outlet for sterling and silver-plate and pewter holloware and flatware.

KENNARD & JENKS
Boston, Massachusetts

Mark: An incised dolphin in a shield.

Silversmiths c. 1875-80.
"The Gorham Mfg. Co. have bought out the entire plant and stock of Kennard & Jenks of Boston and will consolidate it with their plant in Providence." (JC&HR Vol. 11, #6, p. 120, July 1880)

MRS. ANNIE KENNEY
Baltimore, Maryland

Listed in Baltimore City Directories 1867-1873 as a goldsmith and silversmith. Her advertisement says "Mfg. of gold pens."

CHARLES KENNEY
Baltimore, Maryland

Listed in Baltimore City Directories 1867-1868 as a silverplater.

AMBROSE KENT & SONS, LTD.
Toronto, Ontario

Established in 1867 as Kent Bros. Merged with Fairweather Ltd. in 1946 and became Kent-Fairweather, Ltd. Kent sold out in late 1953 and the firm name reverted to Fairweather, Ltd. No silverware is sold there now.

KENT SILVERSMITHS
New York, New York

Founded in 1936 by Lewis E. Ellmore and George Fina, now president. Their factory is in Long Island City, New York. Over a period of years they have purchased the tools and dies of several old manufacturers. They are manufacturers, wholesalers and importers of sterling and silverplate, serving pieces, holloware and novelties; also pewter.

KENT & STANLEY CO., LTD.
Providence, Rhode Island

Partners were E. F. Kent and S. W. Stanley. They were successors to Wm. H. Robinson & Co. who began in 1873. The firm changed to Kent & Stanley in 1888 and was incorporated in 1891. The company owned the Enterprise Building and occupied the top floor. Also housed there were Hamilton & Hamilton, Jr., the Howard Sterling Co. and Parks Brothers & Rogers. Kent & Stanley manufactured silver

souvenir articles. An ad in the City Directory says "rolled plate and silver chains a specialty." The company failed in 1897, went into receivership. The Bassett Jewelry Company, Newark, New Jersey, took over plant and stock in 1898.

WM. B. KERR & CO.
Newark, New Jersey
See Gorham Corporation
(Originally Kerr & Thiery)

Established by William B. Kerr in Newark, New Jersey in 1855. Makers of flat and tableware, gold dresserware and jewelry. Used **fleur-de-lis** trademark in 1892. Purchased by the Gorham Corporation in 1906 and moved to Providence, Rhode Island in 1927.

AMERICAN BEAUTY

H. KESSNER & COMPANY
New York, New York

Listed 1927 KJI as manufacturers of sterling silver, nickel-plated, silver plated, German silver photo frames, mesh bags, and novelties.

KETCHAM & MCDOUGALL
New York, New York

Thimble makers. Ketcham & McDougall was begun as Roshore & Wood in 1830. In 1853 the firm became Roshore & Ketcham; in 1857, Ketcham Bros. & Co., in 1875, Ketcham & McDougall.

KEYSTONE SILVER CO.
Philadelphia, Pennsylvania

Manufacturing silversmiths since 1914. Makers of reproductions in silver and gold; original designing; ecclesiastical goods and restorations.

(On sterling silver)   (On plated silver)

L. KIMBALL & SON
Haverhill, Massachusetts

The business was established by Leverett Kimball in 1840. In 1850 and 1851 Mr. Kimball advertised "burning fluid, lamps, etc." In 1879 his his ads were for

Christmas gifts. In 1891 his ad in the City Directory states "makers of Hannah Duston (also spelled Dustin) and the Bradford Academy souvenir spoons."

Registered U. S. Patent No. 19,222, March 24, 1891. The firm name is listed until 1927, with F. C. Davis and J. D. Folsom, proprietors and called silversmiths, jewelers and opticians.

KIMBALL & RESTAURICK
Boston, Massachusetts

Listed in sterling silver section of 1904 JC as out of business.

K. & R.

STEPHEN C. KIMBLE
Baltimore, Maryland

Silversmith, listed in 1850 census. Born Maryland.

S. KIND & SON
Philadelphia, Pennsylvania

Silversmiths and jewelers. Advertised free catalog in December 1903 Ladies' Home Journal.

KING SILVER CO.
Boston, Massachusetts
See Lunt Silversmiths

Founded in 1955. They purchased the Richard Dimes & Co. c. 1956, and in turn were acquired by Lunt Silversmiths about 1957.

KING'S ENAMEL & SILVERWARE, INC.
New York, New York

Listed KJI 1931 as manufacturers of handmade enamel and sterling, bronze, sterling and gold boudoir sets, frames, cigarette boxes, baby sets, etc.

H. A. KIRBY
Providence, Rhode Island

Retailer of silverware and jewelry. Established in 1886 as Kirby, Mowry & Co. Incorporated in September 1896. Advertised solid gold and diamond jewelry, earrings, scarf pins, brooches, studs, collar buttons and rings. In 1905 the listing was H. A. Kirby Co. and this listing was continued until the death of Henry A. Kirby in 1920.

SAMUEL KIRK & SON, INC.
Baltimore, Maryland

ORGANIZATIONAL TITLES

Kirk & Smith	1815-1820
Samuel Kirk	1821-1846
Samuel Kirk & Son	1846-1861
Samuel Kirk & Sons	1861-1868
Samuel Kirk & Son	1868-1896

Samuel Kirk & Son Co.	1896-1924
Samuel Kirk & Son, Inc.	1924-present

MARKS:

1815-1818	K & S
1818-1821	Kirk & Smith
1821-1846	S. Kirk or Saml Kirk
1846-1861	S. Kirk & Son
1861-1868	S. Kirk & Sons
1868-1896	S. Kirk & Son
1896-1925	S. Kirk & Son Co.
1925-1932	S. Kirk & Son Co. Inc. Sterling
1932-	S. Kirk & Son Sterling

The above were used in conjunction with Baltimore Assay Office marks 1815-1830; with 11/12 or 10.15 1830-1868 (sometimes later); and with 925/1000 c. 1868-1890. Two other curious private marks, one a lion and the other perhaps the figure 11) with embellishment, were used 1829-1830.

In August 1815, 22-year-old Samuel Kirk opened his small shop in Baltimore and founded the oldest surviving silversmithing firm in the United States.

He was born in Doylestown, Pennsylvania in 1793. Through both parents he was descended from English silversmiths of the 17th century: Joan Kirke, registered in Goldsmith's Hall, England 1696-1697 and Sir Francis Child, Lord Mayor of London in 1669 and founder of the Child Banking House.

At 17, Samuel was apprenticed to James Howell, silversmith of Philadelphia and on completing his apprenticeship moved to Baltimore.

In 1815, Samuel Kirk and John Smith entered into a partnership which continued until 1820. In 1846, Samuel Kirk's son, Henry Child Kirk, became a partner and the firm name was changed to Samuel Kirk & Son. In 1861, Charles D. and Clarence E. Kirk also entered the business and the name was changed to Samuel Kirk & Sons. After the Civil War, the two younger brothers left the firm and the name reverted to Samuel Kirk & Son.

After the death of Samuel Kirk in 1872, his son continued alone until 1890, when his only son, Henry Child Kirk, Jr., joined as a partner, retaining the firm name, Samuel Kirk & Son. In 1896, Henry Child Kirk, Sr. formed a corporation and remained as active head until his death in 1914 when his son succeeded as president. Each of these early representatives of the Kirk family served an apprenticeship in the craft and qualified as working silversmiths. Kirk silver continues to be made under the direct supervision and guidance of a member of the Kirk family.

It was Samuel Kirk who introduced the intricate and often imitated Repoussé style of ornamentation to America in 1828. It is often referred to as "Baltimore silver."

Kirk's tradition for fine craftsmanship has brought many famous people to its shop. It is not surprising that when the White House dinner service was in need of repair, Kirk's was selected to renovate the five hundred and fifty pieces of gold flatware that had been in use for state banquets since the administration of President Monroe.

Many famous trophies and presentation pieces have been designed by Kirk's. The most ambitious was the forty-eight piece dinner service commissioned for the old Cruiser **Maryland** in 1905 and now on exhibit at the State House at Annapolis. Nearly two hundred scenes and pictures present a panorama of Maryland's illustrious history.

Kirk silver has always reflected the trends of decorative design. Early pieces were made in the chaste and simple lines of the Georgian era. The China trade is reflected in delicate Oriental lines, and the elaborate ornamentation of the Victorian age produced some magnificent pieces. Contemporary simplicity produces pieces remarkably like those of the very first made by Samuel Kirk.

New techniques, progressive research and new designs have been added to Kirk silver, but, their firm produces prestige merchandise. They pride themselves that hand crafting techniques are still essential in the production of Kirk sterling.

In 1972 the Kirk company added a line of silverplated gift wares.

YEAR	BALTIMORE ASSAY MARK	DOMINICAL LETTERS
1814		B
	ASSAYER'S AND MAKER'S MARKS	
1815	K&S A	A
1816	GF	GF
1817	K.&S. E	E
1818	K.&S. D	D
1819	KIRK & SMITH C	C
1820	KIRK & SMITH A	A OR B
1821	S.Kirk C	G
1822	F	F
1823	Kirk E	E
1824	S.Kirk C	D OR C
1825 1826 1827 no example		B A G

In the absence of any example of the assayer's marks for the years 1825 to 1827 and because of the great number of examples in existence bearing the 1824 marks, it is generally conceded that the 1824 marks were continued through the years 1825, 1826, and 1827.

YEAR	ASSAYER'S AND MAKER'S MARKS	DOMINICAL LETTERS
1828	ZON M.S. F SAM L KIRK	F OR E
1829	S.KIRK D	D
1830	S KIRK KIRK	C

ASSAY MARKS AND DOMINICAL LETTERS WERE NOT USED AFTER 1830

1830 to 1846	SAM L KIRK S.K S.K 11OZ
	S.K 11OZ
	10.15 S.KIRK
	S. KIRK SAM L KIRK 10.15

Year	Mark
1846 to 1861	S.KIRK & SON 11OZ — SK & SON — S.KIRK & SON 10.15 — 11.OZ
1861 to 1868	S.KIRK & SONS 10.15 — S.KIRK & SONS 11 OZ
1868 to 1898	S KIRK & SON 925/1000
1880 to 1890	S.KIRK & SON — S.Kirk & Son 11OZ

YEAR	KIRK'S MAKER'S MARKS	
1896 to 1903 flatware	S.KIRK & SON CO	925/1000
	S.KIRK & SON CO	925/1000
1903 to 1924 holloware	S.KIRK & SON Co. 925	
	S.KIRK & Son Co.	925/1000
1907 to 1914 flatware	S.KIRK & SON CO	925/1000
	S.KIRK & SonCo	925/1000
1903 to 1907 holloware	KIRK Co 925/1000	
	S KIRK & SON CO	925/1000
	S KIRK & SON CO 925/1000	
	S.KIRK & SON Co	
1925 to 1932 holloware	S.KIRK & SON. INC. STERLING	
1927 to 1961 flatware	PAT. S.KIRK & SON STERLING	
1932 to 1961 flatware	S.KIRK & SON STERLING	
1932 to 1961 holloware	S.KIRK & SON STERLING — S.KIRK&SON STERLING	
1959 to 1961 flatware	S.KIRK&SON STERLING	

KIRK INTERNATIONAL
New York, New York

A division of The Kirk Corporation, the parent company of Samuel Kirk & Son, the sterling division, and Kirk Pewter (formerly Hanle & Debler) the domestic pewter division. Kirk International was successor to Eisenberg-Lozano in 1970 though the name was not changed until February 1973.

KIRK & MATZ
Danbury, Connecticut

Advertise "cutlery, silverplate, brassware, Sheffield cutlery, etc." Various articles of silverplate illustrated in advertisements. No answer to recent inquiry.

The Baltimore Assay Office (1814-1830) was established to regulate the quality of silver made or sold there. In addition to the maker's initials or name, the marks adopted were "the shield of the Arms of the State of Maryland in the shape of an oblong square with the corners taken off, and the dominical letter for the year." The shape of the shield was altered in 1824 to an oval. (Baltimore Assay Office stamp for 1824; Samuel Kirk, Baltimore, Maryland)

Early in 1815, continuing through 1823, a third assayer's mark, the head of Liberty, was added. (Baltimore Assay Office stamp for 1826, illustrating the head of Liberty; Simon Wedge, Baltimore, Maryland)

In 1830 the compulsory marking of silver by the Baltimore assayer was modified to the requirement that the maker, in addition to his name or initials, should himself stamp on his silver the figures indicating its purity. From 1830 to the late 1860s the standard of .846, usually expressed as 10.15 was used. (Samuel Kirk, Baltimore, Maryland)

By the late 1860s the sterling standard was more often used by Baltimore silversmiths and was often expressed as 925/1000. (Pen wiper; the bristle brush is missing)

JULIUS KIRSCHNER & CO.
New York, New York

Listed JC 1915-1943. Wholesalers of plated silverware and mesh bags.

JULCKO
(Mesh Bags.)

C. KLANK & SONS
Baltimore, Maryland
See Schofield & Co., Inc.

ORGANIZATIONAL TITLES

Klank & Bro.	1872-1891
Conrad Klank & Sons	1892
C. Klank & Sons Mfg. Co.	1893-1894
C. Klank & Sons	1895-1911

First listed in the Baltimore City Directory in 1872-1873 as Klank & Bro., silverplaters. From 1874-1892 they were listed as silversmiths. Conrad, Frederick W. and George H. Klank were listed as members of the firm.

In 1892 the firm name became Conrad Klank & Sons, silversmiths, with Conrad, Frederick and George H. Jr., listed as members of the firm. The 1893 listing was C. Klank & Sons Mfg. Co., with Conrad listed as manager.

In 1895 the listing was C. Klank & Sons, the members of the firm remaining the same until 1899 when the members were listed as Conrad, F. William, and Herbert Klank and James L. McPhail. This listing continued until 1905 when James L. McPhail, who had also been listed as a member of the firm of A. G. Schultz & Co. during the same period, was no longer listed at either. In 1905 or 1906 C. Klank & Sons was purchased by Heer-Schofield, later Schofield & Co. though it continued to be listed under its own name through 1911.

KLANK MFG. CO.
Baltimore, Maryland

See Sterling Silver Mfg. Co.,
Baltimore, Maryland)

Listed .1892 Baltimore City Directory as silversmiths and silverplaters. George H. Klank, manager.
"The Klank Mfg. Co. made an assignment for the benefit of creditors to Charles O. Stieff." (JC&HR 11-2-1892, p. 8) "The Klank Mfg. Co. was succeeded by The Sterling Silver Mfg. Co. [Baltimore, Maryland]. (JC&HR 2-14-1894, p. 27)

WILLIAM KLANK
Baltimore, Maryland

Listed in Baltimore City Directories 1895-1899 as a silversmith. Not at the same address as C. Klank & Sons.

KNICKERBOCKER SILVER CO.
Port Jervis, New York

Successor to J(ames) A. Babcock in 1894 under William Tuscano as Knickerbocker Mfg. Co.; be-

came Knickerbocker Silver Co. before 1904. Taken over by Crescent Silverware Mfg. Co., Inc. in 1962.

Not used after c. 1900

JACOB KNIPE
Baltimore, Maryland

Listed in Baltimore City Directories 1864-1880 as a silverplater.

WM. KNOLL & CO.
New York, New York

Listed JC 1904 in sterling silver section. Out of business before 1915.

J. B. & S. M. KNOWLES CO.
Providence, Rhode Island

In 1852 Joseph B. Knowles formed a partnership with Henry L. Webster (who had been associated with Jabez Gorham, under the firm name of Webster & Knowles) of Boston. The first shop was located near another firm, Farrington & Salisbury which they soon bought out. The business grew steadily and in 1859 Samuel J. Ladd was admitted to the firm. Webster withdrew from the firm in 1864 and died the following year. The firm name was changed to Knowles & Ladd. In 1875 Mr. Ladd retired and Joseph's brother, Stephen M. Knowles, was admitted, the firm name becoming J. B. & S. M. Knowles. In 1891 J. B. Knowles died and that same year the firm was incorporated. In 1905 the Mauser Mfg. Co. leased the plant of J. B. & S. M. Knowles Co. Notices carried in 1905 trade journals stated that "all the articles hitherto made at the Knowles plant will now be produced by the Mauser Mfg. Co."

RED CROSS

(U. S. Design Patent No. 38-096, April 15, 1902 for spoons)

(On coin silver spoons)

KOECHLIN & ENGLEHARDT
Newark, New Jersey

Earliest record found U. S. Patent 56,499, registered October 2, 1906 for use on sterling and plated silver flat and holloware. Out of business before 1915.

GUSTAVE F. KOLB
New York, New York

Manufacturers, manufacturer's representative and importers of sterling silverware at least as early as 1917.

Gustave Frederick Kolb was born in New York City. At the time the Mt. Vernon, New York, Mauser factory was erected Kolb was general superintendent and treasurer of the company. Later he left to establish his own silversmith business in New York City. He retired in 1921 but continued as a director of the George Borgfeldt Corp. of New York City until his death, August 29, 1945 when he was 80 years old.

Kolb was known not only as a manufacturer and industrialist but was prominent in civic and religious activities. While with the Mauser company he was instrumental in persuading the New York New Haven and Hartford Railroad to build the Columbus Avenue station to accommodate commuters to New York City.

KOONZ MFG. CO.
Greenfield, Massachusetts

Listed JC as manufacturers of sterling silver. Out of business before 1922.

CHARLES KRAEMER
Baltimore, Maryland

Listed in Baltimore City Directory 1882 as a silversmith.

CHARLES M. KRAMER
Baltimore, Maryland

Listed in Baltimore City Directory in 1885 as a silverplater.

KRAUS & JANTZEN
New York, New York
See Kraus, McKeever & Adams

KRAUS, KRAGEL & CO.
New York, New York
See Kraus, McKeever & Adams

KRAUS, McKEEVER & ADAMS
New York, New York

First listed in 1896 as Kraus, Kragel & Co.; in 1904 as Kraus & Jantzen and in 1922 as Kraus, McKeever &

Adams. Trademarks used on sterling silver frames for handbags; 14k gold mountings and sterling silver mountings for leather articles

KRIDER & BIDDLE
Philadelphia, Pennsylvania
See Peter L. Krider Co.

PETER L. KRIDER CO.
Philadelphia, Pennsylvania

CHRONOLOGY

Peter L. Krider	c. 1850-60
Krider & Biddle	1860-c. 1870
Peter L. Krider	c. 1870-1903
Simons Bros. Co.	1903-present

Peter L. Krider (b. Philadelphia, 1821; d. there May 12, 1895) at the age of 14 was apprenticed to John Curry, Philadelphia silversmith, whom he served for six years. On Curry's retirement, young Krider's indenture was transferred to R. & W. Wilson, also silversmiths of Philadelphia. Krider worked with them as a journeyman for 15 months and then made a four-year contract with Obadiah Rich, silversmith in Boston. Two years later Rich sold his establishment to Brackett, Crosby & Brown, Boston silversmiths, with Krider in charge of the business. He later served a short time as foreman in the factory of his old employers, R. & W. Wilson and then went into business for himself. His first order, which was for a tea set, was given by J. E. Caldwell & Co. Krider's business expanded rapidly until he was compelled to find larger quarters and in 1859 took into partnership John W. Biddle, the firm name becoming Krider & Biddle in 1860. During the Civil War Krider served in the army while Biddle maintained the business. Biddle retired five or six years after the War and the firm name became Peter L. Krider Co. About 1888 Krider sold the business to August Weber who later took a partner, W. E. Wood. The business continued to operate under the name Peter L. Krider Co. until 1903 when it was succeeded by Simons Bros. Co., Philadelphia silversmiths established in 1840. The Krider flatware patterns and dies were later sold to the Alvin Mfg. Co. A number of flatware patterns were patented by Krider.

In addition to making a regular line of silverware, flatware as well as holloware, the Krider company was at one time perhaps the largest medal plant in the country. They manufactured medals for the Centennial Commission of 1876; those for the Cincinnati Industrial Exposition; Ohio Mechanics' Institute; National Academy of Design, New York; Georgia State Agricultural Society; Maryland State Agricultural and Mechanical Association; Virginia State Agricultural Society; Massachusetts Humane Society; Pennsylvania State Fair Association; Southern California Horticultural Society; the Agricultural and Industrial Society of Delaware Co., Pa.; Cincinnati High Schools; Industrial Cotton Exposition; the Southern Exposition; the World's Industrial and Cotton Centennial Exposition; Franklin Institute, Philadelphia; the John Scott Legacy, Philadelphia and many others.

KRONHEIMER OLDENBUSCH CO.
New York, New York

Listed in JC 1909--1922 in plated silver section.

LEONARD KROWER & SON, INC.
New Orleans, Louisiana

Established before 1896 as Leonard Krower, wholesalers and jobbers of sterling silver, plated silver, platinum, optical goods, medals, watches, clocks, pearls, diamonds, cut glass and gold jewelry. Listed in JC-K 1943 as Leonard Krower & Son and were incorporated before 1950. Acquired by the Gordon Jewelry Corporation in 1965.

THE FRANK KURSCH & SON CO.
Newark, New Jersey

Listed in JC 1904 in sterling silver section. Out of business before 1915.
    Trademark identical to Shoemaker, Pickering & Co.

L

L'ALLEMAND MFG. CO.
New York, New York

"Ernest A. L'Allemand, doing business as L'Allemand Mfg. Co., manufacturers of electro silver plated ware, N. Y. made an assignment to Oscar L'Allemand. Mr. L'Allemand had bought out his partner, Mr. Stix, two years ago and had not enough capital.
    The business was established many years ago and had been carried on by various firms. E. H. Rowley & Co. had it from 1862-1889 when they were succeeded by Stix & L'Allemand, who dissolved on August 31, 1893, since which time Mr. L'Allemand, who dissolved on August 31, 1893, since which time Mr.

L'Allemand carried on alone." (JC&HR 7-1-1895, p. 10)

P. W. LAMBERT & COMPANY
New York, New York

"P. W. Lambert & Company, N. Y., mfgrs. of standard goods and introducers of novelties such as pocket books, chatelaine bags, ladies' belts — a complete line of silver novelties. In oxidized and EGYPTIAN GOLD. Established 1867." (Adv. JC&HR 11-18-1896, p. 28)

FERDINAND C. LAMY
Saranac Lake, New York

Registered trademark in U. S. Patent Office No. 21,899, October 25, 1892 for use on spoons, forks, knife handles, etc. of souvenir type. Listed in JC as out of business before 1922.

LANCASTER SILVER PLATE CO.
Lancaster, Pennsylvania

"The Lancaster Silver Plate Company was destroyed by fire September 1893." (JC&HR 2-6-1895, p. 26)

LANDERS, FRARY & CLARK
New Britain, Connecticut

Landers, Frary & Clark began as a partnership in 1842 with George M. Landers and Josiah Dewey; became Landers & Smith Mfg. Co. in 1853 and Landers, Frary & Clark in 1865. They purchased the Meriden Cutlery Co. in 1866 and continued to use the Meriden trademark on some sterling wares. Their newly-built Aetna works held this cutlery division. The factory burned in 1874 and was immediately rebuilt.
    The firm's first products were wardrobe hooks. This was later expanded to include other small castings such as drawer pulls, iron coffeepot stands, and sad iron holders. They began the manufacture of cutlery in 1865. They discontinued flatware production c. 1950.
    In 1954 they purchased the Dazy Corp. In 1961 control of the firm was taken over by J. B. Williams Co., a subsidiary of Pharmaceuticals, Inc., and now Landers, Frary & Clark are completely liquidated.

LANDERS FRARY & CLARK
ÆTNA WORKS

(Knife blades with solid silver ferrules; Ivoride handles)

AETNA WORKS	
LANDERS, FRARY &	UNIVERSAL
CLARK	(Used after 1897)

R. LANGE
Baltimore, Maryland

Listed in Baltimore City Directory 1864 as a silverplater.

RALPH LANGE
Baltimore, Maryland

Listed in Baltimore City Directories 1872-1889 as a silverplater.

RUDOLPH LANGE
Baltimore, Maryland

Listed in Baltimore City Directories 1884-1885 as a silverplater at the same address as R. Lange who was listed in 1864.

LA PIERRE MFG. CO.
Newark and New York
See International Silver Co.

The La Pierre company started as early as 1888 in New York where Frank H. La Pierre had a small shop at 18 East 14th St. making a variety of novelties and small wares. In 1895 it was incorporated in New Jersey where they had by that time included quite a variety of dresserware. At this time La Pierre was president and G. H. Henckel, secretary. In 1900 the firm was again incorporated by La Pierre and H. C. Brown. In 1929 the La Pierre business was purchased by the International Silver Company and moved to Wallingford, Connecticut where they enlarged the line to cover more designs and pieces in dresserware.

The La Pierre trademark on sterling silver was made up by the letters F and L to represent the conventional pound sterling mark.

(Used before 1896)

LA SECLA, FRIED & CO.
Newark, New Jersey

Listed in JC 1909-1915 in sterling silver section. Out of business before 1922.

LEBKUECHER & CO.
Newark, New Jersey
See Eleder-Hickok Co., Inc.
*See Hickok Matthews Company
– Silversmiths*

Silversmiths, working c. 1896-1909. Partners were Arthur E. Lebkeucher, Francis (Frank) A. Lebkeucher and Charles C. Wientge, former superintendent and designer for Howard Sterling Company. Name changed by law to F. A. Lester. Taken over by The Eleder Co. in 1918. By 1922 it became the Eleder-Hickok Co., Inc.

TRADEMARK

LEBOLT & CO.
Chicago, Illinois

Registered trademark in U. S. Patent Office No. 70,833-y, October 6, 1908 for manufacture of silverware and jewelry. Listed JC 1915-1922.

LEDIG MFG. CO.
Philadelphia, Pennsylvania

Listed in JC 1896 in plated silver section. Out of business before 1904.

(Solid Plated and Composition Ware.)

LEHMAN BROTHERS SILVERWARE CORP.
New York, New York

Listed 1927 KJI; 1943-73 JCK and 1957-61 JBG as manufacturers of silverplated holloware. No reply to recent inquiry.

LEHMAN SILVER-CRAFT

HENRY L. LEIBE MFG. CO.
Newark, New Jersey
See Archibald, Klement
See C. F. Kees Co.

KARL F. LEINONEN
Boston, Massachusetts

Karl F. Leinonen, born in Turku, Finland in 1866. Served the regular seven year apprenticeship there. He came to the United States in 1893 and worked in a commercial repair shop in Boston. In 1901, when Arthur A. Carey, president of the Boston Society of Arts & Crafts, financed the opening of the Handicraft Shop, where a large number of silversmiths had bench space, he placed Leinonen in charge. He was still in this position in 1932. His son, Edwin, became his assistant.

Now listed in the Boston Directory as Karl F. Leinonen & Sons.

THE LENAU CO.
Attleboro Falls, Mass.

Listed in JC in sterling silver section in 1896. Out of business before 1904.

LENOX SILVER, INC.
New York, New York

Listed directories c. 1950 as manufacturers of sterling silver.

LENOX

LEONARD MFG. CO.
Chicago, Illinois (?)

Manufactured plated silver spoons to commemorate the World's Columbian Exposition in Chicago, 1892.

LEONARD, REED & BARTON
Taunton, Massachusetts
See Reed & Barton

LEONARD, REED & BARTON

(On britannia)

LEONARD SILVER MFG. CO.
Chelsea, Massachusetts

"The Leonard Silver Mfg. Co., manufacturer and distributor, purchased certain assets of Delli Silverplate, San Francisco." (JC-K 3-74, p. 105)

"Leonard Silver Mfg. Co. has entered into a five-year agreement with English Silver Corp., Brooklyn, to market that company's line of silverplated holloware." (JC-K 3-74) No reply to inquiry.

Some products are manufactured by seven different firms in India.

JOSEPH LESHER
Victor, Colorado

Joseph Lesher, a Victor real estate and mining man picked the world's greatest gold mining destrict as the place to distribute his eight-sided silver dollars which he manufactured in a campaign for the free coinage of silver.

One of the rarest items sought by American numismatists, the silver pieces have achieved real value. But in 1900 and 1901, when Lesher was having the coins minted in Denver, they had a value of $1.25 and were issued to merchants to be handed out and redeemed in merchandise. From the high silver content of the coins, Lesher could not have made any money on the arrangement.

No more than 3,500 of the coins were minted. There was a total of 18 varieties, each differing in some minor detail.

The first dies were made by Frank Hurd of Denver. Later dies were made by Herman Otto. The first type, issued in 1900, was 35 mm. across and was stamped one ounce silver, value $1.25. One side had the words, **Jos. Lesher, Referendum Souvenir;** the other side, **A Commodity, Will Give in Exchange for Currency Coin or Merchandise at Face Value.** In order to avoid trouble with the U. S. Government Lesher made his dollars eight-sided, but that did not help. Only a few days after the first coin was issued, government agents called on Lesher to see the dies. Lesher handed them over and then, he reported to the newspapers later, "they pulled out a sack in which they put the dies and walked away, and I never saw them again." The government agents claimed that the silver pieces had the function of coins and were contrary to law. Lesher appealed to Senator Teller for help. Teller took it up with the secretary of the treasury and it was finally agreed that, with certain changes in the design of the coin, the minting could continue.

The second set was issued for exchange of merchandise at A. B. Bumstead. Others were issued for various firms bearing the legend, Trade Mark Reg. U. S. Patent Office No. 36,192, April 9, 1901 Design Patent April 16, 1901. They also bear the altered inscription "Jos. Lesher's Referendum Silver Souvenir Medal."

REFERENDUM

LESSER & RHEINAUER
New York, New York

"Lesser & Rheinauer, silversmiths now at 427 E. 14th St., N. Y., will move their factory and office about May 1 into the Sterling Building, 14 East 17th St. where they will occupy the entire second loft. A. Lesser's Sons, wholesale jewelers, of Syracuse, are members of the firm." (JC&HR 4-14-1897, p. 24)

"A. Lesser's Sons's business closed by the Sheriff." (JC&HR 3-9-1898, p. 19)

F. A. LESTER COMPANY
See Eleder-Hickok Co., Inc.
See Hickok Matthews Company
– Silversmiths
See Lebkuecher & Co.

S. J. LEVI & CO., LTD.
Birmingham, England

Registered trademarks in the United States. Listed 1927 KJI as manufacturers of silverplated tableware and cigarette cases.

LEVIATHAN
PERFECTA
SQUIRREL BRAND

LEVINE SILVERSMITH CO.
New York, New York

Listed 1927 and 1931 KJI as manufacturers of sterling holloware, carving sets and cutlery.

LESCO

LEVITT & GOLD
New York, New York

Listed in JC 1915-1922 in sterling silver section. The trademark was also used on platinum and gold novelties. Listed c. 1935 as Levitt & Co. (?)

CHAS. J. LEWARD
New York, New York

Listed JC in 1896 in sterling silver section. Out of business before 1904.

TRADE MARK.

LEWIS BROS.
New York, New York

Listed in 1896-1904 JC as manufacturers of sterling silver novelties and jewelry. Address was the same as S. M. Lewis & Co. Out of business before 1915.

S. M. LEWIS & CO.
New York, New York

Listed 1896 JC in sterling silver section. Out of business before 1904. Address was the same as Lewis Bros.

S. M. L. & CO.
STERLING

J. A. L'HOMMEDIEU
Mobile, Alabama

Silversmith and jeweler c. 1839-67. Advertised "SILVER WARE, MADE FROM COIN," in the Mobile Directory in 1859. The brothers, William and John, moved to Mobile from Connecticut about 1840. William apparently left the firm about 1850 while John continued until after the close of the Civil War when he returned North and Zadek & Caldwell took over the business. In 1898 Wm. L'Hommedieu was a traveler for G. I. Mix Co.

L'HOMMEDIEU

J. A. HOMMEDIEU

LIEBS SILVER CO., INC.
New York, New York

Listed in JC 1915 as Liebs Co.; became Liebs Silver Co., Inc. before 1922. The last record found was 1931. Manufacturers of sterling silver holloware.

J. ARTHUR LIMERICK
Baltimore, Maryland

Listed in Baltimore City Directories 1903-1904 as successor to Jacob Gminder who began plating silver in 1867.

WILLIAM LINK CO.
Newark, New Jersey

CHRONOLOGY

Wm. Link	1871-82
Link & Conkling	1882-86
Wm. Link	1886-93
Link, Angell & Weiss	1893-c. 1900
Link & Angell	c. 1900-c. 1910
Wm. Link Co.	c. 1910-c. 1915

Established August 1, 1871 by William Link. In 1875 John D. Nesler was admitted to the firm. Nesler retired in 1882 and Addison Conkling was admitted, the firm becoming Link & Conkling. In 1886 Mr. Conkling retired and the business was continued by Link alone until 1893 when it became Link, Angell & Weiss; Link & Angell about 1900 and finally Wm. Link Co. from c. 1910-c. 1915. Listed out of business in 1915. They were manufacturers of sterling and jewelry.

WILLIAM LINKER
Philadelphia, Pennsylvania

Registered trademark in U. S. Patent Office, No. 55,945, August 21, 1906 for gold and silver flatware, holloware and tableware. Out of business between 1909 and 1915. Wm. Linker was a member of the firm of Davis & Galt in 1896.

THE LINCOLN MINT
Chicago, Illinois

No response to inquiries.

LIPPIATT SILVER PLATE AND ENGRAVING CO.
New York, New York

A few years after the company was established Samuel F. B. Morse, inventor of the telegraph and founder of the American System of Electro Magnetic Telegraphy, was president. They registered a trademark November 1, 1870 for silver and plated ware. They also owned a patent, dated April 19, 1871, for a process of putting a satin finish on silver-plated holloware and planned to license manufacturers to use it. It does not seem to have been much used in the early 1870s and the patent terminated in 1878. Morse died in 1872. The concern failed, indicating that they were not successful. In 1878 the patent was used by a few manufacturers according to the catalogs published at that time, and later a similar "satin" finish was given white metal holloware. Much was sold in the cheaper grades as Satin Engraved and Satin Bright Cut.

L. A. LITTLEFIELD SILVER CO.
New Bedford, Massachusetts

An advertisement in an old (c. 1885-85 and unidentified magazine) Littlefield is called a "manufacturer and silverplater of glassware fittings." The business was established in 1884 by _____ Needham and L. A. Littlefield. Needham retired in 1888. The company was incorporated in 1905 under the name L. A. Littlefield Silver Co. It was consolidated with the Rockford Silver Plate Co. in 1909 and moved to Rockford, Illinois. Littlefield was a manufacturer of trimmings for glassware and electroplate. He supplied the silverplated tops for numerous articles of tableware.

P. H. LOCKLIN & SONS
New York, New York

Manufacturers c. 1920-1930 of sterling silverware, vases, candlesticks, salt and pepper shakers, umbrella handles, canes, riding crops, muffineers, novelties, cigar and cigarette holders, and articles of other materials mounted in 14 and 18k white gold and platinum.

MILLIE B. LOGAN
Rochester, New York

U. S. Patent No. 20,375 registered for Millie B. Logan on November 17, 1891 for gold and silver tableware. Listed in JC 1896 among manufacturers of souvenir silverware. Rochester city directory lists her as a manufacturer of ladies' fashionable hair work, hair jewelry, etc., from 1871-c. 1908.

V. LOLLO
Brooklyn, New York

Manufacturers of sterling salt and pepper shakers c. 1950.

VL

THOMAS LONG COMPANY
Boston, Massachusetts

Registered trademark for sterling silver, silverplated flatware, holloware and jewelry. Claims use since Oct. 18, 1946.

H. LORD & CO.
Savannah, Georgia
See Black, Starr & Frost Ltd.

In business c. 1805. Partners were Hezekiah Lord, Cornelius Paulding and Isaac Marquand.

LOTT & SCHMITT, INC.
New York, New York

Listed JC 1915 in sterling silver section. Out of business before 1922.

LOW, BALL & CO.
See Shreve, Crump & Low Co., Inc.

DANIEL LOW & CO.
Salem, Massachusetts

Established in 1867 by Daniel Low as a small jewelry store. Low's reputation as a source of unusual gifts and fine gold and silver articles soon earned a reputation for the store and the confidence of his patrons.

In 1887, when souvenir spoons were being introduced in European cities, Daniel Low took a trip abroad and brought back the idea of making a Witch spoon as a souvenir of Salem and the Witchcraft tradition. His son, Seth F. Low, designed the first Witch spoon. It was made by the Durgin Division of The Gorham Mfg. Co. Its immediate popularity and that of the second Witch spoon which followed shortly afterwards, were largely responsible for the souvenir spoon craze that swept across the country shortly before 1900.

In 1896 Seth F. Low became a partner in the business. On September 1, 1907 the business was incorporated under the name Daniel Low & Co., Inc.

Aware that most of the goods purchased in his store were for gifts, Daniel Low decided to reach out beyond the confines of his own city and in 1893 first published a small catalog to establish a mail order business. The Daniel Low Year Book became a national institution.

WITCH

JOHN J. LOW & CO.
See Shreve, Crump & Low

BENJAMIN F. LOWELL
Malibu Beach, California

Registered trademark for use on handwrought sterling silverware — goblets, trays and flatware. Claims use since Feb. 4, 1946.

MRS. LUCKEY
Pittsburgh, Pennsylvania

Woman silversmith who worked in Pittsburgh between 1830 and 1840.

LUDWIG, REDLICH & CO.
See Elgin Silversmith Co., Inc.
See Redlich & Co.

Registered trademark in U. S. Patent Office No. 21,423, July 5, 1892 for solid silverware and tableware.

LUNT SILVERSMITHS
Greenfield, Massachusetts
See Franklin Silver Plate Company
See Rogers, Lunt & Bowlen

Lunt Silversmiths began with the formation of the A. F. Towle & Son Mfg. Co. in 1880 in Newburyport, Massachusetts. Three years later Anthony Towle and his son left the company and built a new factory in Newburyport under the name A. F. Towle & Son Company. They operated in Newburyport until 1890 when they moved to Greenfield, Massachusetts as a result of the contribution of local financial support. In the early 1890s the firm tried to diversify its operations and went into the manufacture of automobiles and actually manufactured one of the first "horseless carriages" under the name Hertle Horseless Carriages. Lack of proper financing caused the failure of this endeavor and on November 8, 1900 the A. F. Towle & Son Co. failed. George C. Lunt, who had been apprenticed to Anthony Towle as an engraver, obtained financial assistance and established Rogers, Lunt & Bowlen Co., in 1902. Since 1935 the company has used the trade-name LUNT SILVERSMITHS and have trademarked their products LUNT STERLING but the corporate name remains the same.

The Franklin Silver Plate Company of Greenfield, Massachusetts was taken over between 1920-22. With minor exceptions their trademarks have not been used since.

About 1957 the King Silver Company of Boston, including the trademarks and assets of the Richard Dimes Co. was added to the firm. Lunt sterling is noted for fine craftsmanship and good taste in design.
LUNT STERLING

W. H. LYON
Newburgh, New York

Listed in the Newburgh City Directory 1891-1920. His advertisement in the directory stated that Lyon, the Jeweler was sole manufacturer of the Washington Headquarters Souvenir Spoon, in Tea, Coffee, Orange and Sugar Spoons, also Butter Knives, etc. The trademark was the representation of the building known as "George Washington's Newburg[h] N. Y. headquarters." Registered in U. S. Patent Office, No. 18,906, January 17, 1891.

LYONS SILVER PLATE CO.
See Manhattan Silver Plate Co.

M

J. S. MACDONALD CO.
Baltimore, Maryland

J. Stuart MacDonald was listed in Baltimore City Directories under plated silver wares; succeeded by J. S. MacDonald Co. in 1911. Listing continued through 1921.

MACOMBER MFG. CO.
Providence, Rhode Island

Manufacturers of plated silverware c. 1910.

MM Co.

MACFARLANE MFG. CO.
See Bridgeport Silver Plate Co.

R. H. MACY & CO.
New York, New York

Founded by Rowland Hussey Macy of Nantucket Island who went to sea as a whaler when he was only fifteen. At Macy's store he is spoken of as **Captain Macy** — a slight exaggeration.

Nantucketers still speak of "that Macy boy who went to New York and made out all right — even though he did become an off-islander."

He engaged in several business ventures. First, in Boston, where he operated a thread and needle shop — a short-lived venture. His next store was Macy & Company, run in partnership with his brother in Marysville, California, where they were drawn by the Gold Rush.

The family moved back to Massachusetts and in Haverhill he opened the Haverhill Cheap Store.

Finally, in the fall of 1858 he opened his first New York store on 6th Avenue, just below 14th Street.

Macy had some unusual ideas in advertising and believed strongly in the value of this advertising. A distinctive characteristic of this was the introduction of a trademark — a red rooster — used after June 1851 in the Haverhill Store. In New York he adopted a five-pointed red star in 1862 or 1863.

Silverware was first sold in the store in 1874 and was supplied by L. Straus & Sons, wholesalers. Like other large department stores, Macy's had goods marked with their private brands and trademarks.

Chatsworth

(On plated silver)

E. MAGNUS
New York, New York
See Howard Cutlery Co.

ERIK MAGNUSSEN
See August Dingelden & Son

D. J. MAHONEY
New York, New York

Listed in JC in 1896 in sterling silver section. Out of business before 1904.

M

MAJESTIC MFG. CO.
New York, New York

"The Majestic Mfg. Co. of New York was incorporated to manufacture and sell sterling silver, gold and other metal ware. Directors are: Henry L. Fishel, Louis D. Nessler and Theodore F. Fishel, all of New York." (JC&HR 12-25-1895, p. 18) About 1900 the Majestic Mfg. Co. and Fishel, Nessler & Co. were at the same New York address.

This same trademark with the letters "J. O. - N. Y." replacing the word Majestic has been seen on a tea set. The trademark with the letters "F. N. & Co." replacing the word Majestic is attributed in the 1904 JC to Fishel, Nessler & Co.

MAJESTIC SILVER COMPANY
New Haven, Connecticut

Founded in 1910 as The Regal Silver Manufacturing Company by M. L. Baker. Present president is Milton Baker, son of the founder.

From 1910 till 1942 they manufactured silverplated flatware. In the late 1920s the production of stainless steel flatware was begun.

In the early 1930s a separate related firm, The Regal Specialty Mfg. Co., began the manufacture of silverplate and stainless steel flatware. At the end of World War II silverplated flatware was discontinued and now only stainless steel flatware is made.

In late 1945, through internal corporate changes, The Majestic Silver Co. emerged as the parent company and The Regal Specialty Co. continued as the subsidiary.   MAJESTIC

MAJESTIC SILVER CO., INC.
New York, New York

Manufacturers sterling silver holloware and pewter novelties c. 1930.

MALTBY, STEVENS & CURTISS CO.
Wallingford, Connecticut
See International Silver Co.

Successor to Maltby, Stevens & Company's spoon factory, Birmingham, Connecticut, the new company was headed by Elizur Seneca Stevens, Chapman Maltby and John Curtiss. They bought and occupied the old Hall, Elton & Co. plant and manufactured flatware for plating about 1890. In 1896 the company was purchased by the Watrous Mfg. Co., which was one of the original companies to become a part of International Silver Co. in 1898.

(On plated silver)   (On sterling silver)

MANCHESTER MFG. CO.
Providence, Rhode Island
See Baker-Manchester Mfg. Co.
See Manchester Silver Co.

Manufacturers of sterling silver fancy flatware, holloware and novelties. Baker-Manchester Mfg. Co. listed in 1922 JC as successors.

MANCHESTER SILVER CO.
Providence, Rhode Island

Founded in 1887 by William H. Manchester, descendent of an English family of silversmiths. Operations started on Stewart Street under the name W. H. Manchester & Co. They moved to Chestnut Street where Mr. Manchester was associated with a Baker family. From 1904 until 1914-1915, the company name was Manchester Mfg. Co. Manchester moved his operation to the present location on Pavilion Avenue in 1914 or 1915, while the Bakers continued for a time on Chestnut Street under the name Baker-Manchester Co. William Manchester was no longer connected with this operation.

William Manchester had an associate by the name of MacFarland. On his retirement, Frank S. Trumbull, of an industrial family from Connecticut, took his place. When Mr. Manchester and his son retired, the business was owned solely by Frank S. Trumbull until 1947, when E. B. McAlpine and his son, George Wescott McAlpine acquired an interest. Following the death of Mr. Trumbull in 1954 the McAlpine family acquired the entire stock.

Their products are sterling silver flatware and holloware. Everything is marketed under the slogan, "If it's Manchester, it's Sterling."

In 1955 or 1956 they acquired the tools, dies and rights to the flatware patterns formerly produced by Richard Dimes Co.

W. H. MANCHESTER & CO.
Providence, Rhode Island
See Manchester Silver Co.

Manufacturers of sterling silver fancy flatware, holloware and novelties.

MANDALIAN & HAWKINS
North Attleboro, Massachusetts
See Mandalian Mfg. Co.

Founding date unknown. Succeeded by Mandalian Manufacturing Company before 1922.

M & H

MANDALIAN MFG. CO.
North Attleboro, Massachusetts

Successors to Mandalian & Hawkins before 1922. Last record found in 1935.

Manufacturing jewelers, makers of sterling and nickel silver mesh bags and frames.

DEBUTANTE

MANDIX COMPANY, INC.
New York, New York

Importers and wholesalers of pewterware and glassware with pewter trimming c. 1925-30.

JUST ANDERSEN

MANHATTAN SILVER PLATE CO.
Lyons, New York
See International Silver Co.
See Hiram Young & Co.

An unconfirmed source says that the company started as a corporation in 1847 but changed to a partnership in 1865, and remained so until 1885 when it was again incorporated with J. W. Young as president, O. F. Thomas as secretary.

According to the *Jewelers' Weekly* (1890) the company was founded in 1872 and incorporated in 1877. In 1889 or 1890 it was moved from Brooklyn to Lyons, New York when it was bought by Orlando F. Thomas. The *Jewelers' Weekly* (3-6-1890) says that the "Manhattan Silver Plate Co. mark is stamped on their best grades of goods of all kinds. A new line is to appear with Lyons Silver Co. as a trademark." The company manufactured electroplated silverwares and exported, mainly to South America and Australia, nearly one-third its production. This was one of the original companies to become part of The International Silver Co. in 1898. The Manhattan trademark was not used after 1904.

There was a Manhattan Plate Co. listed in the New York City Directory in 1865 which may have been this same company.

Identical to a mark used by Roswell Gleason. Perhaps erroneously attributed to Manhattan Silver Plate Co. in 1904 JC.

MANNING, BOWMAN & CO.
Meriden, Connecticut

E. B. Manning, Middletown, Connecticut was a britannia ware maker from 1850-1875.

Robert Bowman was born in Liverpool England in 1871 and came to this country as a boy. He learned his trade in Middletown, Conn. and after working there a while entered the employ of Samuel Simpson (of later Simpson, Hall, Miller & Co.). He also worked in Baltimore, Md. with Henry Bullard in the silverplating business. At the outbreak of the Civil War he went North again to Middletown and entered into partnership with E. P. Manning and Joseph H. Parsons.

Thaddeus Manning and Manning, Bowman & Company were listed in the Connecticut Business Directory of 1866 as britannia ware manufacturers. The company was founded in 1857 and incorporated in 1887.

Company records do not show just when the manufacture of plated silver products began, but, they are listed in JC from 1896-1915 with trademarks for plated silver. One clue lies in the fact that they won an award at an exhibition of the American Institute of New York in 1869 for plated silverware.

Their advertisement (*Keystone* August 1906) says, "For over 40 years makers of the highest grade of wares in nickel and silverplate."

Best known for their manufacture of electrical appliances, the Manning-Bowman Company is now a Division of the McGraw-Edison Company, Boonville, Missouri.

(Not used after 1898)

MAPPIN & WEBB, LTD.
Sheffield, England

Silversmiths and electroplaters. By appointment to several members of the Royal family and foreign rulers.

John Newton Mappin left the family firm of cutlers Mappin Bros. which he subsequently bought, to found a new firm with George Webb, as his partner. Early in the 1880s they bought the old business of Stephen Smith & Sons (formerly Smith & Nicholson), of Covent Garden, London. In 1896 they bought Heeley Rolling Mills, a high quality foundry started in an old aluminum plant. In 1913 they began the manufacture of a cheaper line under the name Sheffield Silver Plate and Cutlery Company. Now part of British Silverware Ltd.

MAPPIN & WEBB'S
PRINCE'S PLATE

TUSCA

MARCEL NOVELTY CO.
New York, New York

Listed in JC 1896-1904 in sterling silver section. Out of business before 1915.

MARCUS & CO.
New York, New York

There was an I. Marcus, 87 Nassau, New York City in business at least from 1918-27. Manufactured 14K gold and platinum top bar pins, pendants, scarf pins, rings and cuff links.

MARCUS & CO.
New York

(Tentative)

FRED I. MARCY & CO.
Providence, Rhode Island

Frederick I. Marcy (b. Hartland, Vermont 1838; d. Providence, R. I. 1896) was employed for four years with a dealer in tinware, named D. Hoisington. In 1863 he became a traveler with James H. Sturdy, jewelry manufacturer, in Attleboro, and within a year had purchased an interest in the company. In 1867 W. A. Sturdy purchased the business and James H. Sturdy and Marcy moved to Providence where they established the business of Sturdy & Marcy to manufacture jewelry. In 1878 Charles H. Smith became a partner and the name was changed to Fred I. Marcy & Co. Smith retired in 1882 and Marcy continued the business alone. One of their specialties was the "Acme Lever" collar, cuff and sleeve buttons. This type of button was patented August 24, 1881. It was placed on the market and was an immediate success because it "saved time and vexation in dressing." Six thousand different designs were used in their ornamentation — cameos, opals, amethysts, pearls, diamonds, crystal pictures, chasing, engraving and enamel were used on the rolled plate of gold and sterling silver from which they were made. The Marcy trademark is also found on larger silver articles. The business closed shortly before Marcy's suicide in 1896.

MARION MFG. CO.
Salt Lake City, Utah

"The Marion Mfg. Co., Salt Lake City is being organized. They will make a specialty of silverware. The factory is being built like a watch factory so as to have all the light possible. The silverware will be marketed all over the western country." (JW 12-22-1886, p. 716)

MARQUAND & BROTHER
New York, New York
See Black, Starr & Frost, Ltd.

In business 1814-1831. Partners were Isaac Marquand and Frederick Marquand.

MARQUAND & COMPANY
New York, New York
See Black, Starr & Frost, Ltd.

In business 1834-1839. Partners were Frederick Marquand, Josiah P. Marquand and Erastus O. Tompkins. Famed silversmiths and jewelers.

MARQUAND, HARRIMAN & CO.
New York, New York
See Black, Starr & Frost, Ltd.

In business c. 1809-1810. Partners were Isaac Marquand, Orlando Harriman and Cornelius Paulding.

MARQUAND & PAULDING
Savannah, Georgia
See Black, Starr & Frost, Ltd.

Founded c. 1801 and in business until 1810. Partners were Isaac Marquand (who had been apprenticed to his uncle, Jacob Jenning, Norwalk, Connecticut) and Cornelius Paulding.

MARQUAND, PAULDING & PENFIELD
Savannah, Georgia
See Black, Starr & Frost, Ltd.

In business c. 1810-1816. Partners were Isaac Marquand, Cornelius Paulding and Josiah Penfield.

MARSHALL-WELLS HARDWARE CO.
Duluth, Minnesota

Began as the Chapin-Wells Hardware Company in 1886. In 1893, Albert M. Marshall, a Saginaw, Michigan merchant bought out the Chapin interest and the company became the Marshall-Wells Co., hardware wholesalers. Old city directory advertisements indicate that the company first distributed only tools, hardware, cutlery and saddlery. Later their merchandise included everything that could be classified as hardware. It was the largest hardware wholesale distributor in the Northwest and Canada.

November 24, 1908 a trademark, No. 71,473, was registered in their name for silverplated knives, forks and spoons. In an advertisement from the *Zenith Magazine*, their monthly publication, it was noted that cutlery was stamped "manufactured exclusively for Marshall-Wells" and bore the Zenith trademark. Branch jobbing houses were located in Winnipeg (1900), Portland (1901), Spokane (1909), Edmonton (1910), Aberdeen, Seattle, Great Falls, Billings, Minneapolis and Vancouver, B.C. They also had warehouses in Moosejaw, Sasketchewan and Calgary, Alberta.

In May 1955, the trustees of the A. M. Marshall estate sold the controlling interest to Ambrook Industries of New York. At that time Marshall-Wells was the largest wholesale hardware operation in the world.

In 1958, Marshall-Wells and Kelly-How, Thompson, a Midwest hardware distributor merged and in August of that same year the company was sold to Coast-to-Coast stores, and in 1959 Marshall-Wells closed its main office and warehouse in Duluth and moved to New York City.

A 1963 newspaper clipping indicated that the Marshall-Wells Co. of Duluth was still in business, having purchased a St. Louis, Missouri furniture company, but no longer operated as a wholesale hardware distributor.

TH. MARTHINSEN SØLVVAREFABRIKK
Tønsberg, Norway

Established in 1883: now operated by the third generation. Manufacturers of complete lines of sterling and silverplated holloware and flatware. Known especially to collectors in this country through their limited edition enameled and silvergilt Christmas spoons. Products distributed in the U.S. through the Norwegian Silver Corporation.

S Ø L V	P L E T T
(On silver)	(On silverplate)

MARYLAND SILVER CO.
Baltimore, Maryland

Listed in Baltimore City Directories 1906-1908 as silversmiths.

MARYLAND SILVER PLATE CO.
Baltimore, Maryland

Listed in Baltimore City Directories 1889-1899 under plated silverware.

MASCHMEYER RICHARDS SILVER CO.
St. Louis, Missouri

Listed in 1915 JC and 1922 KJI as importer and wholesaler of silver, glassware, leather goods and ivory.

JOHN MASON
New York, New York

"John Mason, 246 Fifth Avenue, formerly with Tiffany & Co., having his factory and salesrooms manned almost entirely by former employees of the above firm, is enabled to furnish exactly the same quality of goods at a very much lower price. High-grade Jewelry, Diamonds, Watches, Silverware, Fancy Goods, Cut Glassware, etc." (Adv. in *Harper's Magazine Advertiser*, November 1890)

MATHEWS & PRIOR
New York, New York

Founding date unknown. Listed in JC in 1904 in sterling silver section as out of business.

N. MATSON
See Spaulding & Co.

Newell Matson was a businessman, not a silversmith. He was born in Simsbury, Connecticut in 1817 and started in business at the age of 15 selling coin silver. He established a small store in Louisburg, Connecticut in 1840. In 1845 he opened a larger store in Owego, New York where he not only sold silverware, but employed several silversmiths whose main output was spoons marked with his name. He started and sold several businesses. One was in Milwaukee, Wisconsin, where he established a partnership of Matson, Loomis & Hoes with a branch in Chicago. The Chicago store grew so rapidly that he sold the Milwaukee store only to be driven out by the fire in 1871. Soon afterwards he began business again, first in his home and later under the name N. Matson & Co., with George E. Johnson, L. J. Norton and W. E. Higby. They carried a large stock of the usual jewelers' goods — the silver being from the Gorham Mfg. Co. Later the firm name became Spaulding & Co. and then Spaulding-Gorham, Inc. from the 1920s to 1943 when the name reverted to Spaulding & Co.

MATTHEWS COMPANY
Newark, New Jersey
*See Hickok Matthews Company
– Silversmiths*

Incorporated in 1907. Merged with Eleder-Hickok Company between 1931-1943 to become Hickok-Matthews Company. Was purchased in 1965 by Wolfgang K. Schroth and is now known as Hickok Matthews Company — Silversmiths, Montville, New Jersey.

(On sterling holloware)

THE MAUSER MANUFACTURING COMPANY
New York, New York

Frank Mauser, silversmith, began the manufacture of fine sterling silver goods in North Attleboro, Massachusetts in July 1887. In March of the following year Frank O. Coombs became a partner. He was designer and chaser for the growing concern. They made "holloware of every description, stationery and toilet novelties and a large variety of miscellaneous articles and sets." In 1890 they were contemplating a move to New York where they planned to increase the capacity of their production. A note in the JC (1-6-1897) says that the "Mauser Mfg. Co., New York, is successor to Frank Mauser & Co."

In 1903 The Mauser Mfg. Co. merged with the Hayes & McFarland Company of Mount Vernon, New York and the Roger Williams Silver Company of Providence, Rhode Island to form the Mt. Vernon Com-

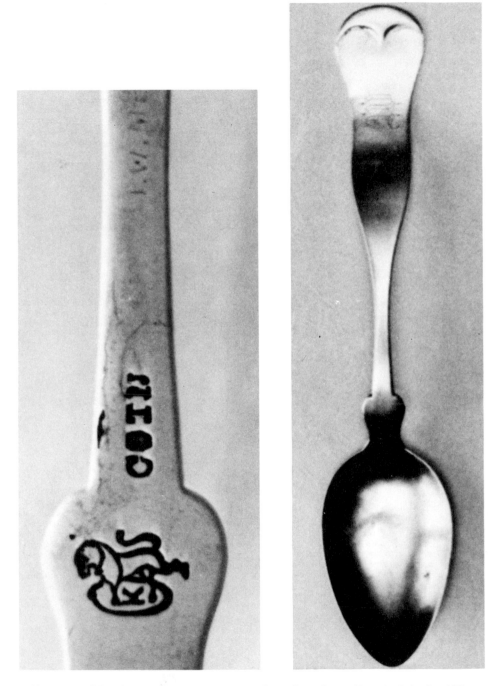

The word COIN began to appear frequently on American silver early in the 19th century and continued to be much used through the 1860s. (J. B. & S. M. Knowles)

Five-piece tea and coffee service marked J. O. Mead & Sons. Bottom of coffee pot showing oval disc bearing Mead trademark. Such soldered on discs were used frequently on pieces actually manufactured by one company to be plated and retailed by another. This apparently was the case here as an almost identical set is illustrated in a Meriden Britannia Company catalog published August 1, 1867.

pany Silversmiths, Inc. which was purchased by the Gorham Corporation in 1913.

The diamond-enclosing-an-M trademark is still listed under Mt. Vernon Company Silversmiths.

Some of their flatware patterns were purchased by the Wendell Mfg. Co., c. 1896-97.

MAUTNER MFG. CO.
New York, New York

Manufacturers of jewelry and silverplated holloware c. 1925-35.

MOREWEAR PLATE
M. M. CO.

THE MAY DEPARTMENT STORES COMPANY
New York, New York
St. Louis, Missouri

Registered trademark in 1949 for use on silverplated holloware.

FRANK T. MAY CO.
New York, New York and
Rutherford, New Jersey

Manufacturers and distributors of sterling silver bags, 14k vanity and ladies' cigarette cases and novelties and jewelry.

Listed in JC-K in 1904-1943

JOSEPH MAYER & BROS.
Seattle, Washington
See E. J. Towle Mfg. Co.

"Joseph Mayer & Bros. had been in business as Empire Jewelry Company." (JC & HR 9-16-1896, p. 20)

"G. A. Schuman, of Attleboro, left last week for Seattle, where he will establish and manage what promises to be the largest jewelry plant on the Pacific Slope. The firm name will be Joseph Mayer & Bro. Mr. Schuman is a designer and toolmaker who has had experience with Gorham, Whiting and Tiffany, and goes under a year's contract. The arrangements as planned are for a big establishment, capable of turning out a great deal of work." (JC&HR 3-2-1898, p. 32)

In addition to jewelry, the Mayer firm made several patterns of flatware and numerous souvenir spoons. Succeeded by E. J. Towle Mfg. Co., c. 1945.

BENJAMIN MAYO
Newark, New Jersey

Silversmith, 1860-1908. Began business as Smith & Mayo in 1860, gold and silver electroplaters. Other Mayos listed at the same residence as Benjamin in the plating business were Arthur, 1869-71; William G. 1869 (moved to Rochester, N.Y., 1871); John B. 1868-71; and Samuel, 1868-71. Benjamin Mayo was listed in the 1871 Newark Directory as a silver plater and manufacturer of silver ware.

JOSEPH B. MAYO
Newark, New Jersey

"Joseph B. Mayo, an old resident of Newark and a former manufacturer of silver plated ware, but now interested in silver mining, is here [Newark] on a visit to his family." (JC&HR 9-21-1892 supplement)

Joseph B. Mayo was a silversmith, working 1868-96. He was a manufacturer of both plated and sterling wares, including cake baskets, card receivers, castors, waiters, pitchers, forks, etc. Also worked in britannia, white metal and solid silver. The compositions required were alloyed in his own factory.

MAYO & CO.
Chicago, Illinois

Listed in JC in 1896 in sterling silver section. Out of business before 1904.

JAMES EDWARD MAZURKEWICZ
Cleveland, Ohio

Silversmith. Mr. Mazurkewicz was born in Cleveland, Ohio and received his education in the Cleveland and Parma Public Schools, the Cleveland Institute of Art and the Syracuse University School of Art. He has been awarded numerous scholarships and awards for the excellence of his work. Among these was an award from the National Sterling Silversmiths Guild of America Student Design Competition. Among his most recent exhibits was "The Goldsmith" at Renwick Gallery, Washington, D.C.

Mr. Mazurkewicz was an instructor at the Syracuse University School of Art and is presently instructor of metalsmithing, both beginning and advanced techniques at the Cleveland Institute of Art. He was recently commissioned to make a trophy presentation piece for Scandinavian Airlines.

THE McCHESNEY CO.
Newark, New Jersey
See Gorham Corporation

Samuel D. McChesney, who died Aug. 1, 1926, age 65 had been connected with the silver business more than 35 years. In January 1890 he went with Wm. B. Kerr, his brother-in-law, founder and head of Wm. B. Kerr Co., Newark, New Jersey, for a number of years. After Kerr's death, McChesney was president of the company until he resigned December 1921 and formed the McChesney Co. which manufactured gold and silver wares in a factory in Newark. He continued there until his death.

His brother, Wm. F. McChesney was treasurer and later president of Dominick & Haff (later sold to Reed & Barton).

It appears that after the death of Samuel D. McChesney, his business was taken over by Dominick & Haff. When that company was sold to Reed & Barton in 1928, what was left of the McChesney business was also taken over by them. The McChesney Company was sold by Reed & Barton in 1931 to the Gorham Company and Wm. F. McChesney went with Gorham. The tools and dies were moved to Providence, Rhode Island.

STERLING

DAVID H. McCONNELL
New York, New York

Earliest record found was registration of U. S. Patent No. 32,828, May 9, 1899 for use on plated flatware. Out of business before 1915.

SO. AM.

H. A. McFARLAND
See Mount Vernon Silversmiths

JOHN M. McFARLANE
See Shreve, Crump & Low Co., Inc.

EDWARD B. McGLYNN
Newark, New Jersey

Listed 1931 KJI as manufacturer of gold and platinum mountings; special order work. In 1950 and 1965 JC-K as maker of sterling silver chalices.

McGLYNN

WALTER H. McKENNA & CO., INC.
Providence, Rhode Island

Established in 1915 as manufacturers of 14k and 10k gold, sterling silver and gold filled jewelry. Also make sterling baby spoons. Still in business in 1965.

MK

JOHN O. MEAD
Philadelphia, Pennsylvania

Britannia ware manufacturer of Philadelphia, John O. Mead, laid the foundation for the important 19th century industry of electroplating silver.

Around 1830-1835 Mead was in charge of the silverplating and gilding work at the N. P. Ames Manufacturing Company of Chicopee, Massachusetts, using the old mercury and acid process.

He went to England to learn the new technique in Birmingham and continued his experiments on his return. Reputedly the first successful American electro-silver plater around 1840-1859.

In 1845 he formed a partnership in Hartford, Connecticut with William and Asa Rogers under the name of Rogers & Mead. This company was soon dissolved.

Mead returned to Philadelphia in 1846 (while William and Asa Rogers founded the firm of Rogers & Bro.) and re-established his business under the name John O. Mead, later J. O. Mead & Sons, the partners at that time being John O. Mead, J. P. Mead and Harrison Robbins. About 1850, the firm name became Filley & Mead (or Filley, Mead & Caldwell). Later still the firm name was changed to Mead & Robbins. One account says that John O. Mead died about 1867 and that the firm of Mead & Robbins was dissolved about 1870. However, there is an item (JC&HR 10-19-1892, p. 27) that says "Frederick Robbins, Philadelphia, has withdrawn from the firm of Mead & Robbins and is making preparations for the establishment of a manufacturing and wholesale silverware house. The old firm will be conducted thereafter by Edmund P. Robbins and will be devoted to the retail business." Mead & Robbins was succeeded by Sackett & Co. in 1893.

Mead & Sons had an extensive business. Their plant employed more than two hundred workmen and they turned out about fifty different designs in tea sets alone. Much of their ware was supplied "in the metal" by Reed & Barton, the plating being done in the Mead plant.

MEAD & ROBBINS
Philadelphia, Pennsylvania
See John O. Mead

MEALY MANUFACTURING COMPANY
Baltimore, Maryland

First listed in the Baltimore City Directory in 1900 as John W. Mealy Son & Company, jewelers. In 1906 John W. was listed as president; Edward H. as treasurer and Charles A. as secretary. In 1908 Allan B. Crouch was listed as secretary and Charles A. as treasurer.

In 1909 Crouch is no longer listed. The company name was listed through 1956.

All these listings are under the head of silversmiths. This listing, in addition to the type of trademark, indicates handwrought silver was made.

MECHANICS STERLING COMPANY
Attleboro, Massachusetts
See Watson Co.

Listed as sterling manufacturer in Jewelers' Weekly 1896. Mark is identical to Watson-Newell, now part of Wallace Silversmiths — a division of Hamilton Watch Co.

"Mechanics Sterling Co. is the flatware branch of Watson, Newell Co., North Attleboro, Mass." (JC&HR) 3-24-1897, p. 17)

Flatware.
MECHANICS STERLING CO.

MEDALLIC ART COMPANY
Danbury, Connecticut

The Medallic Art Co., official medalists for the Society of Medalists, grew out of a small lower Manhattan workshop of the French-born Henri Weil, around the turn of the century. He was joined by his brother, Felix Weil, and the two craftsmen acquired the first modern die reducing machine imported into the United States prior to 1905.

The first medals were produced in 1907 and the Medallic Art Company name first appeared in 1909.

Ten years later, in 1919, an Indiana businessman, Clyde C. Trees, joined the two Weil brothers. In 1927 he assumed the presidency and built the flourishing company into the institution it is today. In 1960 Trees died and his nephew, William Trees Louth, was named president.

Medallic Art Co. is noted especially for its introduction into the United States of the diecutting process which allows fine art medals to be reproduced from sculptor's original large size models. The work of many famous 20th century American sculptors has been reproduced by them.

In addition to finely crafted art medals, they also produce tablets, plaques, emblems and the larger medals known as medallions. Millions of service medals and decorations have been made for the U. S. government.

The key to the production of fine art medals is the Janvier reducing machine. Named after the French engraver Victor Janvier, the device reduces a sculptor's model exactly, cutting a die automatically (rather than by hand) in a pantographic reproduction. It is a little known fact that the Medallic Art Company personnel trained the technicians at the U. S. Mint at Philadelphia after helping that institution obtain its first Janvier machine.

Medallic Art Co. has produced many medals for important occasions, among them are those for the Pulitzer Prize and the inaugural medals for the Presidents Coolidge, Hoover, F. D. Roosevelt, Eisenhower, Kennedy, Johnson and Nixon.

They purchased the medal division of the Aug. C. Frank Co., Inc. of Philadelphia, September 15, 1972. The dies, medal presses and other equipment were incorporated into the Danbury plant soon after that date.

THE MELROSE SILVER CO.
Hartford, Connecticut

Manufactured inexpensive silverplated flatware c. 1900.

COLONIAL PLATE CO.

MERIDEN BRITANNIA COMPANY
Meriden, Connecticut
See International Silver Company

Organized in December 1852 by Horace C. and Dennis C. Wilcox of H. C. Wilcox & Co. Other founders were Isaac C. Lewis of I. C. Lewis & Company; James A. Frary of James A. Frary & Company; Lemuel J. Curtis; William W. Lyman of Curtis & Lyman and John Munson.

Organized for quantity production, their first products were britannia holloware. By 1855 they were also offering plated silver holloware and flatware and German silver articles. Pearl-handled wares were added about 1861.

In 1862 the Rogers brothers who had been making and selling plated silver forks, spoons and other wares were moved to Meriden. Their 1847 Rogers Bros. trademark was an important addition to the Meriden Britannia Company.

In 1896 they ceased stamping their products "Quadruple" plate.

The Meriden Britannia Company officers were among the leaders in the formation of the International Silver Company in 1898.

As early as 1867 the Meriden Britannia Company had a system of stamping nickel silver, silversoldered holloware with a cipher preceding the number and by 1893, nickel silver holloware with white metal mounts had as a part of the number two ciphers. That is, on an article with white metal, 00256, etc. was stamped. This made it quickly understood by the number whether the piece was nickel silver, silver soldered or nickel silver with white metal mounts.

In the production of silverplated flatware one of the biggest improvements was the introduction of sectional plate — depositing an extra amount of silver on spoons, forks, etc., on the parts which are given the hardest wear. A catalog issued in 1871 by MBCo shows a line, more extensive than previously shown, and gives this explanation as to what is meant by "Triple Plate." A portion of the holloware was on nickel silver base, and a part on white metal, both marketed silverplated. They showed the two trademarks and say "goods carrying these trademarks are warranted triple plate and have at least three times the quantity of silver as on single plate."

In 1895 MBCo bought out a small silversmith's shop in New York being run by Wilcox & Evertsen, successors to Rowan & Wilcox, making a quality line of sterling silver holloware, and moved it to Meriden. This was the start of a representative silver holloware line which in 1898 was taken over by the International Silver Company. In 1897 MBCo produced its first sterling silver flatware pattern, *Revere*. MBCo. marks were used until the 1930s.

1847 ROGERS BROS.

(Spoons, Forks, Knives, etc.)

(*Nickel Silver, White Metal Mounted Hollowware.*)

(*Solid Steel, Silver Plated Knives.*)

Meriden Brita Co.
(*Spoons, Forks, Knives, etc.*)

1847 Rogers Bros. ⊕ XII TRIPLE ᵡˢ

(*Nickel Silver, Silver Soldered Hollowware.*)

(*Standard White Metal Hollowware.*) (*Plated Ware.*)

NICKEL SILVER   WHITE METAL

***ROGERS BROS.
Used 1900-1917

(*Holloware.*) (*Flatware.*)

MERIDEN BRITANNIA CO., LTD.
Hamilton, Ontario

Established in 1879 for the production of 1847 Rogers Bros. silverplate, sterling silver flatware, silverplated nickel silver and white metal holloware. Merged with International Silver Co. of Canada, Ltd. about 1912.

MERIDEN CUTLERY COMPANY
South Meriden, Connecticut

This firm began in 1834, when G. and D. N. Ropes manufactured cutlery in Maine. A few years later, A. R. Moen of New York manufactured table cutlery in Wethersfield, Connecticut. The business was acquired by Julius Pratt & Co. of Meriden who continued it for about two years. In 1845, these two firms were consolidated as Pratt, Ropes, Webb & Co. Mr. Ropes erected a factory in Hanover where the business continued until 1855, when the joint stock company Meriden Cutlery Company was formed. One of their specialties was pearl handled cutlery which usually carried the date 1855.

The company was purchased by Landers, Frary & Clark in 1866 which was liquidated in the 1960s.

These two trademarks were used on carving knives with sterling silver blades c. 1900.

The Meriden mark was used by Landers, Frary & Clark on some sterling wares.

(On carving knives with sterling silver blades)

MERIDEN CUTLERY CO.

MERIDEN JLY. MFG. CO.
Meriden, Connecticut

Listed in JC 1915. Became Meriden Jewelry Co. before 1922. Manufacturers of sterling silver and plated silver cigarette cases, fancy pieces and flatware.

(On plated silver)

MERIDEN SILVER PLATE CO.
Meriden, Connecticut
See International Silver Co.

Organized in 1869 by Charles Casper and others. George R. Curtis was president. One of the original companies to become part of the International Silver Company in 1898.

"Robert G. Hill, photographer for the Meriden Silver Plate Co., is said to have discovered a new way of photographing on metal. Colors are reproduced and a likeness on the satin-finished silver background is extremely pleasing." (JC&HR 4-5-1893, p. 55)

(*On Cheaper Grade.*)

EUREKA SILVER PLATE CO.
MERIDEN SILVER PLATE CO.

MERIDEN STERLING CO.
Meriden, Connecticut

Listed in JC 1896 in the sterling silver section. Out of business before 1904.

MERMOD, JACCARD & KING JEWELRY CO.
St. Louis, Missouri

Established in 1829 by Louis Jaccard who was joined by A. S. Mermod in 1845. In 1848, D. C. Jaccard, relative of Louis Jaccard, joined. In 1865 Goodman King became associated with the firm. In 1901 they absorbed the E. Jaccard Jewelry Co. and Merrick, Walsh & Phelphs Jewelry. In 1905 the name of King was added to the firm name.

In 1917 they became part of Scruggs, Vandervoort & Barney but retain their identity as a separate corporate body.

MERMOD & JACCARD CO.
TRIPLE

THE MERRILL SHOPS
New York, New York

Established March 1893 as J. M. Merrill & Co. Listed 1896 as Merrill Brothers & Co., manufacturers of sterling silver and pewter. By 1922 it was The Merrill Co. and The Merrill Shops before 1931.

MERRIMAC VALLEY SILVERSMITHS

A division of Concord Silversmiths Corp., succeeded by Frank M. Whiting & Co. Dies purchased by Crown Silver Co.

MERRIMAN SILVER COMPANY
Attleboro, Massachusetts

"The Merriman Silver Co., Attleboro, are one of the new companies recently started. Their existence dates from the first week of February. If their anticipations are realized they intend to begin the manufacture of staple goods." (JC&HR 3-17-1897, p. 22)

MERRY & PELTON SILVER CO.
St. Louis, Missouri
See Pelton Bros. Silver Plate Co.

Listed JC 1904 as manufacturers of plated silver holloware and flatware. Out of business before 1909. Not listed in St. Louis City Directories which were checked back to 1840.

SECTIONAL PLATE XII
STANDARD PLATE 4
TRIPLE PLATE 12
(Flatware.)

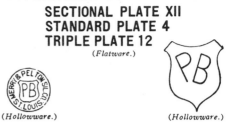

(Holloware.)   *(Holloware.)*

MERWIN-WILSON CO., INC.
New Milford, Connecticut

Company established by the Merwin brothers in 1912 as successors to Bennett Merwin Silver Company. Shortly afterwards one brother was killed.

Roy (?) Wilson joined the remaining Merwin. The company made pewter reproductions and plated silver prize cups, trophies and colonial pewter reproductions until 1935 when they sold out to Robert Oliver who operated under the name of Danforth Company. The company and its molds have changed hands several times since that time and are in use now in the manufacture of pewter reproductions by Woodbury Pewterers.

MESICK MFG. CO.
Los Angeles, California

Manufacturers of sterling and silverplated holloware c. 1950.

METALLURGIC ART CO.
Baltimore, Maryland

Listed in Jewelers' Weekly as manufacturers of sterling silverware in 1896.

First listed in the Baltimore City Directory in 1895 as Victor G. Bloede, Carl Schon, jewelry manufacturers. In 1896 the listing is Metallurgic Art Company. In 1900 Bloede and Carl Schon, Jr. are listed as members of the firm.

In 1901 the Metallurgic Art Company is no longer listed. Bloede is listed as president of Victor G. Bloede, Manufacturing Chemists. Schon is not listed at all, as he moved to Detroit.

METAL PRODUCTS CORP.
Providence, Rhode Island

Manufacturers of plated silverware c. 1920. Out of business before 1922.

METROPOLITAN SILVER CO.
(John Toothill)
New York, New York

Listed in JC in 1896-1904 in plated silver section. Out of business before 1915.

MEYER & WARNE
Philadelphia, Pennsylvania

Silverplaters c. 1859-1880?

WILLIAM B. MEYERS CO.
Newark, New Jersey

Listed JKD as a manufacturer of sterling silver wares and photo frames. Listing found until 1960.

MIAMI SILVER CO.
Cincinnati, Ohio

Listed in City Directories 1903-1912 as silverplaters.

A. MICHELSEN
Copenhagen, Denmark

Anton Michelsen, founder, was born in 1809 and apprenticed to a goldsmith in Odense. He completed his training in Copenhagen, Berlin and Paris. He established his own shop in 1841 and within a few years won approval of the royal court, being designated "Insignia Jeweler" — makers of the official state decorations and Jeweler to His Majesty the King (since 1973 Jeweler to Her Majesty the Queen). The firm has won worldwide recognition for its decorative centerpieces, ornamental goblets, table services and *objets d'art* but is perhaps best known in the U.S. for the annual Christmas spoon and matching fork. Decorative spoons have been among their noted products since 1898 when Michelsen's designed a spoon to commemorate the 80th birthday of King Christian IX. Its success and that of other commemorative spoons led them in 1910 to design and produce the first Christmas spoon, now a yearly tradition.

MIDDLETOWN PLATE CO.
Middletown, Connecticut
See International Silver Co.

One of the early silverware companies that was included in the International Silver Co. The business was first started in 1864 by Edward Payne and Henry Bullard, formerly in the employ of I. C. Lewis, of Meriden, Connecticut, one of the founders of the Meriden Britannia Co. Payne and Bullard formed a partnership doing business in the name of the former, in the manufacture of britannia and plated wares in Middletown. In 1866 the Middletown Plate Co. was incorporated and continued in operation until it became part of the International Silver Co. in 1899.

They not only marketed their products under their own name but also sold holloware to Rogers & Bro., New York, who finished it and marketed it with *their* trademark.

The Superior Silver Co. stamp was used by the Middletown Plate Co. on their low priced merchandise. When they moved to Meriden, June 30, 1899, the International Silver Co. was using Gem Silver Plate Co. stamp on the Wilcox low priced merchandise and rather than have the two competitive stamps, they used the Superior Silver Co. stamp on both and eliminated the Gem Silver Plate Co. stamp.

This trademark adopted about 1866.

MIDDLETOWN SILVER CO.
Middletown, Connecticut

After the business of the Middletown Plate Co. had been taken over by the International Silver Co. in 1899 and moved to other plants, some of the old employees arranged with others to start a new concern, hiring space in the building formerly used by the Middletown Plate Co. The new company went bankrupt, January 6, 1910 but after several reorganizations and changes were still in business as late as 1939. An item in the *Hartford Times* (1-11-1945) indicates that the company was merged with J. A. Otterbein Co. of Middletown. Believed to have been more recently bought by Wallace Silversmiths.

MIDDLETOWN SILVERWARE

(On nickel silver)

(On britannia)

MIDDLESEX SILVER CO.

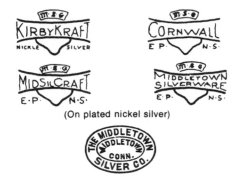

(On plated nickel silver)

HAROLD A. MILBRATH
Milwaukee, Wisconsin

Founded 1952. An individual maker specializing in ceremonial and liturgical arts principally in sterling silver. Communion service appointments and altar appointments in bronze alloys. Makers of holloware, cast and fabricated articles and special jewelry.

(Used on silver, bronze and pewter)

FREDERICK A. MILLER
Brecksville and Cleveland, Ohio

Silversmith. Mr. Miller was born in Akron, Ohio and is a graduate of Cleveland Institute of Art and Western Reserve University. After his discharge from the Army in 1946 he joined the firm of Potter and Mellen, Inc. and is now president and designer of that firm. He studied silversmithing briefly with Baron Erik Flemming and started working in silversmithing and jewelry following the war. He worked mostly in sterling holloware until recently when he became interested in jewelry.

In 1948 Mr. Miller joined the staff of Cleveland Institute of Art as instructor in silversmithing and jewelry where he is presently teaching.

Mr. Miller's work has been exhibited in the Cleveland May Show from 1948 through 1972, where it has won first prize or a special award each year. He has also exhibited in the State Department Exhibition; the Designer-Craftsman Show, first National Exhibition; Rochester Museum Show; Metropolitan Handwrought Silver Exhibition; Newark Museum Show, 1954; Wichita National Exhibition; Los Angeles County Fair; Brussels World's Fair; Museum of Contemporary Crafts, 1961; the Henry Gallery, Seattle; Objects USA; Ohio Designer Craftsman; American Metalsmiths-DeCordova Museum, 1974 and others.

JOHN PAUL MILLER
Brecksville and Cleveland, Ohio

Silversmith affiliated with the Cleveland Institute of Art. Mr. Miller was born in Hintington, Pennsylvania

and educated in Ohio Public Schools. He is a graduate of the Cleveland Institute of Art in Industrial Design. He began making jewelry in 1937 and produced holloware in the middle 1950s. Almost all of his work is done in gold.

Mr. Miller's work has been shown in many exhibitions in the United States and Europe. Examples are in numerous private and public collections. One man shows have been held in the Museum of Contemporary Crafts, New York; the Art Institute of Chicago; the Henry Gallery, Seattle, Washington; and the Wichita Art Association Museum, Wichita, Kansas.

THE MILLER JLY. CO.
Cincinnati, Ohio

Listed in JC 1915 in the sterling silver section and in jewelry. Last listing in 1922.

M Sterling

WM. J. MILLER
Baltimore, Maryland

Listed in Baltimore City Directories 1904-1920 as a silversmith.

MITCHELL & POOL
Baltimore, Maryland

Listed in Baltimore City Directory in 1889 as silverplaters. Succeeded by B. Pool & Company in 1984.

G. I. MIX & CO.
Yalesville, Connecticut

In 1843 Garry I. Mix began the manufacture of spoons and three years later formed a partnership with Charles Parker of Meriden.

"In 1848 Charles Parker and Garry I. Mix began the manufacture of Britannia and German silverware, continuing until 1854, when Mix retired to establish himself in business at Yalesville. Parker and Jeralds (Thomas and Bennet) continued at the old place as the Parker Mfg. Co. In 1857 the old mill and factory buildings were destroyed by fire and a new factory erected.

"In 1876 the Parker Mfg. Co. discontinued the manufacture of German silverware, but the production of Britannia spoons has since been carried on, in a limited way, by Bennet Jeralds.

"G. I. Mix & Co. at Yalesville, are extensive manufacturers of Britannia goods ... In 1886 steam power — 50 horse — was added to the water motor, and the capacity for production was increased." HISTORY OF NEW HAVEN COUNTY CONNECTICUT, Vol. 1. Edited by J. L. Rockey.

"Garry I. Mix died Saturday [dated New Haven, Aug. 15]. He was the leading manufacturer of German silver spoons and tinned ware spoons and edge tools. Some years ago was a State Senator. He built the Baptist Church at Yalesville, mainly at his own expense. In his early business life he manufactured spoons for Russell Hall of Meriden." (JC&HR 8-17-1892, p. 19)

(G. I. MIX & CO.)

CROWN PRINCE
MALACCA PLATED
THE COLUMBIA

JAMES MIX
Albany, New York

The James Mix who designed the James Mix "Albany" souvenir spoon c. 1890 may have been a descendant of James Mix, silversmith in Albany, New York, 1817-1850. His son, James Mix, Jr., was listed in the Albany City Directories as a manufacturing jeweler, 1846-1850.

JAMES MIX

MODERN SILVER MFG. CO., INC.,
Brooklyn, New York

Listed in 1950 JC-K and 1958 JBG as manufacturers of silverplated wares.

HEIRESS

SILVER PLATE

JACOB A. MOLLER
New Rochelle, New York

Listed in 1907 New Rochelle City Directory as a silversmith. No other listing.

MONTGOMERY BROS.
Los Angeles, California

The Los Angeles City Directories list James Montgomery as watchmaker and jeweler from 1883-1886. The first listing for Montgomery Bros. (Jas. A. and Geo. A.) is for the year 1888. The same listing is carried for 1890. No distinction made between retailers and manufacturers in the directories.

On October 27, 1891, Montgomery Bros. registered Patent No. 20,270 for the manufacture of gold, silver and plated articles, flatware and jewelry. Their trademark is listed in JC souvenir section.

MONTGOMERY WARD & CO.
Chicago, Illinois

LAKESIDE BRAND

(First used in 1908 on silverplated flatware made by various manufacturer.)

MONTGOMERY WARD & CO.,

(First used 1887-1888)

PALACE BRAND

(Used 1886)

MONUMENTAL PLATING WORKS
Baltimore, Maryland

Listed in Baltimore City Directories 1887-1912 as silverplaters. Wm. Focke, proprietor.

MOORE BROS.
Attleboro, Massachusetts

Listed in Attleboro City Directories as manufacturing jewelers with John F. and Thomas H. Moore as owners from 1907-1916 and John F., Thomas H. and Charles E. Moore from 1916-1940.

M.B.

MOORE & HOFMAN
Newark, New Jersey
See Schmitz, Moore & Co.

Successors to Schmitz, Moore & Co. between 1915-1922. Succeeded by Moore & Son (?) before 1943.

Manufacturers of sterling silver dresserware, vanity and cigarette cases, tableware and novelties.

JOHN C. MOORE & SON
New York, New York

John Chandler Moore began the manufacture of silverware in 1827 and was later joined in business by his son, Edward C. Moore. John Moore was associated from 1832 to 1836 with the firm of Eoff & Moore (Garrett Eoff). He made silverware for Marquand & Co. and also for their successors, Ball, Thompkins & Black. In 1847 John Moore designed and patented a flatware pattern (Design Patent No. 124, May 29, 1847) that is similar to the *Prince Albert* design of Henry Hebbard, N.Y. silversmith (Directories 1847-49), the *Prince Albert* being derived from the *Albert* design made by C. J. Vander, Ltd. makers of hand forged silver. The same design was shown in an Elkington & Mason Co. catalog of 1851 and described as one of the "current styles in silver-plated wares."

Edward C. Moore learned his trade in his father's shop, and was later taken into partnership, finally succeeding his father on the latter's retirement 1851. Before this an arrangement had been effected to manufacture silverware solely for Tiffany & Co., which was continued until 1868 when, Tiffany & Co. becoming a corporation, they bought the entire Moore plant, Edward C. Moore becoming one of the directors. From its beginnings as a small shop the company developed into an industry giving employment to about 500 men.

J. C. M.

MOORE & LEDING, SILVERSMITHS
Washington, D.C.

Listed in the Washington, D.C. City Directories from 1882 to 1902. Listed as Moore & Leding, 1881-1899, jewelers. Listed as Robert Leding (successor to Moore & Leding (1900-1902), jeweler.

Moore & Leding marketed the "Washington City" and "Mount Vernon" souvenir spoons, both made by The Gorham Company. These two spoons were patented in 1890 and 1891, respectively, and were put on the market shortly after the first Witch spoon designed for Daniel Low Company.

R. L. MOOREHEAD & CO.
Providence, Rhode Island

Listed KJI 1918-19 as manufacturers of sterling and plated wares.

Fruit stand c. 1880. (Meriden Britannia Company)

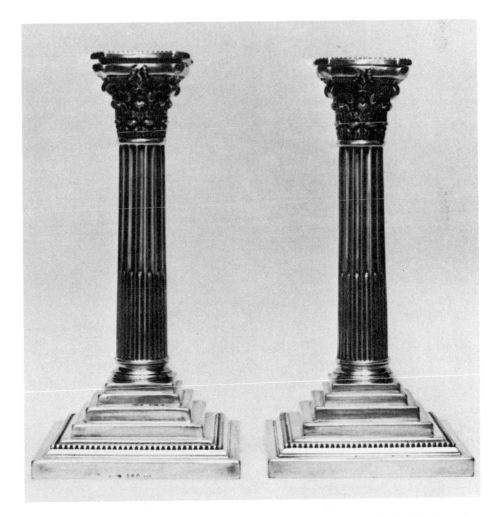

Candlesticks of Italian Renascence Corinthian design. Marked "Made and guaranteed by M. B. Co."

MORGAN MORGAN(S), JR.
New York, New York
See Geo. W. Shiebler & Co.

Morgan(s) was a silversmith in New York City who succeeded to the business of Albert Coles (q.v.) and was in turn succeeded by Geo. W. Shiebler & Co. He is listed in the New York City Directories 1879-80. A flatware design patent was obtained in his name February 5, 1878 and was later made by the Shiebler company.

MORGAN SILVER PLATE CO.
Winsted, Connecticut

"The Morgan Silver Plate Co. of Winsted, Conn. recently purchased the building in which its factory is located." (JW 6-8-1892)

"J. T. Morgan of the Morgan Silver Plate Co., Winsted, Conn. has recovered from an illness of several weeks. Arthur H. Morgan left Feb. 25 on a business trip." (JC&HR 3-6-1895, p. 20)

The Morgan Silver Plate Co. was listed as manufacturers of bookends and bridge accessories. (KJI 1931)

H. R. MORSS & CO., INC.
North Attleboro, Massachusetts

Listed c. 1930-1940. Manufacturers of sterling silver flatware, baby goods and hollow-handled knives, salad sets, etc.

MORSS

Trade Mark

MOSSBERG WRENCH COMPANY
Attleboro, Massachusetts

They advertised (*The Manufacturing Jeweler*, October 15, 1894) as manufacturers of novelties. Illustrated were a knife sharpener of silverplate for office or table use. In the advertisement the patent date of February 23, 1892 is stamped on the knife sharpeners, indicating that they were in business at least that early. A brief notice (JC&HR 2-27-1895, p. 22) states that the Mossberg Mfg. Co., Attleboro, Massachusetts, issued a catalog.

MT. VERNON COMPANY SILVERSMITHS, INC.
Mount Vernon, New York
See Gorham Corporation

Organized in 1914 with Harry A. MacFarland as president. It was the successor of Hayes & MacFarland which began in 1903. The Mauser Mfg. Company of New York and Roger Williams Silver Company of Providence, Rhode Island were part of the merger to form the Mount Vernon Company Silversmiths in 1914.

Purchased by the Gorham Corporation in 1913.

MUECK-CARY CO., INC.
New York, New York

Manufacturers of sterling wares in the 1940s and 1950s. The trademark is now owned by Towle Silversmiths.

THE PETER MUELLER-MUNK STUDIO
New York, New York

Advertised in *The Antiquarian* May 1928 that "The Best traditions of the silversmith's art are mirrored in the work produced under my personal supervision. Here are designed and manufactured candlesticks, tea and coffee sets, tea caddies, bowls, vases, trays, goblets, pitchers, boudoir sets, hand mirrors, perfume bottles, loving cups, brushes, combs and many other miscellaneous items." A teapot with ebony finial and ebony handle is illustrated under the caption "Hand Wrought Silver — Individual pieces or sets designed, reproduced or made to order."

MULFORD, WENDELL & CO.
Albany, New York

Their history can be traced to William Boyd, silversmith (b. 1775-d. 1840) who entered into partnership with Robert Shepard in 1810, under the name Shepard & Boyd (c. 1810-1830). They were succeeded by Boyd & Hoyt (c. 1830-1842); Boyd & Mulford (c. 1832-1842) and Mulford, Wendell & Co. c. 1843.

John H. Mulford and William Wendell, are listed as silversmiths, as are their predecessors.

Mulford and Wendell were also jobbers who did silverplating about 1855. They published an illustrated catalog in 1859.

MULHOLLAND BROS. INC.
Aurora, Illinois

Successor to Aurora Silver Plate Company between 1915-1922. Continued the manufacture of plated flatware and holloware until 1934 when they went out of business. D. E. Mulholland, president; W. S. Mulholland, vice president.

About 1930 it was called Mulholland Silver Co.

JOHN F. MULLER ASSOC., INC.
New York, New York

Listed JBG 1950s and 1960s as manufacturers and importers of silver goods.

MUSIC CENTER MINT
Nashville, Tennessee

No response to inquiries.

S. F. MYERS & CO.
New York, New York

Wholesale jewelers.

In business about 1860 as specialists in plating. (U.S. Patent, February 8, 1887) for jewelry and silverware, plated silver and clocks.

MYRICK, ROLLER & HOLBROOK
Philadelphia, Pennsylvania

In business before 1890. Out of business before 1904. Trademark found on souvenir spoons.

D. NAGIN MFG. CORP.
East Rutherford, New Jersey

Founded July 1957 by Dan Nagin under his own name. In May 1968 the company became D. Nagin Mfg. Corp. Manufacturers of sterling articles, mostly pendants.

NAPIER-BLISS CO.
Meriden, Connecticut
See Napier Co.

Successor to E. A. Bliss Co. about 1915. Succeeded by the Napier Company in 1920.

NAPIER COMPANY
Meriden, Connecticut

CHRONOLOGY

Carpenter & Bliss	1875-82
Carpenter & Bliss, Inc.	1882-83
E. A. Bliss	1883-90
E. A. Bliss, Inc.	1891-1920
The Napier Company	1922-

The original company started in 1875 by E. A. Bliss and J. E. Carpenter, taking over the Whitney & Rice concern where Bliss had been employed as a traveling salesman. At the start it was called Carpenter & Bliss and in 1882 was incorporated. It became the E. A. Bliss Co. by 1883. In 1890 they were offered inducements to move their factory to Meriden, where they incorporated a year later. They were making a variety of jewelry, novelties and staple goods. By 1893 they had added sterling silver novelties.

E. A. Bliss died in 1911 and his son William became active head of the company. In 1915, James H. Napier became associated with the company, and in a reorganization he became general manager. During 1918 they devoted much of their plant to the manufacture of war material. After World War I a large part of their activity was devoted to modern jewelry and many additions to their line of sterling novelties and dresserware. In 1920 Napier was elected president and the name of the company

changed to Napier-Bliss Co. Two years later, the name Napier Company was adopted.

DU BARRY

NAPIER-BLISS
(novelties)

PALM BEACH

SUREFIRE

NACO

NAPIER

NAPIER *Quality*

TRIANON

NASSAU LIGHTER CO.
New York, New York

Listed JC in sterling silver section in 1915. Out of business before 1922.

NATIONAL SILVER COMPANY
New York, New York

Manufacturers of sterling and plated silverware. Began with Samuel E. Bernstein who was first in business in New York in 1890. Became the National Silver Company before 1904.

Cheltenham & Company, Ltd., Sheffield, England, became a division of National Silver Company before 1950; the F. B. Rogers Silver Company was added in February 1955 and in 1956 they purchased the Ontario Manufacturing Company of Muncie, Indiana.

MONARCH SILVER COMPANY and VICEROY SILVER COMPANY are two tradenames recorded in the Trademark Division of the Patent Office by the National Silver Company in 1943 for use on silverplated flatware and cutlery.

N.S.C.

National STERLING

(On sterling)

*N*ASCO

NSC

S.E.B.

(On sterling and silver plate)

Mildred Quality
Silver Plate

National Silver Plate

Lady Berkshire

 Lord Berkshire

IMPERIAL PLATE

PERMA-BRITE

DOUBLE TESTED
SILVER PLATE

National Silver Co.

(On silverplate)

GUILDCRAFT

(On discontinued flatware
produced c. 1955)

NATIONAL SILVER DEPOSIT WARE CO., INC.
New York, New York

Listed KJI 1918-19.
Listed in JC 1922-1950. Manufacturers of silver and gold encrusted glassware, desk sets, ornamental serving trays and silverplated holloware.

T. E. NEILL CO.
Brooklyn, New York

TENCO

NESSLER & CO.
New York, New York

"Nessler & Company was founded in 1869 as Nessler & Redway. It was J. S. & C. L. Nessler in the 70's and Nessler & Bioren later. Still later it was Nessler & Co. It continued until c. 1907 and consisted of father and son. C. L. Nessler died in 1907 and the business was left to his son, Charles F., who continued under the same name. It was incorporated in 1912." (JC-W 2-5-1919)

NEVIUS COMPANY
New York, New York

Reigstered a trademark, No. 48,036, December 5, 1905 for table utensils made of sterling silver. The application was filed by Benjamin C. Nevius, treasurer, who stated that the trademark had been used continuously by them since 1897.
Out of business before 1915.

NEW AMSTERDAM SILVER CO.
New York, New York
See Knickerbocker Silver Co.

NEW ENGLAND SILVER CO.
Deering, Maine

Founded in 1894 by Joseph S. Dunham, son of Rufus Dunham. Joseph had formerly been associated with Stevens, Smart & Dunham

NEW ENGLAND SILVER CO.
QUADRUPLE PLATE.

NEW ENGLAND SILVER PLATE CO.
See Adelphi Silver Plate Co.
See American Silver Co.
See Bristol Brass & Clock Co.

Advertised in *St. Nicholas Magazine*, March 1878 that they furnish "first-class articles at a very low price. A set of six SOLID Silver Tea Spoons for $3.50" or "For 85 cents . . . one set of 6 quadruple tea spoons in case. Fine and heavily plated with pure nickel and coin silver, on a new metal, called Alfenide, which is very similar to the finest English white steel. It contains no *brass* or *German silver* in its composition, and consequently *no poison,* or disagreeable taste." The ad was copyrighted in 1877.

NEW ENGLAND SILVER PLATE CO.
Bridgeport, Connecticut

"The New England Silver Plate Co., Conn. has just been organized. The works will be in West End, Bridgeport. Stockholders are S. C. Osborne, Bridgeport; James Dowdle and D. J. Toothill, Orange, New Jersey." (JC&HR 9-18-1895, p. 26) Not the same New England Silver Plate Co. that was in New Haven, Connecticut.

NEW ENGLAND SILVERSMITHS
New York, New York

Makers of sterling silver goods c. 1950.

NES

NEW HAVEN SILVER PLATE CO.
Lyons, New York

The New Haven Silver Plate Company was established at Lyon, New York in September 1891. The business was purchased by the Manhattan Silver Plate Company of that city in November of that same year. They were successors in 1893 to A. H. Towar & Co, silverplaters in Lyons.
The Manhattan Silver Plate Company, the New Haven Silver Plate Company and A. H. Towar & Co. continued manufacturing operations after being taken over by the International Siver Company.

NEW ORLEANS SILVERSMITHS
New Orleans, Louisiana

Manufacturers of sterling and silverplate reproductions. Founded in 1938 by Karl Dingeldein, native of Hanau, Germany, whose family had been silversmiths since 1720. Mr. Dingeldein died about 1966 and the business was purchased by another young German silversmith, Hans Leutkemeier, originally from Darmstadt. Mr. Luetkemeier began his apprenticeship in Germany in 1952, serving three and a half years as an apprentice. This was followed by five years of working as a jeweler before obtaining full recognition as a goldsmith and silversmith.

(On sterling)

(On silverplate)

NEW YORK SILVER DEPOSIT CO.
Jersey City, New Jersey

Began as New York Silver Deposit Company, founding date unknown. Succeeded by Imperial Art Ware before 1915 and out of business before 1922.

NEW YORK SILVER PLATE CO.
New York, New York
See E. Magnus

"The New York Silver Plate Co., manufacturers of silver plated ware made an assignment. Emil Magnus is president and Stephen C. Duval, secretary. The company was incorporated Sept. 1896 and succeeded to the business carried on at 20 Warren Street by Mr. Magnus who made an assignment July 6, 1896." (JC&HR 8-18-1897, p. 9-10)

NEW YORK STAMPING CO.
Brooklyn, New York
Listed in JC in 1915-1922 in plated silver section.

(*Housefurnishing Goods.*)

NEWBURYPORT SILVER CO.
Keene, New Hampshire

Manufacturers of sterling silver, flat and holloware. Listed in the City Directory of Keene, New Hampshire 1905-1914. The firm was organized in 1904 with John Currier, President; Geo. E Stickney, treasurer; Caleb Stickney and Herbert N. Woodwell, managers. Caleb Stickney was once associated with the Towle Silver Company in Newburyport, Massachusetts and was in charge of the machinery of the new company while Mr. Woodwell did the designing and directed the finances. Woodwell had also been with the Towle Silver Company as an engraver in charge of the engraving room — at one time a most important function. John Currier was a prosperous manufacturer of automobile bodies in Amesbury and it is believed that he provided financial backing but took no active part in the management. The firm was unable to obtain loans from the Newburyport banks and moved to Keene, New Hampshire early in 1905. Woodwell died March 1907

and Stickney and his son assumed full charge. Poor management led the firm into bankruptcy in 1914. The silver stock was bought by Rogers, Lunt & Bowlen.

(*Sterling Silver Ware.*)

N. S. C.

(On plated silver)

WILLIAM F. NEWHALL
Lynn, Massachusetts

First established as a jewelry business by Stephen Cyrus Newhall in 1872. William Frederick Newhall entered the employ of his brother at that time and in 1885, after the death of Stephen, William succeeded to the business. In 1907 he took into partnership his eldest son, Fred Clinton Newhall. The company name became W. F. Newhall & Sons, Inc. before 1922.

Stephen is listed in the Lynn City Directories as a clock repairer, watchmaker and jeweler. William is listed as a clerk, jeweler and optician. Newhall's did special order work, enameling, engraving, die sinking and gold and silverplating.

The 1896-1922 editions of JC carry a trademark (No. 19,751 June 23, 1891 for flat and tableware) that is the handle of a spoon with an old woman and a cat. Newhall's sold many souvenir spoons. Some, at least, carry the Durgin Co. trademark.

There is no record of the shop after 1957.

E. NEWTON & CO.
New York, New York

Listed in JC 1896-1904 in the sterling silver section. Out of business before 915.

STERLING **N**

NIAGARA SILVER CO.
New York, New York
See Oneida Silversmiths
See Wm. A. Rogers, Ltd.

"The Niagara Silver Company has been incorporated to manufacture and sell silver and silver plated ware." (JW 10-11-1899, p. 25)

"The flatware department of the Pairpoint Mfg. Company has been purchased by the Niagara Silver Company." (JC-W 7-4-1900, p. 8)

Wm. A. Jameson was manager of the company.

R. S. MFG. CO.
COIN SILVER METAL
EXTRA COIN SILVER PLATE
EXTRA COIN SILVER No. 12 PLATE

NICHOLS BROS.
Greenfield, Massachusetts

Listed in 1896 Jewelers' Weekly as manufacturers of plated silverware.

NICHOLS BROS.
Greenfield, Mass.
12 dwt.

THE NICKEL SILVER FLATWARE CO.
Unionville, Connecticut

"The Nickel Silver Flatware Co. is in production, putting out, so they claim, not alone unplated, but silverplated and sterling silver." (JC&HR 6-6-1894)

NIEDERER & MOORE
Baltimore, Maryland

Listed in Baltimore City Directory in 1885 as a silversmith.

GEBRUEDER NOELLE
Luedenscheid, Germany

Registered trademark U.S. Patent Office, No. 11,800, December 16, 1884 for knives, forks and spoons. Also, No. 50,984, April 3, 1906 for knives, forks and spoons of britannia.

Listed in JC 1896-1922 in the plated silver section. No record after 1922.

(Knives, Forks, Spoons.)

NORBERT MFG. CO.
New York, New York

Manufacturers of sterling goods since c. 1950. No address listed 1974.

NORTHERN STAMPING & MFG. CO.
Seattle, Washington
See E. J. Towle Mfg. Co.

NORTHAMPTON CUTLERY CO.
Chicago, Illinois

Listed KJI 1918-19 as manufacturers of plated flatware.

NORWEGIAN SILVER CORP.
New York, New York

The Norwegian Silver Corporation is the U.S. distributor of sterling and silverplated holloware, flatware and jewelry made by Th. Marthinsen Sølvvarefabrikk a/s, Tønsberg, Norway, established in 1883 and by David Andersen a/s, Oslo, Norway, established in 1876. Both are third generation silversmithing firms.

NORWICH CUTLERY COMPANY
Norwich, Connecticut
See International Silver Company

Organized and wholly owned by William H. Watrous, of Rogers Cutlery Company, Hartford, Connecticut.

Made cutlery for plating from 1889. Did not use a trademark because they sold their products to other silver manufacturers.

One of the original companies to become part of the International Silver Company in 1898.

WILLIAM NOST CO., INC.
New York, New York

William Nost was a silversmith in New York before 1915. Succeeded by William Nost Company, Inc. before 1922. They made sterling silver holloware.

NOVELTY PLATING WORKS
Baltimore, Maryland

Listed in the Baltimore City Directories 1890-1915 as successors to Schrier & Protze who began silver-plating in 1888.

Anton Protze listed as proprietor 1893-1898. Louis Liepman, proprietor 1899-1915.

NOYES BROTHERS
New York, New York

Wholesalers of silverware and novelties. Begun in New York in 1892 by Pierrepont and Holton Noyes, sons of John Humphrey Noyes, founder of the Oneida Community.

This partnership was dissolved after about two years with Holton going into the restaurant business and Pierrepont Noyes returning to Niagara Falls to develop the Oneida Community silver company.

BENJ. D. NUITZ
Baltimore, Maryland

Listed in 1893 Baltimore City Directory under plated silverware.

NUSSBAUM & HUNOLD
Providence, Rhode Island
See Walter Hunold

 NUSSHOLD

O

OLD NEW ENGLAND CRAFTSMEN, INC.
Newburyport, Massachusetts

Makers of Colonial handwrought solid silver and reproductions. Listed in 1931 KJI. Out of business for many years.

PILLSBURY

PORTSMOUTH
(Reproductions)

OLD NEWBURY CRAFTERS, INC.
Newburyport, Massachusetts

Incorporated in 1916 by silversmiths of long experience. It has been producing and distributing fine handwrought silverware and holloware continuously since that date.

At the present time, the company is the largest producer of handwrought silver in the United States.

In 1964 they purchased the Worden-Munnis Co., founded in Boston in 1940 and are now producing their sterling holloware line.

Each craftsman at Old Newbury Crafters has a personal signature mark that is stamped on each piece of silver flatware.

Personal Signature Marks of the
 Newbury Crafters

Fletcher S. Carter	Robert H. Bean
Chester A. Dow	Chester A. Dow
James F. Harvey	James F. Harvey
Robert H. Lapham	Robert H. Lapham
Gayden F. Marshall	Gayden F. Marshall
Daniel S. Morrill	Daniel S. Morrill
Roger R. Rowell	Roger R. Rowell
Reynolds F. Senior	Reynolds F. Senior
George R. Woundy	George R. Woundy
In use as of June, 1965	In use as of May, 1974

OLIVER MFG. CO.
Los Angeles, California

Manufacturers of sterling novelties c. 1950.

N. & D. ONDERDONK
New York, New York

N. & D. Onderdonk were silversmiths working in New York c. 1800. They are listed in JC in the sterling silver section. Out of business before 1904.

N. & D. O.

ONEIDA SILVERSMITHS
Sherrill, New York

John Humphrey Noyes and a little association of men first began their experiment in communal living at Oneida Creek about 1848.

Their first products were canned fruits and vegetables which found a ready market. Later their chief support came from the manufacture of steel traps.

In 1877 the Oneida Community embarked on the manufacture of tableware. The Wallingford branch made ungraded, tinned, iron spoons in two patterns called "Lily" and "Oval." These two iron spoons were the direct ancestors of the whole line of Community Plate.

By 1878 the mill was turning out steel spoon blanks sold for plating to the Meriden Britannia Company. In 1880 the factory was moved to Niagara Falls.

Their first silverware could not compete with higher quality silver made by other companies. A decision was made to turn out a better quality and better designed line. Their new design called "Avalon" was exhibited in 1901 as the Buffalo Exposition.

In January 1902 the new line of Community Plate was introduced and, but, was not immediately successful. A complete change in advertising methods in high-priced, large-circulation magazines proved enormously effective. It was the first "pretty girl" advertising in America and not only affected the sales of their silver, it also had a profound effect on the whole advertising business. Between 1912-1914 the whole silverware plant was moved from Niagara Falls to Sherrill, New York.

In 1926 they opened a plant, the Kenwood Silver Company, in Sheffield, England and in 1929 bought Wm. A. Rogers, Ltd. Besides the main Wm. A. Rogers, Ltd. plant, they acquired four other factories and their brands; 1881 Rogers; Simeon L. & George H. Rogers Company and Heirloom.

One March 1, 1935, the company name was changed to Oneida, Ltd., and is now commonly known as Oneida Silversmiths.

In 1965 they adopted as their symbol of excellence the Roman cube "tessera hospitalis," which was placed in the hands of a visitor as a pledge of hospitality and friendship. Oneida's tessera is a cube of solid silver, engraved with the company name on all planes. Oneida began production of silverplated holloware in 1926. They sold their Canadian subsidiaries in February 1972.

J. Rogers & Co.

A.1. NICKEL SILVER No. 210

CARBON

N. F. SILVER CO., 1877

SILVER METAL

210 NEARSILVER

U. S. SILVER CO.

ALPHA PLATE

COMMUNITY

COMMUNITY PLATE

DURO PLATE

N. F. NICKEL SILVER

NIAGARA FALLS CO., 1877

O. C.

O. C. LUSTRA

ONEIDA

ONEIDA COMMUNITY DIAMOND
PLATE

ONEIDA COMMUNITY PAR PLATE

ONEIDA COMMUNITY RELIANCE
PLATE

ONEIDA COMMUNITY SILVER
PLATE

PURITAN SILVER CO.

REX PLATE

REX PLATE

RELIANCE

RELIANCE PLATE

TRIPLE PLUS

TUDOR PLATE

ONEIDACRAFT

(Used since Dec. 31, 1925)

ONEIDA STERLING
See Oneida Silversmiths

Production of sterling flatware was begun in 1946.

Oneida Sterling

(Sterling silver flatware. Used since January 25, 1945)

ONODAGO SILVER MFG. CO.
Syracuse, New York

"The Onodago Silver Mfg. Co. of Syracuse have incorporated. Directors are E. P. Goodrich and C. C. Goodrich, of Syracuse, George W. Hills and Frederick W. Chamberlain of Lyons, Elliott M. Tuttle of Munnsville, and S. C. Waterman of Oneida." (JC&HR 4-15-1896, p. 17)

ONTARIO MFG. CO.
Muncie, Indiana
See National Silver Company

Founded 1897. Succeeded by National Silver Company in 1956. Manufactured plated silverware.

HARVEY OSBORN SILVER CO.
Newark, New Jersey

Listed KJI 1918-19 as manufacturers of German silver brushes and mirrors and silver novelties.

OSBORN COMPANY
Lancaster, Pennsylvania
About 1897.

FRANK N. OSBORNE
New York, New York

Listed in JC 1904-1915. May have been wholesale jeweler or distributor.

Also used other trademarks on jewelry sold at the Chicago Columbian Exposition, 1892-1893.

No record after 1915.

XIX CENTURY
HEIRLOOM

No. 23,729 October 24, 1893
For jewelry, spoons, forks, ladles, cutlery, etc.

HEIRLOOM

No. 23,730 October 24, 1893

OVIATT & WARNER
Portland, Oregon

Listed in the Portland City Directory for 1894 and 1895 only. Listed under sterling silver section of the 1896 edition of the JC as out of business in 1896. No information in the Portland newspaper index.

O. & W.

OXFORD HALL SILVERSMITHS, LTD.
New Cassel, L. I. New York

Mentioned in JC-K 1974.

OXFORD SILVERSMITHS CO.
New York, New York

Listed 1918-19 KJI and JC-K 1950 as manufacturers of silverplated wares.

THE PAIRPOINT CORPORATION
New Bedford, Massachusetts

Organized in 1880 as the Pairpoint Mfg. Co., with Edward D. Mandel as president. Thomas J. Pairpoint, for whom the company was named, had most recently been with the Meriden Britannia Company.

Pairpoint served his apprenticeship in Paris and later worked for the prominent firm of Lambert &

Rawlings in London. He was chief designer for the Gorham Manufacturing Company from about 1868 until the late 1870s. During this time he designed many pieces of the Gorham Company's regular line as well as special exhibition pieces.

While employed by the Gorham Company, Pairpoint was one of the six artists who submitted designs for the William Cullen Bryant testimonial vase, presented to the poet June 20, 1876. While he lost the competition to James H. Whitehouse, head designer of Tiffany & Company, his design received favorable press coverage. It was described (Art Journal, 1876) as "a poetical work of Grecian character, gracefully elongated to monumental proportions."

Pairpoint was one of the outstanding proponents of the Renaissance Revival. This was clearly illustrated in "The Century Vase" he and George Wilkinson designed for the Gorham Company and which was exhibited at the Philadelphia Centennial in 1876.

Pairpoint was among the first in this country to visualize silver as an art medium. Repoussé figures on his work were often drawn from mythology and other literature. No doubt the literary character of his work may be ascribed to his association with Morel Ladeuil from whom he gained an interest in Renaissance design.

In 1877 Pairpoint left the Gorham Company to become designer and modeler for the Meriden Britannia Company, Meriden, Connecticut. Shortly before leaving the latter, about August 1879, he prepared a series of articles, "Art Work & Silver," (Jewelers' Circular, September 1879 through March 1880) in which he discussed silver as an art medium. The esteem in which he was held by that publication is reflected in the editorial comment where Pairpoint is spoken of as "one of the most skillful and artistic designers of the present day, having a reputation that is world wide."

This reputation served the newly formed Pairpoint Mfg. Co. well as it soon commanded favorable attention for the design of its products. In 1882 the Jewelers' Circular commented editorially, "The Pairpoint Mfg. Co. is introducing new and more artistic designs by T. J. Pairpoint, a gentleman of rare ability in classical subjects."

On April 1, 1885, Pairpoint severed his connections with the company bearing his name and announced his intention of going into "manufacturing on his own account." There seems to be no record that he really did start a new business. The listing of his name in the Providence, Rhode Island City Directory which had run from 1870 through 1877 and then dropped, reappeared in 1887. The reason for leaving the company is not known. Old-timers there remembered him well but did not know the reason for his leaving.

Pairpoint's obituary (Providence Journal, August 30, 1902, p. 3) says that his death came with slight warning. It went on to say that ". . . for several years past Mr. Pairpoint had been in poor health, but not of a nature to cause great anxiety. [He is said to have been diabetic.] Mr. Pairpoint was well known locally as an expert silversmith and designer, although he had not been actively engaged in business during recent years."

Although T. J. Pairpoint left the company, the tradition of fine design he had established was maintained by the firm. They became one of the country's largest manufacturers of plated silverware

and carried on an extensive export trade, expecially with Austrialia.

In 1894 the Mount Washington Glass Company became part of the Pairpoint organization. This event and their expanded production was noted in the various trade journals.

"The Pairpoint Mfg. Co., owners of the justly celebrated Mt. Washington Glass Co., New Bedford, Mass., contemplate moving their New York business, May 1, from the old stand, 46 Murray St., to Maiden Lane. The new lines of silver plated hollow and glassware and novelties, fine decorated china and glass of this company and their aggregation of rich cut glass tableware, all at popular prices and styles distinctly original, are well calculated to keep this establishment in the front ranks of manufacturers of art wares. An important feature of this establishment is the manufacture from start to finish of special lines of rich cut glass for sterling silver mountings, and manufacturers of sterling silver can avail themselves of the prestige of this company's position to supply designs suited to their requirements and made to the patron's individual suggestions." (JC&HR 3-17-1897, p. 21)

In 1900 financial difficulties of both companies led to their merging to form the Pairpoint Corporation. The combined operations of silverplated wares and glass manufacturing continued successfully until the Depression in 1929, when the company suffered reverses from which it never recovered. Only the glass working part continued under various firm names. Finally, all operations ceased in 1958. The flatware department was purchased by the Niagara Silver Co. in 1900. Some of the dies and patterns were sold to the Rockford Silver Plate Co. Production of glassware resumed on a limited basis in the 1970s.

PAIRPOINT
FLAT 1880 WARE.
BEST
(Flatware.)

BRISTOL PLATE CO.

(Hollowware.)

TRADE MARK.
(Hollowware.)

(On Sheffield reproductions)

PALMER & BACHELDER
Boston, Massachusetts

In the 1860s they purchased Reed & Barton wares "in the metal" and operated their own plating establishment.

PALMER & OWEN
Cincinnati, Ohio

Listed in Cincinnati City Directories 1850-1859 as silversmiths who operated a silverware factory.

Wine bottle holder. A felt lining not only protects the bottle but helps keep the contents cool. (Meriden Britannia Co., patented March 8, 1881)

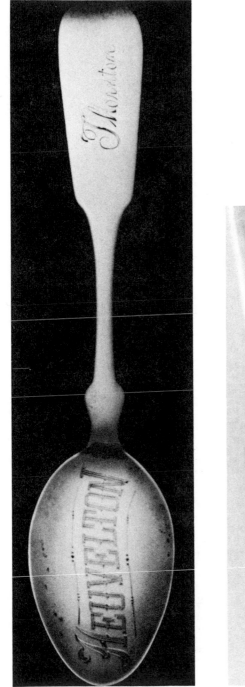

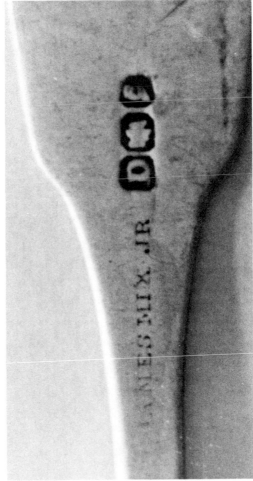

"Pseudo hallmarks" are often accompanied by retailer's marks. (James Mix, Jr., Albany, New York)

PALMER & PECKHAM
North Attleboro, Massachusetts

Listed in JC 1896. Out of business before 1904.

P & P
STERLING.

PARAGON PLATE

A private mail order company (Sears Roebuck & Co.) trademark. Used by International Silver Company c. 1910. In a spiral-bound booklet offered by Follett Studios, Moorhead, Minnesota, there are reprints of pages from various catalogs. On one, there is a teaspoon in the *Royal Oak* pattern "Double Triple Paragon Brand." The ad says it was manufactured by the most renowned firm of silversmiths in the country and will outwear any other brand, including any Rogers brand.

PARKER & CASPER BRITANNIA CO.
See Parker & Casper

PARKER & CASPER CO.
Meriden, Connecticut
See International Silver Co.
See Wilcox Silver Plate Co.

Organized by Charles Casper, John E. Parker, Edmund Parker, Phillip S. Pelton and Samuel L. Dodd, Jr. Incorporated August 6, 1866 with Samuel Dodd, president, under the name Parker & Casper Britannia Co. In May 1867 it became Parker & Caspar Co.

They were specialists in silverplated holloware.

The business was sold in 1869 to the Wilcox Silver Plate Co. which became part of International Silver Co. in 1898.

CHARLES PARKER CO.
Meriden, Connecticut

Spoonmakers c. 1887-1907.

PARKS BROS. & ROGERS
Providence, Rhode Island and New York

Established in 1892 by Geo. W. Parks, Wm. C. Parks and Everett I. Rogers who bought out the American Lever cuff and collar button portion of Howard & Son, the latter devoting all their interests to the silver business. Listed until c. 1930 as manufacturers of 10, 14K gold and gold-filled cuff buttons, collar buttons, cuff links, dress sets, collar pins and grips, bobbettes, scarf pins, lingerie and tie clasps.

G. W. PARKS COMPANY
Providence, Rhode Island

Successors to Hayden Mfg. Co. before 1909. Listed in JC in 1909-1915 as manufacturers of sterling and plated silver. Out of business before 1922.

(On sterling silver)

HOPE SILVER CO.
(On plated silver)

PATENT SILVERWARE MFG. CO.
Buffalo, New York

"The Patent Silverware Mfg. Co. was incorporated for purchasing, selling and manufacturing all kinds of silverware, and to purchase and produce patent rights, etc., patent devices of their own. Frank E. Comstock, Buffalo; B. N. Reynolds, Lakeville, N.Y., and Edith L. Johnston, Wheeling, West Virginia." (JC&HR 11-1-1893 p. 7)

PAUL REVERE SILVER CO., INC.
Boston, Massachusetts

Registered trademark U. S. Patent No. 85,612, March 5, 1912 for plated silverware. Out of business before 1922.

PAUL REVERE

PAYE & BAKER MFG. CO.
North Attleboro, Massachusetts

Successors to Simmons & Paye before 1891. Their first products were souvenir spoons of sterling silver. They also made plated silver table novelties, holloware and Dutch silver reproductions.

Last record found was c. 1935.

Flatware production discontinued c. 1920.

GEO. W. PAYSON & CO.
Baltimore, Maryland

Listed in Baltimore City Directory in 1904 as a silversmith.

C. D. PEACOCK
Chicago, Illinois

Established in 1837 by Elijah Peacock from London. They specialized in clock repairing and adjusting of chronometers for Great Lakes sailing vessels before Chicago was linked to the east by telegraph in 1848 or by railroad in 1852. The company became C. D. Peacock in 1838 and was incorporated in 1860. It was one of the first retail establishments to market flatware stamped with the store name. In 1903 they marketed Gorham's *Cambridge* pattern under the name *Crofut*.

PEERLESS SILVER COMPANY
Brooklyn, New York

Listed 1936 Jobber's handbook as manufacturers of plated wares, pewter salts and pepper sets and novelties. Listed through 1960.

 LA FRANCE

PELTON BROS. SILVER PLATE CO.
St. Louis, Missouri
See Merry & Pelton Silver Co.

Listed in St. Louis City Directories 1872-1900 as manufacturers of plated silverware.

TRIPLE PLATE 12
SECTIONAL PLATE XII
STANDARD PLATE 4
(Flatware.)

(Hollowware.)

J. PENFIELD & COMPANY
Savannah Georgia
See Black, Starr & Frost, Ltd.

In business from 1820-1828. Partners were Josiah Penfield, Moses Eastman and Frederick Marquand.

J. C. PENNEY CO. INC.
The patent number indicates a date of about 1925.

PAT. 72786 J. C. PENNEY CO. INC.

PENNSYLVANIA SILVERWARE COMPANY
Kane, Pennsylvania

Manufacturers of plated silver holloware and soda fountain supplies c. 1920-35.

TRADE MARK
PENNSYLVANIA
SILVERWARE CO
KANE. PA.

D. C. PERCIVAL & CO.
Boston, Massachusetts

Advertised as manufacturers of silverplated novelties (JC&HR 9-14-1892, p. 30)

L. S. PETERSON CO.
North Attleboro, Massachusetts

Manufacturers of novelties of sterling and silverplate c. 1940 to the present. No reply to recent inquiry.

L. S. P.
L. S. P. Co.

J. P. PETTERSON
Chicago, Illinois

Listed c. 1925-43 as manufacturer of handmade sterling silver flatware and holloware; reproductions and special order work.

J. P. P.

W. H. PFEIFFER
Niagara Falls, New York

Listed in the 1890 Niagara Falls City Directory as maker of silver and plated silverware.

F. P. PFLEGHAR & SON
New Haven, Connecticut

The company name first appeared in the New Haven City Directories in 1890. Prior to that Frank P. Pfleghar had been in business alone at that address for a few years. The 1918 Directory lists a change of ownership from Frank P. Pfleghar, Sr. and F. P. Pfleghar to Henry W. Ibelshauser and Max Voight but the business was still operating under the name F. P. Pfleghar & Son. The last listing was in 1919. The type of business was described as "machinists," then "machinists and hardware," or "machinists and hardware mfgrs."

The articles on which the imprint was found are silverplated corn holders. In the Patent Office records Patent #567,284, Sept. 8, 1896 was taken out by Charles W. Stebbins, Hartford, Conn., and assigned to F. P. Pfleghar & Son, New Haven, Conn.

F. P. PFLEGHAR & SON
NEW HAVEN, CONN.
PAT. SEPT. 8 — 96

PHELPS & CARY CO.
New York, New York
See Hartford Sterling Co.
See The Tennant Co.

Listed in JC 1904 in sterling silver section as out of business. Trademark identical to that of Hartford Sterling Co. and The Tennant Co. except for initials in shield. Phelps & Cary business was purchased by the Hartford Sterling Company. H. A. Cary went into business for himself in 1900.

STERLING
TRADE MARK

PHILADELPHIA PLATE CO.
Attributed in *Century of Silver,* to a Division of the International Silver Company. Not confirmed by them.

PHILADELPHIA SILVERSMITHING CO.
Philadelphia, Pennsylvania

In business c. 1890. Listed in JC in sterling silver section 1915-1922. Last record found was c. 1935.

THOMAS PHILE
Baltimore, Maryland

Listed in Baltimore City Directories 1871-1872, 1879-1887 as a whitesmith.

PHILLIPS MFG. CO. INC.
Meriden, Connecticut

Listed 1927 and 1931 KJI as manufacturers of plated holloware and pewterware.

ALBERT PICK & CO.
Bridgeport, Connecticut

Manufacturers of plated silver flatware and holloware. Successors to the E. H. H. Smith Silver Company in 1920. Last appeared in the Bridgeport City Directory in 1927. Said to be still in business.

ACORN BRAND

EVERWEAR

STERLINGUARD

J. V. PILCHER
Louisville, Kentucky

Manufacturers of plated compacts and cigarette cases c. 1940.

PILCHER

W. L. & H. E. PITKIN
Hartford, Connecticut
See Eagle Sterling Company

"The creditors of the firm of W. L. & H. E. Pitkin, Hartford, Connecticut, silverware manufacturers, held a meeting to arrange a compromise. Pitkin had been in business for more than 20 years." (JW 5-5, 1886, p. 20)

"W. L. & H. E. Pitkin were related to John Owen Pitkin and Walter Pitkin in the silver business c. 1830-80 under the firm name J. O. & W. Pitkin. "William Leonard Pitkin, senior member of the former firm of W. L. & H. E. Pitkin, silversmiths and silverplaters, died this week.

Mr. Pitkin was one of the oldest silversmiths in the country and a pioneer in this state [Connecticut] to combine the art with the silver plating business. In 1856 he came to this city and bought out the silversmith and silver plating business then conducted by the late O. D. Seymour. He also bought out a similar business conducted by H. I. Sawyer.

"Early in 1863 Mr. Pitkin's brother, Horace Edward Pitkin, came over from East Hartford and be-

came associated with him in the firm of W. L. & H. E. Pitkin, which continued in existence for more than 31 years. July 1, 1894 they closed out the business and sold the machinery to the Eagle Sterling Company of Glastonbury. Late in the same year both brothers formed a business engagement with the Glastonbury company and have since worked there." (JC&HR 2-27-1895, p. 9)

PITTSBURGH SILVERWARE CO.
Pittsburgh, Pennsylvania

Listed in the Pittsburgh City Directories from 1884 through 1887.

The 1884 directory lists it as the Pittsburgh Silverware Installment Company.

The 1885, 1886 and 1887 directories list it as the Pittsburgh Silverware Company.

The 1887 directory gives the last listing as follows: Pittsburgh Silverware Company, 511 Market St., Manufacturers' Agents for Fine Electro-Plated Ware, Silverware, watches, jewelry leased on easy payments. F. R. Jones, Manager.

No trademark shown.

PITTSBURGH SILVERWARE INSTALLMENT COMPANY
Pittsburgh, Pennsylvania
See Pittsburgh Silverware Co.

Listed in the Pittsburgh City Directory 1884.

GUSTAVUS A. POHLMAN
Baltimore, Maryland

Listed in Baltimore City Directories 1903-1904 as a silversmith.

JOHN POLHEMUS
New York, New York
See Geo. W. Shiebler & Co.

John Polhemus was a silversmith, listed in New York City Directories 1833-40 with the firm of Van Cott & Polhemus, also, Polhemus & Strong, c. 1845 where he made silver for Tiffany & Co. Records in the U. S. Patent Office indicate that he was associated with Henry Hebbard (q.v.) c. 1855 when the two obtained design patents for flatware. This same flatware was later made by the Geo. W. Shiebler & Co. Other flatware design patents obtained in the name of Polhemus from 1860-70 were made by Shiebler and one obtained in 1874 was made by the Whiting Mfg. Co.

POOL & CO.
Baltimore, Maryland
CHRONOLOGY

Mitchell & Pool	1889-94
B. Pool & Co.	1894-99
Pool & Company	1899-1915

Organized in 1889 as Mitchell & Pool, silverplaters; succeeded by B. Pool & Co., 1894; and, by Pool & Company in 1899.

POOLE SILVER CO.
Taunton, Massachusetts

Founded in 1893 in Taunton, Massachusetts with a small two-room factory as manufacturers of plated silverware. Originally called Poole & Roche. Mr.

Poole bought out his partner Mr. Roche and was sole owner until his death when his three sons took over the active management. In 1946 they retired and sold the company to an investment group headed by Sidney A. Kane of Providence, Rhode Island. The company has grown rapidly.

In 1946 a sterling silver department was added and in 1964 a brass division.

Today the company operates the Poole Silver Company for plated holloware, the Bristol Silver division, founded in 1950, for popular priced plated holloware as well as the above. Purchased by the Towle Mfg. Co. in 1971.

(On sterling silver) (*Quadruple Plate.*)

POOLE SILVER CO.
TAUNTON, MASS
NICKEL SILVER

HAND
HAMMERED

TRADEMARK
PEWTER *by* POOLE

(On plated silver)

BRISTOL SILVER CORP.
POOLE STERLING CO.

POPE'S ISLAND MFG. CORPORATION
New Bedford, Massachusetts

Incorporated in 1890 on the island from which it took its name. Horse bits and harness trimming were manufactured at these works. As the company was listed among manufacturers of silverplated wares by the JC 1896 until 1915, some of these trappings must have been plated silver.

NON-CORROSIVE

PORTER BRITANNIA & PLATE COMPANY
Taunton, Massachusetts

Organized in 1859. E. W. Porter of Reed & Barton, became superintendent of the new company. Their products were similar to those made by Reed & Barton. In business at least until the 1870s.

FRANKLIN PORTER
Danvers, Massachusetts

Franklin Porter's early artistic training was at the Rhode Island School of Design, followed by technical training at Browne and Sharpe in Providence. For many years his artistic inclinations took second place to the need to support a family. All the while though he made brass and copper pieces and occasionally silver when he could afford the raw material. In 1924 when he reached his fifty-fifth birthday he was released from his factory job without a pension. On that date, May 9, 1924, he purchased a copy of

Bigelow's *Historic Silver of the Colonies and its Makers* and joined the ranks of American silversmiths. In his journal, Porter wrote "January 1, 1925. Beginning this date, I began the practice of attaching my mark ℉ to every piece of work executed by me on which it is practicable to attach same, together with 'F. Porter' and 'Sterling' in order to distinguish my work, should any of it survive, in years to come, from that of F. Porter, Pewterer, of Connecticut."

Sterling   F. Porter   ℉

H L P

(HLP Mark of daughter, Helen Porter Philbrick, used on silver pins made in 1926)

E S D P

(ESDP Mark of adopted son, used April 1927-May 1928 on flatware)

J. POSNER & SONS. INC.
New York, New York

Manufacturers of silver goods c. 1960.

THE POTOSI SILVER CO.
Birmingham, England

Founded by Levi and Salaman who were electroplaters and silversmiths in 1870. They absorbed the Potosi Silver Company in 1878.

It was succeeded by Barker Bros. Silversmiths, Ltd., Unity Works, Birmingham, England between 1915 and 1922.

On October 19, 1886 they registered a U. S. Patent for plated silver on white metal.

The Potosi Silver Company name was probably derived from the Potosi Mine, discovered in 1545 in the area that was later to be named Bolivia.

(*White Metal.*)

S. C. POWELL
New York, New York

Catalogs of 1900 in existence showing he was in business by then as manufacturer of sterling silver novelties. Out of business before 1909.

PREISNER SILVER COMPANY
Wallingford, Connecticut

Manufacturers of sterling silver articles c. 1935 to the present. No reply to recent inquiry.

P S CO.

PREMIER CUTLERY INC.
New York, New York

Manufacturers of plated silver cutlery c. 1920.

PREMIER SILVER CO.
Brooklyn, New York

Manufacturers of sterling silverware c. 1920.

PRESTO CIGARETTE CASE CORP.
North Attleboro, Massachusetts

Manufacturers of gold, sterling and plated silver cigarette cases c. 1920-1930.

JOHN PRICE
Newark, New Jersey

Optician and silversmith working c. 1840-60. Manufacturer of gold and silver spectacles, silver spoons, etc. Succeeded by his son, Henry M. Price, c. 1860-62.

PRILL SILVER CO., INC.
New York, New York

Edward Prill, Inc. listed in 1936-37. Prill Silver Co. successors (?) c. 1940-45. Manufacturers of sterling articles to the present. No reply to recent inquiry.

J. N. PROVENZANO
New York, New York

In business before 1896. Distributors (?) of sterling silverware, gold and platinum seed pearl and gun metal goods.
  Not listed after 1904.

(On Knives.)

PROVIDENCE STOCK CO.
Providence, Rhode Island

Listed in JC in 1896-1904 in sterling silver section. Subsequent listings are under jewelry and watch attachments, chains, fobs and bracelets. Last record found was 1950.

TRADE   MARK.

PRYOR MFG. CO., INC.
Newark, New Jersey

Listed in JC in 1915 in sterling silver section.
  Consolidated with B. M. Shanley, Jr., Co. between 1915-22.

PUTNAM & LOW
See Shreve, Crump & Low Co., Inc.

QUAKER SILVER CO., INC.
North Attleboro, Massachusetts
See Gorham Corporation

Makers of sterling and silverplated holloware, trophies, novelties and pewterware. In business in North Attleboro, Massachusetts at least as early as 1926. Purchased by the Gorham Corp. in 1959.

NARRANGANSETT
(Used on pewter)

QUAKER
VOGUE

(On silverplate; used since February 1926)

QUAKER VALLEY MFG. CO.
Chicago, Illinois

Trademark used c. 1900 on silverplated articles used in direct sales.

CUVEE

QUEEN CITY SILVER CO., INC.
Cincinnati, Ohio

Manufacturers of plated silver holloware c. 1888. Liquidated in 1949.

COVENANT
(On pewterware)

QUEEN'S ART PEWTER, LTD.
Brooklyn, New York

Founded in 1920 by Anton Theurer and _____ Bower (now deceased). Mr. Theurer was born in Germany and learned the trade of spinning there. He came to this country and started his own business.

He is now retired. John Arcate, with the company since 1960, learned the trade from Mr. Theurer and operates the business today.

QUEEN'S ART PEWTER LTD.

R

RACINE SILVER PLATE CO.
Racine, Wisconsin
See Rockford Silver Plate Co.
See Sheets-Rockford Silver Plate Co.

Founded in 1873 in Racine, Wisconsin. Moved to Rockford, Illinois 1882 and renamed Rockford Silver Plate Co.

"The Guild Stamp Design adopted by the Executive Committee of the United States Guild for flatware, will be used by the Racine Silver Plate Co. on triple plated goods, with ten percent extra weight of silver, without any extra cost. These goods will be sold only to members of the United States and State Associations." (*American Jeweler,* Feb. 1882, p. 44)

"Mr. Purdy of Purdy & Stein is the originator of the stamp." (*American Jeweler,* Feb. 1882, p. 44)

"The Racine Silver Plate Co. (Wisconsin) was moved to Rockford, Illinois." (*American Jeweler,* June 1882, p. 133)

RADAR SILVERSMITHS, INC.
Brooklyn, New York

Manufacturers of sterling lamps and lighters c. 1950.

RA

WILLIAM T. RAE
Newark, New Jersey

Silversmith working c. 1856-64. Successor to A. J. Williams.

RAIMOND SILVER MFG. CO.
Chelsea, Massachusetts

Currently advertise as manufacturers and distributors of sterling and silverplated goods.

"Purchased W. & S. Blackinton Co., Inc. of Meriden, Connecticut, including inventory, materials, existing contracts and tradenames.

"Anthony S. Maisto, independent designer and owner of Maisto Silver, Inc., was named general manager.

"Blackinton was established in 1865 in North Attleboro and moved to Meriden after acquisition by the now defunct Ellmore Silver Co., in 1938." When Ellmore's assets were assigned to creditors in 1960, Blackinton was purchased by Alexander Land of Westport, owners of the present site, who subsequently sold it to a corporation headed by Irving R. Stich, prominent Hartford area builder and developer who backed revitalization of Blackinton in 1961." (*Meriden Journal,* April 26, 1966) Among the products advertised by Raimond's are those of Nils-Johan and Viner's of Sheffield. No reply from Raimond's to recent inquiry.

HARRY S. RAINS
New York, New York
Silverplaters c. 1920.

LA MILITAIRE

RAND & CRANE
Boston, Massachusetts

Successors to C. W. Kennard & Co., Boston in 1886. U. S. Patent registration for HOLMES trademark, May 5, 1891 to be used on solid and plated souvenir spoons and forks.

The company was listed in JC 1896-1922, but the HOLMES trademark was not used after 1903.

HOLMES

THE RANDAHL SHOP
Chicago, Illinois

Julius Olaf Randahl was founder of The Randahl Shop, Park Ridge and Chicago, Illinois. Randahl was born December 21, 1880 in Oëland, Sweden, a small island in the Baltic off the coast of Kalmar. He was apprenticed to a silversmith named J. G. Henshall and after he finished his training he came to the United States in 1901. After working for Tiffany and for Gorham, he worked in his KALO SHOP which made only fine handwrought silver. The shop was first located in Park Ridge and later in Chicago, where it remained until 1971. It closed because of the lack of young silversmiths to enter the business.

In 1910, Randahl, who made only holloware, formed a partnership with Matthias Hanck, a jeweler in Park Ridge. This partnership lasted only one year. The mark used during the partnership was JULMAT, a combination of both their first names.

In 1911 Randahl opened his own business, The Randahl Shop. The early trademark was his initials JOR with a silversmith's hammer drawn through them. Around 1915 the business was moved from Park Ridge to Chicago. It was forced to close during World War I because the men had to go into war work. It re-opened in another location in Chicago in 1919 and in 1930 in still another location closer to the downtown stores, namely Marshall Field's and Peacock's, both of which made a lot of his silver. Sometime in the 1930s the JOR trademark was dropped and the name RANDAHL was used after that. By 1950, both sons were in business with him and they built a factory in Skokie, a suburb just west of Evanston. Randahl's sons, Julius Olaf Randahl, Jr. and E. Scott Randahl, continued the business until 1965 at which time they sold it to Reed & Barton. It is now their RANDAHL division, using the Randahl trademark. The original founder died April 1972.

Randahl Jewelers in Park Ridge and The Cellini Shop in Evanston, Illinois, are owned by the two sons.

RANDAHL

C. RAY RANDALL & CO.
North Attleboro, Massachusetts

Manufacturers of sterling silver, 10k gold and gold-filled bar pins, brooches, necklaces, belt buckles, scarf pins, links and pin sets.

Listed in JC 1915-1922. Last record found was 1935.

STERLING CRR

RANDALL & FAIRCHILD
See Fairchild & Co.

RAY SILVER CO.
Rockford, Illinois

A division of Sheets-Rockford Silver Co.

RAYMOND MANUFACTURING COMPANY
Muncie Indiana

Silverplaters. Out of business before 1920.

SOLID YUKON SILVER WARRANTED

DAVID REAY, JR.
Baltimore, Maryland

Listed in Baltimore City Directories 1865-1873 as a silverplater.

REDDALL & CO., INC.
Newark, New Jersey

Listed as John W. Reddall & Co. in 1896 Jewelers' Weekly.

Listed in JC 1896-1904 in sterling silver section. Out of business before 1909.

REDFIELD & RICE
New York, New York
See Bernard Rice's Sons

"Established in New York City in 1852." (Adv. *New York Tribune,* Nov. 24, 1868)

REDLICH & CO.
New York, New York
See Elgin Silversmith Co., Inc.

Organized February 1890 as Ludwig, Redlich & Co. by Adolph Ludwig, who had for nine years been a designer of silver for Geo. W. Shiebler Co. and A. Alec Redlich, who had been for many years in the diamond business. In the latter part of 1895 Adolph Ludwig sold his interest and the company became Redlich & Co. This firm was taken over in 1946 by the Elgin Silversmith Co. The Redlich trademark is still used. Products are sterling silverware, holloware and 14K gold wares.

TRADE MARK

REED & BARTON
Taunton, Massachusetts

Isaac Babbitt and William W. Crossman, both of Taunton, Massachusetts, formed the partnership of BABBITT & CROSSMAN in 1824 that led to what is now Reed & Barton.

Babbitt had opened a small jewelry store in 1822. The small workshop in the back held his attention more than selling jewelry and repairing watches. Aware of the public's preference for the new britannia ware, he often discussed its properties with his friend, William Porter, who was also a jeweler.

Early in 1824, after much experimenting, Babbitt hit upon the right combination for producing this new alloy.

William Crossman completed his apprenticeship in the jewelers' trade; became dissatisfied with his job in Castleton, Vermont and returned to Taunton.

Babbitt and Crossman decided to pool their resources and experience in a partnership to manufacture britannia ware, though they did not abandon the jewelry store.

They entered this new industry just at the time when mechanization put many establishments, that continued handwrought production, out of business. Because of the uncertainty of their ability to produce and market britannia, they also turned out a great deal of pewter.

Their business prospered so that in 1826 they were able to build a new shop on Fayette Street, equipped with steam power. New machinery was made by Nathaniel Leonard of Taunton. Babbitt was superintendent; William W. Porter, foreman and it is assumed that Crossman managed the jewelry store and sales of the new factory products.

By 1827, with business increasing, more capital was needed so William Allen West bought into the business and a new partnership was formed under the name BABBITT, CROSSMAN & COMPANY. The jewelry store was apparently sold at this time.

On February 18, 1829, Isaac Babbitt sold his interest in the partnership and Zephaniah A. Leonard bought a one-third interest. The new company of CROSSMAN, WEST & LEONARD was formed.

On August 18, 1830 this partnership was dissolved and a joint-stock company, the TAUNTON BRITANNIA MANUFACTURING COMPANY was formed.

On February 16, 1833 the TAUNTON BRITANNIA MANUFACTURING COMPANY was reorganized. When it failed in November 1834, only three people had faith to continue. They were the company agent, Benjamin Pratt; Henry Reed, a spinner and his friend, Charles E. Barton, the solderer.

Barton, brother-in-law of William Crossman, had moved to Taunton from Warren, Rhode Island and started to work in 1827 at the age of 19 as an apprentice.

Henry Good Reed was the son of a family prominent in Taunton for five generations.

Knowledge of britannia manufacturing was their chief asset. To this, Benjamin Pratt contributed his experience in salesmanship. Once again, April 1, 1835, the TAUNTON BRITANNIA MANUFACTURING COMPANY was under new management.

Reed & Barton rented a few of the tools and equipment of the old company while Pratt sold what he could and tried to collect money owed to the company. By the end of 1836, the business had survived and made slight gains. Horatio Leonard transferred to his son, Gustavus, all rights, title and the stock and tools of the business. Soon afterwards an agreement was drawn up that left ownership of the factory itself in the Leonard family and granted to Reed & Barton one-third ownership each in the tools of the company as well as one-third interest in profits. The Taunton Britannia Manufacturing Company remained in legal existence only in the capacity of a landlord. The operating company was known as LEONARD, REED & BARTON and on February 20, 1837 began business under the new name.

The year 1837 was not an auspicious one for a struggling business. More than 600 banks closed their doors. Nine-tenths of the factories of the eastern states were said to have closed. Once again, they managed to survive.

By 1840, Henry Reed and Charles Barton purchased Leonard's interest in the company. Leonard continued to work for the company as salesman-treasurer and the Leonard, Reed & Barton mark was used on some company wares. However, when the company applied for a renewal of their trademark registration, they claimed that the name "REED & BARTON" had been used since August 26, 1840. Possibly both marks were used from 1840 to 1847.

By 1848, Reed & Barton were turning their attention to plated silverware.

The transition from the 1837 Reed & Barton shops to the 1859 factory was gradual, but, inevitable. Specialization emerged through necessity for business growth. New marketing methods were introduced and were extremely successful.

The 1850s, with its demands far exceeding the producing capacities of some large companies, gave rise to a confusing competitive situation. Started by the Meriden Britannia Company, which purchased large quantities of wares from other manufacturers, other companies soon followed. This often placed the manufacturer in the position of competing with his own goods. Goods manufactured by Reed & Barton might be sent to Hartford for a coating of Rogers Bros. silverplate and a Rogers Bros. stamp, and appear in the market in competition with the Reed & Barton plated line.

In the middle 1860s jobbers, and retailers, who operated their own plating shops purchased two-thirds of the factory output. They purchased quantities of wares "in the metal," plated them and sold them with their own trademarks. Practically none of the britannia or plated silver makers could supply a complete line. Reed & Barton bought most of its flatware from Rogers & Brother and the Hartford Manufacturing Company. They produced little of their own flatware except for the hotel trade until the 1860s. Flatware of almost all manufacturers turned up in many different catalogs and with many trademarks. Rogers & Brother, on the other hand, in 1865 was one of Reed & Barton's largest customers for holloware. That is why it is not unusual to find identical pieces of flatware and holloware bearing the trademarks of either company.

The depression of 1866 and 1867 brought about the failure of many jobbing concerns, a large number of whom abandoned plating and confined themselves to wholesale business.

The extension of the market for solid silver services led Reed & Barton into its production in 1889.

On September 13, 1867, Charles Barton died with Henry Reed at his bedside. In 1868 a new partnership, consisting of Henry Reed, Henry Fish and George Babrook who had long been active in mar-

keting, was formed. Each assumed a third interst. The name of the firm continued unchanged. In February, 1888, the company was incorporated.

As early as 1903 Reed & Barton began to reproduce colonial pewter ware which for more than thirty years was popluar and a financial success.

Sterling flat and holloware replaced plated ware in more and more homes so that by 1904 sterling had become the largest selling line produced.

In 1911 a moderately low-priced line was marketed under the name Reed Silver Company. It passed out of existence in 1913 because the ware did not come up to the standard expected of the Reed & Barton name.

In 1913 the Hopewell Silver Company was formed to market a high-quality line of small items. They also put out a line of Lenox china with silver and gold deposit. Both lines failed by 1918.

In 1928 Reed & Barton purchased the Dominick & Haff Company of Newark, New Jersey.

In the 1930s the Viking brand of plated holloware was bought out and terminated in 1941 with the revival of a demand for quality wares.

In 1950 the Webster Company became a subsidiary. The newest facility of the Reed & Barton plant is a modern plated holloware department. The new building replaced seven old ones. Great emphasis is placed on the handling of materials. Raw materials come in at one end and with continuous, in-line production, finished products come out at the other. Reed & Barton's first chased designs were produced in 1852. They first made sterling flatware in 1889.

HOPEWELL
SILVER CO.

(Registered July 29, 1890)

(On sterling silver)

Viking Brand

REED & BARTON
(*Nickel Silver Flatware and Hollowware.*)

GOLDYN-BRONZ

(On plated silver)

REED BARTON

TRADE MARK

(*White Metal Hollowware.*)

𝔗𝔯𝔞𝔡𝔢 𝔐𝔞𝔯𝔨

𝔖𝔱𝔢𝔯𝔩𝔦𝔫𝔤

TRADE MARK

STERLING

REED & BARTON
(On pewter)

SILVER ARTISTS CO.

REED & BARTON
YEAR MARKS

1928	♟ 🎭	1938	⌐	1949	✏
1929	⚲	1939	✳	1950	▦
1930	⚜	1940	☞	1951	△
1931	—⊖	1941	⏝	1952	🐕
1932	⏜	1942	V	1953	⊠
1933	⛄	1943	⏚	1954	♆
1934	⚘	1944	✈	1955	⚓
1935	✿	1945	Ⓐ ♀	1956	♡
1936	☕	1946	✪	1957	⌁
1937	⚓	1947	⚖		
		1948	♘		

From 1928 through 1957 Reed & Barton year-marked their plated holloware with symbols.

REED, BARTON & COMPANY
Taunton, Massachusetts

Set up in 1886 for electroplating. This short-lived enterprise was managed by Edward Barton, son of Charles Barton, and a Waldo Reed, no relation of Henry Reed, but a son-in-law of Charles Barton. They attempted to capitalize on the reputation of the established Reed & Barton name. Bought out in 1892 by Reed & Barton.

REED SILVER COMPANY
See Reed & Barton

REEVES & BROWNE
Newark, New Jersey
See Jennings & Lauter

REEVES & SILLCOCKS
New York, New York
See Jennings & Lauter

THE REGAL SILVER MFG. CO.
New Haven, Connecticut
See Majestic Silver Co.

The Mark of Quality

(Used 1910 to present)

REGAL SPECIALTY MANUFACTURING COMPANY
See Majestic Silver Company

REIBLING-LEWIS, INC.
Providence, Rhode Island

Manufacturers of sterling holloware and jewelry c. 1950.
GOLDEN WHEEL

OTTO REICHARDT CO.
New York, New York

In Directories from c. 1925 through the 1960s. In 1961 listed at a Brooklyn address. Not listed 1973. Manufacturers of sterling wares.

REICHENBERG-SMITH CO.
Omaha, Nebraska
See A. F. Smith

IMPERIAL SILVER PLATE CO.

RENOMMÉE MFG. CO.
Newark, New Jersey

Listed in JC 1896-1904 in sterling silver and jewelry sections.

R. M. CO.

RENTZ BROS.
Minneapolis, Minn.

Listed in 1896 Jewelers' Weekly as manufacturers of sterling silverware. Also importers of jewelry. Last record found was c. 1935.

REVERE SILVER CO.
Brooklyn, New York
See Crown Silver, Inc.

Successor c. 1960 to Revere Silversmiths, Inc., and now a Division of Crown Silver, Inc., New York. Manufacturers of sterling holloware.

BERNARD RICE'S SONS
New York, New York

CHRONOLOGY	
Bray & Redfield	c. 1850-55
Bancroft, Redfield & Rice	1857-71
Redfield & Rice Mfg. Co.	1871-72
Bernard Rice's Sons	1870s-c. 1950

The history of Bernard Rice's Sons can be traced back to Bray & Redfield, established c. 1850-55 by E. D. Bray and James H. Redfield. William Bancroft bought the interest of Mr. Bray about 1857 and at the same time James Rice was admitted to partnership under the name of Bancroft, Redfield & Rice, manufacturers of silverplated ware. On the withdrawal of Bancroft in 1865 the firm name became Redfield & Rice. About 1871 Redfield & Rice was incorporated as Redfield & Rice Mfg. Co.

In 1863 the Hartford Plate Co. was organized by Redfield & Rice in Hartford, Connecticut and operated there until the building was partly destroyed when the foundations gave way in 1865 and the business was moved to Wolcotville. In 1871 the Hartford Plate Co. tools and equipment were sold to the Derby Silver Co.

In 1872 Redfield & Rice went bankrupt. A merger of the Apollo Silver Co., Redfield & Rice and Shepard & Rice formed the company of Bernard Rice's Sons. This took place prior to April 18, 1899 as Patent Office records show the registration of their trademark to be used on plated silverware, under the company name. The company went out of business before 1959.

DORANTIQUE
(Copper and Brass Novelties.)

L'Aiglon
(On silverplate)

Loraline

"BeauXardt"

"ETCHARDT"

"DUTCHARDT"
(On silverplate)

PATRICIA
(On silverplate)

PEWTER BY RICE

MARION PEWTER

(APOLLO STERLING)
(On sterling)

APOLLO STUDIO
NEW YORK
(On silverplate)

B.R.S. CO.
SHEFFIELD
U. S. A.

JOSEPH T. RICE
Albany, New York
See Mulford & Wendell

Silversmith 1813-1853. John H. Mulford was apprenticed to him.

RICHFIELD PLATE COMPANY
See Homan Manufacturing Company

GEO. S. RICHMOND
A catalog published by L. Boardman & Sons September 1880 says that this is a tradename used on their "second quality Britannia spoons."

RICHTER MFG. CO.
Providence, Rhode Island

Manufacturers and importers of sterling silver deposit ware, novelties, and cut glass c. 1915-1920.

RICKETSON COMPANY
Taunton, Massachusetts

Listed in Directories 1955-61 as manufacturers of silverware.

JOHN H. RILEY
Baltimore, Maryland

Listed in Baltimore City Directories 1876-1883 as a goldsmith and silversmith (gold beater).

GOTTLIEB RITTER
Baltimore, Maryland

Listed in Baltimore City Directories 1895-1899 as a silversmith. Succeeded by Ritter & Sullivan in 1900.

RITTER & SULLIVAN
Baltimore, Maryland

Gottlieb Ritter listed in Baltimore City Directories as a silversmith 1895-1899. Joined by Wyndham A. Sullivan in 1900 in the firm of Ritter & Sullivan which continued in business until 1915.

TRADE ⟨R&S⟩ MARK

CHAS. M. ROBBINS
Attleboro, Massachusetts

What is now The Robbins Company was born during the election year of 1892.

Charles M. Robbins, the company's founder, became so interested in the presidential campaign that he designed and produced campaign buttons for his favorite candidate in his own simple shed workshop. This was the start of a business which now has more than 20 general product lines.

At one time, The Robbins Company's jewelry enameling department was the largest in the world.

Principal products today are emblems, service and safety awards, badges, commemorative materials, medallions, insignia, religious and organization jewelry, advertising specialties, souvenirs, premiums and costume jewelry.

Charles Robbins was joined in 1904 by Ralph Thompson, who acquired ownership fo the company in 1910. In 1912, The Robbins Company was formed.

In October, 1961, Robbins acquired a wholly owned Canadian subsidiary, Stephenson, Robbins Company, Ltd., Montreal, Canada.

In July, 1963, The Robbins Company became a wholly owned subsidiary of Continental Communications Corporation of New York. The new owners sold the Canadian subsidiary in 1964. They discontinued the production of plated flatware before 1915.

(Used c. 1900-1926)

(Present mark)

(On sterling silver)

(Used before 1900)

(Flatware.)

(On plated silver)

Reed & Barton's first patented design for a tea service (Design Patent January 12, 1858).

Trademark on waste bowl of Reed & Barton tea set.

Tea and coffee service designed and patented by William C. Beattie (July 25, 1876) for Reed & Barton who exhibited it at the Philadelphia Centennial. Profusely decorated with repoussé chasing and "oxidized and gold-finished" according to the 1877 Reed & Barton catalog, it was admired by members of the Japanese Commission who purchased it for presentation to the Emperor of Japan.

E. M. ROBERTS & SON
Hartford, Connecticut

"They were manufacturers of silver and silverplated wares, established in East Hartford in 1825. The business failed in 1890 and was reported to be taken by Wm. Rogers Mfg. Co., one of the heaviest creditors." (JW 11-13-1890)

ROBESON CUTLERY CO. INC.
Perry, New York

Manufacturers of silverplated steak knives c. 1950-65.

GOURMET CARVERS
ROBESON "SHUR EDGE"

ROCHESTER STAMPING CO.
Rochester, New York

Silverplaters c. 1920.

ROCKFORD SILVER PLATE CO.
Rockford, Illinois
See Sheets-Rockford Silver Plate Co.

ROCKWELL SILVER CO.
Meriden, Connecticut

Founded 1907. Manufacturers of sterling silverware, china, glassware and silver depositware.

(For glass candlesticks ornamented with applied silver. Used since August 10, 1914)

RODEN BROS., LTD.
Toronto, Ontario

In business at least as early as 1891 as Roden Bros. Listed JC 1904-1922. Became Roden Bros., Ltd. between 1904-1915. Distributors of or jobbers (?) of sterling silverware, plated silver, novelties and cut glass.

STERLING SILVER   ELECTRO PLATE

JOSEPH RODGERS & SONS
Sheffield, England

Cutlers, silversmiths and electroplaters for more than two centuries. Also manufacturers of silver and plated wares. Their trademark was probably the oldest in continuous use, being granted in 1682. Registered trademark U. S. Patent Office, No. 16,478, April 9, 1889. For the protection of their reputation for high quality, they have acquired the businesses of all cutlery firms in Great Britain bearing the names "Rodgers" or "Rogers." They are today the best known producers of quality cutlery in Sheffield and the oldest in the world.

            RODGERS

(On sterling silver)   (On plated Silver)

ROEDER & KIERSKY
New York, New York

Listed in JC in 1896 in sterling silver section.

R. & K.
STERLING.

ASA ROGERS, JR. & CO.
See Rogers Brothers

Successors to Rogers & Cole on June 4, 1832 when John A. Cole retired from the firm. The business was bought by William Rogers July 28, 1838.

ROGERS & BRITTIN
West Stratford, Connecticut

Trademark registered May 4, 1880 by Rogers & Brittin, West Stratford, Connecticut for britannia, plated silver and solid silverware.

Succeeded by Holmes & Edwards when it was organized in 1882.

(Britannia, Silver Plated and Solid Ware.)

ROGERS & BRO.
Waterbury, Connecticut
See Rogers Brothers

Started as a partnership with Asa and Simeon Rogers, Leroy S. White and David B. Hamilton. Their first goods were stamped (Star) Rogers & Bro. A-1, causing confusion between their stamp and the one used by the Hartford company which was (Star) Rogers Bros. A-1.

Hamilton's eldest son joined the business after the withdrawal of Asa and Simeon Rogers and in 1886 was one of the organizers of Rogers & Hamilton.

What is believed to be the first fancy pattern made in electroplated ware in this country was the *Olive* design, made in the blank, silverplated and finished for marketing from that plant. Earlier, the *Olive* pattern had been sold here, the blanks being imported from England and only the plating being done in this country.

Rogers & Bro. was exclusively a flatware plant, producing German silver blanks for the trade. By 1869 they were also supplying blanks for many other concerns to plate and finish after stamping them with their own trademarks. This was one of the original companies that became part of the International Silver Co. in 1898.

★ ROGERS & BRO., A 1.
(Best Quality Flatware.)

R. & B.
(Second Quality Flatware.)

★ ROGERS & BROTHER,
(H. H. Knives.)

★ ROGERS & BROTHER, 12
(No. 12 Steel Knives.)

★ R & B
(Pearl Knives.)

(Hollowware.)

ROGERS & BRO.—GERMAN SILVER
(German Silver Flatware, Unplated.)

MANOR PLATE
(on low priced line)

ROGERS BROS.
See Rogers Brothers

In 1847, Asa Rogers, Jr., with his brothers produced and distributed plated silver spoons carrying the ROGERS BROS. trademark.

ROGERS BROTHERS

In 1820 William, the eldest, left the parental farm to become an apprentice to Joseph Church, jeweler and silversmith in Hartford, Connecticut.

In 1825 William became Church's partner in making coin silver spoons stamped, CHURCH & ROGERS. Before 1835, Asa, Jr. and Simeon Rogers were both associated with the firm. William also stamped spoons with his individual (EAGLE) WM. ROGERS (STAR) mark during this time (1825-1841). His spoons are noted for their symmetrical outline, pleasing proportions and fine finish.

Early in 1830 Asa, Jr. formed a partnership with John A. Cole, in New Britain, ROGERS & COLE, to manufacture coin silver flatware.

When Cole retired on June 4, 1832 the name of the firm was changed to ASA ROGERS JR. & CO. with William Rogers as a partner. In 1834 William left the company and Asa, Jr. continued the business alone, moving to Hartford. William continued his partnership with Church while associated with Asa, Jr. in New Britain. This partnership continued until August 2, 1836 when William moved to his own shop, under the name WILLIAM ROGERS. He was one of the first in this country to advertise and manufacture tableware of sterling silver as it had been the general practice to use coin silver.

On July 23, 1838 William bought the spoon manufactory of Asa, Jr. In 1841 Asa, Jr. advertised that he was once again making spoons.

Simeon learned the trade in William's business and in 1841 was admitted as a partner in the jewelry and silverware store, WM. ROGERS & CO., with the new mark, (EAGLE) WM. ROGERS & CO. (STAR) stamped on their coin silver spoons.

About 1843-1844 Asa, Jr. experimented with electroplating in association with Wm. B. Cowles and James H. Isaacson and on November 13, 1845 the COWLES MFG. CO. in Granby was formed to manufacture German and silverplated spoons, forks, etc. Stockholders were Wm. B. Cowles, Asa Rogers, Jr., Jas. H. Isaacson and John D. Johnson. In 1846 Asa, Jr., William and Isaacson left COWLES MFG. CO. and it went out of business a few years later.

In 1845, William and Asa, Jr. in partnership with J. O. Mead, manufactured electroplated silverware in Hartford as ROGERS & MEAD until 1846.

Early in 1847 Asa, Jr., having returned to Hartford, in cooperation with his brothers, produced and distributed silverplated spoons carrying the ROGERS BROS. trademark. Advertisements of this period read as if WM. ROGERS & CO. (composed of William and Simeon) were the producers.

ROGERS BROS. were unable to handle their increasing volume of business, so in 1853 a new company was organized — ROGERS BROS. MFG. CO. William and Asa, Jr. were large stockholders; William was president. Simeon did not join the firm except as a stockholder a few months later.

In 1856 William Rogers left ROGERS BROS. MFG. CO. and with George W. Smith, manufacturer of silverplated holloware, organized ROGERS, SMITH & CO. were consolidated with William as president.

In 1862 the MERIDEN BRITANNIA CO. bought the tools and dies of the company. William joined MERIDEN BRITANNIA CO. to direct production of the 1847 ROGERS BROS. line.

In 1865 William became an organizer and partner in the WILLIAM ROGERS MFG. CO. Associated with him was his son, William Rogers, Jr. They manufactured plated silverware. Asa, Jr. and Simeon, still stockholders in ROGERS BROS. MFG. CO., established ROGERS & BROTHER CO. in Waterbury in 1858. It was incorporated the following year.

Asa, Jr., with his nephew, William H. Watrous, in 1871 organized the ROGERS CUTLERY CO. in Hartford. Frank Willson (Wilson) Rogers, brother of William Rogers Jr., was secretary and a director. They manufactured silverplated flatware and became part of INTERNATIONAL SILVER CO. in 1898. William, Asa, Jr. and Simeon were all employed by MERIDEN BRITANNIA CO. when they died.

ROGERS BROS. MFG. CO.
See Rogers Brothers

Organized 1853, by William and Asa Rogers, Jr. Simeon Rogers became a stockholder in a few months. Consolidated with Rogers, Smith & Co., October 1, 1861 because of financial difficulties.

(Used only 1853-61)

C. ROGERS & BROS.
Meriden, Connecticut
See International Silver Co.

Organized February 26, 1866 by Cephas B. Rogers, Gilbert Rogers and Wilbur F. Rogers when they bought the stock in trade of "one Frary," — probably James A. Frary who had died in December 1865.

Their first products were casket hardware and furniture trimmings. Their use of "C. Rogers & Bros." trademark on silverplated spoons resulted in court action. They were permitted to use the trademark and continued to do so until the concern was bought by International Silver Co. in 1903. Their products were considered an imitation of the original Rogers brothers and none of their trademarks were ever used by International.

SO. MERIDEN SILVER CO. QUADRUPLE
This tradename was used in a holloware catalog of 1899 with the statement that it is "nicely finished but not standard plate," and "made to supply the demand for a good quality of silver plated ware at moderate prices." This bears out the belief that there was no such thing as a standard quadruple plate.

C. ROGERS & BROS., A 1.

ROGERS & COLE
See Rogers Brothers

Organized in 1830 by Asa Rogers, Jr. and John A. Cole in New Britain to manufacture coin silver flatware. Out of business June 4, 1832.

ROGERS CUTLERY CO.
See Rogers Brothers

Founded in 1871. Consolidated with Wm. Rogers Mfg. Co., Hartford, Connecticut in 1879.
Frank Wilson Rogers, usually known as F. Wilson Rogers, son of William Hazen Rogers and brother of Wm. Henry Rogers (who called himself Wm. Rogers, Jr.) was secretary and a director of Rogers Cutlery Co. and also of Wm. Rogers Mfg. Co. when the two companies consolidated.
One of the original companies to become part of the International Silver Co. in 1898.

R. C. CO. AI PLUS

ROGERS CUTLERY CO.

ROGERS CO.

F. B. ROGERS SILVER CO.
Taunton, Massachusetts

Founded 1883 in Shelburne Falls, Massachusetts. Moved to Taunton in 1886, at which time it was incorporated. Successors to West Silver Co. before 1896. Still in business.
Became a division of National Silver Co. in February 1955.

F. B. ROGERS SILVER CO
TAUNTON, MASS.
QUADRUPLE

SHEFFIELD
SILVER METAL
F. B. R.

SHEFFIELD
SILVER ON COPPER
F. B. R.

FRANK W. ROGERS
Hartford, Connecticut

Trademark registered in U. S. Patent Office Dec. 7, 1875 for metal and plated ware, to Frank W. Rogers, Hartford, Connecticut. No record in International Silver Co. that Rogers used this mark.

⊃€ WM. ROGERS' SON ⊄⊅

(Metal and Plated Ware.)

ROGERS & HAMILTON CO.
Waterbury, Connecticut
See International Silver Co.

Rogers & Hamilton Co. was incorporated February 14, 1886 and produced silverplated flatware, taking over the spoon business of Holmes, Booth & Hayden and occupying their building for eight or ten years. President and a stockholder was Charles Alfred Hamilton, who had traveled for Rogers & Brother, Waterbury, for some time. William H. Rogers was made secretary and was a stockholder. Undoubtedly asked to join the company for the use of his name as he was not a silversmith, but was a cigar dealer in Hartford.
One of the original companies to become part of International Silver Co. in 1898.

ROGERS & HAMILTON.

ROGERS & HAMILTON
(on regular grade)

ROGERS & HAMILTON, A 1."

ROGERS & HAMILTON 12

HAMILTON

HAMILTON.
(on finest grade)

HENRY ROGERS, SONS & CO.
Montreal, P. Q.

Listed in JC in 1909 in plated silver section. No record after c. 1915.

TRADE MARK
H.R.S & Co

H. O. ROGERS SILVER CO.
Taunton, [Massachusetts?]

Stamped on a soft metal four-piece tea set, two pieces have the Rogers name while the other two are marked Newburyport Silver Co., Taunton.

H. O. ROGERS SILVER CO.
Taunton

J. ROGERS SILVER CO., INC.
See Oneida Silversmiths

ROGERS, LUNT & BOWLEN CO.
Greenfield, Massachusetts
See Lunt Silversmiths

The Pythagorean symbol R L & B Co. was the original Rogers, Lunt & Bowlen Co. registered trademark. Later, they registered the trademark "Treasure" and used it from 1921 to 1954. This has now been abandoned and only the registered LUNT is used. "Little Men and Little Women" was used solely for sterling silver baby goods. "Wee Folks" was used on some pieces of silverplated babyware.

TRADE MARK STERLING

"Treasure" Solid Silver

*Little Men * Little Women*

ROGERS & MEAD
See Rogers Brothers

In 1845, William and Asa Rogers, Jr. in partnership with J. O. Mead, manufactured electroplated silverware in Hartford under the name Rogers & Mead. This partnership was dissolved in 1846.

ROGERS PARK SILVERWARE CO.
Chicago, Illinois

"The Rogers Park Silverware Co. of Chicago have been closed on chattel mortagages given to the Silver Metal Mfg. Co., Oswego, N. Y." (JC&HR 12-4-1895, p. 26)

ROGERS SILVER PLATE CO.
Danbury, Connecticut

Listed in JC from 1896 through 1922. Founded by Nathaniel Burton Rogers in association with his brothers Cephas B. and Gilbert H. Rogers, who, with another brother, Wilbur F., were principals in the firm of C. Rogers & Bros. of Meriden, Connecticut which later became a part of the International Silver Co.

Rogers Silver Plate Company manufactured silverplated novelties—candlesticks, book ends, pincushions, etc. After the death of the founder, the assets of the company were purchased by Cephas B. (II), who was a manufacturer of electric lighting fixtures and lamps. He continued the manufacture of novelties under his own name until his retirement in the early 1950s.

SIMEON L. & GEO. H. ROGERS CO.
Hartford, Connecticut
See Oneida Silversmiths

In business 1900. Acquired by Wm. A. Rogers Limited in 1918. Purchased by Oneida in 1929.

ACORN

SIMEON L. & GEO. H. ROGERS CO.
S. L. & G. H. ROGERS CO.
S. L. & G. H. R. CO.
ROGERS

ROGERS, SMITH & CO.
See Rogers Brothers

Organized January 1, 1857 by William Rogers, Sr. and George W. Smith. They consolidated October I, 1861 with Rogers Bros. Mfg. Co. because of financial difficulties.

August 12, 1862, the flatware division was sold to the Meriden Britannia Company and the Rogers brothers went to work for them.

Edward Mitchell, formerly with Rogers, Smith & Co. bought the holloware division and on November 6, 1862 organized the Rogers Smith Co. of New Haven for the manufacture of holloware.

On January 13, 1863, the Meriden Britannia Company bought the holloware division of the Rogers Smith & Co. of New Haven. The business continued in New Haven.

In June 1865 the plating shop of the Rogers Smith & Co. of New Haven was moved to Meriden and consolidated with that of the Meriden Britannia Co. on January 1, 1866.

On May 22, 1876, the Meriden Britannia Co. directors voted to bring the business of Rogers Smith & Co. to Meriden on January 1, 1877.

There is merchandise in existence with trademarks bearing the names of Hartford, used from 1857 to 1862; New Haven, 1862 to 1877; West Meriden from 1877 until the early 1880s (when the term West Meriden went out of general use, and Meriden, which was used from that time until about 1918). The Rogers, Smith & Co. as a separate firm was almost non-existent when the International Silver Co. was formed in 1898. It was then simply a trademark that belonged to the Meriden Britannia Co. "Geo. B. White, manager of Rogers, Smith & Co., had been with Young, Smith & Co. which firm had furnished the Rogers brothers with the first imported spoon on which plating had been done."

(JC&HR 10-3-1894, p. 18) Rogers, Smith & Co. were in Hartford 1857-62; in New Haven 1862-77 and in Meriden 1877-98.

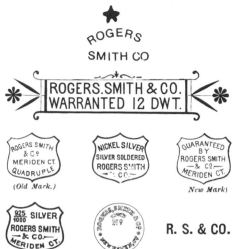

R. S. & CO.

ROGERS & SPURR MFG. CO.
Greenfield, Massachusetts

On the 14th of February, 1879 David C. Rogers and Geo. E. Rogers of Greenfield, Massachusetts made application to the Patent Office for the registry of the trademark shown here to be used by them in the manufacture of table cutlery, forks, etc. Geo. W. Spurr was listed as president and L. C. Pratt as treasurer. They were successors to George W. Spurr & Co. who started in business c. 1873.

WILLIAM ROGERS
See Rogers Brothers

(On coin silver)

WM. A. ROGERS, LTD.
See Oneida Silversmiths

Wm. A. Rogers as a small storekeeper in New York began to stamp the name Rogers on tinned spoons he sold when he found that they sold better with the name Rogers on them. He soon changed to German silver spoons lightly silverplated. He was permitted to use Wm. A. Rogers on his goods if the pieces carried the same amount of silver as the well-known Rogers Bros. standard. They succeeded the Niagara Silver Co. before 1904. And, by 1918 took over the business of Simeon L. & Geo. H. Rogers Co. which had started in Hartford, Conn. in 1900. Were succeeded by Oneida Silversmiths in 1929.

According to Oneida records, Wm. A. Rogers, Ltd. was an Ontario corporation with offices in New York City and factories in Niagara Falls, New York and North Hampton, Massachusetts. The company began making plated silverware in 1894.

The (R) Rogers (R) trademark was first used about 1901. The Warren Silver Plate Co. trademark first used in 1901 was apparently derived from the fact that the New York office was at 12 Warren St.

The 1881 (R) Rogers (R) trademark was first used by Wm. A. Rogers, Ltd. c. 1910.

The Niagara Silver Co. and 1877 N. F. Silver Co. are discontinued trademarks which Oneida acquired through the purchase of Wm. A. Rogers, Ltd.

(Highest Grade Flatware.)

(Cheap to medium grade)

W. R.
(Medium Grade)
(Half Plate Flatware.)

Extra { COIN SILVER } Plate
(Silver Plate on Brass Base.)

Wm. A. Rogers
(12 Dwt. Knives and Forks.)

Wm.A.Rogers A.I.

(R) Rogers (R)
(12 Dwt. Knives and Forks.)

1881 Rogers
QUADRUPLE NEW YORK
(Popular grade)

NIAGARA SILVER CO.
R. S. MFG. CO.
BUSTER BROWN

R. S. MFG. CO.

(Highest Grade Hollowware.)

(Special Knives and Forks Plated with 16 Dwt. Silver.)

OXFORD CUTLERY CO.
WARRANTED NO.12

(Light Plate Knives and Forks.)

NEW YORK
(*Medium Grade*
Hollowware.)

(Cheaper grade)

1877 N.F. Co.

OXFORD SILVER PLATE CO.
(Cheaper grade)

WILLIAM ROGERS & CO.
See Rogers Brothers

Organized in 1841 by William Rogers with his brother, Simeon Rogers who had been apprenticed to him. They used the mark (Eagle) Wm. Rogers & Co. (Star) on their coin silver spoons.

WILLIAM ROGERS, JR.
(William Henry Rogers)
See Rogers Brothers
See Simpson, Hall, Miller & Co.

The original William Hazen Rogers had two sons, William Henry Rogers, and Frank Willson (sometimes spelled Wilson) Rogers. William Henry changed his name to William Rogers, Jr. in order to be more closely associated with his father's well-known name.

In 1868, Wm. Rogers, Jr., together with his father, made a contract with the Meriden Britannia Company for 10 years. Upon the death of his father, in 1873, the contract was to continue with the son until the expiration — which was in March of 1878. Wm. Rogers, Jr. was not successful in renewing the contract with the Meriden Britannia Co., but in that year he did make a 15-year contract with Simpson, Hall, Miller & Co. to superintend their flatware manufacturing and with his permission to use on the silver-plated flatware the trademark (Eagle WM. ROGERS (Star). The contract with Simpson, Hall, Miller & Co. terminated in 1893 and Wm. Rogers, Jr. died in 1896.

The trademark is a very active one today on moderately priced flatware.

⚬ Wm Rogers ★

WILLIAM ROGERS MFG. CO.
Hartford, Connecticut
See Rogers Brothers

Organized 1865 by William Hazen Rogers and his son, Wm. Rogers, Jr. (William Henry Rogers). Were one of the original companies to form the International Silver Co. in 1898.

1846 ⚓ ROGERS ⚓ AA

⚓ R O G E R S ⚓

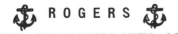

1865. WM. ROGERS M'F'G. CO.
WM. ROGERS & SON.

R. C. CO.
ROGERS NICKEL SILVER
ROGERS CUTLERY CO.

⚓ W. R. & S.   R.C. CO.

Ⓙ Ⓢ Ⓠ

(Jeweler's special quality, used with Anchor Rogers
Anchor Warranted)

CUNNINGHAM SILVER PLATE

(On premium flatware made for
Ocean Spray Cranberry Sauce)

WM. ROGERS MFG. CO., LTD.
Niagara Falls, Ontario

Bought by Wm. Rogers Mfg. Co. (Division of International Silver Co., Meriden, Connecticut in 1905.)

WM. G. ROGERS

Trademark registered U. S. Patent No. 36,147, January 1, 1901 for silverware, knives, forks and spoons.
Listed 1904-1915 in JC plated silver section.

(*Flatware*.)

WILLIAM H. ROGERS
Hartford, Connecticut

Trademark registered U. S. Patent Office, No. 16,007, November 13, 1888 for silver and plated silverware. Out of business before 1915.

⚔ *ROGERS. A1.*

(*Silver and Silver Plated Ware*.)

WILLIAM H. ROGERS CORPORATION
Plainfield, New Jersey

Listed in September 1901 KJI and 1904 JC in plated silver sections. No record in U. S. Patent Office.

Ⓡ

ROGERS, WENDT & WILKINSON
New York, New York

A short-lived firm organized January 1860 to make silverware for Ball, Black & Co. Wendt was John R. Wendt, New York silversmith (q.v.) Wilkinson, designer and superintendent of the Gorham Mfg. Co. The partnership was not of long duration, for in August it was dissolved, and Wilkinson returned to the Gorham Co. in Providence, Rhode Island.

HENRY J. ROHRBACH
Chicago, Illinois

"Silversmith and Manufacturing Jeweler." (Adv. JC &HR 9-27-1893, p. 28)

ROMAN SILVERSMITHS, INC.
Brooklyn, New York

Manufacturers of silverplated goods c. 1950.

LIFETIME

ROSE SILVER CO.
New York, New York

Listed 1922 through 1931 KJI as manufacturers of plated holloware.

J. W. ROSENBAUM & CO.
Newark, New Jersey

Listed JC in 1909-1915 in plated silver section. Out of business before 1922.

FRANCIS ROSENDORN
Baltimore, Maryland

Listed in Baltimore City Directories 1864-1869, 1883-1886 as a silverplater.

ROSENTHAL U. S. A. LTD.
New York, New York

The Rosenthal company was founded in 1879 by Privy Councilor Dr. Philip Rosenthal, the third generation of Westphalian potters and china traders. Rosenthal silver flatware was designed to coordinate with existing Rosenthal chinaware and glassware. The first line of flatware was Bjørn Wiinblad's *Romance* in sterling silver. To coordinate with Tapio Wirkkla's *Variation* pattern, two men, Richard Gump, famous San Francisco retailer, and Karl Gustav Hansen, Danish silversmith, worked together to produce flatware with fluted porcelain handles and contemporary sterling cutting and serving ends. To design a flatware in keeping with its *Classic Modern* designed by Raymond Loewy, Richard Latham of Chicago sculpted in high-gloss silverplate a set of tableware cutlery which is also available in matte finish.

ROSLYN SILVER CORP.
Taunton, Massachusetts

Manufacturers of silverplated wares c. 1950.

CHARLES ROUSH
Baltimore, Maryland

Listed in 1891 Baltimore City Directory under plated silverware.

ROWAN & WILCOX
See Wilcox & Evertsen

ROWLEY MFG. CO.
Philadelphia, Pennsylvania

Listed in JC in 1909 in plated silver section. Out of business before 1915.

LUNA METAL

(Seamless Nickel Silver Hollow Ware.)

ROYAL METAL MFG. CO.
New York, New York

Listed in JC in 1909 in plated silver section. Out of business before 1915.

ROYAL SILVER MANUFACTURING CO.
Newark, New Jersey

Listed in KJI 1918-19 as silversmiths. In 1922 JKD as manufacturers of silver novelties and 1931 issue as makers of ladies' handbag frames.

ROYAL SILVERWARE CO.
Detroit, Michigan

"Rev. Robert J. Service, pastor, Turnbull Avenue Presbyterian Church, resigned to become manager of the business owned by Sherman R. Miller [Royal Silverware Co.] Service replaced by Aubrey W. Knowles, who resigned." (Clipping from unidentified newspaper, dated 1899)

ROY RUBENS SILVERSMITH
Beverly Hills, California

Listed 1961 JBG as silver manufacturers.

A. RUBESCH
Alexandria, Virginia

Silversmith, silverplater and repair service.

RUEFF BROS.
New York, New York

Listed in 1922 KJI as manufacturers of silverplated holloware.

C. F. RUMPP & SONS
Philadelphia, Pennsylvania

Carl Frederich Rumpp, born in Nuertingen, Germany, arrived in this country in 1848 at the age of 20. He brought with him little else but an appreciation of this country and its opportunities, the tools of his trade and a determination to make the best leather goods his thorough apprenticeship had taught him.

Only 25 years after its founding in 1850, the fame of the company had spread through the country and is still considered the standard by which leather goods are judged. Many desk sets, belts, writing cases and travel cases they manufacture are fitted with sterling silver mountings.

RUSSELL HARRINGTON CUTLERY CO.
Southbridge, Massachusetts

The present Russell Harrington Cutlery Company was formed in 1932 through the merger of the Harrington Cutlery Co. and the John Russell Co.

Founded in 1834 by John Russell, descendant of an old New England pioneer family, it was first known as J. Russell & Company Green River Works.

The company became well known for an expression used on the American frontier in the two decades preceding the Gold Rush to California in 1849. This expression, "Up to the Green River," had two meanings — one referred to quality when traders boasted that their goods were "Up to Green River" knives; the other was used when hand-to-hand combat settled personal differences and onlookers shouted, "Give it to him — up to the Green River" — the trademark found near the hilt. (This is the Bowie knife of Texas fame.)

John Russell retired from the firm in 1868, at which time it was incorporated under the name John Russell Mfg. Co. in 1873, it was reorganized and the name was changed to John Russell Cutlery Co. Under this name, in 1881, then located in Turners Falls, they registered a patent for making plated silver knives.

John Russell was the son of the silversmith, also named John Russell, who served his apprenticeship under Isaac Parker.$ The Parker-Russell Silver Shop in Old Deerfield, Massachusetts, is a tribute to Isaac Parker and the first John Russell. Through Parker and his apprentice, American silver craftsmanship can be traced by way of Russell & Ripply, J. Russelll Cutlery, Towle & Sons and Rogers, Lunt & Bowlen to Lunt Silversmiths.

(Used 1881)

J. RUSSELL & CO.
GREEN RIVER WORKS

1834 J. RUSSELL & CO.

"Professional" Pattern

SAART BROS. COMPANY
Attleboro, Massachusetts

Successors to W. H. Saart Co.

Founded by William H. Saart, with his brothers, Albert and Herman. Probably in existence for some time prior to its incorporation in 1906. Frank E. Nolan became principal stockholder in 1937. The business is now conducted by R. J. Nolan, president. Makers of sterling and plated silver holloware, dresserware, cigarette and vanity cases and novelties.

W. H. SAART CO.
Attleboro, Massachusetts
See Saart Bros. Co.

SABEN GLASS CO.
New York, New York

Registered trademark for sterling coasters, holloware, handles for table knives, carving knives, forks, salad forks, silver bands for glass coasters, drinking glasses and water pitchers. Used since Oct. 16, 1949.

SACKETT & CO., LTD.
Philadelphia, Pennsylvania

Successors to Mead & Robbins in 1893 as manufacturers of sterling silver. Out of business before 1904.

F. H. SADLER CO., INC.
Attleboro, Massachusetts

Manufacturers of vanities and compacts c. 1930.

G. T. SADTLER & SONS
Baltimore, Maryland

Philip Sadtler arrived in this country in 1799 and first opened a shop in Baltimore in 1800. For two years he was in partnership with John William Pfaltz. In 1803 he opened his own shop where he carried a full line of optical goods. While there is some question as to whether he was a working silversmith, there is a large quantity of silver bearing his initials P S or his full name. The sons and grandsons continued the business until 1923.

"Philip B. Sadtler, founder of the firm, was born in North Germany. He was a painstaking watchmaker and goldsmith, having obtained his training under the apprenticeship days in the finest horological workshops of Europe. On reaching Baltimore, where he came to seek his fortune in the New World, he renounced his German citizenship and embraced the political and civic faith of America. A man of military training he deeply loved his adopted country, and in 1814 when this city was in danger of capture at the hands of the British, and during the same period of time that Francis Scott Key wrote the immortal song of the nation, Sadtler left his shop, organized and drilled the Baltimore Yeagers. He was made captain of the company which participated in the defense of the city when the British, under General Ross, made their fruitless attack.

"Captain Sadtler died in 1860, and the business which was conducted on Baltimore St., near Charles St., was continued by his son, George T. Sadtler. After the death of George T. Sadtler, in 1888, his sons, George W. and C. Herbert Sadtler, formed the firm of George T. Sadtler & Sons. C. Herbert Sadtler died in 1899 and the business was continued by George W. Sadtler and Fernando Volkmar. George W. Sadtler died two years ago, and Mr. Volkmar became head of the firm at that time." (JC-W 2-5-1919, p. 318)

ST. LOUIS METALCRAFTS, INC.,
St. Louis, Missouri

Manufacturers of sterling and silverplate c. 1950.

(On sterling)

(On silverplate)

ST. LOUIS SILVER CO.
St. Louis, Missouri

First appeared in the 1893 St. Louis City Directory as The St. Louis Silver Plate Company at 207 Chestnut Street and in 1904 as the St. Louis Silver Company at 118 Chestnut. No listing after 1912.

SALES STIMULATORS, INC.
Chicago, Illinois

Registered trademarks for silverplated flatware.

(Claims use since Mar. 5, 1936, on the design; and since Sept. 1, 1948, on the mark in its entirety.)

Queen Esther

(Claims use since Sept. 1, 1948)

SANBORN HERMANOS, S. A.
Mexico, D. F. Mexico

Registered trademark for silverware, including holloware and flatware, made in whole or, in part of, and plated with silver, and ornamental jewelry made of silver.

(Used since Mar. 3, 1931)

SANCRAFT INDUSTRIES
Bronx, New York

Currently doing business in sterling and enameled spoons. Spoons made to order.

SANDLAND, CAPRON & CO.
North Attleboro, Massachusetts

Listed in JC in 1896-1904 in the sterling silver section. Out of business before 1909.

S. C. & Co.
STERLING

J. D. SANFORD & CO.
Granby, Connecticut

Joseph D. Sanford and Lorenzo Peck were in business before 1848 plating and marketing spoons. The business was dissolved c. 1857-58 and Sanford continued at Tariffville. He had some business association with the Cowles Mfg. Co.

PHILIP SAUTER
Baltimore, Maryland

Listed in Baltimore City Directories 1855-1871 as silverplater, manufacturer and dealer in door plates, bell pulls, railing knobs, silver and brass letters and numbers, coffin handles, trimmings, German silver, sheet brass and wire.

P. SAUTER & BRO.
Baltimore, Maryland

Listed in 1864 Baltimore City Directory as silverplaters.

WILLIAM SAUTER
Baltimore, Maryland

Listed in Baltimore City Directories 1865-1886 as silverplaters. Beginning in 1871, coffin trimmings are given special mention.

FREDERICK A. SAWKINS
Baltimore, Maryland

Listed in Baltimore City Directories 1864-1896 as a silverplater.

H. I. SAWYER
See W. L. & H. E. Pitkin

WILLIAM H. SAXTON, JR.
New London, Connecticut

William H. Saxton is listed in the City Directory of New London in 1891 as Collector for port of New London and dealer in watches, clocks and fine jewelry. William H. Saxton, Jr. is listed as watchmaker.

This trademark, No. 20,327 is registered in the name of William H. Saxton, Jr., November 3, 1891, for the manufacture of gold, silver and plated flatware and tableware. The type of trademark would indicate souvenir flatware. Listed 1896 in JC.

MURRAY L. SCHACTER & CO.
New York, New York

Manufacturers(?) of sterling wares c. 1950.

HAMPSHIRE HOUSE

HARVEY M. SCHADE
Brooklyn, New York

The factory of Henry Schade was established in 1873. The earliest listing found was the 1887 City Directory. Listed 1898-1904 in JC as Schade & Co. and variously as Harry M. Schade and Harvey M. Schade as successor before 1915 and out of business before 1922. In the JW 1890 the name is given as Henry Schade. The Brooklyn Plate Co. trademark was derived from the company of that name they succeeded before 1904.

BROOKLYN PLATE CO.

SCHAEZLEIN & BURRIDGE
San Francisco, California

Mark found on King Kamehameha Akahi Dala spoon. They were primarily platers and did repair work. Advertised special order work and badges and insignia. The firm no longer exists but descendants in a related business still advertise special order work.

Schaezlein & Burridge was started by Robert Schaezlein who moved to San Francisco in 1879 (d. c. 1932). The business was continued by his son, Robert Frederick (d. 1960) and now by Robert Frederick, Jr. The present Mr. Schaezlein makes everything he sells, mostly silver buckles with gold appliques of initials for Western outfits and special or-

ders. Also, he produces silver (and gold with gold applique) conchos, etc., for belts and saddles. He still has the screw press his father and grandfather saved from the 1906 earthquake and fire and with which they set up shop right after the fire.

S. & B. S. F. CAL.

SCHARLING & CO.
Newark, New Jersey

John H. Scharling first established his business in 1885; incorporated in 1895. The company manufactured sterling, silverplated and pewter holloware and picture frames, novelties, antique gold and plated filigree frames and silver deposit ware.

He first registered a process for producing raised metallic designs (silver deposit) on glassware March 7, 1893; he registered a second on September 26, 1893. The last listing found for the company was 1931.

(On sterling silver, holloware, picture frames and novelties)

(On sterling silver and nickel silver match cases)

SCHARLING SILVER PLATE

(On silverplated holloware.)

(On pewterware)

NIC. SCHELNIN CO.
New York, New York

Listed in JC in 1904 in the sterling silver and jewelry sections. Out of business before 1909.

WILLIAM SCHIMPER & CO.
Hoboken, New Jersey

Successors (?) to William Schimper, listed as a silversmith in New York in 1841. William Schimper & Co. was listed in JC 1896-1927 as manufacturers of dresserware, bonbon baskets, picture frames, match safes, calendars and hair brushes in sterling and plated silver.

New York, New York
See Adelphi Silver Plate Co.

Made sterling silverware c. 1890-97. Later made silver and gold plated wares as Adelphi Silver Plate Co.

JEROME N. SCHIRM
Baltimore, Maryland

Listed in 1901 Baltimore City Directory as a silversmith.

E. SCHMIDT & CO.
Philadelphia, Pennsylvania

Listed JKD 1918-19 as silversmiths.

SCHMITZ, MOORE & CO.
Newark, New Jersey

Manufacturers of sterling silver dresserware. Listed in JC in 1915. Succeeded by Moore & Hofman between 1915-1922.

SCHOFIELD CO., INC.
Baltimore, Maryland
See Baltimore Silversmiths Mfg. Co.
See Jenkins & Jenkins
See C. Klank & Sons

Founded in 1903 by Frank M. Schofield as the Baltimore Silversmiths Mfg. Co.

Schofield was from a family of silversmiths and worked as a die-cutter. He is said to have cut the dies for the "Baltimore Rose" for The Stieff Company.

Heer-Schofield Co. was the company name from about 1905-1928 when it was changed to Frank M. Schofield Co.

Around 1930 it was changed to Schofield Co. and incorporated a few years later.

Manufacturers of sterling silver flatware and holloware, Schofield Co., Inc. Operated 1948-65 by Berthe M. Schofield, late widow of the founder.

Their trademark has been unchanged except that the letter B in the diamond was changed to an H when the company name was changed to Heer-Schofield.

In 1905 they bought out C. Klank & Sons which continued to be listed under its own name through 1911. Shortly after 1915 they also purchased the tools and dies of Jenkins & Jenkins and also the Farreals Co. Schofield's purchased by Oscar Caplan & Sons in1965.

Schofield Co. bought by the Stieff Co. in 1967.

MILTON J. SCHREIBER
New York, New York

Registered trademark for use on holloware made in part of, or plated with, precious metal. Used since April 28, 1949.

STERLON

A. B. SCHREUDER
Syracuse, New York
See Syracuse Silver Mfg. Co.

Andrew B. Schreuder was born in Norway, 1828. Listed in Utica, New York City Directories in 1852-1853 as a silversmith and later joined the firm of Hotchkiss & Schreuder in Syracuse. The exact date of the founding of the A. B. Schreuder Company not located.

Succeeded by Syracuse Silver Mfg. Co. in 1895.

H. & S.

SCHRIER & PROTZE
Baltimore, Maryland

Listed in 1888 Baltimore City Directory as silverplaters. Firm name changed to Novelty Plating Works in 1890.

A. G. SCHULTZ & CO.
Baltimore, Maryland

Listed in Baltimore City Directories 1899-1950 as manufacturers of sterling silver holloware.

Successors to Schultz & Tschudy & Co., first listed in 1898. Andrew G. Schultz and Otto Rosenbauer were listed as members of the firm. From 1902-1905, James L. McPhail was also listed as a member of the firm and was listed at C. Klank & Sons during those same years.

(Hollow Ware.)

SCHULTZ, TSCHUDY & CO.
Baltimore, Maryland

Listed in 1898 Baltimore City Directory as silversmiths. Succeeded by A. G. Schultz & Co. in 1899.

SCHULZ & FISCHER
San Francisco, California

Began the manufacture of silverware in San Francisco in 1868 and occupied a prominent position as workers in precious metals. Their first listing in the San Francisco Directory was in 1869.

Their products included spoons, forks, and table silverware, as well as presentation pieces. One of their epergnes was 27 inches high — the largest piece of its kind made on the Pacific Coast. They were also importers of plated silverware and fine table cutlery.

Company name Schulz & McCartney after 1887.

"Wm. Schulz, 230 Kearny St., San Francisco, California, is recorded as a manufacturing silversmith and probably has a shop on a small scale. (JC&HR 9-8-1897, p. 20)

The trademark was based on the California State Seal which is reproduced here also. No matter the size of the piece of silver, the mark is always tiny — no more than 3 mm. It was used with COIN and STERLING.

SCHWEITZER SILVER CORP.
Brooklyn, New York

Manufacturers of sterling holloware c. 1950 to the late 1960s. A division of Lord Silver, Inc.

SCIENTIFIC SILVER SVC CORP.
New York, New York

Listed JBG 1957 and 1961 as manufacturers.

SCOFIELD & DE WYNGAERT
Newark, New Jersey

Listed 1904 JC in the sterling silver section and in 1915 in jewelry. Became F. P. Scofield & Company before 1922 after which no further listing was found.

SEARS ROEBUCK & CO.
Chicago, Illinois

A number of silverplated flatware patterns were made for them by various silver manufacturers and sold under the tradenames and trademarks illustrated here.

ALASKA METAL
(Used since 1908)

SALEM SILVER PLATE
(First used in 1914)

CAMBRIDGE SILVER PLATE
(First used c. 1909)

FASHION SILVER PLATE

PARAGON

PARAGON EXTRA

HARMONY HOUSE PLATE
(made by R. Wallace & Co.)

JACOB SEEGER
Baltimore, Maryland

Listed in Baltimore City Directories 1864-1869 as a silverplater.

SELLEW & COMPANY
Cincinnati, Ohio

The Cincinnati City Directory lists Sellew & Company as pewterers in 1834. The 1836-1837 Directory lists Enos and Osman Sellew, makers of britannia ware.

About 1860 they discontinued making pewter and devoted their attention to britannia ware.

Out of business in the late 1870s.

SELLEW & CO.
CINCINNATI

(On britannia)

SENECA SILVER CO.
Salamanca, New York

In business about 1900.

Trademark is Seneca Silver Co., Quadruple, Salamanca, N. Y. with an Indian profile in the center.

WILLIAM H. SEYFER
Baltimore, Maryland

Listed in 1884 Baltimore City Directory as a silversmith.

JOS. SEYMOUR MFG. CO.
Syracuse, New York

CHRONOLOGY	
Joseph Seymour	1835
Willard & Hawley	1844-c. 1850-51
Norton & Seymour	1850-51
Joseph Seymour & Co.	1851-87
Joseph Seymour, Sons & Co.	1887-98
Joseph Seymour Mfg. Co.	1898-1905

The company was founded by Joseph Seymour, born 1815, near Albany, New York. At the age of 14 he went to New York to apprentice himself to a leading silversmith. He worked there as a silversmith in 1835 and in the early 1840s in Utica. He became associated with Willard & Hawley (1844-51) in the establishment of a silverware factory in Syracuse, of which he later became owner. About 1850-51 he became a partner in Norton & Seymour (B. R. Norton). The company name was changed to Norton, Seymour & Co., after 1850. Shortly afterwards he went into business for himself under the name of Joseph Seymour & Co. Seymour's sons, Joseph, and E. G., and George F. Comstock, Jr., were admitted to partnership and about 1887 the firm name became Joseph Seymour, Sons & Co. In 1896 the stock was advertised for sale and in 1898 a new company, the Joseph Seymour Mfg. Co., was organized to carry on the manufacture of silverware. This too, went out of business about 1905.

Joseph Seymour patented a process in 1859 for making spoons (Pat. #25,765).

The company manufactured fine silverware. They were one of the first companies to make tableware in patterns, *Cable, Bridal Wreath, Prairie Flower, Corn, Tulip, Cottage, Plain, Thread* and *Prince Albert* being among them. Regrettably, much of their ta-

Candy or nut dish. The "hand" trademark with the word "HAND" enclosed conveys the message that the bowl was handwrought. (A. G. Schultz, Baltimore, Maryland)

Martelé bowl made by the Gorham Company silversmiths under the direction of William Christmas Codman. Entirely hand wrought, these articles made in *l'art nouveau* style, were 950/1000 fine silver.

bleware was made by melting down tons of old Hudson Valley silversmiths' work.

J. S. & Co.

(c. 1850-1887)

★ S ★

* S *
(1887-c. 1900)

(c. 1900-c. 1909)

O. D. SEYMOUR
Hartford, Connecticut
See W. L. & H. E. Pitkin

Oliver D. Seymour, silversmith, maker of coin silver spoons was in business in Hartford c. 1845 as a partner in the firm of Seymour & Hollister (Julius Hollister). Their business was succeeded by W. L. & H. E Pitkin.

The following account appeared in the *Hartford Daily Courant*, December 12, 1848.

NOTES BY A MAN ABOUT TOWN
Number VI

"In our last number we had not completed our exploration of the old jail building and its environs. We will this morning look a little farther among the various colonies which swarm this busy hive. And first we will step into the Spoon Manufactory of Mr. O. D. Seymour — Silversmith.

"The 'raw material' here consists of pure coin, mostly American half dollars — rather a queer article to be sure, and confounding some of our previous notions as to the meaning of the term 'raw material.' Just see those bags of Uncle Sam's precious metal — all of them doomed to be here melted down with as little remorse as the nabob's son usually melts down the dollars of his father.

"Some fifty of those half dollars are run into a bar of about eighteen inches in length. This bar is passed through a steam rolling mill and flattened, and afterwards hammered into a strip of the proper thickness for a spoon, and about half an inch in width, It is now cut into pieces, each piece designed for a spoon, but having no 'spoon fashion' or shape, about it. One end of this then, by a succession of blows skillfully applied with a 'peen' or oval faced hammer, spread out into the shape of a leaf for the bowl, and the other end formed in like manner for the handle. The whole spoon is then smooth hammered or planished upon an anvil, and brought to a uniform thickness and perfectly flat. During this process the silver by repeated heatings has become blackened to the color of iron. By boiling it in vitriol the white color is again restored.

"The bowl is now shaped and the tip formed in a die by 'swedging' or forcing these parts with a steel die into a spoon shaped cavity or matrix, formed in a block of lead. This completes the form. They now go into the hands of the filer, who trims them — next to a brush scouring wheel, which revolves rapidly in a lathe, where they are scoured smooth by a mixture of scotch stone in oil; and thence to the hands of the 'finisher,' who either polishes or burnishes them as the purchaser may direct, or as fancy may dictate.

"That lady who has just entered, you see has a broken spoon in her hand. She very honestly supposes that spoons are run in a mould, and has brought hers to be run over. She is not alone in the error — others are calling in constantly on the same errand, and probably nine tenths of our good citizens who are in the constant use of this now com-

mon utensil, entertain a like opinion — block tin, iron or pewter spoons, are indeed cast; but silver ones are always wrought with a hammer, and generally in the mode described.

"The polishing dust and oil, after use, become so imbued with particles, as to sell at the rate of six dollars per pound; and the very sweepings of the floor and common rubbish of the room are all saved for the filings and impalpable silver dust which they contain, and sold for $25 per hogshead.

"This concern employs from twelve to fourteen hands; feeds some fifty or more persons dependent; and turns off per annum $25,000 worth of silverware, consisting of tea and tablespoons, cream and sugar spoons, dessert knives and forks, etc. &c., &c., which find a market all over the States of New England and New York, and to some extent over other portions of the Union.

"Just examine those elegant silver and pearl handled butter knives. What beautiful things! How finely formed and highly wrought."

B. M. SHANLEY, JR. CO.
See Pryor Mfg. Co., Inc.

Consolidated with Pryor Mfg. Co. between 1915 and 1922. Last record found was c. 1935.

SHAPLEIGH HARDWARE COMPANY
St. Louis, Missouri

Established by A. F. Shapleigh. Their 1915-16 General Hardware Catalog has a photograph of the founder under which there is the statement "Established this Business in St. Louis, 1848." This same catalog illustrated and described "Peerless Silver Flat Ware" under the name Diamond Brand. It is described as "An entirely New Alloy of Metals Containing over 5% Sterling Silver; it is of a Pure White Silver Color Through and Through and will Retail its Luster Until Worn Out. Unlike Silver Plated Ware this Metal May be Scoured without any Injury to the Surface."

They also advertised "Lashar Silver Flat Ware" as "Lashar Silveroid Metal is not Plated, but Possesses the Same Color as Pure Silver Through and Through." Nickel silver tea and tablespoons were listed under the trademark "Bridge," and "Bridge Cutlery Co." Among their other offerings were tinned steel spoons and aluminum ones.

DIAMOND EDGE

GEORGE B. SHARP
Philadelphia, Pennsylaniva

Silversmith in Philadelphia c. 1848-1850.

This mark is an example of a type of quality mark used by a few American silversmiths. The American shield was used as a quality mark.

George and William Sharp worked together, perhaps a bit earlier. Their silver was stamped W. & G. SHARP.

George Sharp made silver for Bailey & Co. (later Bailey, Banks & Biddle). A Bailey & Co. advertisement of 1850 includes this mark accompanied by the statement that "All Silver Ware sold by them manufactured on the premises — Assayed by J. C. Booth, Esq., of the U. S. Mint.''

George Sharp is recorded as working as a silversmith in Danville, Kentucky c. 1850-70.

CHARLES C. SHAVER
Utica, New York

Charles C. Shaver was born in Germany. He served his apprenticeship under Willard & Hawley (William W. Willard and John D. Hawley) of Syracuse. He moved to Utica in 1854 and was listed there in the City Directories as silversmith and jeweler until 1858.

From 1858-62 he was not listed, but returned in 1863 where he continued in business until his death in 1900.

GEORGE E. SHAW
Putnam, Connecticut

Listed in JC 1896-1922 in sterling silver section.

The Gen. Putnam trademark was registered in U. S. Patent Office, No. 19,736, June 16, 1891, for flatware, solid and plated. This trademark was for two souvenir spoons to commemorate the Revolutionary hero.

GEN. PUTNAM

ALEX SHEARS
Baltimore, Maryland

Listed in the 1850 Census as a silversmith in Baltimore. Born Maryland.

SHEETS-ROCKFORD SILVER PLATE CO.
Rockford, Illinois

CHRONOLOGY

Racine Silver Plate Co.	1873-82
Rockford Silver Plate Co.	1882-1925
Sheets-Rockford Silver Plate Co.	1925-56

The company was founded in 1873 as the Racine Silver Plate Co., in Racine, Wisconsin. In 1882 the factory there burned. The stockholders decided to rebuild in Rockford, Illinois and erected the new factory there that same year. They made silverwares for the United States Jewelers' Guild (also called Jewelers' Crown Guild) which sold only through jewelry stores. About 1925 the company was bought by Raymond Sheets and became the Sheets-Rockford Silver Plate Co. The manufacture of flatware was discontinued but silverplated holloware was produced. Later Mr. Sheets operated it as a resilvering plant. The stock of the old company was purchased by S. L. & G. H. Rogers and records removed or destroyed. The Sheets-Rockford Silver Co. name appears in the City Directories through 1956.

SHEFFIELD CUTLERY CONCERN
Boston, Massachusetts

Published an illustrated catalog in 1882. Plated silver novelties, including fancy figure napkin rings were illustrated.

SHEFFIELD SILVER CO.
Brooklyn, New York

Registered trademark U. S. Patent Office, No. 107,747, December 28, 1919 for plated silverware and holloware.

Incorporated in the State of New York in 1908. Their basic product is plated silver holloware.

They were moved from New York to Norton, Massachusetts and became a division of Reed & Barton Silversmiths in 1974.

(1908-1950)

THE SHEFFIELD SILVER CO.
MADE IN U. S. A.

(1950-present)

SHELDON & FELTMAN
Albany, New York
See Smith & Company

Britannia workers 1846-1848. Thought to have made a small quantity of palted silver with the mark below. The upper ones most certainly were used only on britannia wares. Succeeded by Smith & Feltman in 1849; and by Smith & Co. in 1853.

SHEPARD MFG. CO.
Melrose Highlands, Mass.

Chester Shepard and his son, Chester Burdelle, moved from Connecticut to Melrose, Massachusetts in 1892 or 1893 and established their silversmith business there. For several years they claimed to be the only concern of importance which made a specialty of souvenir spoons, although their products embraced napkin rings and other fancy articles in flatware. The elder Shepard died July 11, 1902. Chester B. continued the business for several years but it passed to a younger brother, Llewlyn in a family disagreement and the factory closed in 1923.

On leaving the Shepard Company, Chester B. worked for several years for the Mt. Vernon Silver Co. In 1918 he founded a second Shepard Mfg. Co. in Detroit, organized for the manufacture of silverplated interior hardware for limousines such as Cadillac, Durant and LaSalle. He sold the business in 1925 and died two years later.

S

SHEPARD & RICE
See Bernard Rice's Sons

SHERIDAN SILVER CO., INC.
Taunton, Massachusetts

Originated in 1944 as the C & C Silver Company by Joseph Caiozzo and Harry Carmody. Incorporated in 1946 as Sheridan Silver Co., Inc. The largest of the independent silver manufacturers. Their production is limited to plated silver holloware.

SILVER ON COPPER

EMMONS F. SHERMAN
Baltimore, Maryland

Listed in 1868-1869 Baltimore City Directory as a silverplater.

GEORGE W. SHIEBLER & CO.
New York, New York

Geo. W. Shiebler was first employed as a salesman for the firm of Jahne, Smith & Co. in 1867. He remained with them until the deaths of both Jahne and Smith about 1870-71 when the firm was succeeded by Hodenpyl, Tunison & Shiebler, manufacturers of gold chains. In 1873 or 1874 Shiebler purchased the business of Coles & Reynolds, manufacturers of silver spoons. On March 4, 1876, with a force of five men, he began business under his own name. A few months later he bought out the business of John Polhemus, an old and recognized silversmith and merged this plant with his own. A short time later he purchased the factory of M. Morgan, who had succeeded Albert Coles, another silversmith. This plant he merged with the others. The flatware dies of A.&W. Wood and Henry Hebbard and Hebbard & Polhemus were added to his plant. He also succeeded Theo. Evans & Co., probably in the 1870s. A few years later he moved the factory operations to Brooklyn. On January 1, 1892 the firm was incorporated. George W. Shiebler was president and Wm. F. Shiebler, treasurer. It was out of business before 1915. In 1892 there were reported negotiations underway to combine with the Gorham Company but no confirmation has been found.

In the beginning the Shiebler firm made only spoons and forks but this was gradually expanded until they produced the largest line of novelties in silver extant at the time. They were especially noted for their medallion work, inspired by the excavations at Pompeii and Herculanaeum and their transparent enamel work. Raised Greek mottoes appeared on the articles giving them the appearance of the antique. This type of work was applied to brooches,

sleeve buttons and bangles and was later extended to forks, spoons and holloware. Oxidized silver had until then been a failure on the market but when introduced by Shiebler met with instant success. Another one of his innovations was silver leaves tinted in all the rich autumn colors. This work was applied to spoons, berry bowls, pitchers and other articles. Shiebler is also credited with the introduction of Renaissance open-work style in jewelry, bonbonnières, dishes, trays and spoons.

(Old Mark.)

(Mark of an old silversmith named Platt, whose business was acquired by Shiebler. Probably firm of Platt & Brothers, thimble makers, N. Y. C. 1836-46.)

SHIELDS, INC.
Attleboro, Massachusetts

Founded c. 1920 as the Fillkwik Company, it was incorporated in 1936 under the present name. In January 1939 the company was bought by Rex Products Corporation of New Rochelle, New York.

During World War II, Shields produced insignia and medals, and now manufactures men's jewelry, fancy display and jewelry boxes.

SHIRLEY METALCRAFT, LTD.
Williamsburg, Virginia

Founded in 1955 by Shirley Robertson. He started working on castings in 1953 in a garage and expanded into the present location in 1955. Only the highest quality, lead-free, heavy gauge pewter is used in the handcrafted Shirley pewter. About a hundred different articles are made and include reproductions and adaptations of old designs as well as his own designs. Among them are bowls, trays, candlesticks, coffee and tea services, mugs, etc.

SHIRLEY
(Intaglio script)

Another mark: Colonial powder horn in Williamsburg with Shirley, Hand Made, Williamsburg, Va.

SHOEMAKER, PICKERING & CO.
Newark, New Jersey

Listed in JC 1896 in sterling and jewelry sections. Out of business before 1915.

Trademark identical to Frank Kursh & Son, Co.

SHREVE & CO.
San Francisco, California

Two brothers, George C. and S. S. Shreve first opened a jewelry shop in 1852 and were active in its management all their lives. The company was incorporated shortly before 1900.

Ownership and management has remained in the

hands of San Franciscans, though since 1912 no member of the Shreve family has been part of the corporation.

Shreve & Co., a San Francisco institution with a history almost as old as the city itself, has made silver services for several battleships and cruisers; the State of California's gift to Queen Elizabeth on her coronation; gifts for the delegates at the founding of the United Nations and has fashioned pieces to the special orders of kings, presidents, shahs, sheiks and people of the entertainment world. They also produce 20 exclusive flatware patterns.

In 1915 they bought the Vanderslice Company.

Shreve & Co. manufactured their first flatware in 1904.

"Obituary Geo. C. Shreve. B. Salem, Mass. about 65 years ago. He died after an illness of more than a year. He lived in Saco, Maine with his sister, Mrs. Calef, and was in the store of his half-brother, Benjamin, in that town. When a boy he shipped as a sailor aboard a coasting vessel on the Atlantic Coast, with his brother Samuel. After this he was with Kingsley & Shreve, at 22 Maiden Lane, N. Y. He came to California by way of Cape Horn, arriving in San Francisco in 1852. The same year he went into partnership with his brother Samuel S. Shreve, in the jewelry business. While on the way east, a few years later, S. S. Shreve was drowned near the Isthmus of Panama. According to their prior agreement, the surviving brother became sole owner of the business. Some years later George Bonney and Albert J. Lewis were associated with him, the three forming the firm of Geo. C. Shreve & Co." (JC&HR 10-25-1893, p. 13)

"George R. Shreve elected president of Shreve & Co., succeeding the late Al J. Lewis. Bruce Bonney elected treasurer. Mr. Bonney until recently had been manager of the New York wholesale department of Gorham Mfg. Co., in whose employ he had been for about 19 years. Mr. Bonney's uncle, Geo. Bonney is the largest stockholder in Shreve & Co." (JC&HR 10-16-1895, p. 23)

(Little used after 1918)

SHREVE & CO.

(Not used after January 1894)

SHREVE, CRUMP & LOW CO., INC.
Boston, Massachusetts

CHRONOLOGY

John M. McFarlane	1796
Jones & Ward	1809
Baldwin & Jones	1813
Putnam & Low	1822
John J. Low & Co.	1828
John B. Jones Co.	1838
Jones, Low & Ball	1839
Low, Ball & Co.	1840
Jones, Ball & Poor	1846
Harris & Stanwood	1847
Henry B. Stanwood	
Jones, Ball & Co.	1852
Jones, Shreve, Brown & Co.	1854
Shreve, Brown & Co.	1857
Shreve, Stanwood & Co.	1860
Shreve, Crump & Low Co.	1869
Shreve, Crump & Low Co., Inc.	1888

According to tradition, John McFarlane, originally from Salem, proprietor of a modest watchmaker's shop in 1796, was the founder of the company that is now known as Shreve, Crump & Low Co., Inc.

In the early 1800s Jabez Baldwin moved to Boston and formed a copartnership with a neighboring craftsman, and under the title of Baldwin & Jones continued the business begun by McFarlane.

Among the apprentices of Jabez Baldwin in Salem were John J. Low and Edward Putnam, who in 1822 established the firm of Putnam & Low. Three or four years later they separated and in 1839 John J. Low and his brother Francis, joined with George B. Jones, son of Mr. Baldwin's partner. In 1852 Benjamin Shreve was admitted to the firm and 17 years later Charles H. Crump joined. In 1888 the firm was incorporated as Shreve, Crump & Low Company under the law of Massachusetts, with Benjamin Shreve as president.

The Shreve, Crump & Low Company tradition so ably started by the Salem craftsmen and apprentices almost 150 years ago is being carried on today by Richard Shreve, great-grandson of the first Shreve.

The company does no manufacturing, but, has always sold designs made by the finest of American silversmiths; some of the designs being created exclusively for them.

SHREVE, TREAT & EACRET
San Francisco, California

Jewelers and silversmiths. Young George Shreve withdrew from Shreve & Co. and with Treat and Eacret formed the new firm in 1912 around the corner from the old one and were in business until c. 1940.

The last Directory entry was for 1941 when silversmithing was mentioned. Oddly, in the 1945-46 Directory the name is back in the listing with the note "See Granat Bros." who may have bought the firm but if they did so they did not stay at the same location but moved or located elsewhere.

VICTOR SIEDMAN MFG. CO., INC.
Brooklyn, New York

Manufacturing silversmiths c. 1920-1930. Makers of sterling silver holloware, picture frames and candlesticks.

A. L. SILBERSTEIN
New York, New York

Successor to Silberstein, Hecht & Co. before 1904.

Succeeded by Griffon Cutlery Works before 1915. Still in business under that name.

Griffon

(All Above on Cutlery.)

GRIFFON

SILBERSTEIN, HECHT & CO.
New York, New York

Founding date unknown.
Succeeded by A. L. Silberstein before 1904. Manufacturers of sterling silverware.

SILBERSTEIN, LA PORTE & CO.
Providence, Rhode Island
New York, New York

"Silberstein, La Porte & Co. importers of cutlery, N.Y. This firm also manufactures sterling silver cutlery, with a factory in Providence, Rhode Island. Griffen[sic!] trademark." (JC&HR 6-23-1897, p. 36) Probably related to above.

SILO SILVER MFG. CO.
New York, New York

Listed 1927 KJI as manufacturers of silverplated wares.

SILVER BROTHERS
Atlanta, Georgia

Registered trademark for sterling silver and silverplated flatware and holloware and jewelry.

(Used since June 1, 1950)

THE SILVER CITY PLATE CO.
Meriden, Connecticut

"The Silver City Plate Co. has begun the manufacture of Britannia ware in Meriden. Harry Felix, formerly with the Toronto Silver Plate Co., is associated with three others in the enterprise." (JW 1-23-1895, p. 3) Eugene H. Ray, also with the company, had learned his trade from Simons & Miller Co., in Middletown.
In 1908 the International Silver Co. bought from the receivers the business and tools they could use.

SILVER COUNSELORS OF HOME DECORATORS, INC.
Newark, New York

Successors between 1943 and 1950 to Home Decorators, Inc.

State House ⚜ Sterling

Inaugural   *Formality*

SILVERART
New York, New York

Listed 1957 and 1961 JBG as manufacturers of silverware.

SILVERCRAFT CO. INC.
Boston, Massachusetts

Listed JC-K 1950 as manufacturers. Owned now by Raimond Silver Manufacturers.

SILVERCRAFT

SILVER METAL MFG. CO.
Lyons and Oswego, New York

"A stock company has been organized to manufacture table ware from a metal recently invented by D. J. Toothill. The new firm will be known as the Silver Metal Mfg. Co. of Lyons." (JW April 1892)
"The Silver Metal Mfg. Co. recently moved from Lyons, N. Y. to Oswego, N. Y. started up last Monday." (JC&HR 8-31-1892, p. 17)

SILVER PLATE CUTLERY CO.
Birmingham, Connecticut

This concern, as the name indicates, made cutlery, and some of it was silverplated. They were in business as early as 1884 and continued until some time after 1896. Some of their products they sold to other manufacturers, such as Holmes & Edwards, Wm. Rogers Mfg. Co., etc., furnishing lines particularly suitable for the firms doing the marketing.

THE SILVERSMITHS CO.
SILVERSMITHS STOCKS CO.

"The Silversmith's Co. incorporated, the present companies comprised in the new organization . . . . Gorham, Whiting, Dominick & Haff, Geo. W. Shiebler and Towle Mfg. Co." (JC&HR 12-14-1892, p. 22) Nothing ever came of this. A few years later, however, Wm. B. Durgin Co., W. B. Kerr Co., The Mount Vernon Co. and Whiting Mfg. Co. became a part of the Gorham Company.

F. W. SIM & CO.
Troy, New York

Registered U.S. Patent June 6, 1891 for manufacture of souvenir sterling silverware. No other record.

SIMMONS & PAYE
North Attleboro, Mass.
See Paye & Baker

"Simmons & Paye, manufacturers of souvenir spoons, etc., will show their goods in Denver in 1898." (JC&HR 12-15-1897, p. 26)
They sold some of their patterns and dies to the Wendell Mfg. Co.

S. & P.

SIMONS BRO. & CO.
Philadelphia, Pennsylvania

Simons, Bro. & C. was established in 1840 by George W. Simons, father of John F. Simons, Frederick M. Simons and Edwin S. Simons, who were later members of the firm. Some years subsequent to 1840, Peter B. Simons joined his brother, the firm becoming George W. Simons & Bro. In 1861 Thomas Maddock was admitted to an interest in the business, and later, S. B. Opdyke, the firm name changing to Simons, Bro., Opdyke & Co. Some years later Mr. Opdyke retired, as did subsequently the elder Simons, the firm continuing under the name of Simons, Bro. & Co. It is now Simons Bros. Co.

George W. Simons was born in Philadelphia in 1819 and learned there the trade of making silver thimbles and pencils. These were the company's first products. Gradually they increased the scope of their activities and produced many exclusive patterns of tea sets and tableware, comb tops, cane and umbrella heads as well as their well-known thimbles. They were successors to Peter L. Krider Co. in 1903. Their flatware patterns and dies and Simons Bros. patterns and dies were sold to the Alvin Mfg. Co. in 1908 and they discontinued flatware manufacture entirely.

ESTABLISHED 1840

SIMONS & MILLER PLATE CO.
Middletown, Connecticut

Apparently begun by workmen previously associated with the Middletown Plate Co. Listed in the Middletown Directory in 1870. A price list for 1874 is in existence. The New England business directory for 1867 lists Simons, Lawrence & Co. Britannia makers of Middletown, Conn. — probably their predecessors.

SIMPSON-BRAINERD CO.
Providence, Rhode Island

Listed JC 1915-1922 in plated silver section.

ENGLISH SILVER

SIMPSON, HALL, MILLER & CO.
Wallingford, Connecticut
See International Silver Co.

Samuel Simpson was well-known for his britannia ware in Wallingford. In 1866 he organized Simpson, Hall, Miller & Co. to do silverplating. He was extremely successful and in 1878 made a contract with William Rogers, Jr., to supervise the manufacture and marketing of Simpson, Hall, Miller & Co. Rogers "Eagle" Brand.

In 1895 they started the manufacture of sterling silverware and were one of the original companies to become part of the International Silver Company in 1989. The Wallingford factory became International's sterling center.

Their sterling flatware produced after 1895. The same mark continued by International Silver Co.

(Flatware.)

(Hollowware.)

(Cheaper Grade.)

AMERICAN SILVER PLATE CO.

SIMPSON NICKEL SILVER CO.
Wallingford, Connecticut
See International Silver Co.

Incorporated in 1871 by Samuel Simpson, E. W. Sperry, Albert A. Sperry, Alfred W. Sperry and R. L. McChristie. They made nickel silver flatware blanks which were sold to Simpson, Hall, Miller & Co. for plating and marketing. They did not use a trademark because they sold their products to other silver manufacturers. They began the manufacture of sterling silver flatware shortly before the organization of the International Silver Co. The nickel silver operations were moved to other factories after the company became part of the International Silver Co. in 1898.

SINCLAIR MFG. CO.
Chartley, Massachusetts

Listed in 1950 JC-K under sterling.

B. & J. SIPPEL LTD.
Sheffield, England

Registered trademark for flatware.

SIPELIA

(Used since August 13, 1934)

JAMES SISSFORD
Baltimore, Maryland

Listed in the 1850 Census as a silversmith. Born in the District of Columbia.

WM. AND GEO. SISSONS
Sheffield, England

Successors to Smith, Sissons & Co. who were makers of Sheffield plate and silversmiths in 1848.

Listed in JC 1909-1922 in sterling and plated silver sections.

W. S.

C. S.

(On plated silver)

(On sterling silver)

A. F. SMITH CO.
Omaha, Nebraska

Founded in 1894 as Reichenberg-Smith Co., wholesale jewelers. A. F. Smith, President, Louis Reichenberg, Vice President and Max Reichenberg, Sec. Last listed under this name in 1905.

The 1906 City Directory carries the listing of the A. F. Smith Co. with Arthur F. Smith as President. They were incorporated in 1932. In 1936 the listing is A. F. Smith & Co. with G. A. Smith as President-treasurer; L. P. Smith, Vice President and A. F. Smith, Secretary.

The 1938 listing is Smith & Co., with Franklin & Gordon A. Smith (sons) listed as owners. The 1941 listing is A. F. Smith & Co., Inc. and is the last listing under the Smith name.

It was later known as the Allgaier-Smith Co., Inc. in 1942; Allgaier Jewelry Co. in 1945 and John Byrne Inc. 1948-1964.

SMITH & COMPANY
Albany, New York

Listed in the Albany City Directory 1846-1848 as Sheldon & Feltman, Brittania [sic] and Argentina Manufactory. Listed 1849-1853 as Smith & Feltman, Argentine and Brittannia Works. Listed 1853-1856 as Smith & Company, Argentine and Brittania Works.

The Argentina and Argentine are thought to have been britannia ware plated with silver.

C. R. SMITH PLATING COMPANY
Providence, Rhode Island

"The C. R. Smith Plating Company was established in 1890." (JW 3-30-1892)

E. H. H. SMITH KNIFE CO.
Bridgeport, Connecticut

In business in 1899 as manufacturers of plated silver knives. Out of business before 1915.

Probably related to E. H. H. Smith Silver Co. but this could not be established.

(Knives.)

E. H. H. SMITH SILVER CO.
Bridgeport, Connecticut
See Albert Pick & Co., Inc.
See Blackstone Silver Co.

The E. H. H. Smith Silver Company was first listed in the Bridgeport City Directory in 1907. Listed in the JC in 1904. U. S. Patent No. 44,191 was issued in their name on February 14, 1905. They were manufacturers of "artistic cutlery and sterling effects in quintuple plated spoons and forks." They were last listed in the 1919 City Directory and were succeeded by the Albert Pick Company in 1920.

Reorganized as Blackstone Silver Co. in 1914. Sold to Bernstein (of National Silver Co.?) in 1943.

× × ⑤ × ×

◁ **S** ▷

(Flatware.)

SMITH & FELTMAN
See Smith & Company

SMITH & FELTMAN
ALBANY

FRANK W. SMITH SILVER CO., INC.
Gardner, Massachusetts
See The Webster Co.

Frank W. Smith (b. March 13, 1848; d. August 2, 1904), son of Dr. William A. and Susan F. (Durgin) Smith was born in Thornton, New Hampshire. He entered the employ of his relative, William B. Durgin, silversmith in Concord, New Hampshire and remained with him in various capacities until 1886 when the Smith family moved to Gardner, Massachusetts. He established his silversmith's factory that year. He had two sons, William D. and Frank H., the former associated with him in business.

Sterling flatware and holloware were the principal products of the factory. For a time, Arthur J. Stone, expert in handwrought silver and designer, was associated with the firm.

In October 1958 all of the flatware tools and dies, along with the trade name and trademark, were purchased by the Webster Company and the flatware portion of the business moved to North Attleboro, Massachusetts.

TRADE MARK.
925/1000 FINE

FREDERICK L. SMITH
Denver, Colorado

The business was first listed as the C. H. Green Jewelry Company in 1889 with F. L. Smith as secretary-treasurer and L. H. Gurnsey, manager. In 1890 it was known as the C. H. Green Jewelry Company with the Gurnsey name no longer listed. In 1892 the name was changed to the Green-Smith Watch and Diamond Company. Harper's Magazine, July 1892, carried an advertisement listing them as manufacturers of souvenir spoons made of Colorado silver, "Protected by letters Patent, dated Feb. 16, 1892." In 1894 the business listing was dropped and the only entry was under Smith. In 1895 the listing was Frederick L. Smith as manager of John W. Knox — successor to Green-Smith Company.

GEORGE W. SMITH
Albany, New York
See Rogers Brothers

Holloware silverplater in Albany, New York before he joined with Wm. Rogers and founded the Rogers, Smith & Co. of Hartford, Connecticut in 1856. Went out of business in 1862.

LAWRENCE B. SMITH CO.
Boston, Massachusetts

Founded in Boston in 1887. Made sterling and plated silverware. Out of business about 1958.

SMITH & MAYO
Newark, New Jersey

Benjamin J. Mayo and Edwin B. Smith were gold and silverplaters c. 1860.

SMITH METAL ARTS COMPANY
Buffalo, New York

Registered trademark for use on trophies, vases, bowls, photograph frames, smoking accessories, desk accessories, etc., all embossed, ornamented or plated with silver.

SILVERCREST

(Used since January 1920)

SMITH, PATTERSON & CO.
Boston, Massachusetts

Founded in 1876, became part of Jordan Marsh, New England's largest department store, in 1956. Agents for "several of the best manufacturers." Importers of watches, clocks, silverware and jewelry.

RICHARD SMITH
Newark, New Jersey

Richard Smith was a jeweler who sold under the name of the Newark Jewelry Store 1850-1898. He had been with Baldwin & Smith. Advertised in the Newark Directory 1854 a large variety of silverware "manufactured in the best style warranted of the finest quality," and in the 1859 Directory "Not only do I claim superiority so far as artistic design and perfect finish are concerned but every article made is guaranteed to equal the best American coin. . ."

SMITH & SMITH
Attleboro, Massachusetts
See Wallace Silversmiths

Manufacturers of sterling cigar boxes and novelties.
Specialize in reproductions of early American, English and Dutch pieces in sterling.
A division of Wallace Silversmiths.

S & S

W. D. SMITH SILVER CO.
Chicago, Illinois

Rudolph J. Bourgeois, vice-president of the company, registered U.S. Patent No. 148,714 on November 22, 1921 for the manufacture of silverware, particularly holloware, flatware, jewelry and precious metal ware. In applying for this patent registration, it was stated that this trademark had been used continuously since 1913.
The company was incorporated under the laws of Delaware and was located in Chicago.

(Nickel Silver Hollowware.)   *(Plated Flatware.)*

ALBERT SMYTH CO., INC.
Baltimore, Maryland

Listed 1965 JC-K. 1974 listing has no address.

SMYTH

EDWIN V. SNYDER
Philadelphia, Pennsylvania

Listed JKD 1918-19 as a silversmith.

SOCIÉTÉ PICARD FRERES
Paris, France

Registered trademarks U. S. Patent Office No. 30,171, June 8, 1897 for table, kitchen, dresserware and utensils of copper and pure silver. No record after c. 1920.

PARIS

BI-METAL
CUIVRE
ET
ARGENT PUR

Bté S G.D.G.

A. M. SOFFEL CO., INC.
Newark, New Jersey

Manufacturers (?) of sterling silverware c. 1920-30.

SOUTHERN SILCO
Hartsville, South Carolina

Name found stamped on silverware.

SOUTHINGTON CUTLERY CO.

Advertised holloware and knives (JC&HR December 1886) "Mfg. fine silver Plated Ware." (Adv. JC&HR March 1887)
"The Southington Cutlery Co. sent out circulars stating that their Britannia department will be reorganized as a separate concern under the name

Southington Silver Plate Co." (JC&HR 11-30-1892, p. 4)

SOUTHINGTON CO.
See Barbour Silver Co.
See International Silver Co.

Also used name of company in a circle with TRIPLE.

SOUTHINGTON CO.

A. S. SOUTHWICK & CO.
Providence, Rhode Island

"Established in 1874 as Vose & Southwick." (JW 3-30-1892)
　　Manufacturers of silverwares.

GEORGE A. SPARKS
Brooklyn, New York

Manufacturers (?) of plated silver c. 1920.

S-C-A G

J. E. SPARKS
Brooklyn, New York

Manufacturer (?) of sterling silver c. 1920.

$ Spark $

SPAULDING & CO.
Chicago, Illinois

Founded in 1855 under the name of S. Hoard & Co. In 1888 it was incorporated under the name of Spaulding & Company, Inc., taking over, at that time, the business of N. Matson & Co. (q.v.)

On November 2, 1888 Levi Leiter of Chicago and Edward Holbrook of New York, representing the interests of the Gorham Mfg. Co. of Providence, and Henry A. Spaulding, formed a corporation to manufacture and retail watches, clocks, jewelry, diamonds, silverware, silverplated ware, objects of art and other related merchandise, with Henry A. Spaulding as its first president. In the 1920s the Gorham Mfg. Co. acquired control of Spaulding & Co. and the name changed to Spaulding-Gorham, Inc. On June 1, 1943 the entire interests of Spaulding-Gorham, Inc. were acquired by Gordon Lang, at which time the name was changed to Spaulding & Company. On October 1, 1973 ownership was acquired by Stewart S. Peacock.

Spaulding & Co.'s English sterling has its own Guildhall registered London hallmark. They have long been noted for their handforged silver by Fletcher of London as well as flatware by eminent American silversmiths.

REGISTERED LONDON HALLMARK

SPAULDING-GORHAM, INC.
See Spaulding & Co.

D. S. SPAULDING
Mansfield, Massachusetts

Listed in JC 1896-1922 in sterling and plated silver sections.

(Sterling Silver Top and Plated Back
(On sterling silver)

(On plated silver)

SPENCE, GAVEN & CO.
Newark, New Jersey

Listed as silversmiths 1859-1916 in Newark City Directories.

SPENCE & CO. STERLING

GAVEN & SPENCE

G. SPENCE (straight line) with pseudo hallmarks, lion, head leopard

G. SPENCE (in half circle) with lion passant, D. Head.

BEN. SPIER
New York, New York

Successor to Spier & Forsheim about 1909. Wholesaler (?) of silverware, jewelry and related articles.

SPIER & FORSHEIM
New York, New York
See Ben. Spier Co.

Listed JC 1896. Succeeded by Ben. Spier Co. c. 1909.

WILLIAM SPRATLING
New Orleans, Louisiana
Taxco, Mexico

Spratling had taught architecture at Tulane University, New Orleans. In 1925 he traveled to Mexico and decided to settle in Taxco where he was one of the pioneers in reviving the art of silversmithing there. He started a shop with six boys whom he trained. Incorporating old Aztec designs and *ranchero* motifs the shop turned out fine work, much of it combining wood and metal. In 1944 he was sent to Alaska by the U. S. Dept. of Interior where he trained Alaskan Indians in the art of silversmithing. Spratling left behind a legacy of many silversmiths in both areas, trained in the highest standards of craftsmanship. He himself was killed in an automobile accident in August, 1967.

SPRINGFIELD SILVER PLATE CO.
Springfield, Ohio

"The Springfield Silver Plate Co., Springfield, Ohio, have incorp. to mfg. casket hardware, novelties and to do electroplating. Incorporators are: Ed. N. Lupfer, Charles H. Hiser, W. H. Reania, Paul A. Staley and W. W. Diehl. Lupfer has conducted a successful similar business for three years." (JC&HR 1-22-1896, p. 21)

GEORGE W. SPURR & CO.
Greenfield, Massachusetts
See Rogers & Spurr Mfg. Co.

S. & S. NOVELTY CO.
Providence, Rhode Island

Manufacturers (?) of plated silver novelties c. 1915-1922.

STANDARD MFG. CO.
Winsted, Connecticut

"The Standard Mfg. Co., Winsted, Conn., who began the mfg. of silverplated table knives, have increased their working capital and are turning out considerable quantities of goods." (JC&HR 3-16-1898, p. 40)

STANDARD SILVER CO. OF TORONTO
Toronto, Canada
See International Silver Co.
See International Silver Co. of Canada, Ltd.

When the Acme Silver Co. of Toronto was liquidated in 1893 it was sold to W. K. George and others who formed the Standard Silver Co., Toronto, Ltd., for the production of silverplated flatware and holloware and hotel ware. Merged with International Silver Co. of Canada, Ltd. about 1912.

(*E. P. on Copper.*)

MANF'D AND GUARANTEED BY

TRADE MARK FOR HOLLOW WARE.

MONARCH SILVER CO.

STANDARD SILVERWARE COMPANY
Boston, Massachusetts

Retailer and jobber of plated silverware. First appeared in the Boston City Directories in 1883, which probably means that it was founded the previous year. Last listed in 1921. Edward C. Webb was head of the firm and was associated with it from about 1903 through 1921.

NEVADA SILVER METAL

STANLEY & AYLWARD, LTD.
Toronto, Canada

Wholesalers of plated silver holloware c. 1920.

THEODORE B. STARR
New York, New York

In business c. 1900-1924. Succeeded by Reed & Barton.

I. J. STEANE & CO.
Hartford, Connecticut and New York
See Barbour Silver Co.

Isaac J. Steane, a watchmaker at Coventry, England, came to America about 1866 to collect a bad debt. He was forced to take over his debtor's stock, which he auctioned off at a profit of $6,000. He continued in the auction business for some time; returned to England, wound up his business affairs and came again to the United States where he formed the firm of Steane, Son & Hall, consisting of Isaac J. Steane, Isaac J. Steane, Jr., and J. P. Hall. Mr. Hall retired in 1886 and the firm name was changed to I. J. Steane & Co.

Mr. Steane bought the Taunton Silver Plate Co., and took stock to New York for auction. He later bought the Albany Silver Plate Co., combining the affairs of these two companies with that of I. J. Steane & Co.

In the early 1880s, Mr. Steane purchased the old silverware stock of the Cromwell Plate Co., of Cromwell, Connecticut. The sale was made by A. E. Hobson, who in 1881 had left the Meriden Britannia Co. to become a salesman for Cromwell.

About this same time, the Barbour Bros. Co. was formed by S. L. Barbour, from Chicago, joined by his brother Charles, who was in business in New Haven. I. J. Steane & Co. produced the goods that the Barbour Bros. Co. marketed. Mr. Hobson was associated with I. J. Steane at this time. At the suggestion of W. H. Watrous, the business was moved to Hartford and two years later the Hartford Silver Plate Company business was also acquired. Mr. Steane, Sr. retired and returned to England in 1888.

The I. J. Steane Co., the Barbour Bros. Co. and the Barbour Hobson Co., all of Hartford, united to form the Barbour Silver Company in 1892.

Steane introduced many European designs into this country by purchasing silver articles in Europe and bringing them to be copied here.

STEANE, SON & HALL
New York, New York
See Barbour Silver Co.
See I. J. Steane & Co.

THE STEEL-BRUSSEL CO.
New York, New York

Listed in JC 1896 in sterling silver section. Out of business before 1904.

TRADE MARK

STERLING

H. STEINACKER
Baltimore, Maryland

Listed in 1868-1869 Baltimore City Directory as a silverplater.

STERLING COMPANY
Derby, Connecticut

Published illustrated catalogs of fine silverware in 1893 and 1898. On the catalogs is the statement, "Established 1866."

STERLING CRAFT
Toronto, Canada

Sterling silver manufacture (?) c. 1920. Related (?) to Spurrier & Co., London.

STERLING SILVER MFG. CO.
Baltimore, Maryland

"The Sterling Silver Manufacturing Company, Baltimore, Md. which by an infusion of new blood and fresh capital, emerged from the Klank Mfg. C., recently passed the first twelfth month of their existence with a good yearly record. They manufacture solid silver holloware and flatware, and a full line of white metal goods, besides doing considerable repairing and replating. Their new and original designs in hollowware have proved very taking. Factory at 110 W. Fayette St., office and salesroom at 17 N. Liberty St." (JC&HR 2-14-1894, p. 27)

THE STERLING SILVER MFG. CO.
Providence, Rhode Island

Listed in the City Directories 1909-1932. Samuel A. Schreiber, president-treasurer; Max L. Jocby vice-president; L. C. McCaffrey, sec. Manufacturing silversmiths. Made sterling flat and holloware and souvenir spoons.

Their flatware dies were purchased by Saart Bros.

STERLING SILVER SOUVENIR CO.
Boston, Massachusetts

In business before 1890. Advertised that they were makers of sterling silver souvenirs. Out of business before 1915.

LOUIS STERN CO., INC.
Providence, Rhode Island

Established in 1871 as chainmakers and silversmiths. Wholesalers of chains, bags, watch bracelets, bracelets, knives, buckles and jewelry. Last record found 1950.

LS. & Co.

S. STERNAU & CO.
Brooklyn, New York and New York, New York

Proprietors were Sigmund Sternau and Charles Nelson.

Listed in 1896 Jewelers' Weekly as manufacturer of plated silver chafing dishes and miscellaneous lines. Last record c. 1920.

(*Metal Wares.*)

STEVENS & LEITHOFF
Irvington, New Jersey

Listed JC 1915 in sterling silver section. Out of business before 1922.

STEVENS SILVER CO.
Portland, Maine
See Colonial Silver Co.

CHRONOLOGY

Stevens & Smart	1879-1883
Stevens, Smart & Dunham	1884-1886
Stevens & Smart	1887-1890
Stevens, Woodman & Co.	1890-1891
Woodman-Cook Co.	1892-1893
Stevens Silver Co.	1893-1899

The firm of Alfred A. Stevens was listed in 1879 and known as Stevens & Smart (Alfred A. Stevens and Nehemiah Smart), manufacturers of britannia wares until 1883 when it was succeeded by Stevens, Smart & Dunham (Joseph Dunham). It became Stevens, Woodman & Co., (Fred H. Woodman). They advertised that they did silverplating. Woodman-Cook succeeded in 1892. They manufactured silverplated wares. Edward B. Cook was president; C. H. Fessenden, vice president and Fred H. Woodman, treasurer. This was succeeded by the Stevens Silver Co. incorporated in 1893. Alfred A. Stevens was president. He left Woodman-Cook to firm the Stevens Silver Company which later became the Colonial Silver Co.

THE STIEFF COMPANY
Baltimore, Maryland

Founded in 1892 as The Baltimore Sterling Silver Company by Charles C. Stieff. In 1904 the corporation name was changed to The Stieff Company.

They are manufacturers of sterling silver flatware and holloware. Their "Rose" pattern is so identified with Baltimore that it is often called "Baltimore Rose." They are the exclusive makers of Williamsburg Restoration, Historic Newport and Old Sturbridge Village sterling silver and pewter reproductions.

Their appointment to make sterling silver holloware and flatware reproductions for Williamsburg was in September 1939. They began the production of pewter August 19, 1951, after receiving the appointment but because of the tin shortage caused by the Korean war, their first shipments were not made until August 1953.

They bought the Schofield Co. in 1967.

STIEFF STERLING

"Hallmark" used on Williamsburg Restorations. Used in Virginia in the 17th and 18th centuries as a shipper's or maker's mark. Used in England as early as the 16th century — apparently to indicate the highest quality.

Since 1901 the Stieff Company has used year markings on their sterling silver holloware.

1901 ①	1929 ⌀ or 🖋	1946	L
1902 ②	1930 ☆	1947	M
1903 ③	1931 ⚘ or Ψ	1948	N
to	1932 ➵	1949	O
1916 ⑯	1933 ⚲ or ⚓	1950	P
1917 ⬭ or ◇	1934 ⌷ or ⛃	1951	R
1918 △	1935 ✓ or ✓	1952	S
1919 ○	1936 A	1953	T
1920 ⌒ or ⌓	1937 B	1954	U
1921 —	1938 C	1955	W
1922 +	1939 D	1956	X
1923 ⧧ or ++	1940 E	1957	Y
1924 ⧣	1941 F	1958	Z
1925 ⬠	1942 G	1959	1
1926 ⬡ or ◇	1943 H	1960	2
1927 ☾ or ⌒	1944 J		
1928 卍	1945 K		

1961	3
1962	4
1963	5
1964	6
1965	7
1966	8
1967	9
1968	10
1969	11
1970	12
1971	13
1972	14
1973	15
1974	16

STIEFF-ORTH CO.
Baltimore, Maryland

Not listed in Baltimore City Directories which were checked from the 1890s through the 1930s. Listed in JC 1909 sterling silver section. Out of business before 1915.

JAMES H. STIMPSON
Baltimore, Maryland

Listed Baltimore City Directories 1851-1868, variously as "zink works," "chemist" and "manuf'g chemist and patentee of ice pitcher, etc." James H. Stimpson was the son of James Stimpson, inventor of the double-wall ice pitcher. James H. Stimpson invented and patented a triple-wall ice pitcher and several styles of butter coolers. Though listed as a "chemist" the inventory of his estate revealed that his "chemical works" was actually a silverplating establishment.

(On britannia)

G. B. STOCKING
Tacoma, Washington

Jeweler, watchmaker, optician 1893-1896. Registered U.S. Patent No. 22,807, April 18, 1893 for manufacture of jewelry, spoons and other flatware.

RHODODENDRON

ARTHUR J. STONE
Gardner, Massachusetts
See Stone Associates

STERLING

STONE ASSOCIATES
Gardner, Massachusetts

Founded by Arthur J. Stone (b. September 26, 1847; d. 1938), who was born in Sheffield, England. After an apprenticeship of seven years and a working practice as a designer and chaser for ten years, he came to this country in 1884 and was employed by Wm. B. Durgin, in Concord, New Hampshire. He later became superintendent and designer of the Frank W. Smith Silver Shop in Gardner, Massachusetts.

Stone opened his own shop in 1901 with the assistance of his young American wife. There handwrought silverware was made.

In 1913 he received the first medal for excellence in craftsmanship and service given by the Society of Arts and Crafts of Boston.

At first he worked alone, gradually adding assistants until he had twelve in number. He retired in 1937 at the age of ninety and sold the shop to Henry Heywood of Gardner. Mr. Heywood continued the business for a short period and following his death his sons carried it on until the mid-fifties. Mr. Stone's associates and successors followed his own high standards until they went out of business.

When Stone was in charge of the shop he insisted that each craftsman should sign his work, so each had his initial stamped under the STERLING mark on holloware and after the STERLING on flatware. Below is a list* of the Stone craftsmen and their dates as nearly as they can be reconstructed. The initials used to identify their work precede the names:

L—Lamphrey 1908-1911
W—Alfred Wickstrom 1912-1915
C—David Carlson 1916-1921 (flatware)
B—George Blanchard 1906-1908 (flatware)
ᴔ—Charles Brown 1911-1936 (to the end of Stone's ownership) (flatware)
H—Arthur Hartwell 1910-1936, to end of Stone's ownership (holloware)
T—Herbert Taylor 1908-1936, to end of Stone's ownership
E—George C. Erickson (q.v.) 1918-1932 (flatware) (He went into business for himself and still works in Gardner.
G—Herman W. Glendenning (q.v.) 1920-1936 (flatware and holloware) to end of Stone's ownership. He worked for George C. Erickson until 1971. Now works for himself in Gardner.

C—Edgar Caron 1924-1936, to end of Stone's ownership (holloware)
U—Earl Underwood 1918-1924 and 1928-1930 (holloware)

* Most of the information regarding craftsmen's marks reprinted from the Magazine *Silver*, Sept.-Oct. 1973 by permission.

The silversmith's mark used by Arthur Stone consisted of a chasing hammer whose head formed the "A" for Arthur with the handle continuing on to cross the "T" in Stone.

When Heywood took over the shop the mark was changed to three Ss with the hammer handle crossing through each.

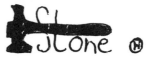

The three S mark was soon discarded and the original mark used again with the addition of a small oval panel at the end of Stone. The oval panel contained an "H".

STONE STERLING SILVER CO.
New York, New York

Registered their trademark U. S. Patent Office, No. 28,350, June 4, 1896 for silverware and jewelry. Listed in JC 1896. Out of business before 1904.

MAX H. STORCH
New York, New York

Registered trademarks for use on silverplated and sterling flatware and other tableware.

(Used since 1949)

(Used since 1950)

L. S. STOWE
See H. J. Webb & Co.

Stowe was born August 9, 1834, and orphaned at the age of 12. He was "bound out" to a farmer. When he was 18 he began training in the jewelry trade. He started in business in Gardner, Massachusetts in 1855. He moved to Springfield in 1864. Sold out to Webb in 1900 and died in 1924." (Clipping from unidentified newspaper dated 1924)

— 164 —

A. STOWELL, JR.
Baltimore, Maryland

Silversmith c. 1855. Listed as member of firm Gould, Stowell & Ward in 1855-1856 Baltimore City Directory.

STRATHMORE CO.
Providence, Rhode Island

Manufacturers of sterling flatware and plated silverware, holloware, picture frames and gift shop novelties. Listed 1915 through 1927.

SOLID STRATHMORE SILVER
T.S. CO.
STRATHMORE MESH
DIAMOND MESH

NATHAN STRAUS-DUPARQUET INC.
New York, New York

Tradename filed Sept. 7, 1950 for use on silverplated flatware. Claims use since January 1931.

NASTRAUS

STRAUSS SILVER CO., INC.
New York, New York

Manufacturers and importers of solid and silverplated Dutch silver novelties. Late 1920s and 1930s.

R. STRICKLAND & CO.
Albany, New York

Ralph Strickland listed in Albany City Directories 1857-1884 as manufacturer of plated wares.

Trademark is the company name and Albany, N. Y. in a circle.

STRONG & ELDER CO.
No address

Listed in JC 1896 sterling section as out of business.

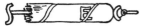

STRONG MFG. CO.
Winsted, Connecticut

In 1856, Markham and Strong of East Hampton, Connecticut made a small line of coffin tacks, screws and handles from white metal. Mr. Markham continued the business while the two Strongs, David and Clark were in the Union service. In 1866 David Strong bought out the company and moved to Winsted, Connecticut. The articles were considered of great beauty and were silver plated. It is reported that General Grant's casket was adorned with gold handles made by them. Also, handles and plates were furnished for the caskets of ex-president Harrison and Cornelius Vanderbilt. The company is last listed in 1934 city directory. No trademark has been located.

ARTHUR STUART COMPANY
Albuquerque, New Mexico

The company was established in 1949 and operated, according to the 1959 Albuquerque City Directory, by Arthur H. Spiegel. The above trademark and the sterling flatware pattern names *Empress Carlotta* and *Fidelity* were registered on the same date. Four additional sterling silver flatware pattern names,

Queen of Scots, Ceremonial, Crescendo and *Breath of Spring*, were registered November 10, 1949. The designs originated in Albuquerque and were sold on a direct mail basis from there. The silver was manufactured in Meriden, Connecticut by the Amston Company. When Amston went into bankruptcy in 1960, the Arthur Stuart Company was dissolved.

(No. 598,123, filed May 25, 1950; claims use since August 15, 1949.)

STUDIO SILVERSMITHS
Division of Hannon & Smith Co., Inc.
Hawthorne, New Jersey

Founded in 1950 as Hannon & Smith Co. by Jack Hannon and Elmer Smith, both deceased. Now owned by Elmer Smith's widow, since remarried, Margaret Smith Gunster. Manufacturers of 24K gold plate, silverplate, crystal combined with gold and silverplate. Products include holloware, salad bowls, salad servers, gold and silver footed crystal bowls, candelabra, centerpieces, etc.

SSS

STURDY & MARCY
See Fred I. Marcy & Co.

SUCKLING, LTD.
Birmingham, England

Successor to Wm. Suckling & Sons between 1915-1922. Manufacturers of plated silverware.

WYNDHAM A. SULLIVAN
Baltimore, Maryland

Listed in Baltimore City Directories 1900-1915 as a silversmith in the firm of Ritter & Sullivan.

SUMMIT SILVER INC.
New York, New York

Advertised 1965-74. Advertising says "two-tone decorative silverplate that never needs any polishing . . . From the famous HOKA silversmiths in Western Germany." Distributors (?) only. No answer to inquiries.

SUNDERLIN COMPANY
Rochester, New York

This silversmithing business began with three Burr brothers; Albert, who was apprenticed to Erastus Cook, and died shortly after starting his jewelry business; Alexander J., who was Albert's apprentice and Cornelius. The business went through a series of partnerships from 1838 and was known as C. A. Burr & Company after the death of the two brothers. In 1864 it was sold to Sunderlin & Weaver; became Sunderlin & McAllister; L. Sunderlin & Company and in 1944 was the Sunderlin Company. Out of business in 1952.

SUPERIOR SILVER COMPANY
See Middletown Plate Co.
See Wilcox Silver Plate Co.

The Superior Silver Co. marks were used by the Middletown Plate Co.
The Superior marks first read "Superior Silver Co." and later read "Superior Silver Plate Co." This change may have been after the Middletown Plate Company moved to Meriden and the Superior line was transferred to Wilcox Silver Plate Company.

(Registered April 3, 1906; first use claimed February 6, 1906; renewed in 1926)

SUPREME SILVER CO.
New York, New York

Manufacturers of sterling silver holloware and repair work c. 1930.

SUTTON HOO JEWELERS
Colorado Springs, Colorado

Founded November 1972 by Bob Newell and Charles Lamoreaux. They make one-of-a-kind jewelry and holloware of sterling silver and gold. The firm was joined in 1974 by Lewis Ridenour, silversmith, who concentrates on holloware and flatware. Bob Newell (b. December 6, 1940) received his education at the New Mexico Military Institute and studied the art of *cire perdue* with the master technician from New Gold Company. Charles Lamoureaux (b. December 26, 1950) received his education at the University of Kansas. Lewis Ridenour, (b. July 8, 1949) was educated at Northwest Missouri State College and the University of Kansas.

Bob Newell   Charles Lamoreaux   Lewis Ridenour

(Shop stamp)

THE SWEETSER CO.
New York, New York

Gold and silversmiths c. 1900-1915.

CHAS. N. SWIFT & CO.
New York, New York

Listed JC 1904 sterling silver section. Out of business before 1915.

SYRACUSE SILVER COMPANY
Syracuse, New York

First listed in Syracuse City Directory in 1940 as manufacturers of silverplated holloware, novelties, trophies, also plating. Ernest Kauer, owner. The 1946-56 Directories list Mrs. Edith O. Kauer as owner and the 1965-66 telephone directory lists only her home address.

SYRACUSE SILVER MFG. CO.
Syracuse, New York
See Lesser & Rheinauer
See A. B. Schreuder

"The sterling silver manufacturing plant of A. B. Schreuder, which has been in existence for 40 years, goes into the hands of the Syracuse Silver Mfg. Co. The latter is a new organization formed by the partners in the firm of A. Lesser's Sons, wholesale jewelers. Members of the company are Simon Lesser, S. Harry Lesser and Benjamin Lesser. They will manufacture sterling silver novelties. Benjamin Lesser will be manager." (JC&HR 2-20-1895, p. 10)

Listed 1896-1904 in JC as manufacturers of sterling silverware. Syracuse Silver Mfg. Co. listed in Syracuse, New York City Directories 1895-1900. Under the first listing, J. Barton French was president and business manager, A. Hubbs, Secretary and E. Elmer Keeler, treas. In 1896-1897, Benjamin F., Simon and Solomon H. Lesser were listed as owners. In 1898-1900, it was listed as Silverware Manufacturers, A. Lesser's Son. In 1900, the listing was A. Lesser Son, watch materials.

TABER & TIBBITS, INC.
Wallingford, Connecticut

Listed in the City Directory 1919-1941. Makers of silverplated hollowares and novelties. Trademark was a tabor (small drum).

The firm was started in 1919 by Charles H. Tibbits and R. H. Taber, his son-in-law. They were succeeded by Silvercraft Co.

TALBOT MFG. CO.
Providence, Rhode Island

Manufacturers of cigarette cases in the 1920s.

TALCO

H. H. TAMMEN CURIO CO.
Denver, Colorado

In business from c. 1881 to 1962. Was purchased by Con Becker in 1957 and is now the Thrift Novelty Company.

First begun by H. H. Tammen as a curio shop, the business was expanded to include the manufacture and wholesaling of souvenir novelties and jewelry. Among their widely distributed souvenirs were sterling silver spoons depicting people and places of the West. By 1887, after several moves for expansion, a museum established in connection with the business, advertised that "it was lighted by electric light," and was considered a place no traveler should miss. The business managed to survive the panic of 1893 and went on to become the largest of its kind in the West.

TAUNTON BRITANNIA MANUFACTURING COMPANY
Taunton, Massachusetts
See Reed & Barton

The Taunton Britannia Manufacturing Company was the successor to Crossman, West & Leonard when the need for additional capital for expansion brought about the establishment of this joint-stock company on August 18, 1830.

There were eight shareholders in the new company. Of these, only William Crossman, Haile N. Wood, Daniel Cobb and William West were experienced in the britannia business. James Crossman had been a merchant tailor, real estate investor and was at that time a director of the Cohannet Bank in Taunton. Haile Wood, Sr., dealt in real estate and Horatio and Z. A. Leonard were prominent in the metal and textile trades.

Immediately a new factory at Hopewell, on the Mill River, was built. Water was planned as the main source of power, but the old steam engine from the Fayette Street shop was installed for power during summer droughts.

By 1831, the manufacturing of britannia ware had all been shifted to the new factory. Throughout that year, many additions to their product line were added. Among them were castor frames, tankards, church cups, christening bowls, soup ladles and candlesticks. In 1832, toast racks, soda dispensers and fruit dishes were added. Sales of the tea sets, that had been the backbone of the business, dropped after 1831.

The Taunton Britannia Manufacturing Company was noted for the production of some of the most beautiful lamps made in America. New designs in these lighting devices and an increased supply of whale oil on the market promoted their popularity.

Castor sets were to be found on every dining table in America; many of them were made by this company. Their revolving sets were considered the epitome of luxurious living.

In 1832, William Crossman, William West and Zephaniah Leonard sold their interests in the company to Horatio Leonard and in 1833, Isaac Babbitt, superintendent of the plant, left the company.

On February 16, 1833, a new corporation, with Horatio Leonard, James Crossman, Haile Wood, Daniel Cobb and Haile N. Wood was formed under the same name — the Taunton Britannia Mfg. Company. General business uncertainty of the period, competition from other britannia ware establishments, as well as a strong preference for foreign articles brought about the total failure of the company in November, 1834.

Three people still had great faith in the enterprise. They were the company agent, Benjamin Pratt; Henry Reed, a spinner; and his friend, Charles E. Barton, the solderer. On April 1, 1835, they reopened the factory and eventually formed what is now Reed & Barton.

T. B. M. CO.
TAUNTON BRIT.
MANFG. CO.

TAUNTON SILVERSMITHS

A subsidiary of Lenox, Inc. The Taunton Collection, a line of silverplated holloware, is offered only to Lenox dinnerware dealers. Introduced late in 1974.

ANDREW A. TAYLOR
Newark, New Jersey

Listed from c. 1930 to 1973 as manufacturer of sterling silver holloware. No longer listed.

DAVID TAYLOR JEWELRY CO.
New York, New York

Registered trademark for use on flatware, holloware, insignia, service medals and costume jewelry made of or plated with gold, silver, or other precious metals, all for use of officers and enlisted men of the Armed Forces of the U.S.

(Used since April 15, 1945)

F. C. TAYLOR & CO.
Baltimore, Maryland

Listed in 1881 Baltimore City Directory as silverplaters.

THE TENNANT COMPANY
New York, New York
See Hartford Sterling Co.
See Phelps & Cary Co.

Silversmiths before 1896. Makers of holloware and dresserware in sterling silver only. Trophies, presentation pieces. Succeeded (?) by Hartford Sterling Co. c. 1901. Trademark is identical to one used by Hartford Sterling Co. and by Phelps & Cary Co., with the exception of the initials in the shield.

THIERY & CO.
Newark, New Jersey

Listed JC as jewelers; out of business before 1909. Trademarks found on souvenir spoons.

THE THOMAE CO.
Attleboro, Massachusetts

Chas. Thomae & Son, Inc. was established August 1, 1920 by the late Charles Thomae and his son, Herbert L. Thomae. They make novelty goods of 14k gold and sterling silver, religious medals, photo etching on gold and silver and make bronze memorial plates and signs.

Charles Thomae was superintendent of the Watson Co. for several years and developed enameling and a line of novelties and dresserware till it reached the importance of a separate business. The Thomae Co. was formed as a division of the Watson Co. In 1920, Charles Thomae resigned from both firms and started a new business with the name of Chas. Thomae & Son.

The firm's founder died in 1958. It is now run by his two sons Herbert L., President and Charles G. Thomae.

The trademark ⚓ has been used with little change since 1920 and was a personal mark used by Charles Thomae to mark his own work before that.

THOMPSON, HAYWARD & CO.
Mechanicsville, Mass.
See Walter E. Hayward Co., Inc.

THOMPSONS
ERNEST THOMPSON, JR.
Damariscotta, Maine

A husband and wife team, trained as silversmiths and jewelers in both the craft and design. They have a second generation joining their forces. They are involved primarily in silversmithing in the traditional manner but are also equipped for small productions.

They make reproductions of historical and domestic as well as ecclesiastical articles — monstrances, croziers, processional crosses, chalices, ciboria, pectoral crosses, candlesticks, pyxes, etc., in both traditional and contemporary designs. Their work is primarily handwrought.

The Thompsons also do designing to order, chasing, enameling, inlay and encrustation, engraving, spinning and finishing, and the other processes necessary to a complete silversmithing operation.

E. T. Thompson (intaglio; single or double line)
E. T. Thompson (cameo; single line)
Also Reproduction and Sterling Silver (cameo)

THORNTON BROTHERS
New York, New York

"The Thornton Brothers were established in 1877." (JW 4-6-1892) Listed 1927 JKD as manufacturers of emblems.

THORNTON & CO.
New York, New York

Manufacturers of sterling silverware. Successors May 26, 1896 of Holbrook & Simmons; later Holbrook & Thornton. Went into receivership September 16, 1896.

H. & S.

Old Mark of
Holbrook & Simmons.

TIFFANY & CO., INC.
New York, New York

CHRONOLOGY

Tiffany & Young	1837
Tiffany, Young & Ellis	1852
Tiffany & Company	1853
Tiffany & Co., Inc.	1868

Founded by Charles L. Tiffany in 1837 with John B. Young under the name Tiffany & Young. They first stocked their store with stationery, Chinese bric-a-brac, fans, pottery, umbrellas and desks. They purchased almost all of their silverware from John C. Moore who had begun the manufacture of silverware in 1827 and who was later joined in business by his son, Edward C. Moore.

Called Tiffany, Young & Ellis in 1852. Became Tiffany & Co. in 1853.

In 1868 Tiffany was incorporated and the silverware factory of the Moores became part of the organization with Edward C. Moore becoming one of its directors. From then on, and until Mr. Moore's death the silverware made in the factory bore not only the mark "Tiffany & Co." but also the letter "M."

Ever since then, both the name Tiffany & Co., and the initial of the incumbent company president appear on all Tiffany-made silver.

In 1852 Tiffany introduced the English sterling silver standard to America for Tiffany silver. This standard was later adopted by the U.S. Government and made into Federal law determining the minimum amount of fine silver required for articles marked "Sterling Silver."

Soon after the company was incorporated the manufacture of electroplate was added.

Recent Tiffany Presidents

Louis de Bèbian Moore	1947-1955
William T. Lusk	1955-1967
Farnham Lefferts	1967-1973
Henry B. Platt	Incumbent

TIFFANY YOUNG & ELLIS

J.C.M

20

(*Used 1850-52.*)

TIFFANY & Co
271 BROADWAY

TIFFANY & Co
271 BROADWAY

TIFFANY & Co

•

G & W

(Grosjean & Woodward)

300   **323**

J. C. M.

(*Used 1852-53.*)

2
TIFFANY & CO.
LATE
TIFFANY, YOUNG & ELLIS
550 BROADWAY
720

TIFFANY & Co
6601

G&W   G&W
ENGLISH STERLING
925-1000
4
550 BROADWAY, N.Y.

(*Used 1854-55.*)

TIFFANY & CO.
657
GOLD & SILVERSMITHS
2712
550 BROADWAY

TIFFANY & CO.
295
ENGLISH STERLING
925-1000
•
550 BROADWAY

(*Used 1854-70.*)

TIFFANY & CO
1063
STERLING
M
1100
UNION SQUARE

(Used 1870-75)

TIFFANY & CO
MAKERS
STERLING-SILVER
925-1000
M

(*Used 1875-91.*)

TIFFANY & CO
● 0 7 4   MAKERS   7 1 8 4
STERLING SILVER
925-1000
T

(*Used 1891-1902.*)

TIFFANY & CO.	TIFFANY & CO
12345 MAKERS 67890	14786 MAKERS 5885
STERLING SILVER	STERLING SILVER
925-1000	925-1000
M	C

(*Used since 1902.*)

The figures at the right and left of the word "Makers" are the pattern and order numbers, and vary accordingly.

Mark in use 1902-07	Mark in use 1907-38	Present Mark in use since 1938
TIFFANY & CO	TIFFANY & CO	TIFFANY & CO
14786 MAKERS 5885	12345 MAKERS 67890	MAKERS
STERLING SILVER	STERLING SILVER	STERLING SILVER
925-1000	925-1000	12345
C	M	M

TIFFANY & CO
1824
QUALITY
925-1000
5731
UNION SQUARE
10

TIFFANY & COMPY
M
136

The following marks were used on silverware made for International Expositions in addition to the usual one:

1893	1900	1901
World's Columbian Exposition Chicago.	*Exposition, Universelle, Paris.*	*Pan-American Exposition, Buffalo.*

TIFFT & WHITING
North Attleboro, Mass.
See Gorham Corporation

Founded in 1840 in North Attleboro, Massachusetts. Succeeded by Whiting Manufacturing Company, Newark, New Jersey in 1866. Purchased by the Gorham Corporation in 1905.

TILDEN-THURBER CO.
Providence, Rhode Island

Roots of Tilden-Thurber Company go deep into the history and business development of Rhode Island. In 1856, when the doors of the new firm opened, the sign above the window read GORHAM CO. AND BROWN. Gorham Thurber, great-grandfather of today's president, was listed as one of the officers. An unusually active man in business, in addition to his interest in Gorham Co. & Brown, he formed a co-partnership with John Gorham, forming the firm of Gorham & Thurber, one of the predecessors of the Gorham Manufacturing Company.

In 1878, Gorham Co. & Brown moved across the street from its first location and changed its name to Henry T. Brown & Co. Members of the board were Mr. Brown, Henry Tilden and Gorham Thurber. The firm remained there until 1895 when it moved into the present Tilden-Thurber building. Gorham Thurber died shortly afterwards.

In March, 1880, the name of the firm was changed to Tilden-Thurber & Co. In the same year, William H. Thurber, grandfather of the present officers and son of Gorham Thurber, joined the firm, becoming a partner in 1885.

On June 23, 1892, the company became incorporated under the present name Tilden-Thurber Corporation. At this time Henry Tilden was elected President and William H. Thurber, Treasurer. William H. Thurber's contributions to the development of the company were an increased volume of business and addition of a number of new departments added to the original line of jewelry and silverware. Following Mr. Tilden's death in 1907, Mr. Thurber was elected President and Treasurer.

Henry C. Tilden, son of Henry Tilden, joined the firm and became manager of the sterling silver department. In 1915, he moved to Chicago and joined Spaulding & Co., leading jewelers and eventually became president of that firm.

In 1956, when the company celebrated its 100th anniversary, Frederick B. Thurber was President and William Gorham Thurber, Treasurer. Tracy Gorham Thurber, son of W. G. Thurber, joined the

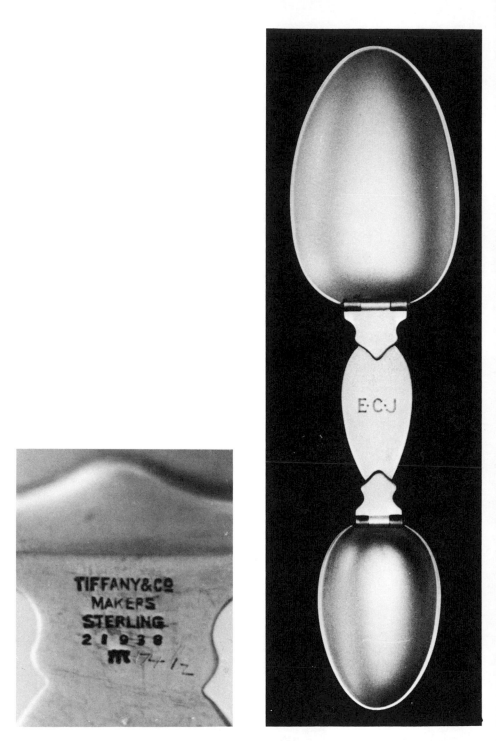

Since its incorporation 1868 Tiffany's silver has been marked not only "Tiffany & Co." but also with the initial of the incumbent company president. (Tiffany & Co.)

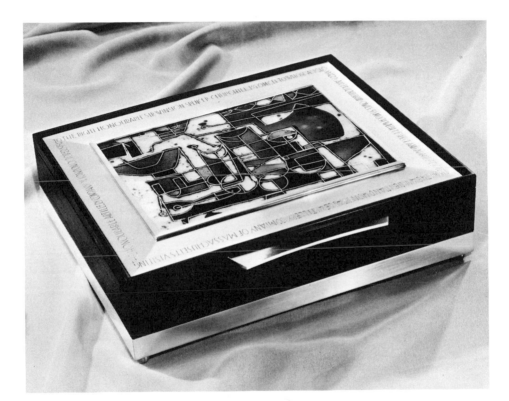

Cigar box made for Sir Winston Churchill by the Towle Silversmiths of Newburyport, Massachusetts. Climaxing their first official visit to London in 316 years (October 1954) the Ancient and Honorable Artillery Company of Massachusetts presented the silver cigar box to Prime Minister Churchill — made to the exact measurement of his large cigars. The box is of silver and Gaboon ebony. A plaque on the top is of cloisonné enamel, with 118 pieces of silver wire separating the fourteen colors. Engraved around the top is: "To the Right Honourable Sir Winston Churchill, K. G., O. M., C. H., to whom Anglo-American Friendship owes so much, with respect and admiration from the Ancient and Honorable Artillery Company of Massachusetts, visiting the Honourable Artillery Company of London, October, 1954." The Artillery Company seal is inside the hinged top. *The Towle mark is on the bottom of the box.*

company in 1951. Another son, William H. Thurber, is currently President.

Since 1878, Tilden-Thurber has been noted as the source of rare and beautiful importations. Fine paintings and etchings are displayed in the Tilden-Thurber Art Galleries.

Working with the Gorham Manufacturing Company, Tilden-Thurber furnished a complete sterling silver service for the Battleship **Rhode Island**, later placed on display in the State House. They also furnished the silver service for the Cruiser, **Providence**, later exhibited at Brown University.

Service to the community and active interest in its employees have been outstanding characteristics of this company. This has been demonstrated in the establishment of a Brown University scholarship for a local student; assistance in the establishment of a rigorous educational and training program for jewelers; a company-paid pension plan and, most recently, a profit-sharing plan for employees.

TILLINGHAST SILVER CO.
Meriden, Connecticut

Manufacturers of sterling silver hollow handle serving pieces. In business c. 1920-1935.

TILLINGHAST SILVER CO.

EDWARD TODD & CO.
New York, New York

Edward Todd & Co. began as Smith & Todd in 1851, as successors to Bard Brothers & Co. The changes have been from Smith & Todd to Mabie, Todd & Co. and then to Edward Todd & Co. They were manufacturers of sterling silverware and gold pens.

Another account reads: "The Edward Todd Co. was formed in 1869. He had previously been with E. G. Bagley, which company was founded in 1843. It continued until 1851. C. F. Newton succeeded in 1859 and was succeeded by Newton, Kurtz & Co. which continued for 10 years when Edward Todd & Co. was formed. The company was incorporated in 1897." (JC-W 2-5-1919) It was still listed in business in 1927 JKD.

EUGENE S. TONER CO.
New York, New York

Manufacturers (?) of sterling silverware. Listed JC 1909 as out of business.

Note similarity of trademark to that of Depasse Mfg. Co.

JOHN TOOTHILL
See Metropolitan Silver Co.

TOOTHILL & McBEAN SILVER CO.
Ottawa, Illinois

Listed JC 1898 in plated silver section. Out of business before 1904.

QUADRUPLE PLATE

Toronto, Canada

Founded in 1882 by James A. Watts, formerly sales representative of the Meriden Britannia Co. of Connecticut, and others to manufacture a complete line of silverplated and sterling wares in Canada. Around 1885 they began the production of Holmes & Edwards flatware under license. In addition to their own productions they had some silver made for them by Henry & Leslie, silversmiths in Montreal. This silver bears the marks **STERLING⊛ ⊞T.S.P.**

The Toronto Silver Plate Co. was absorbed by the Wm. A. Rogers Co. about 1914 and when that company was sold to Oneida in 1929 the Toronto company marks were no longer used.

STERLING
STERLING⊛ ⊞T.S.P.

(On sterling silver)

Sterling marks not used after 1915.

(On plated silver holloware)

TORONTO SILVER PLATE CO.
(Flatware.)

TORSIL METAL
TORSIL STEEL
TORSIL E. P.—N. S.

(Knives.)

JOHN TORSLEFF
Boston, Massachusetts

John Torsleff first appears in the Boston City Directory of 1857; at that time associated with Thomas Barker & Co., silverplated ware, along with one Charles Anthes. From 1858 through 1860 Torsleff and Anthes were in business together, and from 1861 through 1863 (the last listing) John Torsleff, silverplated ware, was in business at 334 Washington St. He lived in Chelsea, Mass. Either this John Torsleff or John Torsleff, Jr., died about 1869.

Some pieces of his manufacture are of thin sterling with decorative elements of cast brass, silverplated.

J. TOSTRUP
Oslo, Norway

Founded in 1832 by Jacob Ubrich Holfeldt Tostrup, great-grandfather of the present manager. Makers of all kinds of flatware and holloware. The firm has won many international awards for the excellence of its work. They were influential in 19th century revival of filigree work and were especially noted for their *plique à jour* enamels.

(Both marks for use on flatware and holloware, made of or plated with precious metal. Registered in the U.S. in 1949. Norwegian registration 1947.)

A. H. TOWAR & CO.
Lyons, New York
See New Haven Silver Plate Co.

A. F. TOWLE & SON CO.
Greenfield, Massachusetts
See Lunt Silversmiths
See Rogers, Lunt & Bowlen
See Towle Silversmiths

A. F. Towle & Son, successors to Towle & Jones, were the links between the Moultons, of Newburyport, and the Towle Silversmiths. Anthony F. Towle was an apprentice to William Moulton IV and bought his business and that of Joseph Moulton IV in 1873. In 1882, with others, the business was incorporated as Towle Silversmiths. Anthony F. Towle & Son moved to Greenfield, Massachusetts in 1890 and operated until 1902. At that time their business was taken over by Rogers, Lunt & Bowlen, now known as Lunt Silversmiths.

They were manufacturers of both sterling and plated silverware. Registered trademark, U. S. Patent Office, No. 27,286, November 19, 1895 for electroplated ware.

"Anthony F. Towle, b. Newburyport, Dec. 12, 1816. He learned silversmith trade with the late firm of N. & T. Foster, and in 1855 established the firm of Towle & Jones, jewelers and silversmiths. Subsequently the firm name was changed to Towle, Jones & Co. and

A. F. Towle & Son. Under the last firm name, in 1880, the manufacture of silverware was established in this city [Newburyport] by the deceased. Mr. Towle retired from active business in 1892. He leaves three children. Mrs. E. B. Horn of Boston, and Edward B. and William A. Towle of Newburyport." (JC&HR 4-7-1897, p. 19)

E. J. TOWLE MFG. CO.
Seattle, Washington

Began as Joseph Mayer & Bros. 1898; Jos. Mayer, Inc. before 1922; Northern Stamping & Manufacturing Co. (still used for some items) and was succeeded by E. J. Towle Manufacturing Company c. 1945.

Were wholesalers of diamonds, watches, jewelry, sterling silverware, plated silver goods, cut glass and optical goods.

Medals and other presentation pieces have been and are still made. Some of the finest die work in the country is still done by this company.

Their work is now mainly the designing and manufacturing of silver jewelry, charms, religious goods and souvenir silverware.

E. J. T. Co.

ESTABLISHED 1895

TOWLE SILVERSMITHS
Newburyport, Massachusetts

William Moulton II, born in 1664, settled in old Newbury, later Newburyport, to become the first silversmith in a long lineage of craftsmen now the Towle Silversmiths. He was succeeded by Joseph I, William III (who moved to Marietta, Ohio and became not only the first silversmith in The Northwest Territory, but, also one of the founders of Marietta), Joseph II, Joseph III, Ebenezer, William IV, Enoch, Abel and Joseph IV — all silversmiths.

Anthony F. Towle and William P. Jones, apprentices of William IV, began business under the name Towle & Jones in 1857, later buying the business of William IV and Joseph IV. Anthony F. Towle and Edward F., his son, engaged in business as A. F. Towle & Son in 1873, and this partnership was the germ of the A. F. Towle & Son Co., Inc. in 1880, which in 1882 became the Towle Manufacturing Company, Anthony F. Towle and Edward F. Towle retiring. The company is now known as the Towle Silversmiths.

About 1890 the familiar "T enclosing a lion" was first used as a trademark. It is said to have been designed by Anthony Towle from the family coat of arms.

In 1890 the manufacture of holloware began at the Towle company under Richard Dimes who later went to Frank W. Smith, Gardner, and finally established his own business in Boston.

The Towle firm made plated flatware from 1906-1909. It was gradually discontinued, the last pattern was *Chester*. The stock was sold to Samuel Weare.

They have been leaders in establishing an exhibit gallery where artist-silversmiths skills are presented to the public. Other exhibits of silver craftsmanship have been prepared in cooperation with museums.

In the 1940s Mueck-Cary Co. was purchased by Towle and the trademark now belongs to them. Carvel Hall, a subsidiary manufacturing fine cutlery, is in Crisfield, Maryland.

(On plated silver)

La Fayette Silverware   Paul Revere Silverware

(On sterling silver)

(Mueck-Cary)

TOWLE MFG. CO.

THE MOULTON MAKER'S MARKS

WILLIAM MOULTON 1720–1793	W.MOULTON	WM
	W.Moulton	W·M
JOSEPH MOULTON 1724–1795	I·MOULTON	I·M J·M
JOSEPH MOULTON 1744–1816	J·M MOULTON MOULTON	
	I·M I·MOULTON MOULTON	
WILLIAM MOULTON 1772–1861	W·MOULTON W·M	
	W·MOULTON W·M	
EBENEZER MOULTON 1768–1824	W·MOULTON W·MOULTON	
	MOULTON	
ENOCH MOULTON 1780–1815	E·MOULTON E·MOULTON	
	E·MOULTON	
ABEL MOULTON 1784–1840	AM ·M· A·MOULTON	
JOSEPH MOULTON 1814–1903	J·MOULTON J·MOULTON	
TOWLE & JONES 1857–1873	TOWLE & JONES	
A. F. TOWLE & SON 1873 Inc. 1880 1882	A. F. TOWLE & SON	

NOW

THE TOWLE SILVERSMITHS

IRA STRONG TOWN & J. TOWN
Montpelier, Vermont

Advertised 1830-1838 as clockmakers and silversmiths — "silver work of every description manufactured to order on short notice."

IRA S. TOWN & ELIJAH B. WITHERELL
Montpelier, Vermont

Successors to Ira Strong Town and J. Town. Formed a partnership that took over the business until it was dissolved in 1845. Advertised that "they made all the silverware bought at their shop and it was warrented to be the best quality."

THE TOWNSEND, DESMOND & VOORHIS CO.
New York, New York

Listed JC 1896-1904 in sterling silver section. Out of business before 1909.

T. D. & V. CO. STERLING.

TRINAC METALCRAFTS INC.
Brooklyn, New York

Manufacturers of pewterwares. In business now. No reply to inquiries.

J. W. TUCKER
San Francisco, California

Listed in City Directories from 1852 as a jeweler and importer. He was a retailer of first quality silver, many pieces of which bear his mark — though no known pieces can actually be attributed to his workmanship or to his shop. Tucker died in 1876 but the business was continued under his name for another ten years. The last listing was in 1886. Occasional directory entries mention "mfgr." before and after his death but may refer only to repair work or possibly special orders.

TUCKER & PARKERHURST CO.
Ogdensburg, New York

Successors to Bell Bros. in 1898. Out of business before 1904.

JAMES W. TUFTS
Boston, Massachusetts

Trademark registered February 2, 1875 for plated silverware by James W. Tufts, Medford, Massachusetts. Incorporated 1881. Out of business before 1915.

Tufts started his business career as an apprentice in the apothecary store of Samuel Kidder in Charlestown, Massachusetts. He soon went into business for himself and became the proprietor of a chain of three pharmacies. His interest in the concoction of syrups and other products sold at the soda fountain led to the manufacture of these products. His next step was to branch out into the manufacture of the apparatus used in drugstores. The soda fountain of that time was a magnificent piece of equipment.

Many were of Italian marble and the metal parts were silverplated. From the silverplating of fountain parts, Tufts branched out in 1875 into the manufacture of an extensive line of silverplated items such as pitchers, dishes and bases. The business, which had been conducted under Tufts' name, was consolidated in 1891 with other soda fountain companies and became the American Soda Fountain Company, the largest in its field. By 1895 Tufts turned the active management of his business over to others because of his health. In search of a more healthful climate and atmosphere, he purchased 5,000 acres in the sandhills of North Carolina and founded the resort town of Pinehurst. He died there February 2, 1902.

TUTTLE SILVER CO.
Boston, Massachusetts
See Tuttle Silversmiths

TUTTLE SILVERSMITHS
Boston, Massachusetts

In 1890, Boston silversmith Timothy Tuttle was first commissioned by wealthy families to copy old English silver. His original pieces were dated in the English custom with the crest of the reigning monarch. During the term of office of President Calvin Coolidge, Tuttle adopted this custom, marking each piece with a crescent and the initials of the incumbent President of the United States. Today this date mark is unique with Tuttle.

Timothy Tuttle used the Pine Tree Shilling symbol as his trademark. The Pine Tree Shilling was one of the earliest silver coins minted in the American colonies by Hull and Sanderson in 1652. Used as the Tuttle trademark it is the stamp of quality and prestige appearing on all Tuttle sterling pieces, including authentic reproductions of Early American, European and modern design.

In 1915, the company was listed as Tuttle Silver Co. By 1922, it was incorporated.

In 1955 Tuttle Silversmiths was purchased by R. Wallace & Sons Mfg. Co. (now Wallace Silversmiths) and became an acquisition of the Hamilton Watch Company of Lancaster, Pennsylvania when Hamilton purchased Wallace Silversmiths in December 1959. Every piece of Tuttle silver is sterling. They make no plated silver.

FINE STERLING

TIMOTHY TUTTLE
Boston, Massachusetts
See Tuttle Silversmiths

Silversmith in Boston, Massachusetts in 1890. Founder of Tuttle Silversmiths.

TYSON, TRUMP & CO.
Baltimore, Maryland

Listed in 1867-1868 Baltimore City Directory as silverplaters.

U

UNGER BROS.
Newark, New Jersey

CHRONOLOGY

Unger Brothers	1872-1879
(William, George, Frederick, Herman and Eugene)	
Unger Brothers	1879-1904
(Herman and Eugene)	
Unger Brothers, Inc.	1904-1919
(Herman and Eugene; Philemon O. Dickinson)	

William Unger was a partner of Thomas A. Edison from 1870 to 1872 in the Newark Telegraph Works. This firm was dissolved that year and the five brothers organized Unger Brothers for the manufacture and sale of pocket knives and hardware specialties. They began the manufacture of silver jewelry in 1878. Three of the brothers, William, George and Frederick died that year and the two surviving brothers, Herman and Eugene reorganized the business, retaining the name Unger Brothers.

When Eugene Unger married Emma L. Dickinson, daughter of Philemon Dickinson, in 1880, a new dimension was added to the firm. It was Dickinson who was the designer of the extensive line of Art Nouveau articles made by the Unger firm and now so avidly sought by collectors.

January 21, 1904 the firm was incorporated. The last of the Unger brothers died in 1909 and by 1910 the dies for the Art Nouveau patterns were no longer used; a simpler, more rectilinear line being produced. In 1914 the firm ceased production of silver articles entirely to manufacture airplane parts. In 1919 the business was sold.

The trademark of the Unger Brothers, an interlaced U and B, was stamped on all Unger silver with the exception of some jewelry made after 1910. This jewelry is of light weight and of lesser quality than the original work.

UNITED STATES SILVER CO., INC.
New York, New York

Manufacturers of plated wares. First listing found was 1948. Still listed. No response to inquiry.

UTOPIAN SILVER DEPOSIT & NOVELTY CO.
New York, New York

Listed JC 1915 in sterling silver section. Out of business before 1922.

THOMAS J. VAIL
Connecticut
See American Sterling Co.
See Curtisville Mfg. Co.
See Williams Bros. Mfg. Co.

During the Civil War Thomas Vail produced war materials. Between 1865 and 1869 Vail probably was

in the silver plating business as in the Hartford Directory for 1869 he is listed as manufacturer of German Silver and plated ware, etc. In 1871, The American Sterling Company took over the property from the trustee, Leavitt Hunt.

VALENTINE LINSLEY SILVER CO.
Wallingford, Connecticut
See Wallace Bros. Silver Co.
See The Wallingford Co.

Listed in the City Directory 1895-1899. Makers of plated silverware. Succeeded by The Wallingford Co. in 1899.

V. L.
(Silver Plated Hollowware.)

MADE AND PLATED BY WALLACE BROS. SILVER CO.

VAN BERGH SILVER PLATE CO.
Rochester, New York

Founded 1892 by Frederick W. Van Bergh and Maurice H. Van Bergh, who were President and Secretary, respectively. A third brother is said to have joined the firm in 1898 (not confirmed). The company was incorporated July 1, 1904. In 1925 all assets were transferred to a new corporation, The Van Bergh Silver Plate Company, Inc., set up by Oneida Community Limited. This new corporation was merged into Oneida Community Limited in 1926 and moved from Rochester to Oneida, New York.

BRITANNIA METAL CO.

CLARENCE A. VANDERBILT
New York, New York

Manufacturers of sterling silverware, baskets, salt and peppers, cups, candlesticks, cigarette cases, vanity cases, picture frames, napkin rings and flasks from c. 1909-1935.

STERLING—V

STERLING

W. K. VANDERSLICE & CO.
San Francisco, Calif.

Vanderslice learned silversmithing in Philadelphia and was active in that city as a silversmith c. 1840-57.

He founded the W. K. Vanderslice Co. in San Francisco in 1858 or 1859. It was the pioneer silverplate company west of the Rockies. It was sold to Shreve & Co. in 1915.

JOHN T. VANSANT & BROTHER
Philadelphia, Pennsylvania

Vansant & Co. was listed as silversmiths in 1850. John T. Vansant Mfg. Co. listed around 1887 to 1905.

"John T. Vansant & Brother, manufacturers of silverware, Philadelphia, who have been in financial difficulties recently were sold out by the sheriff." (JW 8.18-1886, p. 984)

ERSKINE V. VAN HOUTEN
White Plains, New York

Listed 1931 to 1950 as manufacturers of table glassware (apparently silver depositware).

VAUGHAN PEWTER SHOP
Taunton, Massachusetts

Lester H. Vaughan was a manufacturer of pewterware c. 1930-1950. Originally L. H. Vaughan; later Vaughan Pewter Shop.

P. M. VERMASS
Minneapolis, Minnesota

Successors to F. L. Bosworth before 1921. They were jobbers who bought wares "in the metal" and plated them in their own shop. No record after 1922.

VERNAY & LINCOLN
Attleboro, Massachusetts

Silver manufacturers. "Vernay & Lincoln are doing quite a business. Their facilities for turning out work are excellent and their prices reasonable." (Jeweler, Silversmith & Watchmaker, Oct. 1877)

VICTOR SILVER CO.
See International Silver Co.

Trademark of Derby Silver Co. on less expensive line. Variation used after 1922 by International on silverplated flatware for hotels, restaurants, etc.

VICTOR S. CO.

VINEGAR BROS.
New York, New York

Listed 1927 KJI as manufacturers of silverware.

VINER'S OF SHEFFIELD
Sheffield, England

Founded in 1907. Britain's largest silver trade's manufacturer. The plant is almost entirely automated. Their 1960 cutlery was 85% electroplate and in 1967 75% stainless steel. They have factories in Hong Kong and in Japan. They bought two fine old Sheffield firms of cutlers, Thomas Turner and Harrison Bros. and Howson. They manufacture 60% of the current lightweight sterling tableware, mostly traditional designs. These are distributed in the United States through Raimond Silver Mfg. Co., Inc.

GEO. L. VOSE MFG. CO., INC.
Providence, Rhode Island

Successor to Geo. L. Vose & Co. between 1904-1915. Manufacturing jeweler. Last listed c. 1920.

W

A. L. WAGNER MFG. CO., INC.
New York, New York

Listed 1927 KJI as manufacturers of silverplated and sterling silver holloware.

J. WAGNER & SON, INC.
New York, New York

First listed in JC in 1909 as the Central Sterling Company. Succeeded by Weber-Wagner Co. between 1909 and 1915. Listed as Weber-Wagner & Benson Co., Inc. 1915-1931 and as J. Wagner & Son, Inc. in 1950. Not listed in 1965.

Manufacturers of sterling silver holloware.

Used since 1909

THE WALDO FOUNDRY
Bridgeport, Connecticut

Listed in JC 1896-1904. Out of business before 1915. Manufacturers of aluminum-gold flat and tableware.

Note similarity to trademarks of the W. H. Glenny & Co. and H. H. Curtis & Co.

(Aluminium-Gold Flat and Table Ware.)

A silver bowl made for Queen Elizabeth and presented by the Ancient and Honorable Artillery Company of Massachusetts. The bowl is of silver with plique á jour enamel on the body. The small holes drilled through the silver have been filled with transparent green enamel. The inscription reads: "An offering to Her Majesty Queen Elizabeth II, Captain General Honourable Artillery Company, from the Ancient and Honorable Artillery Company of Massachusetts, October, 1954." The seal of the Artillery Company is inside. *The Towle mark is underneath.*

The Massachusetts Company is the third oldest military organization in the world, dating to 1638 when Governor Winthrop granted its charter. The oldest is the Swiss Guard at the Vatican and the second oldest is the Ancient and Honourable Company of London.

Silverplated cake dish. *Paisley* is the pattern name, the stamping of which is a 20th century practice. (Wilcox Silver Plate Co., Div. of International Silver Company)

WALDORF SILVER CO.
See Woodman-Cook Co.

Trademark of Woodman-Cook Co.

WALDORF SILVER CO.

WALLACE BROS. SILVER COMPANY
Wallingford, Connecticut
See Wallace Silversmiths

In July 1875, Robert Wallace and his sons, Robert B., William J., Harry L., George H., Frank A., and sons-in-law, W. J. Leavenworth and D. E. Morris formed a co-partnership with the name Wallace Brothers to manufacture plated silver flatware of cast steel. On June 23, 1879 the corporation of R. Wallace & Sons Mfg. Co. bought the business of Wallace Brothers.

QUADRUPLE
PLATE

ESSEX SILVER CO.
ESSEX SILVER CO.
QUAD PLATE

(Silver plated britannia)

MADE AND PLATED BY WALLACE BROS. SILVER CO.

R. WALLACE & SONS. MFG. CO.
Wallingford, Connecticut
See Wallace Silversmiths

Successor to Wallace, Simpson & Co. in 1871. Name changed to Wallace Silversmiths in 1956.

"The first spoons made in this country of German or nickel silver were manufactured by Robert Wallace in 1835. From that date to January 1, 1897, we manufactured more than 5 million dozen nickel silver spoons, forks, etc. . . . and not one single one bore our name or trademark — these goods having been made for other firms who have built up on our skill and workmanship a world-wide reputation for the quality and durability of such wares. On January 1, 1897, we began to place our nickel silver flatware on the market bearing our name, which is a guarantee of both the quality and durability of the goods so stamped. They are plated with FINE SILVER, in the following grade: EXTRA or STANDARD which we plate 20 PER CENT heavier than the regular standard. TRIPLE and SECTIONAL PLATES. The stamps and trademarks are:

1835 R. Wallace AI for Extra Plate
1835 R. Wallace XII for Sectional Plate.
1835 R. Wallace 6, 9 or 12 for Triple Plate"
(Adv. JC 7-2-1898, p. 6)

TRADE **1835** MARK
R·WALLACE
(Flatware.)
(Used since 1897)

(Nickel Goods.)

(Hollowware.)

900
(Steel Flatware.)

Trade Mark.

R·W·&·S·
Sterling.

(On sterling silver knives about 1898)

TRADE MARK
RW&S
STERLING

R. WALLACE
(Silver Soldered.)
SILVER SOLDERED

LUXOR PLATE
FORTUNE SILVER PLATE
ANDOVER SILVER PLATE CO.

ADAMS MANUFACTURING CO.
WALLINGFORD CO. SECTIONAL
WALLINGFORD CO. AI

MELFORD
SILVERPLATE
ON COPPER

M**ELFORD**
SILVER PLATE

MELFORD
E.P.W.M.

MELFORD
E.P.N.S.

ANDOVER S. P
E P N S

LUXOR PLATE—WALLACE
The Wallace silverplate flatware dies were sold to the International Silver Co. in 1954.

WALLACE SILVERSMITHS
Wallingford, Connecticut

CHRONOLOY
Robert Wallace	1834
Robert Wallace & Co.	1855
Wallace, Simpson & Co.	1865
R. Wallace & Sons Mfg. Co.	1871
Wallace Silversmiths	1956

ROBERT WALLACE was born in Prospect, Connecticut in 1815. He was the grandson of James Wallace, who had come from Scotland and settled in Blandford, Mass., late in the 18th Century. At 16, Robert was apprenticed to Captain William Mix of Prospect to learn the art of making britannia spoons. Two years later, in 1833, he set up shop in an old grist mill to make spoons on his own. About a year later he saw a German silver spoon, made by Dixon & Sons of Sheffield, England. He recognized its superior strength and color and with Deacon

Almer Hall (later head of Hall, Elton & Co.) began the manufacture of German silver spoons — the first in this country.

From 1834 to 1849 he made these spoons for Deacon Hall, for Hall, Elton & Co., and in 1849 entered into a co-partnership with J. B. Pomeroy to manufacture them on contract for Fred R. Curtis Co. of Hartford and made britannia spoons for Hall, Elton & Co. and Edgar Atwater of Wallingford.

In 1854, Robert decided to take up farming, but soon returned to Wallingford to continue the manufacture of German silver forks, spoons and similar articles with Samuel Simpson of Wallingford. This ten-year partnership was formed May 1, 1855, under the name of R. WALLACE & CO.

On May 15, 1855, Simpson's partners in the Meriden Britannia Co., H. C. Wilcox, W. W. Lyman and Isaac C. Lewis, were admitted, with the firm name remaining the same. This contract was terminated in 1865 when a new contract was made and the corporation WALLACE, SIMPSON & CO. was organized.

In 1870, Wallace purchased two-thirds of Simpson's interest and in 1871 bought the remainder. On July 17, 1871 the corporate name was changed to R. WALLACE & SONS MFG. CO. with his two sons, Robert B. and William J. and a son-in-law, W. J. Leavenworth members of the firm.

In 1875 the company started production of forks and spoons of sterling. In July 1875, Robert Wallace with his sons, Robert B., William J., Henry L., George H., Frank A. and sons-in-law W. J. Leavenworth and D. E. Morris formed a co-partnership under the name of WALLACE BROTHERS for the manufacture of silverplated flatware on a base of cast steel. Manufacture of silverplated holloware also began at this time. On June 23, 1879, the corporation of R. WALLACE & SONS MFG. CO. acquired and took over the business and good will of WALLACE BROTHERS

New machinery and mass production methods made possible great expansion. All types of flatware, holloware, dresser silver and practically all lines of articles in which silver is a component, as well as stainless steel, were added.

In 1924 a Canadian plant was opened in Cookshire, Quebec, for production of tinned spoons and forks. In 1944 sterling flatware was added to the line. In 1945 the Canadian branch was incorporated as R. WALLACE & SONS OF CANADA, LTD. It was sold in 1964.

In 1934, William S. Warren, designer for the company, conceived the idea of three-dimensional flatware patterns — for which the Wallace Company is noted. The Watson Company of Attleboro, Mass. was bought by Wallace in 1955, moving to Wallingford in 1956. The name R. WALLACE & SONS MFG. CO. was changed to WALLACE SILVERSMITHS in 1956. The Tuttle Silver Company and Smith & Smith were acquired by Wallace and moved to Wallingford. WALLACE SILVERSMITHS, in 1959 was purchased by the Hamilton Watch Company of Lancaster, Pennsylvania and is now a Division of that firm. Manufacturing continues in Wallingford, but office facilities are in Lancaster.

They made silverplated flatware from 1877 to 1941; silverplated hotel flatware continued until 1953.

THE WALLINGFORD CO., INC.
Wallingford, Connecticut
See Wallace Bros. Silver Co.

The Wallingford Co. was listed in the City Directory 1903-1941.

ESSEX SILVER CO.
(Quadruple Plate.)

V. L.
(Silver Plated Hollowware.)

MADE AND PLATED BY WALLACE BROS. SILVER CO.

ESSEX SILVER CO. QUADRUPLE PLATE

THE ESSEX SILVER PLATE CO

JOHN WANAMAKER
Philadelphia, Pennsylvania

Founded 1861 as Wanamaker & Brown. Became John Wanamaker in 1870. It was the first American system store — actually a collection of exclusive stores under one roof.

Like Marshall Field's, Macy's and others, they sold silverware stamped with their own trademark.

(On silverplate)

ANDREW E. WARNER, JR.
Baltimore, Maryland

Listed in Baltimore City Directories as a goldsmith and silversmith from 1864 till 1893. Listed as Andrew

E. Warner & Son, 1867-1870. Andrew E. is listed alone from 1874-1889. The listing from 1890-1893 is A. E. Warner.

ANDREW E. WARNER, SR.
Baltimore, Maryland

Andrew Ellicott Warner was born in 1786 and died in 1870. He was listed as a goldsmith and silversmith from c. 1805 till his death.
Andrew and Thomas H. Warner (1780-1828) worked together c. 1805-1812.

GEORGE C. WARNER
Baltimore, Maryland

Listed in 1855-1856 Baltimore City Directory as a silver chaser.

WARNER MFG. CO.
Greenfield, Massachusetts

Manufacturers of silverplated flatware c. 1905-1909. They were among the first manufacturers to supply retail outlets with flatware stamped with private brand names.

WARNER SILVER MFG. CO.
Chicago, Illinois

Incorporated in March 1894 with Augustus Warner, P. B. Warner and Cassius C. Palmer. Out of business before 1915.

THOMAS H. WARNER
Baltimore, Maryland

Thomas H. Warner c. 1780-1828. He and Andrew Ellicott Warner worked together c. 1805-1812. From 1814 to 1824, and perhaps longer, Thomas H. Warner was assayer for the city of Baltimore. His duty was to "test silverwares to see that they were of no less fineness than eleven ounces pure silver to every pound troy."

WARREN MANSFIELD CO.
Portland, Maine .

An advertisement in Leslie's Magazine, November 1904 carried the statement that they were goldsmiths and silversmiths, established in 1867. They are not listed in the Portland City Directories.
They published an illustrated catalog with price list of jewelry, spoons, tableware, watches, etc. in 1900. Another catalog, dated 1907, illustrated an extensive line of silverware. No trademark is shown.

WARREN SILVER PLATE CO.
New York, New York
See Oneida Silversmiths
See Wm. A. Rogers, Ltd.

Warren Silver Plate Company was a trademark first used in 1901 by Wm. A. Rogers Company on their medium grade holloware. The name apparently was based on the fact that the New York Office was located at 12 Warren Street.

NEW YORK
(*Medium Grade* Holloware.)

WARWICK STERLING CO.
Providence, Rhode Island

John F. Brady, treasurer of the company, registered the lower trademark, U.S. Patent Office No. 97,038 on May 19, 1914 to be used on sterling silver, flatware, holloware, tableware, dresserware, desk articles, sewing articles, silver trimming for leather, glass, wood, metal, fabrics and jewelry. He stated that this trademark had been used continuously since January 1, 1913. No record after 1922.

GEORGE WASHINGTON MINT
New York, New York
Out of business.

WATROUS MFG. CO.
Wallingford, Connecticut
See International Silver Co.

Started as Maltby, Stevens & Company, later Maltby, Stevens and Curtiss. Incorporated as Watrous Mfg. Co. in 1896.
The largest part of their business had been the making of German silver spoon blanks which they had sold to others, where they were plated and trademarked for the market. When the Watrous Co. was organized in 1896 most of the product was furnished to the Wm. Rogers Mfg. Co. in Hartford. After 1898 the spoons they made were distributed among several of the International Silver factories and they also added smaller articles and novelties which they made in sterling. Among these were vanity cases, dorine boxes, match boxes, belt buckles and small holloware. These were distributed through regular trade channels.
They were one of the original companies to become part of the International Silver Co. in 1898.

STERLING.

(*Silver Plated on Nickel Silver Holloware.*)

ALEXANDRA SOLOWIJ WATKINS
Brunswick, Maine

Listed as a silversmith in the "Handcraft Trails in Maine," 1966 edition. Recent inquiry returned as undeliverable by Post Office.

THE WATSON & BRIGGS CO.
Attleboro, Massachusetts

In the 1934 dresserware catalog Watson & Briggs is given as the successor to the Thomae Co.

WATSON COMPANY
Attleboro, Massachusetts
See Wallace Silversmiths

CHRONOLOGY	
Cobb, Gould & Co.	1874-1880
Watson & Newell	1880-1886
Watson, Newell & Co.	1886-1895
Watson, Newell Co.	1895-1919
Watson Company	1919-1955

The company began with the partnership of Cobb, Gould & Co. in 1874. With these two were associated Clarence L. Watson and Fred A. Newell.

By 1894 and continuing through 1919, C. L. Watson and Fred A. Newell were in control. At first they produced jewelry principally but soon began the production of souvenir spoons. A little later they added silverplated flatware, holloware and novelties. Later the business was confined to sterling flatware and holloware.

About 1900 they made a line of sterling holloware for Wilcox & Wagner which was sold under the Wilcox & Wagner trademark. When Wilcox & Wagner gave up operating as selling agents about 1908, Watson continued the line and took over their New York office. Wilcox & Wagner started business after being associated with the Wilcox & Evertsen line which business had been sold to the Meriden Britannia Co.

J. T. Inman, also of Attleboro, bought the souvenir spoon dies from the Watson Co. The balance of the business was purchased by R. Wallace & Sons (now Wallace Silversmiths). In 1964 these same souvenir spoon dies were sold to Whiting & Davis who are producing the spoons stamped with their own trademark.

(1879-1905)

(1905-1929)

(1910-)

JULIUS R. WATTS & CO.
Atlanta, Georgia

Established in 1888 and listed in the Atlanta City Directories through 1958-1959. They are listed as watchmakers and more recently as jewelers and watch inspectors. The Uncle Remus trademark was stamped on souvenir spoons.

(On Souvenir Spoons.)

JOHN WAUBEL
Baltimore, Maryland

Listed in the 1864 Baltimore City Directory as a silverplater.

WAYNE SILVER CO.
Honesdale, Pennsylvania

"The Wayne Silver Co. of Honesdale, Pa. was incorporated. Directors are: L. J. Dorflinger, Thomas B. Clark, Wm. B. Holmes, Walter A. Wood and Grant W. Lane. They manufacture fancy and useful articles of silver, not plated, with the possible exception of knives and forks." (JC&HR 3-13-1895, p. 14)

"Operations began in the Wayne Silver Co.'s factory. The building is completed and mechanics are making models, dies, etc. Tea sets, berry sets, cake baskets and fancy and useful articles of various kinds will be made of sterling silver. E. Newton, formerly with Tiffany & Co., N. Y., is the manager of the factory." (JC&HR 9-25-1895, p. 14)

Listed out of business before 1904.

TRADE MARK

WAYNE SILVERSMITH, INC.
Yonkers, New York

Makers of handwrought sterling silver articles from c. 1950 to the present. No response to recent inquiry.

J. P. WEATHERSTONE
Chicago, Illinois

Advertised in the *American Jeweler*, Sept. 1892, p. 3, as a manufacturer of sterling and coin silverware. He advertised that special pieces in silver could be made on short notice. Prices for making over old silver were quoted at 45¢ per ounce, an extra charge for hand engravings.

WEB SILVER COMPANY, INC.
Philadelphia, Pennsylvania

Successors to the Web Jewelry Manufacturing Co. between 1950-1965. In 1952 they acquired the sterling flatware dies and patterns formerly used by the Weidlich Sterling Spoon Company, Bridgeport, Connecticut.

GEORGE W. WEBB
Baltimore, Maryland

George W. Webb was born in 1812 and died in 1890. The earliest record found for his goldsmithing and silversmithing was an advertisement stating that his business was established in 1850. He is listed in the Baltimore City Directories as George W. Webb until 1865-1866 when the name was changed to Webb & Company. G. W. Webb, A. Remick and W. H. Sexton, partners. This listing continued until 1877 when it changed to Geo. W. Webb & Co. The latter listing continued through 1886.

H. J. WEBB & CO.
Springfield, Massachusetts

Successors to L. S. Stowe & Co. between 1896 and 1904. Jobbers and retailers of silver and jewelry. Out of business before 1915.

JOHN WEBB
Baltimore, Maryland

John Webb is listed by Pleasants and Sill (see bibliography) as a silversmith in Baltimore c. 1827-1842. In the Baltimore City Directories John Webb is listed 1855-1856 as a goldsmith. The 1864 listing is in the name John Webb, Sr. The 1865-1866 listing is John Webb, jeweler.

WEBER-WAGNER & BENSON CO., INC.
See J. Wagner & Son, Inc.

WEBER-WAGNER CO.
See J. Wagner & Son, Inc.

WEBSTER COMPANY
North Attleboro, Massachusetts
See Reed & Barton
See Frank W. Smith Silver Co., Inc.
See G. K. Webster Co.

Founded by George K. Webster in 1869 in North Attleboro under the name of G. K. Webster & Company. As the business grew, Mr. Webster purchased the interest of his partners. It operated under his direct supervision throughout his lifetime.

On January 1, 1950 it became a subsidiary of Reed & Barton of Taunton, Massachusetts. It continues its independent operation as The Webster Company.

The principal product has always been articles made of sterling silver. They are mostly baby goods, dresserware and picture frames.

In October 1958 they purchased the Frank W. Smith Silver Co. Inc. and all the tools and dies, along with the tradename and trademark. The flatware portion of this business was moved to North Attleboro from the original location in Gardner, Massachusetts.

Trademark now owned by the Webster Co. Division of Reed & Barton Silversmiths.

CLARENCE B. WEBSTER
Brooklyn, New York

CHRONOLOGY
Frederick S. Hoffman
Webster Brother & Co.
A. A. Webster & Co.
Clarence B. Webster

The company began as Frederick S. Hoffman (q.v.) founding date not known; succeeded by Webster Brother & Co., and then by A. A. Webster & Co. in 1886; became Clarence B. Webster before 1904. A. A. Webster was formerly with E. G. Webster & Bro.

Manufacturers of sterling silver goods, 14K and 18K gold novelties and leather goods with silver mountings.

E. G. WEBSTER & SON
Brooklyn, New York
See International Silver Co.

CHRONOLOGY
Webster Mfg. Co.	1859-1873
E. G. Webster & Bros.	1873-1886
E. G. Webster & Son	1886-1928

In 1859 Elizur G. Webster (1829-1900) bought Henry L. Webster's (formerly with Jabez Gorham) store and with his brother, A. A. Webster, started a small manufacturing business in Brooklyn in the early 1860s under the name of Webster Mfg. Co. In 1873 the firm name became E. G. Webster & Bros. and with the retirement of his brother in 1886, he took in his son, Fred H. Webster under the name E. G. Webster & Son. After his father's death, Fred H. Webster continued the business until it was sold to the International Silver Co. in 1928 and moved from Brooklyn to Meriden, Conn.

Their main line was silverplated holloware, much of it on German silver. It was well known for its highly chased holloware and English reproductions. The business was combined with the Barbour Silver Co. factory "A" plant in Meriden. Fred H. Webster continued with the firm, but retired a few years before he died in 1941.

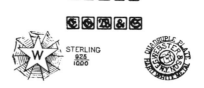

(On sterling silver)

Brooklyn S.P. Co. Quadruple Plate
(On napkin rings)

G. K. WEBSTER
North Attleboro, Massachusetts
See Reed & Barton
See Webster Co.

"G. K. Webster, North Attleboro, Born Wentworth, N. H., 1850. Attended common schools there until old enough to attend academy at Newbury, Vt. from which he graduated. In 1868 he went to New Jersey and worked for the then Raritan and Delaware railroad in the office of the repair shop. Later he went to Lawrence, Massachusetts and worked at the drug business for three years and in Boston for two years for a wholesale drug concern. He then moved to N. Attleboro and engaged in the drug business for himself. In 1879 he sold out and began manufacturing and making a general line [sterling and jewelry] and also novelties." (Obit. *Manufacturing Jeweler*, 10-2-1894, p. 60)

The company was succeeded by the Webster Co. soon after his death.

H. L. WEBSTER & CO.
See J. B. & S. M. Knowles
See Gorham Corporation

W. E. WEBSTER CO.
Providence, Rhode Island

Registered trademark U.S. Patent Office, No. 27,241, November 19, 1895 for sterling silver, rings, pins and ornamental jewelry. Out of business before 1904.

WEE CHERUB MFG. CO.
Houston, Texas

Manufacturers (?) of sterling novelties c. 1950.

WEE CHERUB

THE WEIDLICH BROS. MFG. CO.
Bridgeport, Connecticut

Founded in 1901 in Bridgeport, Connecticut. Specialized in sterling and plated trophies. Went into voluntary dissolution in 1950. No connection with Weidlich, Inc. 140 Hurd Avenue, Bridgeport, Connecticut.

POMPEIAN GOLD
THE WARNER SILVER CO.

FVFR DRY
(On salt & pepper sets)

AVON
(On sterling)

MAYFLOWER
(On pewter)

WEIDLICH STERLING SPOON CO.
Bridgeport, Connecticut

Related to Weidlich Bros. Mfg. Co. of Bridgeport. Made sterling silver souvenir spoons and sterling silver flatware (U.S. Patent 103,304, March 30, 1915). In 1952 the Web Jewelry Mfg. Co., now the Web Silver Co., Inc., silversmiths in Philadelphia, acquired the sterling flatware dies and patterns. No connection with present Weidlich, Inc., 140 Hurd Avenue, Bridgeport, Connecticut.

E. M. WEINBERG & CO.
New York, New York

Listed JC 1915 in plated silver section. Out of business before 1922.

Note similarity of trademark to that of F. G. Whitney & Co., Attleboro, Massachusetts.

WEINMAN CO.
Philadelphia, Pennsylvania

Manufacturers of plated silverware in Philadelphia c. 1900-1915.

BRAZIL SILVER

WEIZENNEGGER BROS.
Newark, New Jersey

Listed JC 1909-1922 in sterling silver section, manufacturers of mesh bags, dealers in diamonds.

WELLS, INC.
Attleboro, Massachusetts

Purchased R. Blackinton & Co., in 1967. Wells manufactures charms and other fine jewelry.

WELSH & BRO.
Baltimore, Maryland

Listed in Baltimore City Directories 1887-1909 under plated silverware.

Successors to Canfield Bros. & Co.

"Welsh & Bro. of Baltimore designed and manufactured the Communion service presented by the Altar Guild of Mt. Calvary Protestant Episcopal Church to the Rev. Geo. A. Leakin." (JC&HR 4-20-1898, p. 28)

WENDELL MANUFACTURING COMPANY
Chicago, Illinois

Founded by Charles Wendell c. 1850. Became the Wendell Mfg. Co. by 1885; incorporated May 1889. Manufacturers of sterling silver badges. Around 1896-97 they acquired some of the flatware patterns and dies of the Mauser Mfg. Co. Retail or wholesale outlet in New York listed as Wendell & Co. 1904-1909. Not listed in Chicago City Directories.

They made sterling wares for Marshall Field & Co., some of which were marked with trademarks of both. Discontinued flatware production c. 1900.

J. R. WENDT & CO.
New York, New York

In business c. 1855-1870. John R. Wendt had a shop in the building erected at Broadway & Prince Street, New York, in 1859 by Ball, Black & Co., then the largest jewelry store in America. The factory occupied the two upper floors, and they worked on orders from the jewelry firm below.

The firm was, during and immediately following the Civil War, the most prominent maker of silver flatware in the country being well-known throughout.

For a brief period — January to August 1860 — Wendt was one of the partners in Rogers, Wendt & Wilkinson (q.v.).

Wendt's business was sold in two parts, one part going to the Whiting Mfg. Co. and the other to Adams & Shaw Co. and later to Dominick & Haff.

THE WESSELL SILVER CO.
New York, New York

"The Wessell Silver Co. of 1945 Park Avenue, N. Y. made an assignment Wednesday. The company began business in July 1893. W. Emlen Roosevelt, president and Charles Wessell, secretary. The original incorporators were C. A. Wessell, R. A. Mead and Arthur Cristodoro. The company manufactured a composition metal called Wessell silver, which they recently began to make into spoons, forks and other tableware." (JC&HR 5-5-1897, p. 18)

WEST SILVER CO.
Taunton, Massachusetts

Founded in Taunton, Massachusetts in 1883. F. B. Rogers successors before 1896.

WESTBROOK BRITANNIA COMPANY
Portland, Maine

Listed in 1869-1885 City Directories. William Wallace Stevens, owner.

WESTERLING COMPANY
Chicago, Illinois

Founded in 1944 by Jack Luhn, Les Hedge and Glenn Olmstead as the Easterling Co. A direct sales company handling only sterling silver flatware. Tableware lines were diversified to include china, crystal, cook-and-serve wares and others. The sterling inventory and pattern rights were sold to the Westerling Co. in March 1974. These six patterns are manufactured by the Gorham Company for Westerling.

WESTERN SILVER WORKS, INC.
New York, New York

Listed 1927 KJI as manufacturers of silverplated ware.

WESTMORLAND STERLING CO.
Wallingford, Connecticut

Westmorland was created in 1940 through the cooperative efforts of Wearever Aluminum Inc. and Wallace Silversmiths. War-time priorities made it necessary to diversify hence the idea of selling sterling flatware on a direct-to-consumer basis was developed. Wearever developed the marketing programs and Wallace Silversmiths manufactured five sterling silver flatware patterns, exclusive to that organization. In 1966, Wallace assumed the marketing responsibility for Westmorland and reorganized the marketing program by establishing franchised dealers and continues to manufacture the same five patterns.

C. A. WETHERELL & CO.
Attleboro, Massachusetts

Listed in Jeweler's Weekly, 1896 as manufacturers of sterling silverware. Listed in Attleboro City Directories 1892-1897 as manufacturing jewelers.

WHITE SILVER CO.
Taunton, Massachusetts

Manufacturers of plated silver holloware, prize cups and pewterware c. 1900-1930.

H. L. WHITE & CO.
Providence, Rhode Island

In business c. 1852. Succeeded by J. B. & S. M. Knowles in 1891.

WHITING & DAVIS CO., INC.
Plainville, Massachusetts

Began as a small chain manufacturing company c. 1876. Operated by William Wade and Edward P. Davis. C. A. Whiting, while still a young boy, entered the business as an unskilled worker. He worked as an artisan, salesman and partner, finally becoming owner in 1907.

Years of experimenting led to the development of the first chainmail mesh machine shortly after 1907. Whiting & Davis is now the world's largest manufacturer of mesh products including such items as safety gloves and aprons, mesh handbags and purse accessories, and jewelry. They also produce an outstanding line of antique reproduction jewelry — many pieces copies of museum masterpieces.

In 1964 they purchased the J. T. Inman Company and integrated the complete manufacturing facilities into their main plant. The souvenir spoon equipment, dies and tools were bought from the Watson Company by J. T. Inman. The balance of the business was sold to the Wallace Company. These dies are now used to make souvenir spoons. There are approximately 3,000 designs, according to the Executive Vice President, George J. LeMire. They will be stamped, whenever possible, with the Whiting & Davis registered trademark.

W. & D.

FRANK M. WHITING CO.
North Attleboro, Massachusetts
See Ellmore Silver Co.

CHRONOLOGY

Holbrook, Whiting & Albee	-1878
F. M. Whiting & Co.	1878-1891
F. M. Whiting	1891-1895
F. M. Whiting Co.	1895-1896
Frank M. Whiting & Co.	1896-1940

Frank M. Whiting, son of William D. Whiting, founder of the Whiting Mfg. Co. had been associated with his father in that company. Prior to 1878 he left the company and formed the firm of Holbrook, Whiting & Albee, who began the manufacture of silverware in North Attleboro, Massachusetts. In 1878, Frank M. Whiting bought out his two partners and continued business under the firm name of F. M. Whiting & Co. In 1881 his father, William D. Whiting, became a partner, the firm name remaining the same until his father's death in 1891, when it was changed to F. M. Whiting. The following year Frank M. Whiting died and the business was continued by his widow, mother and two sisters. In 1895 it was converted into a stock company under the name F. M. Whiting Co. About 1940 it became a division of the Ellmore Silver Co. which went out of business c. 1960. The sterling flatware dies were bought by the Crown Silver Co.,

New York. It is believed that they are no longer being used.

Action brought by the Whiting Mfg. Co. against the F. M. Whiting Co. in 1896 resulted in F. M. Whiting agreeing to change their name to Frank M. Whiting & Co. The suit was to restrain the defendant company from using a griffin trademark which testimony showed led to confusion with the mark of the Whiting Mfg. Co. trademark.

(Not used after 1896)

WHITING MFG. CO.
Providence, Rhode Island
See Gorham Corporation

Originated by Albert T. Tifft and William. D. Whiting in 1840 as Tifft & Whiting, to manufacture jewelry. They later added ladies' silver combs and small holloware. For a brief time, prior to 1858, the firm was Whiting, Fessenden & Cowan (W. B. Fessenden, q.v.), located in North Attleboro, Massachusetts. It became Whiting Mfg. Co. in 1866. After the factory in North Attleboro was destroyed by fire, they moved to Newark, New Jersey. In 1910 it was moved again to Bridgeport, Connecticut where a large modern plant was erected, and a complete line of silverware was produced. The company was purchased by the Gorham Company in 1926 and moved to Providence, Rhode Island. The Whiting mark is still used.

WHITING M.F.G. CO
YEAR MARKS

Mark	Year	Mark	Year
♣	1905	(symbol)	1915
(symbol)	1906	(symbol)	1916
(symbol)	1907	⅃	1917
∞	1908	˥	1918
(symbol)	1909	⊐	1919
(symbol)	1910	X	1920
(symbol)	1911	⊔	1921
(symbol)	1912	⌐	1922
△	1913	⊏	1923
(symbol)	1914	L	1924

CHARLES WHITLOCK
Baltimore, Maryland

Listed in the 1850 Census as a silversmith in Baltimore. Born in Maryland.

F. G. WHITNEY & CO.
Attleborough, Massachusetts

Trademark registered July 12, 1881 for use on jewelry. Note similarity to trademark of E. M. Weinberg & Co. of New York.

WHITNEY JEWELRY COMPANY
Boston, Massachusetts

First listed in the Boston City Directories in 1883; probably founded the previous year. It was first listed as Whitney Brothers, jewelers. The brothers were: Edwin A. Whitney of Watertown, Massachusetts, and later of Newton, Massachusetts, and Albert E. Whitney of Fitchburg, Massachusetts. Albert E. was not connected with the firm by 1894, when it was listed as E. A. Whitney Company, watches and jewelry. Was in business through 1911.

U.S. Patents Nos. 19,778 through 19,992 were registered in the name of Edwin A. Whitney, June 30, 1891, for use on gold, silver and plated flatware Barbara Frietchie No. 19,788.

Columbus Before the Queen
No. 19,778

Columbus and the Egg
No. 19,779

Monitor & Merrimac
March 9, 1862
No. 19,791

Gettysburg, July 1863,
No. 19,789

The March to the Sea
No. 19,781

Barbara Frietchie
No. 19,788

Fort Smith
No. 19,790

Antietam, September 17, 1862,
No. 19,992

The **Santa Maria**, No. 19,780

Appomattox, April 9, 1865
No. 19,782

July 4, 1776, No. 19,784

General Stonewall Jackson,
No. 19,785

Sheriden's Ride
No. 19,783

"The Seven Days" battle used in spoon bowl, General Robert E. Lee is the trademark, No. 19,786

Signing the Emancipation Proclamation, January 1, 1863, No. 19,787

There is a discrepancy between the historical scenes listed in the trademark description and those actually shown. Numbers 19,784 and 19,790 are listed as "July 4, 1776" and "Fort Smith." The two scenes shown are actually of Harpers Ferry, Oct. 17, 1859 and Fort Sumpter, April 12, 1861.

H. F. WICHMAN
Honolulu, Hawaii

Manufacturing silversmiths and jewelers. Began in 1890 as Gomes & Wichman. Became H. F. Wichman in 1891 and continues in business under that name.

An order for heroic medals from His Majesty, King David Kalakaua, in 1877 provided the financial base for the beginning of the firm.

H. F. WICHMAN

HENRY WIENER & SON
New York, New York

Distributors (?) of sterling silver mesh bags c. 1920.

PICADILLY

CHAS. C. WIENTGE CO.
Newark, New Jersey

Charles C. Wientge designed silverware for the Howard Sterling Co. Providence, Rhode Island, c. 1891-93 and was a silversmith working for himself in Newark, 1893-96; employed by Lebkuecher & Co., Newark in 1896.

WILCOX BRITANNIA CO.

See International Silver Co.
See Wilcox Silver Plate Co.

WILCOX & EVERTSEN

New York, New York
See International Silver Co.

Successors to Rowan & Wilcox, who started under that name the latter part of 1889. Became Wilcox & Evertsen in 1892 with Robert M. Wilcox and Henry H. Evertsen as partners. They were makers of sterling silver holloware. In 1896 the company was purchased by the Meriden Britannia Co. and moved to Meriden, Connecticut.

They made a beautiful line of sterling holloware and started a sterling flatware line. After the formation of the International Silver Co., in 1898, the tools and equipment for flatware were moved to Wallingford, Connecticut and used space in the Simpson Nickel Silver plant while the holloware was made in Meriden. When more room became necessary they consolidated in 1929 in Wallingford with other sterling lines in the old Simpson, Hall, Miller & Co. buildings.

For their flatware markings see the International Silver Co.

H. C. WILCOX & CO.

Meriden, Connecticut
See International Silver Co.
See Meriden Britannia Co.

Organized in 1848 by Horace C. and Dennis C. Wilcox to market the products of Meriden's britannia ware. A forerunner of Meriden Britannia Co.

WILCOX-ROTH CO.

Newark, New Jersey

Listed in JC 1909 in sterling silver section as out of business.

WILCOX SILVER PLATE CO.

Meriden, Connecticut
See International Silver Co.
See Superior Silver Co.

Organized in 1865 by Jedediah and Horace Wilcox, Charles Parker, Aaron Collins and Hezekiah Miller and others to make holloware as Wilcox Britannia Co. In 1867 the name was changed to Wilcox Silver Plate Co. In 1869 they purchased the Parker & Casper Co. They were one of the original companies to become part of the International Silver Co. in 1898.

STERLING   **PEWTER**
                  BY
                  WILCOX
                  (Pewter Hollowware)

WILCOX & WAGONER

New York, New York

Listed in JC 1904 in sterling silverware and cut glass sections. Bought by the Watson Co. before 1905.

WILEY-CRAWFORD CO., INC

Newark, New Jersey

Manufacturers of gold and sterling silver novelties, card trays and jewelry c. 1915-1922.

WILKINSON SWORD CO.

London and Sheffield, England

Manufacturers of plated silver swords. Listed JC 1909-1922.

WILLIAMS BROS. MFG. CO.

Naubuc, Connecticut
See American Sterling Co.
See F. Curtis & Co.
See Curtisville Mfg. Co.
See Thomas J. Vail

James B. and William Williams bought the American Sterling Company and founded the Williams Bros. Mfg. Co., in 1880. Manufacturers of plated silver spoons, forks and a general line of flatware. They went out of business in June 1950.

American Sterling Co. used as a brand name on some of their silverplated ware.

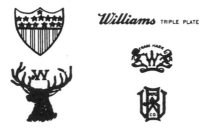

Williams TRIPLE PLATE

ROGER WILLIAMS SILVER CO.
Providence, Rhode Island
See Gorham Corporation
See Mt. Vernon Co. Silversmiths, Inc.

The Rogers Williams Silver Co. was successor c. 1900 to Howard Sterling Silver Co. It was merged in 1903 with the Mauser Mfg. Co. of New York and Hayes & McFarland of Mount Vernon, New York to form the Mt. Vernon Company Silversmiths, Inc. which was bought by the Gorham Corporation in 1913.

For a brief time c. 1911 control of the Roger Williams Silver Co. was transferred to the Silversmiths' Co. of New York, under the management of Theo Bender, Wm. Linker, from David & Galt, silversmiths of Philadelphia, was associated with the firm.

U.S. Patent No. 36,769, July 16, 1901 for certain named metalwares — whole or in part of silver.

R & W

Trademark used continuously since June 1, 1901.

JAMES A. WILLIG
Baltimore, Maryland

Listed in the 1850 Census as a silversmith. Born in Pennsylvania.

JOHN W. WILLSON
Baltimore, Maryland

Listed 1867-1869 Baltimore City Directories as silverplaters.

WILMORT MFG. CO.
Chicago, Illinois

Manufacturers of sterling and plated silverware and novelties c. 1920-1930.

(Silver Plated Hollowware)

WM. WILSON & SON
Philadelphia, Pennsylvania

Patent Office records show the registration of two trademarks by William Wilson & Son in 1883. They were also listed in JC in 1896 and 1904 and were out of business before 1909.

Robert Wilson was listed in New York City Directory in 1805 and Philadelphia City Directories 1816-1846. Robert Wilson and William Wilson (R. & W. Wilson) listed in Philadelphia Directories 1825-1850. Wm. Wilson & Son, silversmiths, Philadelphia, listed in *Jeweller, Silversmith & Watchmaker*, 1877.

U.S. Patent No. 9,949, January 9, 1883 for sterling silverware.

U. S. Patent No. 9,950, January 9, 1883 for electroplated wares.

WILTON BRASS FOUNDRY
Columbia, Pennsylvania

Manufacturers of articles that are "hand-cast in sand, hand-polished. The beauty and weight of pewter, . . . [made of] a secret fusion of 10 metals. . . ."

WINDSOR SILVER CO., INC.
Brooklyn, New York

Listed 1966-1973 JC-K under sterling and plated holloware. No reply to recent inquiry.

WINNIPEG SILVER PLATE CO., LTD.
Winnipeg, Manitoba

Listed JC 1915-1922 in plated silver section.

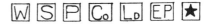

WOLF & KNELL
New York, New York

Manufacturers and importers c. 1900 of antique silver in Dutch, French and English designs. Decanters, tea and coffee sets, vases, spoons, tea strainers, etc. O. Buchholz, U.S. and Canadian representative. Factory at Hanau, Germany.

WOLFENDEN SILVER COMPANY
North Attleboro, Massachusetts
See Crown Silver, In.

Successor to J. W. Wolfenden Corp. Founded in 1919 by John W. Wolfenden and now a Division of Crown Silver Inc., New York. Dies and equipment were moved to the Crown factory in New York in 1955.

(Used since May 24, 1949)

WOOD & HUGHES
New York, New York
See Gorham Corporation
See Graff, Washbourne & Dunn

CHRONOLOGY

Gale, Wood & Hughes	1833-1845
Wood & Hughes	1845-1899

In 1833 William Gale formed a partnership with Jacob Wood and Jasper H. Hughes, under the name Gale, Wood & Hughes. Wood and Hughes had both served apprenticeships under Gale. Jacob Wood and Jasper H. Hughes remained in the partnership until 1851, the year of the death of the founder. Then Charles Hughes and Stephen T. Fraprie entered the business. Jasper H. Hughes retired in 1856, the business being continued by the three remaining partners until 1865. In that year Henry Wood and Dixon G. Hughes were admitted and succeeded to the business as equal partners after the death of Charles Wood in 1881, Charles H. Wood in 1883 and S. T. Fraprie in 1889. They manufactured a general line of sterling silverware and were noted for the excellence of their work. Succeeded by Graff, Washbourne & Dunn in 1899.

(*Used* 1833 *to* 1871.)

WωH.
(*Used since* 1871.)

N. G. WOOD & SONS
Boston, Massachusetts

Registered trademark U.S. Patent Office, No. 20,515, December 29, 1891 for spoons, gold, silver and plated.

Listed JC 1896-1922 in sterling silver section. The trademark illustrated was for souvenir spoons made to commemorate the Boston Tea Party and was discontinued before 1922.

MRS. SARAH B. DICKINSON WOOD
Niagara Falls, New York

The House of Dickinson, well-known jewelry firm of Buffalo was founded by Thomas V. Dickinson in 1849. Associated with him were his wife, Elizabeth, and later his son, Alfred; his grandson, Alfred. Now the great grandson Alfred Dickinson is in charge of the business.

The founder was granted a patent on July 21, 1891 for the manufacture of silver, flat and tableware, using the buffalo head trademark that his daughter (later Mrs. Sarah B. Dickinson Wood) used on souvenir silverware. According to Alfred III, they have no records that the Dickinsons actually manufactured these items themselves. They were probably made for them by one of the many companies who did this sort of work and stamped it with the trademark of the wholesaler or retailer.

WOODBURY PEWTERERS
Woodbury, Connecticut

Founded in 1952 by R. C. Holbrook and L. R. Titcomb when they acquired the tools, etc. of the Merwin & Wilson Co., New Milford, Connecticut and the Danforth Pewter Co., Woodbury, Connecticut and used them as the nucleus for developing a product line of early American pewter reproductions, later expanded to include a separate line for the Henry Ford Museum.

(Under each mark)

The ATC Hallmark on Pewter indicates that the finest quality metal has been used in its manufacture. The Hallmark guarantees that the metal contains only tin, and very small percentages of copper and antimony, as hardening agents. It is the quality mark of Pewter!

WOODMAN-COOK CO
Portland, Maine
(See Stevens Silver Co.)

Began as Stevens & Smart 1879-1883. Manufacturers of britannia ware. Became Stevens, Smart & Dunham 1884-1886; Stevens & Smart, 1887-1890; Stevens, Woodman and Company, 1891-1892 and Woodman-Cook Company 1893-1914. Manufacturers of plated silverwares. Edward B. Coon, president; C. H. Fessenden, vice-president; Fred H. Woodman, treasurer.

"Fred H. Woodman, of Woodman-Cook Co. Born Palmyra, Maine, December 28, 1855. At the age of 18 taught school and soon after he was engaged in the business department of a cotton mill. Later he bought an interest in the business of Stevens & Smart, manufacturers of silver plated ware, Portland. The business was founded in 1878 by Rufus [?] Dunham, who had been making Britannia ware since 1837. Later the firm became Stevens, Woodman & Co. and finally it was incorporated as Woodman-Cook Co." (JC&HR 3-1—1897, p. 19)

WALDORF SILVER CO.

WOODS & CHATELLIER
New York, New York

Successor to Stephen Woods before 1904. Manufacturers of sterling cases, novelties, boxes and jewelry. Listed JC 1904-1922.

STEPHEN WOODS
Newark, New Jersey
See Woods & Chatellier

RICHARD M. WOODS & CO.
New York, New York

Successor to Woodside Sterling Company c. 1920. Makers of sterling silver holloware, dresserware and novelties. Around 1940 also listed as wholesalers.

WOODSIDE STERLING CO.
See Richard M. Wood & Co.

Listed 1896 Jewelers' Weekly. Listed 1904 JC. Succeeded by Richard M. Woods & Co. c. 1920.

JAMES T. WOOLLEY
Boston, Massachusetts

James T. Woolley was born in Providence, Rhode Island in 1864. He learned the silversmithing craft in The Gorham Company. For eighteen years he was foreman at Goodnow & Jenks (q.v.) in Boston. For two years he shared bench room with George J. Hunt at 79 Chestnut St. though they worked independently. Around 1908 he opened his own shop in the Studio Building in adjacent Lime Street. Many of his pieces are excellent adaptations of colonial silver.

WORDEN-MUNNIS CO., INC
Boston, Massachusetts

Silversmiths and goldsmiths, founded in 1940. Makers of early American, English and Irish reproduc-

tions. The company was purchased in 1964 by Old Newbury Crafters who are producing the sterling holloware line.

WORLD HAND FORGED MFG. CO.
New York, New York

Manufacturers of silverplated wares c. 1950.

WORTZ & VOORHIS
New York, New York

Listed in JC 1896 in sterling silver section. Out of business before 1915.

Trademark identical to D. C. Bourquin.

WÜRTTEMBERGISCHE METALLWARENFABRIK (WMF)
Geislingen, Germany

Founded in 1853 by Daniel Straub (1815-1889), a miller who had been repairing tools and railway construction equipment. Under the name Straub & Schweizer they produced tableware from silver-plated copper sheets. In 1880 Straub & Schweizer joined with A. Ritter & Co. of Esslingen which had been founded in 1871 for the manufacture of silver-plated wares. In 1883 a glass works was added and in 1897 WMF took over Schauffler & Safft of Göppingen, makers of light holloware. They advertised under the WMF-IKORA name "The original tarnish-resistant silverplate." Stainless steel tableware, multicolored "Ikora: metal and bronze castings were 20th century introductions. The company was especially noted for its Art Nouveau styles c. 1900. Still in business. Distributed in this country through WMF-IKORA.

WYMBLE MFG. CO.
Newark, New Jersey

About 1886 a new method of depositing silver on non-metallic articles was discovered. Among the companies founded for the purpose of decorating articles by this process was the Wymble Mfg. Co. organized in September 1890. Justus Verschuur, artist and designer, was one of the founders. The firm set up a handsome and extensive display of its wares in the American jewelry and silverware exhibit at the World's Columbian Exposition held in Chicago in 1893-94. The company went into receivership in March 1895 and the Alvin Mfg. Co. purchased the entire stock and fixtures.

YORK SILVER CO.
New York, New York

PAT JANE

Listed 1950 JC-K under sterling.

HIRAM YOUNG & COMPANY
New York, New York

In the 1860s they purchased Reed & Barton wares "in the metal" and operated their own plating establishment.

In 1860-62 the firm was listed at 20 John St., New York, at the same address as the Manhattan Plate Co. In 1868, the *Jewelers' Weekly* says that the Manhattan Plate Co. was a trademark used by Henry Young and Henry C. Reed, whose factory was at 227 6th St.; showroom at 8 Maiden Lane. In 1870-72 this Henry C. Reed is identified as the one connected with Reed & Barton Co. In 1879 there is a reference to "the old Manhattan Plate Co. now owned by Hiram Young."

OTTO YOUNG & COMPANY
Chicago, Illinois

Established in 1865. Importers, manufacturers and wholesalers of all types of silverware and jewelers' merchandise.

Successors in 1880 to William B. Clapp, Young & Co.

An illustrated catalog of 1893 (courtesy of the Whittelsey Fund, Metropolitan Museum of Art) depicts silverware, jewelry, optical goods, clocks and watches.

Succeeded by A. C. Becken Co. c. 1924.

ZELL BROS.
Portland, Oregon

Listed in 1950 JC-K under sterling. They advertise Reed & Barton collector's limited edition Damascene plates. These are made of sterling or silverplate.

UNASCRIBED MARKS

 STERLING

 STERLING

SILVER ON COPPER

Rosebud

TRADE NAMES

A. 1. NIKEL SILVER No. 210 . . . . .ONEIDA
ACORN BRAND . . . . .ALBERT PICK & CO.
ALASKA METAL . . . . .SEARS ROEBUCK & CO.
ALBANY SILVER PLATE . . . . .INSILCO
ALDEN . . . . .DERBY SILVER CO.
ALPHA PLATE . . . . .ONEIDA
ALUMINUM SILVER . . . . .DANIEL & ARTER
AMERICAN SILVER CO. . . . . .INSILCO
AMERICAN SILVER PLATE CO. . . . . .SIMPSON, HALL, MILLER & CO.
AMSILCO . . . . .INSILCO
ANDERSON, JUST . . . . .MANDIX CO.
APOLLO . . . . .BERNARD RICE'S SONS
ARGENLINE . . . . .DANIEL & ARTER
ARMETALE . . . . .WILTON BRASS FOUNDRY
ARROW PLATE . . . . .GLASTONBURY SILVER CO.
A. S. Co. . . . . .AMERICAN SILVER CO.
ATLANTIC SILVER PLATE CO. . . . . .RUEFF BROS.
ATLAS SILVER PLATE . . . . .INSILCO
AVON SILVER PLATE . . . . .INSILCO
AZTEC COIN METAL . . . . .HOLMES & EDWARDS CO.
BALTCO . . . . .BALTES-CHANCE CO.
B. B. & CO. . . . . .BARDEN BLAKE & CO.
BANQUET PLATE . . . . .GORHAM
BEACON SILVER CO. . . . . .AMERICAN SILVER CO.
BEACON SILVER CO. . . . . .F. B. ROGERS SILVER CO.
BEAUXARDT . . . . .BERNARD RICE'S SONS
BᴺE . . . . .BENJAMIN F. LOWELL
BENGAL SILVER . . . . .DANIEL & ARTER
BERKELEY . . . . .BENEDICT MFG. CO.
BREWSTER . . . . .INSILCO
BRIDGE . . . . .SHAPLEIGH HARDWARE CO.
BRISTOL CUTLERY CO. . . . . .AMERICAN SILVER CO.
BRISTOL PLATE CO. . . . . .PAIRPOINT MFG. CO.
BRISTOL SILVER CORP. . . . . .POOLE SILVER CO.
BRITANNIA ARTISTIC SILVER . . . . .M. T. GOLDSMITH
BRITANNIA METAL CO. . . . . .VAN BERGH SILVER PLATE CO.
BROOKLYN PLATE CO. . . . . .SCHADE & CO.
B. R. S. CO. SHEFFIELD, U.S.A. . . . . .BERNARD RICE'S SONS
B. S. CO. . . . . .BIRMINGHAM SILVER CO.

```
BS CO. .............................................INSILCO
B.S. Co. ...................................HOLMES & EDWARDS SILVER CO.
BURMAROID................................................DANIEL & ARTER
CAMBRIDGE SILVER PLATE ........................SEARS ROEBUCK & CO.
CAMELIA SILVERPLATE .............................................INSILCO
CARAVELLE ...........................................SUMMIT SILVER CO.
CARBON............................................................ONEIDA
CARLTON SILVERPLATE ............................................ONEIDA
CARVEL HALL..............................CHAS. D. BRIDELL, INC.
CARV-EZE ..........................................................INSILCO
THE CELLAR SHOPS ............................RAYMOND BRENNER
CENTURY STERLING ............................................INSILCO
CHASE ........................................MAX H. STORCH
CHATSWORTH .....................................R. H. MACY & CO.
CHICAGO SILVER PLATE CO. ...............ELGIN-AMERICAN MFG. CO.
COLONIAL PLATE CO. ..........................MELROSE SILVER CO.
COLUMBIA ...............................MIDDLETOWN PLATE CO.
COLUMBIAN SILVER CO. ...............................QUEEN SILVER CO.
COMMUNITY ......................................................ONEIDA
CONNECTICUT PLATE CO. ...................ADELPHI SILVER PLATE CO.
CONNECTICUT PLATE CO. ...........................J. W. JOHNSON
COURT SILVER PLATE .............................................INSILCO
CRESCENT SILVER CO...........................ALBERT G. FINN SILVER CO.
CROSBY .............................................A. COHEN & SONS
CROWN GUILD.........................ROCKFORD SILVER PLATE CO.
CROWN GUILD ...............................JEWELERS' CROWN GUILD
CROWN PRINCE....................................G. I. MIX & CO.
CROWN SILVER CO. ...............................AMERICAN SILVER CO.
CROWN SILVER CO. ..............................................INSILCO
CROWN SILVER PLATE CO. ........................AMERICAN SILVER CO.
CUNNINGHAM SILVER PLATE CO. ..................WM. ROGERS MFG. CO.
CUVEE .........................................QUAKER VALLEY MFG. CO.
DEEP SILVER ....................................................INSILCO
DEERFIELD SILVER PLATE ........................................INSILCO
DEKRA ...........................................ARGENTUM SILVER CO.
DEPOS-ART ......................................CANADIAN JEWELERS
DIAMOND EDGE ...............................SHAPLEIGH HARDWARE CO.
DISTINCTION ....................................HOME DECORATORS
DORANTIQUE .......................................BERNARD RICE'S SONS
DOUBLE-TESTED SILVERPLATE ......................NATIONAL SILVER CO.
DU BARRY .............................................NAPIER COMPANY
DUNGEON ROCK .....................................H. M. HILL & CO.
DUNKIRK ..........................GOLD RECOVERY & REFINING CORP.
DURO PLATE ....................................................ONEIDA
DUTCH SILVER NOVELTIES ...............JOHNSON, HAYWARD & PIPER CO.
EAGLE BRAND..............................SIMPSON, HALL, MILLER & CO.
EASTERN SILVER CO...............................AMERICAN SILVER CO.
EASTERN SILVER CO................................................INSILCO
1847 ROGERS BROS. .............................................INSILCO
1847 ROGERS BROS. ...........................MERIDEN BRITANNIA CO.
1857 WELCH-ATKINS ...........................AMERICAN SILVER CO.
1865 WM. ROGERS MFG. CO. ......................................INSILCO
```

```
ELMWOOD PLATE ...................................................GORHAM
EMBASSY SILVER PLATE ...........................................INSILCO
EMPIRE ART SILVER ...........................................E. & J. BASS
EMPIRE SILVER COMPANY ...........................BENEDICT MFG. CO.
EMPRESS WARE ...............................NEW YORK STAMPING CO.
ENGLISH SILVER .............................SIMPSON-BRAINERD CO.
ENGLISH STERLING ...................................TIFFANY & CO.
ESSEX SILVER CO. ..............................WALLINGFORD CO.
ETCHARDT .................................BERNARD RICE'S SONS
EUREKA SILVER PLATE CO. ...................MERIDEN SILVER PLATE CO.
EVERWEAR ........................................ALBERT PICK & CO.
EVOLUTION ........................................NAPIER COMPANY
FASHION PLATE ...............................SEARS ROEBUCK & CO.
FASHION SILVER PLATE ........................SEARS ROEBUCK & CO.
FORTUNE SILVER PLATE ...................R. WALLACE & SONS MFG. CO.
GEE-ESCO .................................GLASTONBURY SILVER CO.
GEM SILVER CO. .......................................INSILCO
GEORGIAN .........................................BENEDICT MFG. CO.
GERMAN SILVER.....................................HOLMES & EDWARDS
GOLD ALUMINUM ...................................HOLMES & EDWARDS
GOLDYN-BRONZ .....................................REED & BARTON
GONDOLA SILVER ...................................CARLBERT MFG. CO.
GOPHER BRAND........................................F. L. BOSWORTH CO.
GUILDCRAFT ........................................NATIONAL SILVER CO.
HAMPSHIRE HOUSE ...........................MURRAY L. SCHACTER & CO.
HAR-MAC ...................................HARPER & MACINTIRE CO.
HARMONY HOUSE PLATE AA + .......................SEARS ROEBUCK & CO.
H. B. & H. A1 .........................HOLMES, BOOTH & HAYDENS
HARMONY HOUSE PLATE ..........................SEARS ROEBUCK & CO.
HARVEST ........................................ELLMORE SILVER CO.
HICKS SILVER CO. ..............................A. R. JUSTICE CO.
HOLD-EDGE .............................................INSILCO
HOLMES & EDWARDS ...................................INSILCO
HOLMES & TUTTLE ...................................INSILCO
HOPE SILVER CO. ..............................GEO. W. PARKS CO.
H. & T. MFG. CO. .....................................INSILCO
IMPERIAL PLATE ...............................NATIONAL SILVER CO.
IMPERIAL SILVER PLATE CO. ..........................A. F. SMITH CO.
INDEPENDENCE BRAND .......................AMERICAN SILVER CO.
INDEPENDENCE TRIPLE ..................................INSILCO
INDIANA BRAND ..............................ANCHOR SILVER PLATE CO.
INDIAN SILVER .................................DANIEL & ARTER
INLAID ..............................................INSILCO
INSICO .............................................INSILCO
INTERNATIONAL .....................................INSILCO
INTERNATIONAL SILVER CO. ...........................INSILCO
I.S.C.O. ............................................INSILCO
I.S. CO. ............................................INSILCO
JAPANESE SILVER ...............................DANIEL & ARTER
J (CROWN) G .............................ROCKFORD SILVER PLATE CO.
J. ROGERS & CO. ....................................ONEIDA
KENSICO ...........................................INSILCO
```

```
KENSINGTON SILVER PLATE ............................................INSILCO
KIRBYKRAFT ...............................MIDDLETOWN SILVER CO.
KRANSHIRE .....................................A. COHEN & SONS
LADY BERKSHIRE ............................NATIONAL SILVER CO.
LAKESIDE BRAND ..........................MONTGOMERY WARD & CO.
LASHAR ................................................INSILCO
LAXEY SILVER ...............................DANIEL & ARTER
LESCO ....................................LEVINE SILVER CO.
LEVIATHAN .................................S. J. LEVI & CO.
LIFETIME ......................................ZELL BROS.
LORALINE ...............................BERNARD RICE'S SONS
LORD BERKSHIRE ...........................NATIONAL SILVER CO.
LULLABY STERLING ...............................ALVIN
LUNA METAL .................................ROWLEY MFG. CO.
LUXOR PLATE ......................R. WALLACE & SONS MFG. CO.
MALACCA PLATED ...............................G. I. MIX & CO.
MANOR PLATE ..........................................INSILCO
MARIE LOUISE .................................R. BLACKINTON
MARION PLATE CO. ......................BERNARD RICE'S SONS
MARION SILVERPLATE ...............................INSILCO
MEDFORD CUTLERY CO..........................A. R. JUSTICE CO.
MEDFORD SILVER CO. ..................R. WALLACE & SONS MFG. CO.
MELODY SILVER PLATE ...............................INSILCO
MEXICAN CRAIG ...................HOLMES & EDWARDS SILVER CO.
MEXICAN SILVER ...................HOLMES & EDWARDS SILVER CO.
MIDDLESEX SILVER CO. ......................MIDDLETOWN SILVER CO.
MILDRED QUALITY SILVER PLATE ...................NATIONAL SILVER CO.
M. M. CO. ...................................MACOMBER MFG. CO.
MONARCH SILVER CO. .........................STANDARD SILVER CO.
MONARCH SILVER CO. ......................KNICKERBOCKER SILVER CO.
MONARCH SILVER CO. .........................NATIONAL SILVER CO.
MOREWEAR PLATE ............................MAUTNER MFG. CO.
MONTAUK SILVER CO............................J. W. JOHNSON
NACO ......................................NAPIER COMPANY
NARRAGANSETT PEWTER .......................QUAKER SILVER CO.
NASCO ....................................NATIONAL SILVER CO.
NATIONAL CUTLERY CO. .....................ROCKFORD SILVER PLATE CO.
N. E. S. P. CO. ...........................................INSILCO
NEVADA SILVER ................................DANIEL & ARTER
NEVADA SILVER METAL ....................STANDARD SILVERWARE CO.
NEW ENGLAND SILVER PLATE ...............................INSILCO
NEW ENGLAND CUTLERY CO..........................AMERICAN SILVER CO.
NEWFIELD SILVER COMPANY ..............BRIDGEPORT SILVER PLATE CO.
NEWPORT STERLING ............................................GORHAM
N. F. NICKEL SILVER CO., 1877 ...............................ONEIDA
NIAGARA FALLS CO., 1877 ...............................ONEIDA
NICKELITE SILVER .....................GOLDSMITH'S CO. OF CHICAGO
NOBILITY PLATE ...........................EMPIRE CRAFTS CORP.
NORMAN PLATE ..............................STANLEY & ALYARD
NORTH AMERICA ...........................JAMES J. DAWSON CO.
NO-TARN ................................................INSILCO
N.S.C. ....................................NATIONAL SILVER CO.
```

```
O.C. .................................................................ONEIDA
O.C. EXTRA .......................................................ONEIDA
OHIO SILVER PLATE CO. ...............................QUEEN SILVER CO.
OLD COMPANY PLATE..........................................INSILCO
OLD ENGLISH BRAND B ........................AMERICAN SILVER CO.
ONEIDA................................................................ONEIDA
ONEIDA PAR PLATE .............................................ONEIDA
ONEIDA RELIANCE PLATE ....................................ONEIDA
ONEIDA SILVERPLATE ..........................................ONEIDA
ONEIDACRAFT ......................................................ONEIDA
OXFORD SILVER PLATE CO. ......................WM. A. ROGERS LTD.
PALACE BRAND ............................MONTGOMERY WARD & CO.
PALLADIANT ........................................................INSILCO
PALM BEACH .........................................NAPIER COMPANY
PARAGON ....................................SEARS ROEBUCK & CO.
PARAGON EXTRA .........................SEARS ROEBUCK & CO.
PEQUABUCK MFG. CO. ..........................AMERICAN SILVER CO.
PERFECTA ..........................................S. J. LEVI & CO.
PERMA-BRITE ....................................NATIONAL SILVER CO.
PILGRIM ............................................FRIEDMAN SILVER CO.
POMPEIAN GOLD ............................WEIDLICH BROS. MFG. CO.
PONTIFEX ..............................................R. BLACKINTON
POPPY ....................INTERNATIONAL-COMMONWEALTH SILVER CO.
PRESTIGE PLATE ...................................HOME DECORATORS
PRINCE'S PLATE ...................................MAPPIN & WEBB
PROVIDENCE SILVER PLATE CO.................AURORA SILVER PLATE CO.
PURITAN SILVER CO. ...........................................ONEIDA
QUEEN ESTHER ................................SALES STIMULATORS
R. & B. ...............................................................INSILCO
R. C. CO. ...........................................................INSILCO
R. COIN ..............................................A. DAVIS CO.
R. COIN ..........................................M. C. EPPENSTEIN
RELIANCE ..........................................................ONEIDA
RELIANCE PLATE ................................................ONEIDA
R SPECIAL .........................................A. DAVIS CO.
REVELATION SILVER PLATE .......................................INSILCO
REVERE .............................................BENEDICT MFG. CO.
REV-O-NOC..........................HIBBARD, SPENCER, BARTLETT & CO.
REX PLATE .........................................................ONEIDA
RICHFIELD PLATE COMPANY ...............................HOMAN MFG. CO.
RIVERTON SILVER CO. .........................................A. R. JUSTICE
ROGERS CUTLERY CO. ...........................................INSILCO
ROGERS & HAMILTON ...........................................INSILCO
ROYAL CREST STERLING ....................EMPIRE CRAFTS CORP.
ROYAL FAMILY ...................................SABEN GLASS CO.
ROYAL PLATE CO..................................................INSILCO
ROYAL PLATE CO. ..............................AMERICAN SILVER CO.
ROYAL PLATE CO. ..................................J. W. JOHNSON
ROYAL SILVER .....................................LEDIG MFG. CO.
R. S. MFG. CO. ...................................NIAGARA SILVER CO.
SALEM SILVER PLATE ..........................SEARS ROEBUCK & CO.
SALDSICO WARE ..............................ST. LOUIS SILVER CO.
```

```
S. E. B. . . . . . . . . . . . . . . . . . . . . . . . . . . . . . . . . . . . . . . . . . . . . .NATIONAL SILVER CO.
SHADOARDT . . . . . . . . . . . . . . . . . . . . . . . . . . . . . . . . . . . . .BERNARD RICE'S SONS
SHEFFIELD H. S. CO. . . . . . . . . . . . . . . . . . . . . . . . . . .HEMILL SILVERWARE INC.
SHEFFIELD PLATED CO. . . . . . . . . . . . . . . . . . . . . . . .HOLMES, BOOTH & HAYDENS
SHEFFIELD PLATED CO. . . . . . . . . . . . . . . . . . . . . . . . . . . . . . . . . . . . . . .INSILCO
SILVER ARTISTS COMPANY . . . . . . . . . . . . . . . . . . . . . . . . . . .REED & BARTON
SILVER CREST . . . . . . . . . . . . . . . . . . . . . . . . . . . . .SMITH METAL ARTS CO.
SILVER CRAFT . . . . . . . . . . . . . . . . . . . . . . . . . . . . . . . . . . . .FARBER BROS.
SILVERGRAMS . . . . . . . . . . . . . . . . . . . . . . . . .CHICAGO MONOGRAM STUDIOS
SILVER HARVEST . . . . . . . . . . . . . . . . . . . . . . . . . . . . .ELLMORE SILVER CO.
SILVEROIN . . . . . . . . . . . . . . . . . . . . . . . . . . . . . . . . . . .BRISTOL MFG. CO.
SILVER METAL . . . . . . . . . . . . . . . . . . . . . . . . . . . . . . . . . . . . . . . . .ONEIDA
SILVER WELD (knives) . . . . . . . . . . . . . . . . . . . . . . . . . . . . . . . . . . . .INSILCO
SKYSCRAPER . . . . . . . . . . . . . . . . . . . . . . . . . . . . .BERNARD RICE'S SONS
SO. AM. . . . . . . . . . . . . . . . . . . . . . . . . . . . . . . . . . .DAVID H. MCCONNELL
SOCIAL SILVER . . . . . . . . . . . . . . . . . . . . . . . . . . . . .DELLI SILVERPLATE
SOLID YUKON SILVER WARRANTED . . . . . . . . . . . . . . . . . . . .RAYMOND MFG. CO.
SO. MERIDEN SILVER CO. QUADRUPLE . . . . . . . . . . . . . . . .C. ROGERS & BROS.
SOMERSET . . . . . . . . . . . . . . . . . . . . . . . . . . . . . . . . . . . . . . . .W. BELL CO.
SOUTHINGTON COMPANY . . . . . . . . . . . . . . . . . . . . . . . . . . . . . . . . . .INSILCO
SOVEREIGN PLATE . . . . . . . . . . . . . . . . . . . . . . . . . . . . . . . . . . .P. W. ELLIS
SQUIRREL BRAND . . . . . . . . . . . . . . . . . . . . . . . . . . . . . . . . .S. J. LEVI & CO.
STANDISH. . . . . . . . . . . . . . . . . . . . . . . . . . . . . . . . . . . .BENEDICT MFG. CO.
STAR CUTLERY CO. . . . . . . . . . . . . . . . . . . . . . . . . .ELGIN-AMERICAN MFG. CO.
STATE HOUSE STERLING . . . . . . . . . . . . . . . . . . . . . . . .HOME DECORATORS
STERLING B . . . . . . . . . . . . . . . . . . . . . . . . . . . . . . . . . . . . .BATTIN & CO.
STERLING G . . . . . . . . . . . . . . . . . . . . . . . . . . . . . . . . . . .F. S. GILBERT
STERLINGUARD. . . . . . . . . . . . . . . . . . . . . . . . . . . . . . .ALBERT PICK & CO.
STERLING PLATE ◁ B ▷ . . . . . . . . . . . . . . . . . . . . . . .AMERICAN SILVER CO.
STERLING SILVER PLATE CO. . . . . . . . . . . . . . . .HOLMES, BOOTH & HAYDENS
STERLING SILVER PLATE CO. . . . . . . . . . . . . . . . . . . . . . . . . . . . . . . . .INSILCO
STERLON . . . . . . . . . . . . . . . . . . . . . . . . . . . . .MILTON J. SCREIBER
STRAND . . . . . . . . . . . . . . . . . . . . . . . . . . . . . . . . . . . . . . . . . . . .INSILCO
STRATFORD SILVER PLATE CO. . . . . . . . . . . . . . . . . . . . . . . . . . . . .INSILCO
STRATFORD PLATE . . . . . . . . . . . . . . . . . . . . . . . . . . . . . . . . . . . .INSILCO
STRATFORD SILVER CO. . . . . . . . . . . . . . . . . . . . . . . . . . . . . . . . . . .INSILCO
SUFFOLK SILVERPLATE . . . . . . . . . . . . . . . . . . . . . . . . . . . . . . .GORHAM
SUPER-PLATE . . . . . . . . . . . . . . . . . . . . . . . . . . . . . . . . . . . . . . . . .INSILCO
SUPERIOR . . . . . . . . . . . . . . . . . . . . . . . . . . . . . . . . . . . . . . . . . . .INSILCO
SUPREME SILVER PLATE . . . . . . . . . . . . . . . . . . . . . . . . . . . . . . . . .INSILCO
SUREFIRE . . . . . . . . . . . . . . . . . . . . . . . . . . . . . . . . . .NAPIER COMPANY
SUSSEX . . . . . . . . . . . . . . . . . . . . . . . . . . . .HEMILL SILVERWARE CO.
TABARD SILVER. . . . . . . . . . . . . . . . . . . . . . . . . . . . . .BENEDICT MFG. CO.
TAUNTON SILVER PLATE CO. . . . . . . . . . . . . . . . . . . . . .I. J. STEANE & CO.
THE COLUMBIA . . . . . . . . . . . . . . . . . . . . . . . . . . . . . . . .G. I. MIX & CO.
JOHN TOOTHILL . . . . . . . . . . . . . . . . . . . . . . . .METROPOLITAN SILVER CO.
TORSIL METAL . . . . . . . . . . . . . . . . . . . . . . . . .TORONTO SILVER PLATE CO.
TORSIL E. P. - N. S. . . . . . . . . . . . . . . . . . . . . .TORONTO SILVER PLATE CO.
TRIPLE PLUS . . . . . . . . . . . . . . . . . . . . . . . . . . . . . . . . . . . . . . . .ONEIDA
TUDOR PLATE . . . . . . . . . . . . . . . . . . . . . . . . . . . . . . . . . . . . . . . .ONEIDA
TWINKLE STERLING . . . . . . . . . . . . . . . . . . . . . . . . . . . . . . . .GORHAM
210 NEARSILVER . . . . . . . . . . . . . . . . . . . . . . . . . . . . . . . . . . . . .ONEIDA
```

UNION SILVER PLATE CO. .HOLMES, BOOTH & HAYDENS
UNION SILVER PLATE CO. . . . . .INSILCO
UNITED JEWELERS' CROWN GUILD . . . . .JEWELERS' CROWN GUILD
UNIVERSAL . . . . .LANDERS, FRARY & CLARK
U. S. SILVER CO. . . . . .ONEIDA
VIANDE . . . . .INSILCO
VICTOR S. CO. . . . . .INSILCO
VOGUE . . . . .GORHAM
WARNER SILVER COMPANY .WEIDLICH BROS. MFG. CO.
WARWICK . . . . .W. BELL CO.
WEARWELL . . . . .GOTHAM SILVER CO.
WMF . . . . .WÜRTTENBERGISCHE METALLWARENFABRIK
WELCH SILVER . . . . .AMERICAN SILVER CO.
WILCOX SILVER PLATE CO. . . . . .INSILCO
WM. ROGERS MFG. CO. . . . . .INSILCO
WM. ROGERS & SON . . . . .INSILCO
WORLD . . . . .INSILCO
X S TRIPLE . . . . .INSILCO
YOUREX . . . . .GEORGE E. HERRING
Y STERLING . . . . .W. F. CORY & BRO.
YUKON SILVER . . . . .CATTARAUGUS CUTLERY CO.
ZENITH . . . . .MARSHALL-WELLS HARDWARE CO.

KEY TO UNLETTERED TRADEMARKS

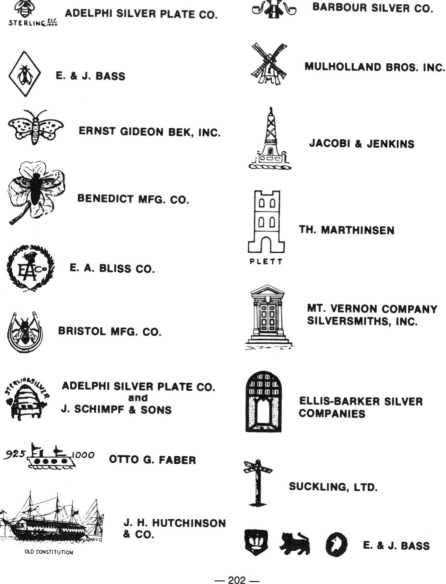

STERLING **ADELPHI SILVER PLATE CO.**

E. & J. BASS

ERNST GIDEON BEK, INC.

BENEDICT MFG. CO.

E. A. BLISS CO.

BRISTOL MFG. CO.

ADELPHI SILVER PLATE CO.
and
J. SCHIMPF & SONS

925 1000 **OTTO G. FABER**

J. H. HUTCHINSON & CO.

OLD CONSTITUTION

BARBOUR SILVER CO.

MULHOLLAND BROS. INC.

JACOBI & JENKINS

PLETT **TH. MARTHINSEN**

MT. VERNON COMPANY SILVERSMITHS, INC.

ELLIS-BARKER SILVER COMPANIES

SUCKLING, LTD.

E. & J. BASS

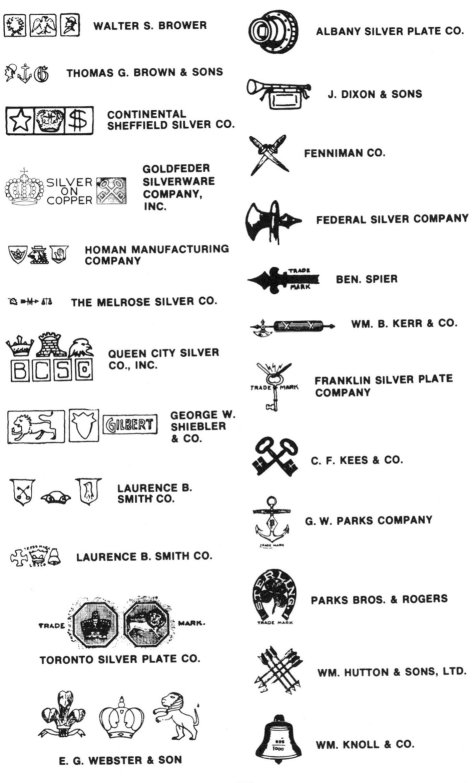

WALTER S. BROWER

THOMAS G. BROWN & SONS

CONTINENTAL SHEFFIELD SILVER CO.

GOLDFEDER SILVERWARE COMPANY, INC.

HOMAN MANUFACTURING COMPANY

THE MELROSE SILVER CO.

QUEEN CITY SILVER CO., INC.

GEORGE W. SHIEBLER & CO.

LAURENCE B. SMITH CO.

LAURENCE B. SMITH CO.

TORONTO SILVER PLATE CO.

E. G. WEBSTER & SON

ALBANY SILVER PLATE CO.

J. DIXON & SONS

FENNIMAN CO.

FEDERAL SILVER COMPANY

BEN. SPIER

WM. B. KERR & CO.

FRANKLIN SILVER PLATE COMPANY

C. F. KEES & CO.

G. W. PARKS COMPANY

PARKS BROS. & ROGERS

WM. HUTTON & SONS, LTD.

WM. KNOLL & CO.

ST. LOUIS METALCRAFTS, INC.,

 WM. AND GEO. SISSONS

 TH. MARTHINSEN

 POOLE SILVER CO.

 ELLIS-BARKER SILVER COMPANIES

 J. TOSTRUP

 THE POTOSI SILVER CO.

 FINE ARTS STERLING SILVER COMPANY

 KENT & STANLEY CO., LTD.

 BROWN & WARD

 MERMOD, JACCARD & KING JEWELRY CO.

 REDDALL & CO., INC.

 SOCIÉTÉ PICARD FRERES

 DAVIS & GALT

 WM. B. KERR & CO.

 WILLIAM LINKER

 JOSEPH MAYER & BROS.

 TOWLE SILVERSMITHS

 INTERNATIONAL SILVER CO.

OLD NEW ENGLAND CRAFTSMEN, INC.

 SOCIÉTÉ PICARD FRERES

DOMINICK & HAFF

 MERRIMAC VALLEY SILVERSMITHS

 H. H. CURTIS & CO.

 STERLING — MECHANICS STERLING COMPANY and WATSON COMPANY

 THE MAUSER MANUFACTURING COMPANY

 REDLICH & CO.

BACHRACH & FREEDMAN

 C. E. BARKER MFG. CO.

SACKETT & CO., LTD.

 MISS SARAH B. DICKINSON and MRS. SARAH B. DICKINSON WOOD

THE MERRILL SHOPS

  A. L. SILBERSTEIN

 JACK BOWLING

 A. L. SILBERSTEIN

ALBERT FELDENHEIMER

TILDEN-THURBER CO.

 ELLIS-BARKER SILVER COMPANIES

BARKER BROS. SILVER CO., INC.

 MAX HIRSCH

 POTOSI SILVER CO.

 LEHMAN BROTHERS SILVERWARE CORP.

 BLACK, STARR & FROST, LTD.

 S. J. LEVI & CO., LTD.

  THORNTON & CO.

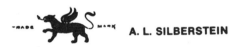

MAYO & CO.

 MERIDEN BRITANNIA COMPANY

 MANNING, BOWMAN & CO.

 OLD NEWBURY CRAFTERS, INC.

 WM. B. DURGIN CO.

 A. G. SCHULTZ & CO.

  WILLIAM C. FINCK CO.

 J. T. INMAN & CO.

 SHREVE, CRUMP & LOW CO., INC.

 BARKER BROS. SILVER CO.

 J. W. ROSENBAUM & CO.

H. J. WEBB & CO.

 COLONIAL SILVER COMPANY, INC.

HENRY C. HASKELL

 TUTTLE SILVERSMITHS

 MAJESTIC SILVER COMPANY

 TIMOTHY TUTTLE

 GENOVA SILVER CO., INC.

 HAWTHORNE MFG. CO.

 MERIDEN BRITANNIA COMPANY

 CHARTER COMPANY

CHARTER COMPANY

 PRILL SILVER CO., INC.

 CHARTER COMPANY

 ST. LOUIS METALCRAFTS

 ECKFELDT & ACKLEY

 GEBRUEDER NOELLE

 LOTT & SCHMITT, INC.

 NEW ORLEANS SILVERSMITHS

 SIMEON L. & GEO. H. ROGERS CO.

 NEW ORLEANS SILVERSMITHS

 ELLIS-BARKER SILVER COMPANIES

 W. E. WEBSTER CO.

 STANDARD SILVER CO. OF TORONTO

J. J. COHN

 NORBERT MFG. CO.

 GALT & BRO., INC.

 WATSON COMPANY

MT. VERNON COMPANY

 MATHEWS & PRIOR

GALT & BRO., INC.

HANLE & DEBLER, INC.

GALT & BRO., INC.

 SCHULZ & FISCHER

MEDALLIC ART COMPANY

 MILLIE B. LOGAN

 UTOPIAN SILVER DEPOSIT & NOVELTY CO.

 DANIEL LOW & CO.

 ROGER WILLIAMS SILVER CO.

 E. A. BLISS CO.

 AUG. C. FRANK CO., INC.

 FERDINAND C. LAMY

 R. GLEASON & SONS

 WILLIAM F. NEWHALL

  HARRIS & SCHAFER

 WILLIAM H. SAXTON, JR.

 N. G. WOOD & SONS

 ROMAN SILVERSMITHS, INC.

 H. G. HUDSON

 SUTTON HOO JEWELERS

 MERIDEN BRITANNIA COMPANY

 MONTGOMERY BROS.

 WILCOX & EVERTSEN

 L. KIMBALL & SON

 H. H. TAMMEN CURIO CO.

 H. G. HUDSON

THOMAS F. BROGAN

 BASCH BROS. & CO.

 R. BLACKINTON & CO.

 BROWN & BROS.

 DAY, CLARK & CO.

M. EISENSTADT JEWELRY CO.

 COMMONWEALTH SILVER CO.

 FUCHS & BEIDERHASE

 HERBST & WASSALL

 THE FRANK KURSCH & SON CO.

SUTTON HOO JEWELERS

HERBERT COCKSHAW, JR.
and
HOWARD & COCKSHAW CO.

Sterlin E   JAMES E. BLAKE CO.

 BARKER BROS.
SILVER CO., INC.

 AUGUST DINGELDEN & SON

ERIK MAGNUSSEN

 ELLIS-BARKER
SILVER COMPANIES

 J. F. FRADLEY & CO.

TRADE MARK

THE BASSETT JEWELRY CO.

 H. A. KIRBY

 TOWLE SILVERSMITHS

 ALBERT J. GANNON

D. C. BOURQUIN

GLOSSARY

Acanthus: A form of ornamentation taken from the acanthus leaf, originally used extensively on the Corinthian capital throughout the Renaissance period, 16th–17th centuries.

Ajouré: A French term applied to metalwork which is pierced through, perforated or openwork.

Alaska Silver: Base metal of secret composition. According to contemporary ads, "Its purpose is to imitate solid silver at a fraction of the cost." It is subject to damage if left 12 hours or more in acid foods, fats or grease. It is also a tradename used on silverplated flatware sold by Sears Roebuck & Co., c. 1908. In the 1908 catalog was the statement that Alaska Metal was their special formula of composition metal made to imitate solid silver. Contains no silver.

Albata: Alloy of nickel, copper, and zinc, forming a silvery white metal.

Alchemy: A superior pewter used in the 16th and 17th centuries for making spoons and plates; an alloy of tin and copper.

Alcomy: An alloy of various base metals.

Alfenide: "Spoons made of alfenide similar to finest English white metal. Contains no brass or German steel." (Clipping dated March 18, 1878, *St. Nicholas Magazine*.)

Alloy: A substance composed of two or more metals intimately united, usually intermixed when molten.

Alpacca: German silver and nickel silver; are synonymous trade names of an alloy of copper, nickel and zinc.

Aluminum Silver: A composition of aluminum and silver which is much harder than aluminum. It takes a high polish. Air does not affect the color. The proportion of ingredients varies. One of three parts silver and ninety-seven parts aluminum makes an alloy similar in appearance to pure aluminum but is much harder and takes a better polish.

Annealing: Reheating of silver to keep it malleable while it is being worked.

Anvil: An iron block on which metal is hammered and shaped.

Apocryphal: Classical term for a fake.

Applied: Certain parts, such as spouts, handles, covers, et cetera, are sometimes made separately and applied with solder.

Apprentice: One who is bound by indentures to serve another person with a view of learning a trade.

Argentine: An alloy of tin and antimony used as a base for plating; nickel silver; German silver; also "British plate"; known in China as Paktong. Bradbury says, "Credit [is] due to W. Hutton & Sons, of Sheffield, for being the first firm to manufacture spoons and forks from the newly-invented metal called Argentine, in the year 1833."

Assay: The test made to prove that the metal is of the required quality.

Baltimore Assay Marks: Starting in 1814, silver made in Baltimore was marked at a hall and identified by a date letter; this compulsory marking was abolished in 1830.

Base Metal: An alloy or metal of comparatively low value to which a coating or plating is normally applied.

Bat's-wing Fluting: Gadrooning, graduated and curved to resemble the outline of a bat's wing and encircling holloware.

Beading: A border ornament composed of small, contiguous, bead-like, half-spheres. Popular in late 18th century.

Beakhorn: A sharply pointed anvil.

Bell Metal: A variety of Sheffield Plate consisting of an unusually heavy coating of silver, introduced in 1789 by Samuel Roberts.

Black Pewter: An alloy of 60 per cent tin and 40 per cent lead. Used for making organ pipes and candle molds.

Bleeding: The technical term applied to pieces of plate whereon the copper base is exposed.

Bobèche: Flat or saucerlike rings placed around candle bases to stop wax drippings.

Bright-cut Engraving: A particular form of engraving popular about 1790, in which the metal is removed by bevelled cutting tools.

This gives a jewel-like, faceted sparkle to the surface.

Bright Finish: Highly polished, mirror-like finish produced by use of jeweler's rouge on a polishing wheel.

Britannia: A silver-white alloy composed largely of tin hardened with copper and antimony. Closely akin to pewter, yet differing in the higher proportion of tin, the addition of antimony and the omission of lead, resulting in a more silvery appearance than is possible with the pewter mixture. It often contains also a small quantity of zinc and bismuth. A common proportion is 140 parts of tin, three of copper and ten of antimony.

Bronze: An alloy chiefly of copper and tin.

Buffing: Removal of the outer layer of metal with a flexible abrasive wheel or a soft mop, exposing a shiny undersurface but imparting no additional hardness.

Burnisher: Tool with hard, polished working surface such as agate, for burnishing gold and silver.

Burnishing: Electro deposits consist of a multitude of small crystals, with intervals between them, and with facets reflecting the light in every direction. The deposited metal is hardened by burnishing and forcing into the pores of the underlying metal. The durability is thus increased to such an extent that, with the same amount of silver, a burnished article will last twice as long as one which has not been so treated.

Butler's Finish: Satin finish produced by a revolving wheel of wire which makes many tiny scratches, giving the article a dull appearance. Patented by James H. Reilly, Brooklyn Silver Co.

C: (See Coin.)

Cable: Molding like twisted rope, derived from Norman architecture.

Cast: Formed in a mold, i.e., handles, ornaments, et cetera are often cast separately.

Chafing-dish: One dish or vessel within another, the outer vessel being filled with hot water and in direct contact with the heat source and an inner container for food.

Chamber-candlestick: A tray candlestick in the form of a circular dish stand with a handle.

Champleve: Enameling by cutting troughs in the metal into which the frit is melted; the surface is ground flush and polished.

Chasing: A cold modeling process of ornamenting metal by hammers. Also called embossing.

Cloisonné: Enameling by melting the frit into areas defined by wire soldered to surface to be decorated.

Coin: By 1830, COIN, PURE COIN, DOLLAR, STANDARD, PREMIUM or C or D were used to indicate 900/1000 parts of silver.

Coin Silver: 900/1000 fine, with 100/1000 of copper. Used by early silversmiths to whom sterling was not available.

Commercial Silver: 999/1000 fine or higher.

Craig Silver: Similar to German silver. Used for making knives.

C-scroll: Usually applied to the shape of a handle in the form of the letter C; also called 'single scroll'.

Cut-cardwork: Silver work in which conventional designs of leaves and flowers are cut from thin sheet-silver and applied to a silver surface.

Cutler: One who makes, deals in, or repairs utensils or knives.

Cutlery: Knives having a cutting edge.

D: (See Coin.)

Date Letter; Date Mark: Proper assay marks on English silver, the date being indicated by a letter of the alphabet. Some American silver is date marked. (See Gorham, Kirk, Tiffany, and Tuttle.)

Dish Cross: An x-shaped support for a dish, some with spirit lamps for warming food.

Dish Ring: A silver stand particularly identified with Irish silver, and sometimes called a potato-ring.

Dollar: (See Coin.)

Dolphin: The sea dolphin used as a sculptured or carved motif.

Domed: Spheroid form of cover, first used in 1715 on tankards, teapots and coffeepots.

Domestic Plate: Silverware for home use.

Double-scroll: A sinuous line of S-shape, or composed of reverse curves, used especially in design of handles.

Drawing Irons: Metal parts of a drawing bench, through which silver is drawn.

Electrolysis: Conduction of an electric current by an electrolyte of charged particles.

Electroplate: Articles consisting of a base metal coated with silver by the process of electrolysis.

Electrotype: Copy of art object produced by electroplating a wax impression. Much used in the nineteenth century to reproduce antique objects. Now employed in the production of facsimile plates for use in printing.

Electrum: A natural pale-yellow alloy of gold and silver. Also, an imitative alloy of silver, 8 parts copper, 4 nickel, and 3½ zinc.

Embossing: Making raised designs on the surface of metal from the reverse side, strictly applicable only to hammered work (Repoussé).

Engraving: Cutting lines into metal with a scorper or graver.

EPC: Electroplate on copper.

EPBM: Electroplate on britannia metal.

Epergne: An elaborate centerpiece, especially for a dining table; an ensemble of cups and vases for holding fruits, flowers, et cetera.

EPNS: Electroplate on nickel silver.

E.P.N.S. — W.M.M.: Electroplate on nickel silver with white metal mounts.

EPWM: Electroplate on white metal.

Etching: Surface decoration bitten-in with acid.

Ewer: A jug or pitcher having a wide spout and a handle.

Feather Edge: Decoration of edge of spoon-handle with chased, slanting lines. An engraved, decorative design.

Fine Pewter: Eighty per cent tin and 20 per cent brass or copper. Used for making plates because of the smooth surface, attractive color and strength.

Fine Silver: Better than 999/1000 pure. It is too soft for practical fabrication, and is mainly used in the form of anodes or sheets for plating.

Flagon: Large vessel for serving wine or other liquors.

Flash Plate: Unbuffed, cheap plated ware.

Flat Chasing: Surface decoration in low relief. Popular in England in early 18th century, and widely used in America, 1750–1785.

Flatware: Knives, forks, spoons and serving pieces.

Fluted: A type of grooving.

Foreign Silver: Other than English sterling, is sometimes of uncertain silver content, in some instances running considerably below the coin standard. The fineness is often stamped on the article. In the Scandinavian countries and Germany solid silver tableware 830/1000 fine has been standardized, and the stamp "830" signifies this silver content.

Forging: The shaping of metal by heating and hammering.

Fusion: An act or operation of melting, as the fusion of metals. Usually accomplished by the application of intense heat.

Gadroon: A border ornament radiating lobes of curved or straight form. Used on rims and feet of cups, plates and other vessels from late 17th century.

German Silver: A silver-white alloy consisting principally of copper, zinc and nickel. During World War I this name was dropped by many and the term nickel silver used.

Gold Aluminum: A solid alloy used for flatware made by Holmes & Edwards Silver Co., Bridgeport, Connecticut. Marked with a trademark WALDO HE preceded by a symbol used by the Waldo Foundry which probably made the metal. Flatware made only in *Rialto* pattern which was also made in silverplate.

Gold Plating: The covering of an article with gold.

Goldsmiths' Company: The organization under whose jurisdiction and regulation the English silver industry has been conducted.

Graver: Tool used to engrave silver.

Hallmark: The official mark of the English Goldsmiths' Company used on articles of gold and silver to indicate their genuineness.

Hollow Handle (H. H.): Handles made of two halves soldered together. Knives, especially, need the thickness provided for comfortable use, controlled handle weight and balance.

Holloware: A general term for articles in the form of hollow vessels, such as mugs, ewers, teapots, coffeepots, bowls and pitchers also includes trays, waiters, meat and chop plates and flat sandwich trays.

Holloware Pewter: Eighty per cent tin and 20 per cent lead, used for making teapots, tankards, coffee pots and liquid measures.

Ingot: A bar of silver or other metal.

Katé: A Malayan weight equal to 11.73 ounces. Tea was sold by the kate (pronounced katde). It became "caddy" — hence tea caddy. Also spelled kati.

Lashar Silver: A process invented by Thomas B. Lashar of the Holmes & Edwards Silver Co., whereby the copper and zinc from the surface of nickel alloy was removed, leaving only the nickel exposed.

Latten: An alloy of copper and zinc; brass.

Limoges: Enamel painted on metal, covering the surface.

Maker's Mark: The distinguishing mark of the individual goldsmith.

Malleable: Capable of being extended or shaped by beating with a hammer; ductile.

Matted-ground: A dull surface made by light punchwork, to secure contrast with a burnished surface.

Metalsmith: One versed in the intricacies of working with metals.

Nickel Silver: An alloy of nickel, copper and zinc.

Niello: Deep-line engraving on gold or silver with the lines filled with copper, lead and sulphur in borax, forming a type of black enamel which is fired and polished.

Non-tarnishing Silver: Produced by alloying silver with cadmium or by the application of a thin plating of rhodium or palladium on the surface.

N.S.: Nickel silver.

Onslow Pattern: Design for flatware shaped as a volute scroll.

Ormolu: "Ground gold," literally. Ground gold leaf used as a gilt pigment. Also, brass made to look like gold.

Oxidizing: Accented beauty of ornamentation by the application of an oxide which darkens metal wherever applied. Shadows and highlights are created which give depth and character.

Patina: Soft luster caused by tiny scratches that come with daily use.

Pewter: An alloy of tin and copper or any alloy of the low-melting-point metals, including tin, lead, bismuth and antimony. Sad pewter is the heaviest, but not the best. The higher the tin content, the better the pewter.

Pinchbeck: An alloy of copper or zinc used to imitate gold. Invented by Christopher Pinchbeck (1670–1732), London. Also called "Chapman's" gold or Mannheim gold.

Pit Marks: Minute holes usually found on lead or soft metal borders.

Planishing: To make smooth or plain. Oval-faced planishing hammers are used to conceal hammer marks used in forming a piece.

Plate: Used in England and on the Continent when referring to articles made of precious metals.

Plique-á-jour: Translucent enamel without a metal backing, enclosed within metal frames, giving a stained glass or jewel-like effect

Premium: (See Coin.)

Pricking: Delicate needle-point engraving. Pricked initials were often used on early pieces.

Pseudo Hall-marks: Devices used to suggest English hall-marks.

Pure Coin: (See Coin.)

Raising: Formation of a piece of holloware beginning with a flat circle of silver. It is hammered in concentric circles over a succession of anvils with frequent annealings.

Rolled Plate: (See Sheffield Plate.)

Rope-molding: A type of gadroon bordering made up of reeds and flutes slightly spiralled.

R.P.: Rolled Plate.

Repoussé: Relief ornament hammered from the under or inner side of the metal. Usually given added sharpness of form by surface chasing of detail and outline. Has been practiced from early times. Introduced to this country by Samuel Kirk in 1828.

Satin Finish: (See Butler's Finish.)

Scorper: Small chisel for engraving. The blades are of various shapes.

Sheffield Plate: True Sheffield plate was produced by fusing, with intense heat, a thin sheet of silver to one or both sides of a thick sheet of copper. The composite metal was then rolled down to the proper thickness for fabrication. Invented by Thomas Boulsover about 1743 Frequently called "Old Sheffield Plate" to distinguish it from electroplate.

Silver Edge: An ornamental border of solid silver.

Silverite: "A combination of tin, nickel, platinum, etc." according to advertisements.

Silverplate: A base metal, usually either nickel silver or copper, coated with a layer of pure silver by electroplating.

Spinning: Process used for forming holloware. A metal plate is cut to proper size, placed against a chuck in a lathe, where pressure against it with a smooth revolving instrument produces the desired form.

Stake: An iron anvil or tongue, on which a silver object is formed.

Stamping: Impressing of designs from dies into the metal by means of heavy hammers. Often followed by hand chasing to sharpen up design details.

Stamping Trademarks and Stock Numbers: As early as 1867, the Meriden Britannia Co. had a system of stamping nickel silver, silver soldered holloware with a cipher preceding the number, and by 1893, nickel silver holloware with white metal mounts had as a part of the number two ciphers. That is, on a waiter with white metal, 00256, etc. would be stamped. This made it quickly understood by the number whether the piece was nickel silver, silversoldered or nickel silver with white metal mounts.

Standard: (See Coin.)

Sterling Silver: 925/1000 fine, with 75/1000 of added metal, usually copper, to give it strength and stiffness. This is the standard set by the United States Government in the Stamping Act of 1906, and any article stamped "sterling" is of assured quality. It appears on Baltimore silver, 1800–1814, and after 1860, elsewhere.

Stoning: Polishing of silver with an emery-stone.

Swaged: Shaped by the process of rolling or hammering.

Tempering: Strengthening of metal by heat.

Touch: Maker's mark, impressed with a punch.

Touchstone: A hard siliceous stone or modern square of Wedgwood on which a piece of silver or gold of known quality can be rubbed to compare its mark with that of a piece being assayed.

Town Mark: The mark assigned to a city and applied as a hallmark to denote the location of manufacture.

Trademark: Symbol or tradename by which a manufacturer may be identified. Widely used in this country as a guarantee of quality. A distinction should be made between a trademark and a hallmark, as required by English and other European countries. Because the United States has never had a goldsmiths' or silversmiths' hall, there are no true hallmarks on American silver.

Trifle Pewter: Sixty per cent tin and 40 per cent lead. Of a darker color and softer than better grades of pewter, it was short lived. The alloy was altered to 83 parts tin and 17 parts antimony and was made into spoons, saltshakers, buttons and similar articles which could not be finished on a lathe. Workers in this alloy were called "triflers."

Vermeil: Gold plating process developed in France in the mid 1700s. France banned production of vermeil early in the 19th century because the process involved the use of mercury. Present-day vermeil is produced by a safe electrolytic process.

Victorian Plate: Plated silver ware made during the period c. 1840–1900 by the process of electrolysis.

Waiter: A tray on which something is carried; a salver.

White Metal: An alloy usually containing two or more of the following elements — tin, copper, lead, antimony and bismuth. The color depends on whether lead or tin predominates. The more tin the whiter the color.

Whitesmith: A planishing smith; superior workman in iron, comparable to the armorer. Also a worker in pure tin of the "block" variety, not cast, but hammered and battered, planished and "skum." Originally "whitster."

SILVERPLATE SPECIFICATIONS

When plated silver production first began, some manufacturers either ignored indicating the quality or marked their products "Triple" or "Quadruple" plate. About this, the JEWELERS' CIRCULAR had this to say:

SILVER PLATED WARE

NOTE: — Manufacturers of silver plated flatware, in addition to their trade-mark, stamp the quality upon their goods, almost all of them adopting the same signs and figures. These quality signs and figures are as follows:

A.I......................represents standard plate
XII ....represents sectional plate
4 ....represents double plate, tea spoons
6 ....represents double plate, dessert spoons and forks
8 ....represents double plate, table spoons
6 ....represents triple plate, tea spoons
9 ....represents triple plate, dessert spoons and forks.
12 ....represents triple plate, table spoons.

There is an amount of cheap plated ware on the market stamped with the names of fictitious companies, such as "Quadruple Silver Plate Co." "Royal Sterling Plate Co.," etc. These goods are furnished, bearing no stamp, to department storekeepers, conductors of gift enterprises and jobbers of cheap merchandise, who stamp the goods themselves with such names as suit their fancy. It is, therefore, practically impossible to trace these stamps.

FOR FLATWARE

Half plate: 1 troy oz. per gross of teaspoons

Standard plate: 2 troy oz. per gross of teaspoons

Double plate: 4 troy oz. per gross of teaspoons

Triple plate: 6 troy oz. per gross of teaspoons

Quadruple plate: 8 troy oz. per gross of teaspoons

Federal specification: 9 troy oz. per gross of teaspoons

These specifications produce a thickness whose range is from 0.00015 to 0.00125 in. — the latter equivalent to 1 troy oz. per square ft. Federal specifications call for an average of 0.000125 in. thickness to be reinforced by silver to a minimum of 0.00180 in. on the backs of spoon bowls and fork tines.

FOR HOTELWARE – HOLLOWARE

Federal specification plate: 20 dwt. per sq. ft.

Extra heavy hotel plate: 15 dwt. per sq. ft.

Heavy hotel plate: 10 dwt. per sq. ft.

Medium plate: 5 dwt. per sq. ft.

Light plate: 2 dwt. per sq. ft.

The Federal specification is for 0.00125 in., the same thickness required for flatware. Light plate is 0.000125 in., slightly less than the half plate under flatware.

TABLE OF EQUIVALENTS

TROY WEIGHT

POUNDS		OUNCES		PENNYWEIGHTS (dwts.)
1	=	12	=	240
		1	=	20

SILVER STANDARDS

.846 = 10.15 (Used in Maryland c. 1840–c. 1860) = $\dfrac{10.75}{12}$

.892 Standard for U.S. coins 1792–1837

.900 (Standard for U.S. coins after 1837) = 10.8 = $\dfrac{10 \text{ oz. } 16 \text{ dwts.}}{12}$

.917 = 11 = $^{11}/_{12}$ Baltimore standard during Assay Office period. 1814–1830.
Midway between coin and sterling.

.925 = 11.1 = $\dfrac{11 \text{ oz. } 2 \text{ dwts.}}{12}$ The sterling standard. Used often in Baltimore c. 1800–1814.
Not used consistently elsewhere in the U.S. until c. 1865.

.958 = 11.5 = $\dfrac{11 \text{ oz. } 10 \text{ dwts.}}{12}$ The Britannia standard.

BIBLIOGRAPHY

Abbey, Staton. *The Goldsmiths and Silversmiths Handbook.* New York: Van Nostrand, 1952.

Albany Silver. Albany, New York: Albany Institute of History and Art, 1964.

Alexander, S. E. "Tiffany's Sterling: History and Status," *National Jeweler,* June, 1963.

American Church Silver of 17th and 18th Centuries Exhibited at the Museum of Fine Arts, July to December, 1911. Boston: Boston Museum of Fine Arts, 1911.

"American Silver," *American Magazine of Art,* August 1919, v. 10, p. 400.

Antiquarian Magazine. 1924–1933.

Antiques Digest. Frederick, Maryland: Antiques Publications, Inc., 1951–1952.

Antiques Magazine. New York: 1922–1975.

Attleboro Daily Sun, Anniversary Edition. Attleboro, Mass.: 1964.

Avery, Clara Louise. "New York Metropolitan Museum of Art, American Silver of the 17th and 18th centuries." *Metropolitan Museum of Art Bulletin.* 1920.

Avery, Clara Louise. "New York Metropolitan Museum of Art, Exhibition of Early American Silver." *Metropolitan Museum of Art Bulletin.* December, 1931.

Avery, Clara Louise. *Early American Silver.* New York: The Century Company, 1930.

Bartlett, W. A. *Digest of Trade-Marks. (Registered in the U. S.) for Machines, Metals, Jewelry and the Hardware and Allied Trades.* Washington, D.C.: Gibson Bros., Printers, 1893.

Bent, Dorothy. "A Fascinating Biography of Knives and Forks." *Arts and Decoration.* Vol. 25, June, 1926.

Bigelow, Francis Hill. *Historic Silver of the Colonies and its Makers.* New York: The Macmillan Company, 1917.

Biographical History of the Manufacturers and Business Men of Rhode Island at the Opening of the Twentieth Century. Providence, Rhode Island: J. D. Hall & Co., 1901.

Bishop, J. Oleander. *A History of American Manufacturers from 1808–1860,* 2 vols. Philadelphia: Young & Co., 1861.

Boger, H. Batterson and Boger, Louise Ade. *The Dictionary of Antiques and the Decorative Arts.* New York: Charles Scribner's Sons, 1957.

Bolles, Albert S. *Industrial History of the United States from the Earliest Settlements to the Present Time.* Norwich, Conn.: 1879.

Bradbury, Frederick. *History of Old Sheffield Plate.* J. W. Northend, Sheffield, England, 1912; reprinted 1968.

Brix, Maurice. *List of Philadelphia Silversmiths and Allied Artificers, 1682–1850.* Philadelphia: Privately printed, 1920.

The Bromwell Story. Washington, D.C.: D. L. Bromwell, Inc., pamphlet, no date.

Buck, J. H. *Old Plate, Its Makers and Marks.* New York: Gorham Manufacturing Company, 1903.

Buhler, Kathryn C. "Silver 1640–1820," *The Concise Encyclopedia of American Antiques.* New York: Hawthorn Books, Inc., Vol 1., no date.

Burton E. Milby. *South Carolina Silversmiths 1690–1860.* Charleston: The Charleston Museum, 1942.

Bury, Shirley. *Victorian Electroplate.* Country Life Collectors' Guides. The Hamlyn Pub. Group, London, 1971.

Carlisle, Lilian Baker. *News and Notes.* Vermont Historical Society, no date.

Carlisle, Lilian Baker. *Vermont Clock and Watchmakers, Silversmiths and Jewelers, 1778–1878.* Burlington, Vermont, 1970.

Carpenter, Ralph E. Jr. *The Arts and Crafts of Newport.* Rhode Island: Preservation Society of Newport County, Pittshead Tavern, 1954.

Catalog of an Exhibition of Paintings by Gilbert Stuart, Furniture by the Goddards and Townsends, Silver by Rhode Island Silversmiths. Rhode Island School of Design, Providence, Rhode Island: 1936.

"A Cincinnati Industry, Homan & Co., the largest manufacturers of fine silver-plated ware in the city," *The Watch Dial,* July 1888.

Clarke, Hermann Frederick, *John Coney, Silversmith 1655–1722.* Boston: Houghton Mifflin Company, 1932.

Clarke, Hermann Frederick and Foote, Henry Wilder. *Jeremiah Dummer, Colonial Craftsman and Merchant 1645–1718.* Boston: Houghton Mifflin Company 1935.

Clarke, Hermann Frederick. *John Hull, Builder of the Bay Colony.* Portland, Me.: The Southworth-Anthoensen Press, 1940.

Clark, Victor S. *History of Manufacturers in the United States.* New York: Carnegie Institute of Washington, 1929.

Clearwater, Alphonso T. *American Silver, List of Unidentified Makers and Marks.* New York: 1913.

A Collection of Early American Silver. New York: Tiffany and Company, 1920.

Colonial Silversmiths, Masters & Apprentices. Boston Museum of Fine Arts, 1956.

Comstock, Helen. "American Silver," *The Concise Encyclopedia of Antiques.* New York: Hawthorn Books, Inc.

"The Craft of the Spoonmaker." *Antiques,* 1929.

Crosby, Everett Uberto. *Books and Baskets, Signs and Silver of Old Time Nantucket.* Nantucket, Mass.: Inquirer and Mirror Press, 1940.

Crosby, Everett Uberto. *95% Perfect.* Nantucket, Island, Mass.: Tetaukimmo Press, 1953.

Crosby, Everett Uberto. *The Spoon Primer.* Nantucket, Mass.: Inquirer and Mirror Press, 1941.

Currier, Ernest M. *Early American Silversmiths, The Newbury Spoonmakers.* New York: 1929.

Currier, Ernest M. *Marks of Early American Silversmiths, List of New York City Silversmiths 1815–1841.* Portland, Me.: The Southworth-Anthoensen Press. 1938; reprinted 1970 by Robert Alan Green.

Curtis, George Munson. *Early Silver of Connecticut and Makers.* Meriden, Conn.: International Silver Company, 1913.

Cutten, George Barton. *Silversmiths of Georgia.* Savannah, Ga.: Pigeonhole Press, 1958.

Cutten, George Barton. *Silversmiths of Northampton, Massachusetts and Vicinity down to 1850.* Pamphlet.

Cutten, George Barton. *Silversmiths of North Carolina.* Raleigh, N. C.: State Department of Archives & History, 1948.

Cutten, George Barton and Cutten, Minnie Warren. *Silversmiths of Utica.* Hamilton, New York: 1936.

Cutten, George Barton. *Silversmiths, Watchmakers and Jewelers of the State of New York Outside New York City.* Hamilton, N. Y.: Privately printed, 1939.

Cutten, George Barton. *Silversmiths of Virginia.* Richmond, Va.: The Dietz Press, 1952.

Cutten, George Barton. *Ten Silversmith Families of New York State.* Albany, New York: State Historical Assoc., 1946.

Danbury (Conn.) News-Times, December 2, 1938.

Davis, Charles H. S. *History of Wallingford, Connecticut.* Published by author, 1870.

Davis, Fredna Harris and Deibel, Kenneth K. *Silver Plated Flatware Patterns.* Dallas, Texas: Bluebonnet Press, 1972.

Day, Olive. *Rise of Manufacturing in Connecticut, 1820–1850.* Yale University Press for Tercentenary of Conn.

Depew, Chauncey M. *One Hundred Years of American Commerce.* D. O. Haynes & Co., 1895, Vol. 2.

Descriptive Catalogue of Various Pieces of Silver Plate forming Collection of the New York Farmers 1882–1932.

Detroit Historical Society Bulletin. Detroit, Mich.: November, 1952.

Dreppard, Carl W. *The Primer of American Antiques.* Garden City, N. Y.: Doubleday & Company, Inc., 1954.

Duhousset, Charles. *l'Art Pour Tous.* Paris: 1879.

Durrett, Colonel Reuben T. *Traditions of the Earliest Visits of Foreigners.* (Filson Club Publications No. 23) Louisville, Kentucky: John P. Morton & Co., 1908.

Dyer, W. A. "Early American Silver," *Arts and Decoration.* VII (May 1917)

Early American Spoons and Their Makers. Editor and Publisher, Golden Anniversary Issue, July 21, 1934.

Early Connecticut Silver 1700–1830. Gallery of Fine Arts. New Haven, Conn.: Yale University Press, Connecticut Tercentenary Commission, 1935.

Early, Eleanor. *An Island Patchwork.* Boston: Houghton Mifflin Company, 1941.

Early New England Silver lent from the Mark Bortman Collection. Northampton, Mass.: Smith College Museum of Art, 1958.

Eaton, Allen H. *Handicrafts of New England.* New York: Harper & Brothers Publishers, 1949.

Eberlein, H. D. "Early American Silver," *Arts and Decoration.* XI (August 1919).

Eberlein, Harold D. and McClure, Abbot. *The Practical Book of American Antiques.* Garden City, New York: Halcyon House, 1948.

Edmonds, Walter D. *The First Hundred Years, 1848–1948, Oneida Community.* Oneida, N.Y. : Oneida Ltd., 1958.

Ellis, Leonard Bolles, *History of New Bedford and its Vicinity, 1602–1892.* Syracuse, New York: D. Mason & Company, Publishers, 1892.

Ensko, Robert. *Makers of Early American Silver.* New York: Trow Press, 1915.

Ensko, Stephen. *American Silversmiths and Their Marks.* New York: Privately printed, 1927.

Ensko, Stephen. *American Silversmiths and Their Marks II.* New York: Robert Ensko, Inc., Privately printed, 1937.

Ensko, Stephen. *American Silversmiths and Their Marks III.* New York: Robert Ensko, Inc., Privately printed, 1948.

Exhibition of Old American and English Silver. Pennsylvania Museum and School of Industrial Art, 1917.

Fisher, Leonard Everett. *The Silversmiths.* New York: Franklin Watts, Inc.

Flynt, Henry N. and Fales, Martha Gandy. *The Heritage Collection of Silver, Old Deerfield, Massachusetts:* The Heritage Foundation, 1968.

Forbes, Esther. *Paul Revere and the World He Lived In.* Boston: Houghton Mifflin Co., 1942.

Freedley, E. T. *Philadelphia and its Manufacturers,* 1857.

Freeman, Larry and Beaumont, Jane. *Early American Silversmiths and Their Marks.* New York: Walpole Society, 1947.

French, Hollis. *Jacob Hurd and His Sons Nathaniel and Benjamin, Silversmiths.* Printed by the Riverside Press for the Walpole Society, 1939.

From Colony to Nation, Exhibit. Chicago, Illinois: Chicago Art Institute, 1949.

Galt & Bro., Washington, D. C.: Pamphlet, no date.

Gibb, George S. *The Whitesmiths of Taunton, A History of Reed and Barton.* Cambridge, Mass.: Harvard University Press, 1946.

Gillespie, Charles Bancroft. *An Historic Record & Pictorial Description of the Town of Meriden.* Meriden, Conn.: Journal Pub. Co., 1906.

Gillingham, H. E. "Silver," *Pennsylvania Magazine of History and Biography,* 1930–1935.

Gorham Silver Co. *The Gorham Manufacturing Company Silversmiths.* New York: Cheltenham Press, 1900.

Goyne, Nancy A. "Britannia in America, the introduction of a new alloy and a new industry," *Winterthur Portfolio II,* Winterthur, Delaware, The Henry Francis Dupont Winterthur Museum, 1965.

Graham, James Jr. *Early American Silver Marks.* New York: James Graham Jr., 1936.

Greene, Welcome Howard. *The Providence Plantations for Two Hundred and Fifty Years.* Providence, R.I.: J. A. & R. A. Reid Publishers, 1886.

Grimwade, A. G. "Silver, " *The Concise Encyclopedia of Antiques.* New York: Hawthorn Books, Inc.

Halsey, R. T. Haines. *New York Metropolitan Museum Catalogue of Exhibition of Silver Used in New York, New Jersey, and the South.* Metropolitan Museum of Art, 1911.

Hardt, Anton. *Souvenir Spoons of the 90's.* New York: Privately printed, 1962.

Harrington, Jessie. *Silversmiths of Delaware 1700–1850.* Delaware: National Society of Colonial Dames of America, 1939.

Heller, David. *History of Cape Silver, 1700–1750.* 1949.

Hiatt, Noble W. and Lucy F. *The Silversmiths of Kentucky.* Louisville, Ky.: The Standard Printing Co., 1954.

"Highlights of the House of Kirk," *Hobbies.* August, 1939.

Hill, H. W. *Maryland's Silver Service.* Baltimore, Maryland: Waverly Press, Inc., 1962.

Hipkiss, E. J. *Boston Museum of Fine Arts Philip Leffingwell Spaulding Collection of Early American Silver.* Cambridge, Mass.: Harvard University Press, 1943.

Historical and Biographical Sketch of the Gorham Manufacturing Company. Reprint of booklet issued, 1878.

History of New Haven County, Connecticut. Edited by J. L. Rockey, Vol. One

History of the Spoon, Knife and Fork. Taunton, Mass.: Reed & Barton, 1926.

Hittell, John S. *Commerce and Industries of the Pacific Coast of North America.* San Francisco: A. L. Bancroft & Co., 1882.

Hoitsma, Muriel Cutten. *Early Cleveland Silversmiths.* Cleveland, Ohio: Gates Publishing Co., 1953.

The House of Kirk, Our 150th Year, 1815–1965. Baltimore: Samuel Kirk & Son, Inc., 1965.

Hoving, Walter. "The History of Tiffany," *Christian Science Monitor.* April 9, 10, 11, 1959.

"How America's $400 Million-a-Year Silver Manufacturing Industry Grew," *The Jewelers' Circular-Keystone,* Directory Issue. Philadelphia, Pa.: 1965.

Hower, Ralph Merle. *History of Macy's of New York, 1858–1919.* Cambridge, Mass.: Harvard University Press, c. 1943.

Hughes, G. Bernard. "Sheffield Plate," *The Concise Encyclopedia of Antiques.* New York: Hawthorn Books Inc., Vol. Two.

Hughes, Graham. *Modern Silver.* New York: Crown Pub., Inc., 1967.

Humphreys, Mary Gay. "Maiden Lane of the Past and Present," *Jewelers'Circular & Horological Review,* Nov. 28, 1894.

Hungerford, Edward. *The Romance of a Great Store (Macy's).* New York: Robert M. McBride & Co., 1922.

Index of Trademarks Issued from the United States Patent Office, 1881.

Jacobs, Carl. *Guide to American Pewter.* New York: McBride, 1957.

James, George B., Jr. .*Souvenir Spoons,* Boston, Mass.: A. W. Fuller & Co., 1891.

Jayne, H. F. and Woodhouse, S. W., Jr. "Early Philadelphia Silversmiths," *Art in America.* IX (October 1921).

Jeweler Buyers' Guide, A McKenna Publication. New York: Sherry Publishing Co., Inc., 1957, 1958, 1960.

The Jewelers' Circular & Horological Review. New York: D. H. Hopkinson, no date.

The Jewelers' Circular-Keystone. Philadelphia Pa.: Chilton Publication, 1869–1975.

The Jewelers' Circular-Weekly, 50th Anniversary

Number. New York: Jewelers' Circular Pub. Co., 1919.

The Jewelers' Dictionary. New York: The Jewelers' Circular-Keystone, no date (c. 1950).

Jobbers' Handbook. 1936–1937.

Johnson, J. Stewart. "Silver in Newark, A Newark 300th Anniversary Study," *The Museum*, New Series, Vol. 18, Nos. 3 & 4. The Newark Museum, 1966.

Jones E. Alfred. *Old Silver of Europe and America*. Philadelphia: Lippincott Co., 1928.

Keddell, E. Avery. "Romance of the Spoon," *Art Journal*. January 1907.

Keir, Robert M. *Manufacturing in Industries of America*. Roland Press, 1928.

Kelley, Etna M. *The Business Founding Date Directory, (1687–1915)*. Scarsdale, N.Y.: Morgan & Morgan, 1954.

"Kentucky Silversmiths before 1850," *Filson Club History Quarterly*. XVI, No. 2, April 1942, 111-126.

Kerfoot, J. B. *American Pewter*. Boston and New York: Houghton Mifflin Co., 1924.

The Keystone Jewelers' Index. Phila.: The Keystone Publishing Co., 1922, 1924, 1927, 1931.

Kirk in U. S. Museums. Baltimore, Maryland: Samuel Kirk & Son, Inc., 1961.

Kirk Sterling—A Complete Catalog of America's Finest Sterling by America's Oldest Silversmiths. Baltimore: 1956 (?).

Knittle, Rhea Mansfield. *Early Ohio Silversmiths and Pewterers 1787–1847*. (Ohio Frontier Series.) Cleveland, Ohio: Calvert-Hatch Company, 1943.

"Knives for a Nation," *Industry September, 1961*.

Kovel, Ralph M. and Kovel, Terry H. *A Directory of American Silver, Pewter and Silverplate*. New York: Crown Publishers, 1961.

Lambert, Isaac E. *The Public Accepts; Stories Behind Famous Trademarks, Names and Slogans*. Albuquerque, N. M.: Univ. of N. M. Press, 1941.

Langdon, John Emerson. *Canadian Silversmiths & Their Marks, 1667–1867*. Lunenberg, Vermont: The Stinehour Press, 1960.

Langley, Henry. "Silverplating in California," *The Pacific Coast Almanac for 1869*, San Francisco, 1869.

Lathrop, W. G. *The Brass Industry in the United States*. Mt. Carmel, Conn.: Wilson H. Lee Co., 1926.

Laughlin, Ledlie I. *Pewter in America*. Boston: Houghton Mifflin Co., 1940.

Macomber, Henry P. "The Silversmiths of New England," *The American Magazine of Art*. Oct. 1932.

The Magazine SILVER (formerly Silver-Rama). 1968–1975.

Masterpieces of New England Silver 1650–1800. Gallery of Fine Arts, Yale University, 1939.

May, Earl Chapin. *A Century of Silver 1847-*

1947. New York: Robert McBride Co., 1947.

Mazulla, Fred M. and J. *The First Hundred Years, Cripple Creek and the Pikes Peak Region*. Denver, Colorado: A. B. Hirschfeld Press, 1956.

Meeks, E. V. *Masterpieces of New England Silver*. Cambridge: Harvard Univ. Press, 1939.

"Men Who Developed the Silver Plated Ware Industry," *The Jewelers' Circular & Horological Review*, Oct. 3, 1894.

Meriden, the Silver City. Connecticut Tercentenary Committee, 1935.

The Meriden Daily Journal, 50th Anniversary Number. April 17, 1936.

Miller, V. Isabelle. *Silver by New York Makers, Late Seventeenth Century to 1900*. New York: Women's Committee of the Museum of The City of New York, 1938.

Miller, William Davis. *The Silversmiths of Little Rest, Rhode Island*. D. B. Updike, The Merrymount Press, 1920.

National Jeweler's Speed Book, No. 11, National Jeweler, c. 1930.

The National Jewelers' Trade and Trade-Mark Directory, 1918–19. Chicago: The National Jeweler, 1918.

Nationally Established Trade-Marks. New York: Periodical Publishers Assoc. of America, 1934.

"New England Silversmiths, news items gleaned from Boston newspapers, 1704–1705." *Art in America*, (February 1922), 75.

The New England States. William T. Davis, Ed. Vol. II: 832,833.

New York State Silversmiths. Eggertsville, N. Y.: Darling Foundation, 1965.

New York Sun. Antiques section.

Okie, Howard Pitcher. *Old Silver and Old Sheffield Plate*. New York: Doubleday, Doran and Company, 1928.

"Old American Silver," *Country Life in America*. February 1913–January 1915.

Ormsbee, Thomas H. *Know Your Heirlooms*. New York: The McBride Co., 1956

Parke-Bernet Galleries catalogue. January 1938–1975.

Elias Pelletreau, Long Island Silversmith and his Sources of Design. Brooklyn, N.Y.: Brooklyn Institute of Arts and Sciences, Brooklyn Museum, 1959.

"Pennsylvania Museum and School of Industrial Art Loan exhibition of Colonial Silver, special catalogue." *Pennsylvania Museum Bulletin*. No. 68, June 1921.

Percy, Randolph T. "The American at Work, IV: Among the Silver-Platers," *Appleton's Journal*, New Series, No. 30. (Dec. 1878).

"Philadelphia Silver 1682–1800," *Philadelphia Museum Bulletin*, LI, No. 249 (Spring 1956).

Philbrick, Helen Porter. "Franklin Porter, Silversmith (1869–1835)" *Essex Institute Historical Collections, Annual Report, 1968–69*, Salem, Massachusetts.

Phillips, John Marshall. *American Silver*. New York: Chanticleer Press, 1949.

"Pioneers of the American Silver Plate Industry," *Hobbies*. April, 1947.

Pleasants, J. Hall and Sill, Howard. *Maryland Silversmiths, 1715–1830*. Baltimore: The Lord Baltimore Press, 1930; reprinted 1972 by Robert Alan Green.

Porter, Edmund W. "Metallic Sketches," *Taunton Daily Gazette*. March 19, 1906–Sept. 28, 1907.

Prime, Alfred Coxe. *The Arts & Crafts in Philadelphia, Maryland and South Carolina, 1721–1785*.

Prime, Alfred Coxe. *The Arts & Crafts in Philadelphia, Maryland and South Carolina, 1786–1800*.

Prime, Mrs. Alfred Coxe. *Three Centuries of Historic Silver*, Philadelphia: Pennsylvania Society of Colonial Dames of America, 1938.

Purdy, W. Frank. "Developments in American Silversmithing," *The Art World*, May 1917.

Rainwater, Dorothy T. *Sterling Silver Holloware*. A Catalog reprint, American Historical Catalog Collection. Princeton, New Jersey: The Pyne Press, 1973.

Rainwater, Dorothy T. and Felger, Donna H. *American Spoons, Souvenir & Historical*. Nashville, Tennessee: Thomas Nelson Inc., and Hanover, Pennsylvania: Everybodys Press, 1968.

Rainwater, Dorothy T. and Rainwater, H Ivan. *American Silverplate*. Nashville, Tennessee: Thomas Nelson Inc., and Hanover, Pennsylvania: Everybodys Press, 1972.

Randolph, Howard S. F., "Jacob Boelen, Goldsmith of New York and his family circle," *New York Genealogical and Biographical Record*. October, 1941.

Report of the Eighth Industrial Exhibition of the Mechanics Institute, 1871. San Francisco, 1872.

Retrospect, A publication of the Historical Society of Glastonbury, Conn. No. 10, Feb. 1948.

Revi, Albert Christian. *Nineteenth Century Glass*. New York: Thomas Nelson & Sons, 1959.

Roach, Ruth Hunter. *St. Louis Silversmiths*. Privately printed, St. Louis, 1967.

Robertson, Constance, *The Oneida Community*. Pamphlet, no date.

Roe, Joseph Wickham. *Connecticut Inventors*. Tercentenary Commission of Connecticut, N.Y. Press, 1934.

Rogers, Edward S. *The Lanham Act and the Social Function of Trade-Marks, in Law and Contemporary Problems*. Durham, S. C. Quarterly, pub. by Duke Univ. School of Law, V. 14, No. 2, 1949.

"The Rogers Manufacturing Company," *The American Jeweler*, March 1882.

William Rogers and his Brothers in the Silverware Industry. Philadelphia: Keystone, Keystone Publishing Company, August and September, 1934.

Romaine, Lawrence B. *A Guide to American Trade Catalogs, 1744–1900*. New York: R. R. Bowker Company, 1960.

Rosenbaum, Jeanette. *Myer Myers, Goldsmith*. Philadelphia: Jewish Publication Society of America, 1954.

Rumpp, Leaders for a Century in Fine Leather Goods. Philadelphia: C. F. Rumpp & Sons, Inc., 1950.

Sabine, Julia. *Silversmiths of New Jersey*. Proc. of the New Jersey Historical Society, July–October, 1943 (Newark, 1943).

Schild, Joan Lynn. *Silversmiths of Rochester*. Rochester, N. Y.: Rochester Museum of Arts and Sciences, 1944.

Seeger and Guernsey. *Cyclopaedia of the Manufacturers and Products of the United States*. New York: 1890.

Selwyn, A. *The Retail Jeweller's Handbook*. New York: McBride Company, 1947.

Semon, Kurt M. *A Treasury of Old Silver*. New York: McBride Company, 1947.

"Silver by New York Makers," *Museum of the City of New York*. New York: 1937.

"The Silversmiths of New England," *American Magazine of Art*. October, 1932.

"The Silverware Industry in America," *The Jewelers' Circular-Keystone*. New York: November and December 1946.

"The Silverware Industry, Early Workers in Silver," *The Keystone*, November, 1899.

Sniffen, Philip L. *A Century of Silversmithing*. Reed & Barton Silversmiths. Taunton, Massachusetts: 1924.

Snow, Wm. G. "Early Silver Plating in America," *Metal Industry*, New York: June 1935.

Snow, Wm. G. "Silverplating in Connecticut, Its Early Days," *United States Investor*, May 18, 1935.

Souvenir Spoons of America. New York: The Jewelers Circular Publishing Co., 1891.

The Spinning Wheel, Hanover, Pa.: 1945–1975.

The Spoon from Earliest Times. Meriden, Conn.: International Silver Company, 1915.

Sterling Flatware Pattern Index. N. Y. and Phila.: Jewelers' Circular-Keystone, 1949.

Stieff Sterling Silver, The Stieff Company. Baltimore: Barton-Gillet, c. 1930.

The Story of Daniel Low. Salem, Mass.: Daniel Low & Co., Catalog for 1917.

The Story of Sterling. Newburyport, Mass.: The Towle Silversmiths, 1954.

The Story of Sterling. New York: Sterling Silversmiths Guild of America, 1937.

The Story of the House of Kirk. Baltimore: Samuel Kirk & Son, Inc., 1914 and 1939.

Stow, M. *American Silver*. New York: Barrow & Co. 1950.

Stutzenberger, Albert. *The American Story in Spoons*. Louisville, Ky.: Privately printed,

1953.

"Tammen Curio Company of Denver," *Denver Post*. January 29, 1957.

"Tammen's Curio Shop," *Rocky Mountain Life*. Denver, Colorado: March 1949.

Taylor, Emerson. *Paul Revere*. New York: Dodd, Mead & Co., 1930.

Taylor, Gerald. *Silver*. London: Unwin Brothers, Ltd. 1956.

Thorn, C. Jordan. *Handbook of American Silver and Pewter Marks*. New York: Tudor Publishing Company, 1949.

Those Green River Knives. Russell Harrington Cutlery Company (Reprinted in part from Indian Notes, Vol. IV, No. 4 Museum of the American Indian, Heye Foundation, New York: October, 1927.

"Three Centuries of European and American Silver," *M. H. de Young Memorial Museum Bulletin*. San Francisco: October 1938.

"Charles L. Tiffany and the House of Tiffany & Co.," *Jewelers' Circular & Horological Review*, February 7, 1894.

Tilton, George P. *Colonial History* (catalogues of Benjamin Franklin, La Fayette, Paul Revere, Newbury and Georgian flatware patterns in addition to the histories of the persons and places.) Newburyport, Mass.: Towle Manufacturing Company, 1905.

Trade Marks of the Jewelry and Kindred Trades, New York and Philadelphia: Jewelers' Circular-Keystone Publishing Co., 1869, 1896, 1898, 1904, 1910, 1915, 1922, 1943, 1950, 1965, 1969, 1973.

Tryon, R. M. *Household Manufactures in U. S.* Chicago: University Press, 1917.

Turner, Noel D. *American Silver Flatware, 1837–1910*. Cranbury, New Jersey: A. S. Barnes & Co., Inc., 1972.

Twyman, Robert W. *History of Marshall Field & Co., 1852–1906*. Philadelphia: University of Pennsylvania Press, 1954.

U. S. Bureau of the Census, Digest of Accounts of Manufacturing Establishments in the United States and of Their Manufacturers. Washington, D.C.: 1823.

U. S. Tariff Commission. A Survey of the various types of silverware, the organization of the industry and the trade in silverware, with special reference to tariff consideration. Washington, D. C.: U. S. Gov't Printing Office, 1940. Report No. 139, Second Series.

Wallace, Floyd, Sr. *Wallace News*. June 1947. Credit to Miss Emma Dray.

Wardle, Patricia. *Victorian Silver & Silver Plate*. Victorian Collector Series. Thomas Nelson & Sons, 1963.

Wendt, Lloyd & Kogen, Herman, *Give the Lady what She Wants*. History of Marshall Fields, Chicago: Rand McNally, c. 1952.

Wenham, Edward. *Practical Book of American Silver*. New York and Philadelphia: J. B. Lippincott Co., 1949.

Westman, Habakkuk O. "The Spoon: Primitive, Egyptian, Roman, Medieval & Modern," *The Transactions of the Society of Literary and Scientific Chiffoniers*. New York: 1844.

White, Benjamin. *Silver, its History and Romance*. New York and London: Hodder & Stoughton. 1917.

White, Richard L. "A Century of Inventions for the American Home," *The Newcomen Society in North America*, lecture, 1955.

Williams, Carl Mark. *Silversmiths of New Jersey 1700–1825*. Philadelphia: G. S. McManus Co., 1949.

Woolsey, Theodore S. "Old Silver," *Harper's Magazine*, 1896.

Wroth, Lawrence C. *Abel Buell of Connecticut, Silversmith, Typefounder, and Engraver*. 1926.

Wyler, Seymour B. *The Book of Old Silver*. New York: Crown Publishers, 1937.

Wyler, Seymour B. *The Book of Sheffield Plate, Including Victorian Plate*. New York: Crown Publishers, 1949.

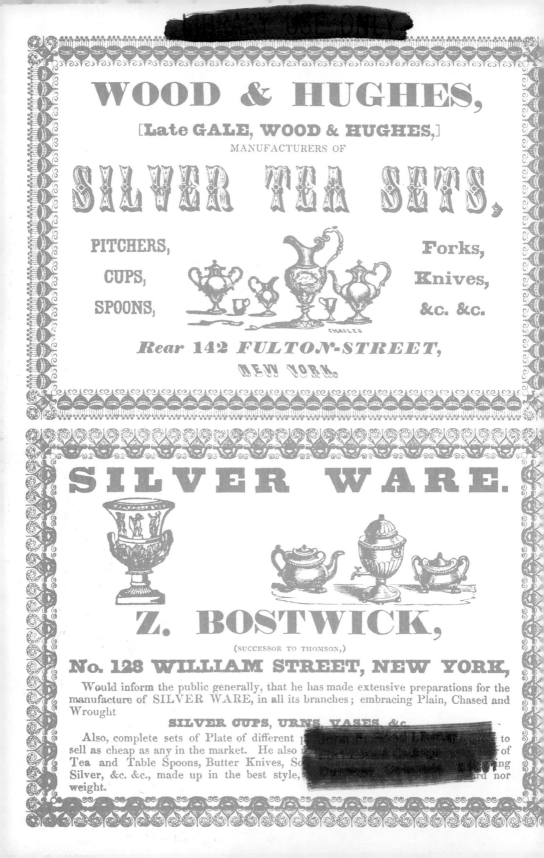

WOOD & HUGHES,

[Late GALE, WOOD & HUGHES,]

MANUFACTURERS OF

SILVER TEA SETS,

PITCHERS,

CUPS,

SPOONS,

Forks,

Knives,

&c. &c.

CHARLES

Rear 142 *FULTON-STREET,*

NEW YORK.

SILVER WARE.

Z. BOSTWICK,

(SUCCESSOR TO THOMSON,)

No. 128 WILLIAM STREET, NEW YORK,

Would inform the public generally, that he has made extensive preparations for the manufacture of SILVER WARE, in all its branches; embracing Plain, Chased and Wrought

SILVER CUPS, URNS, VASES, &c.

Also, complete sets of Plate of different p............................ to sell as cheap as any in the market. He also .... of Tea and Table Spoons, Butter Knives, So................................ Silver, &c. &c., made up in the best style, ... nor weight.